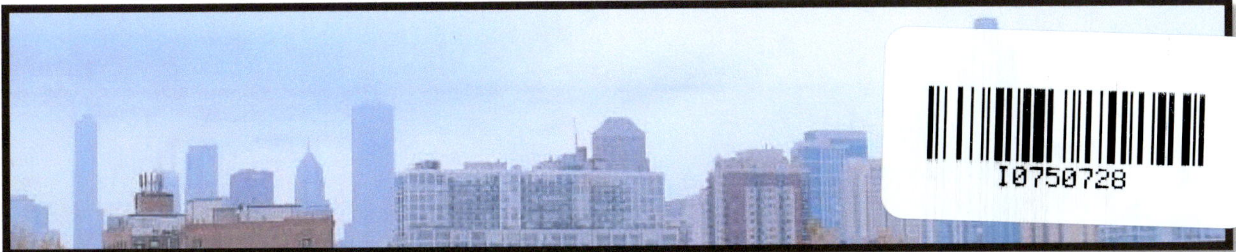

Chicago.

A Photographic Essay.

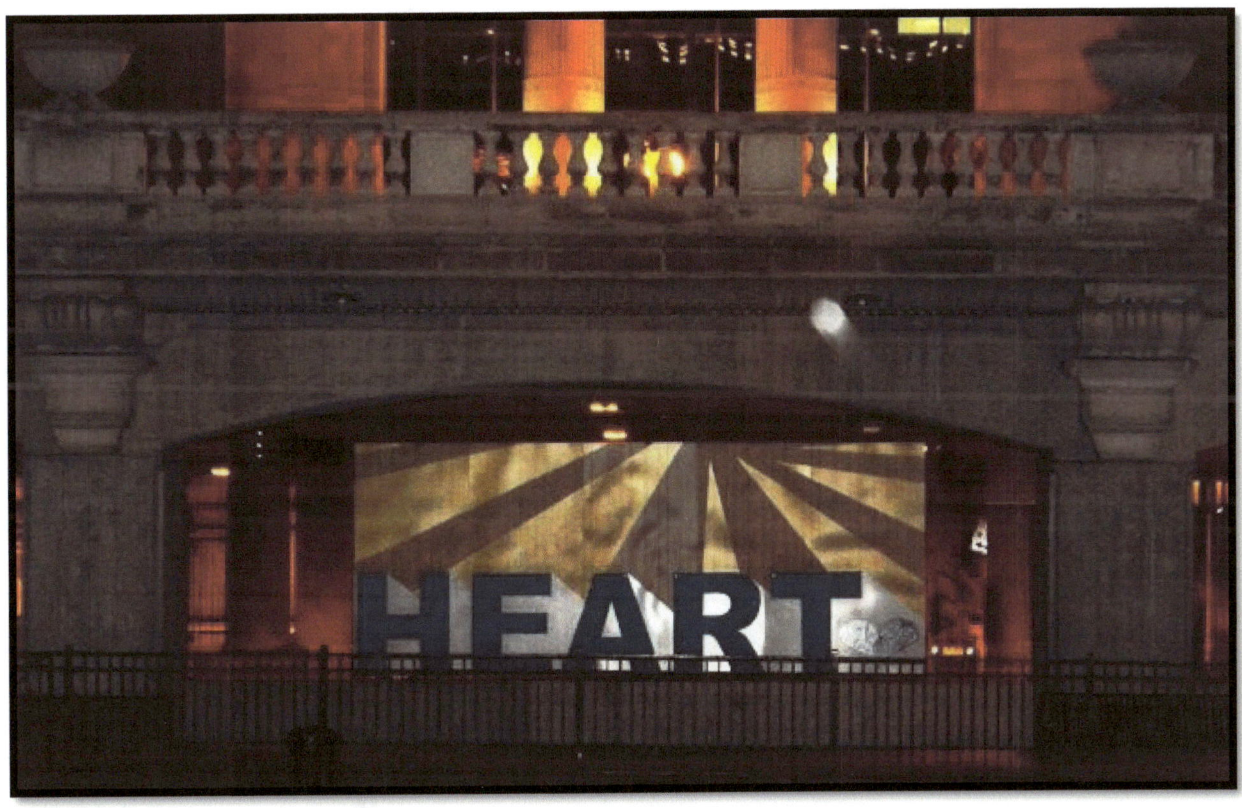

John William Thomas and Mary Rainer Skala

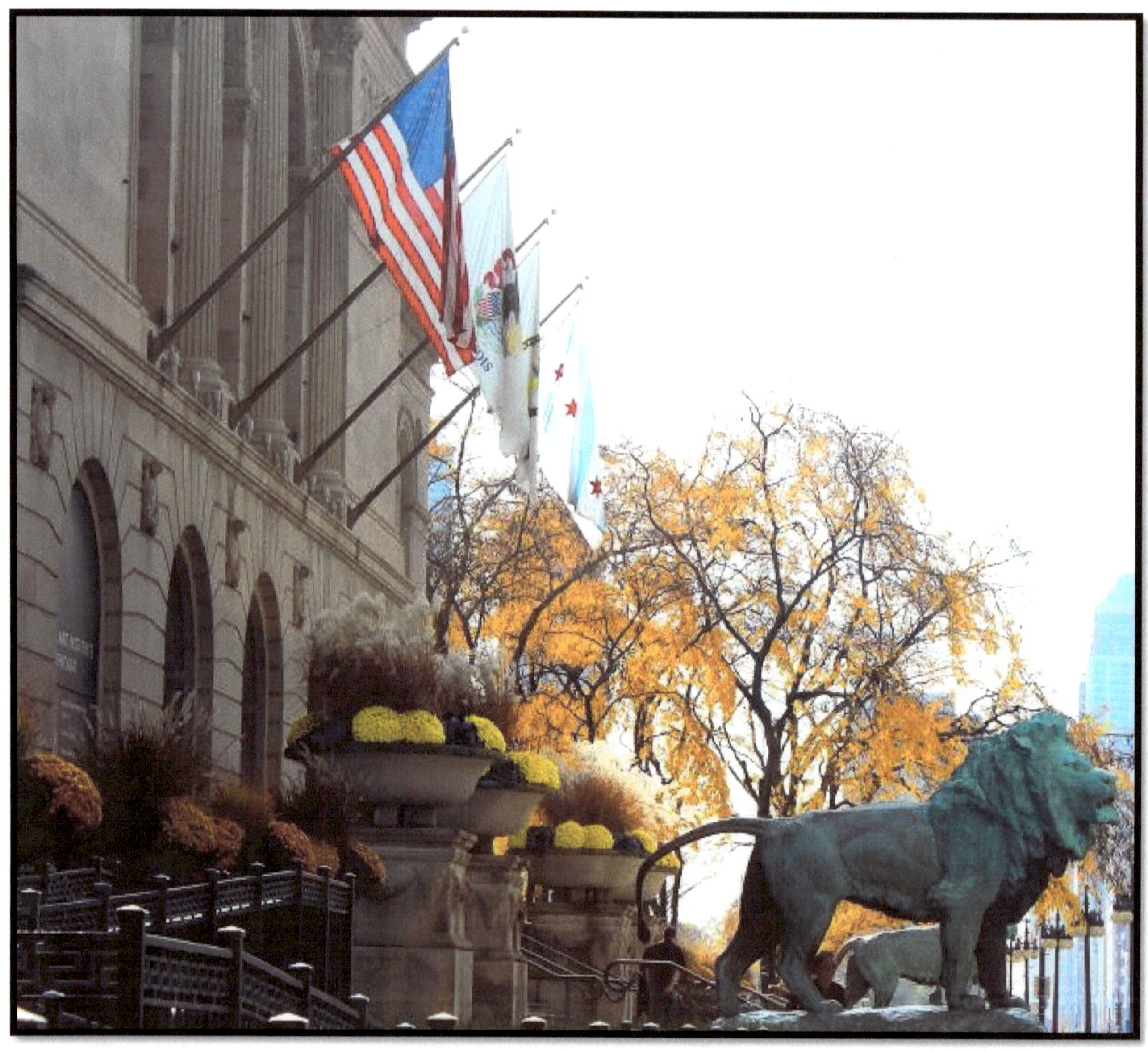

"Chicago is an October sort of city even in spring." —**Nelson Algren**

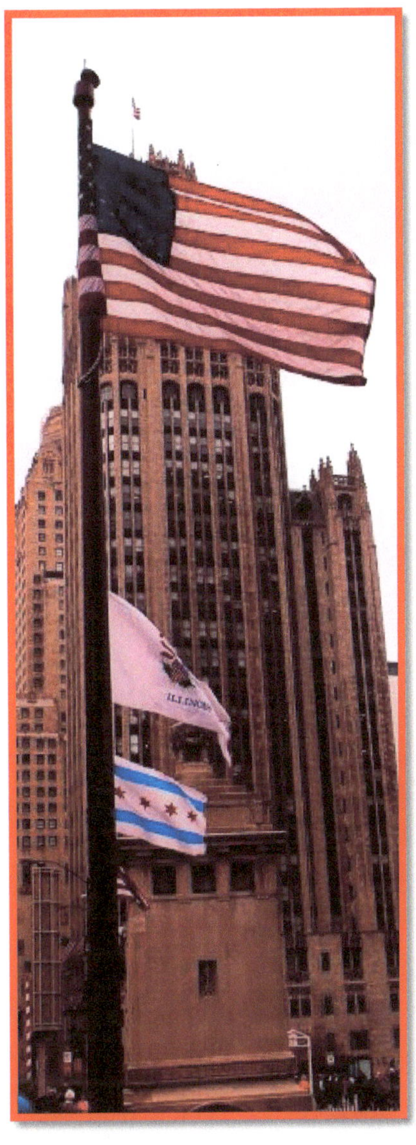

"New York is one of the capitals of the world and Los Angeles is a constellation of plastic, San Francisco is a lady, Boston has become Urban Renewal, Philadelphia and Baltimore and Washington wink like dull diamonds in the smog of Eastern Megalopolis, and New Orleans is unremarkable past the French Quarter. Detroit is a one-trade town, Pittsburgh has lost its golden triangle, St. Louis has become the golden arch of the corporation, and nights in Kansas City close early. The oil depletion allowance makes Houston and Dallas naught but checkerboards for this sort of game. But Chicago is a great American city. Perhaps it is the last of the great American cities." **Norman Mailer,** ***Miami and the Siege of Chicago, 1968***

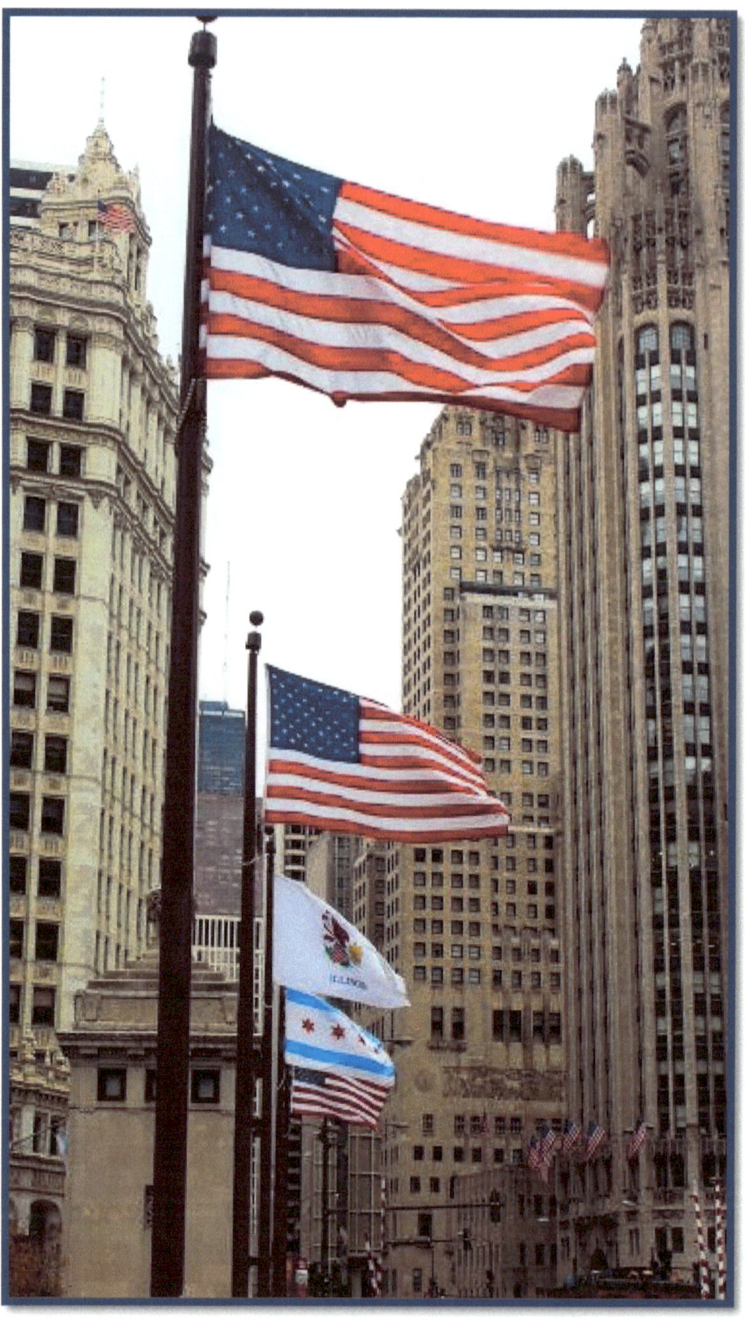

"We struck the home trail now, and in a few hours were in that astonishing Chicago–a city where they are always rubbing a lamp, and fetching up the genii, and contriving and achieving new impossibilities. It is hopeless for the occasional visitor to try to keep up with Chicago– she outgrows her prophecies faster than she can make them. She is always a novelty; for she is never the Chicago you saw when you passed through the last time." **Mark Twain "*Life on the Mississippi*," 1883**

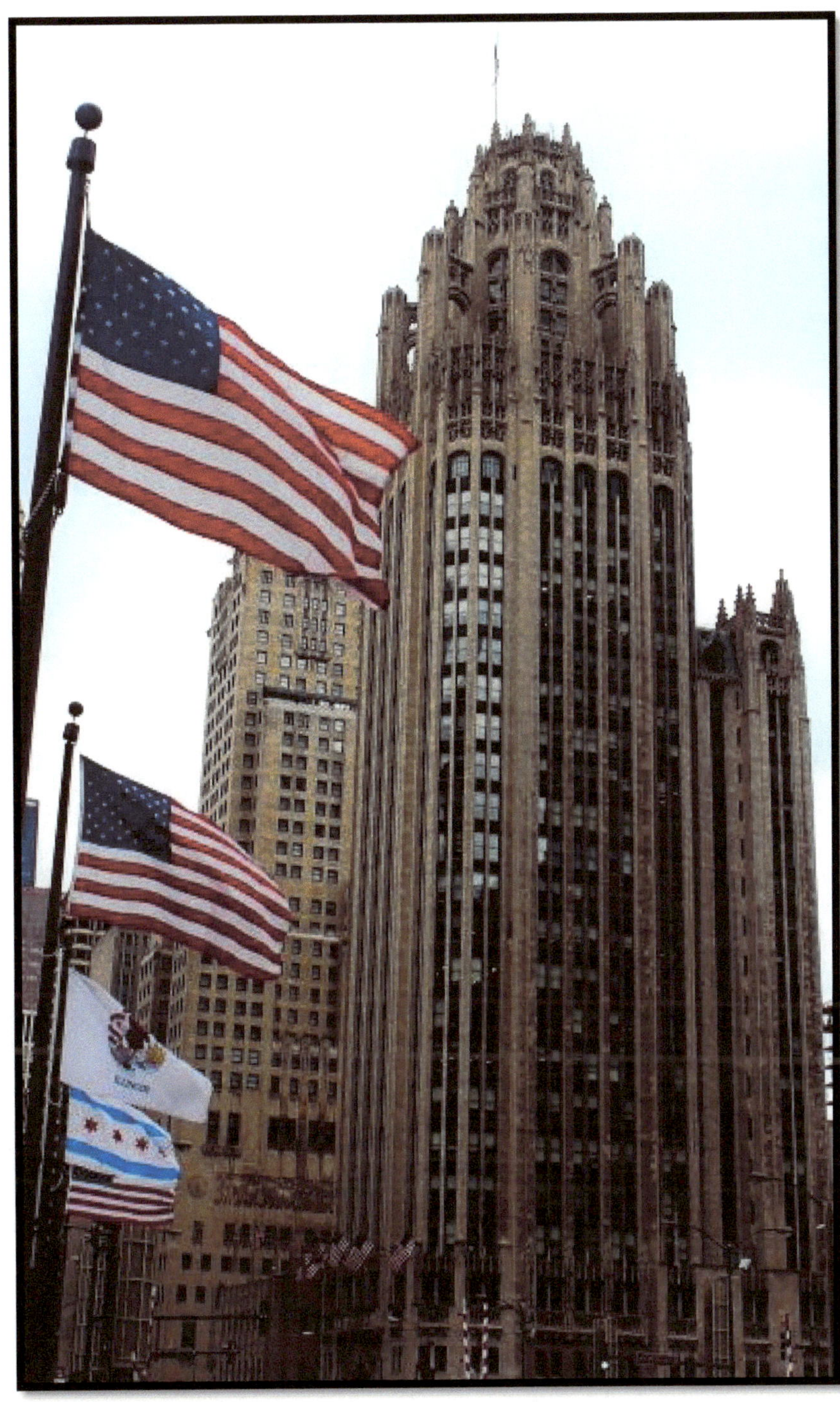

"Chicago still remains a Mecca of the Midwest— people from both coasts are kind of amazed how good life is in Chicago, and what a good culture we`ve got. You can have a pretty wonderful artistic life and never leave Chicago." **Harold Ramis**

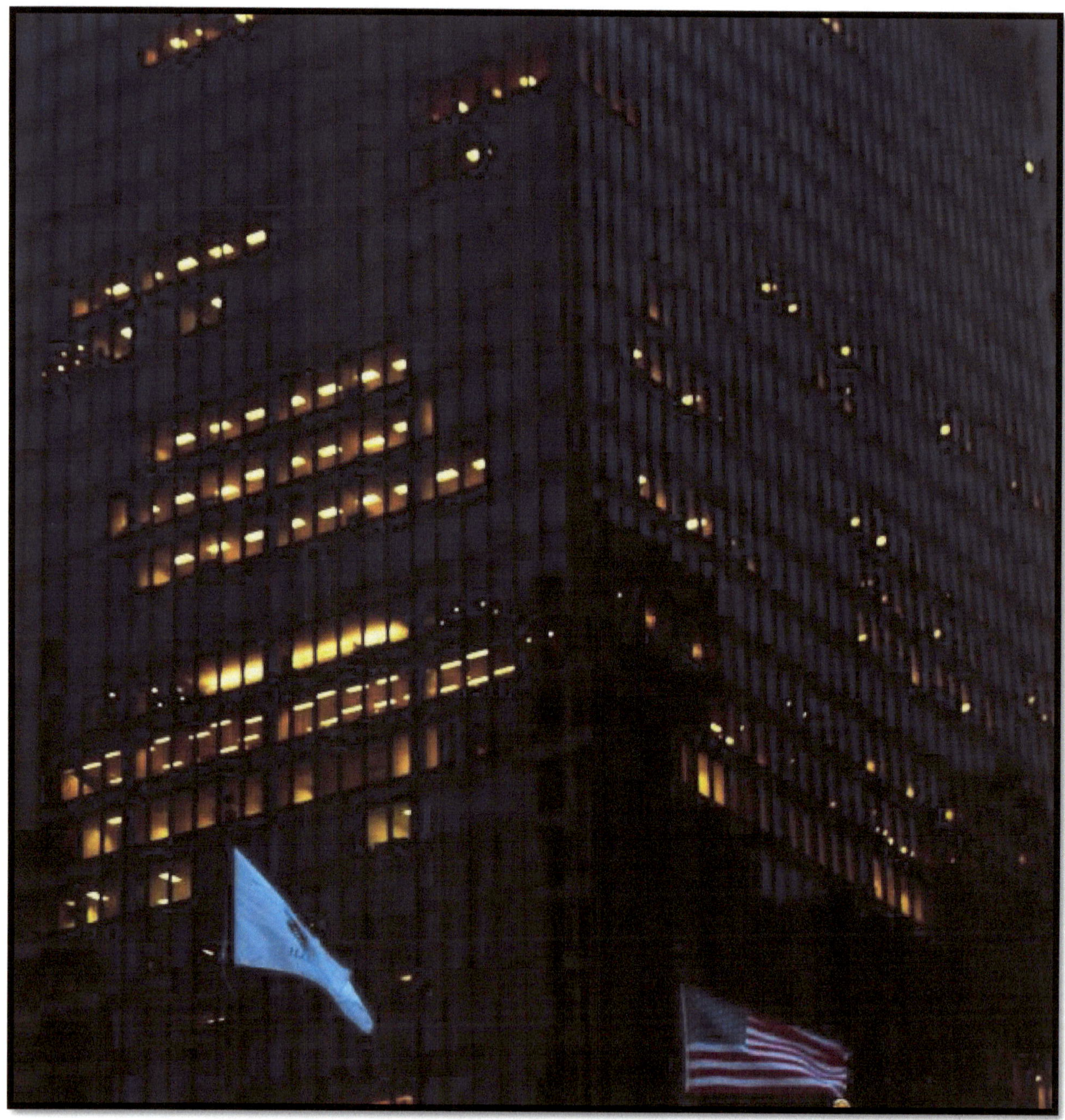

“The thing about Chicago is that it really isn't like any other place. The architecture and the layout of the city are the best. I'm from the Midwest, and consider myself a Midwesterner. I feel most at home there. I love California. I have great friends in California. I just have always considered Illinois to be home.” **Vince Vaughn**

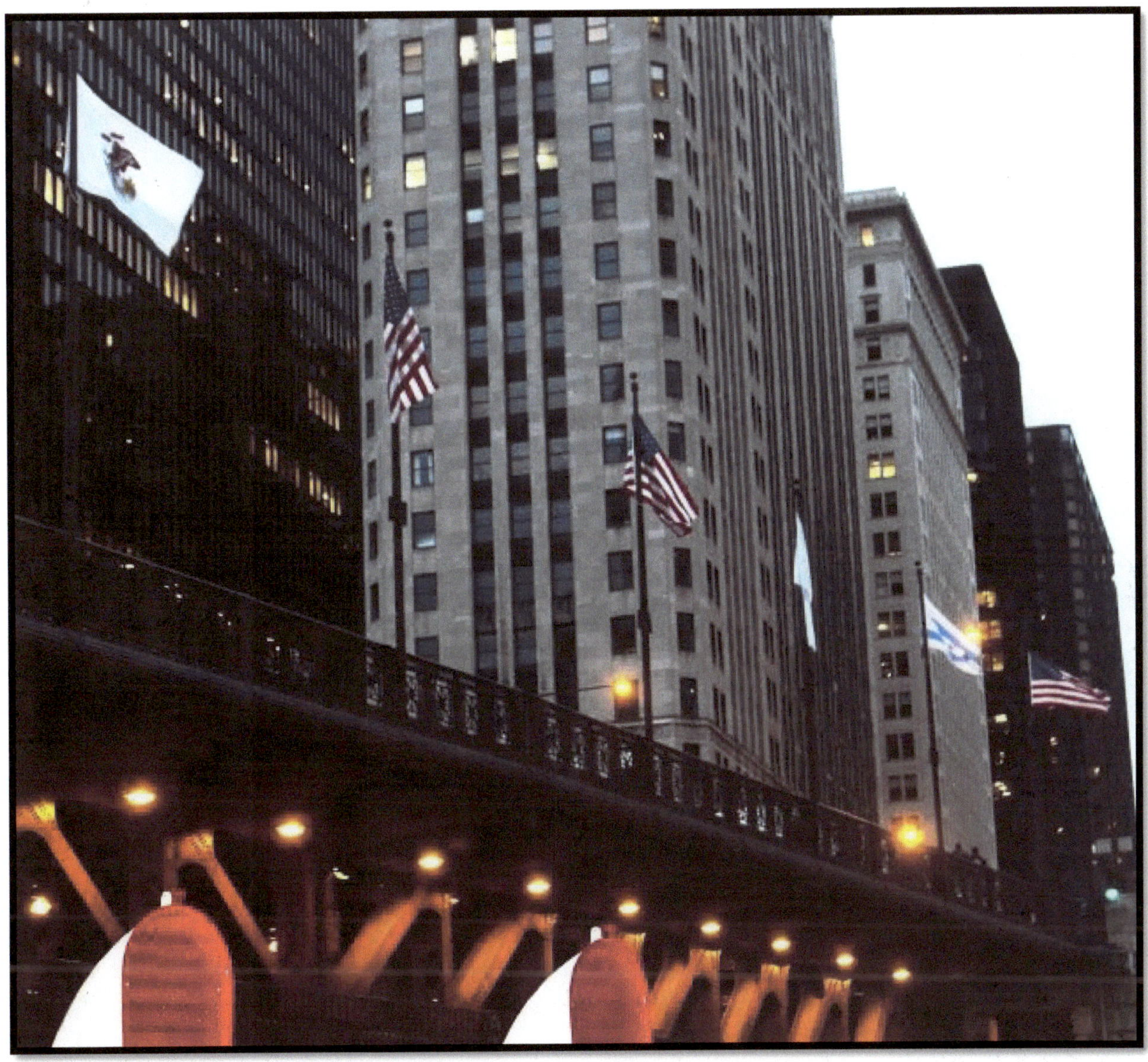

"There was no need to inform us of the protocol involved. We were from Chicago and knew all about cement." **Groucho Marx, pressing his hands into the cement at Grauman's Chinese Theater in Hollywood**

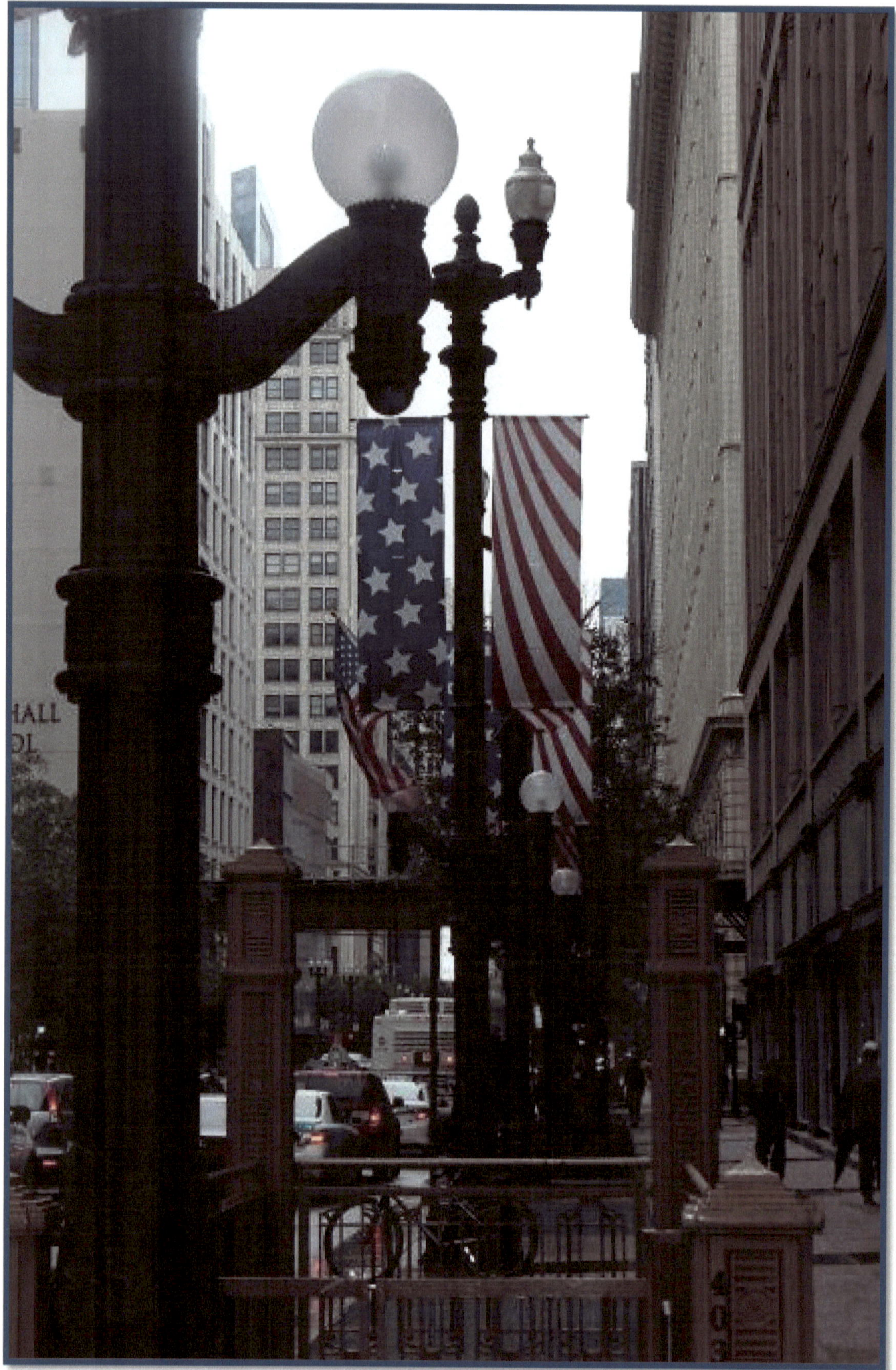

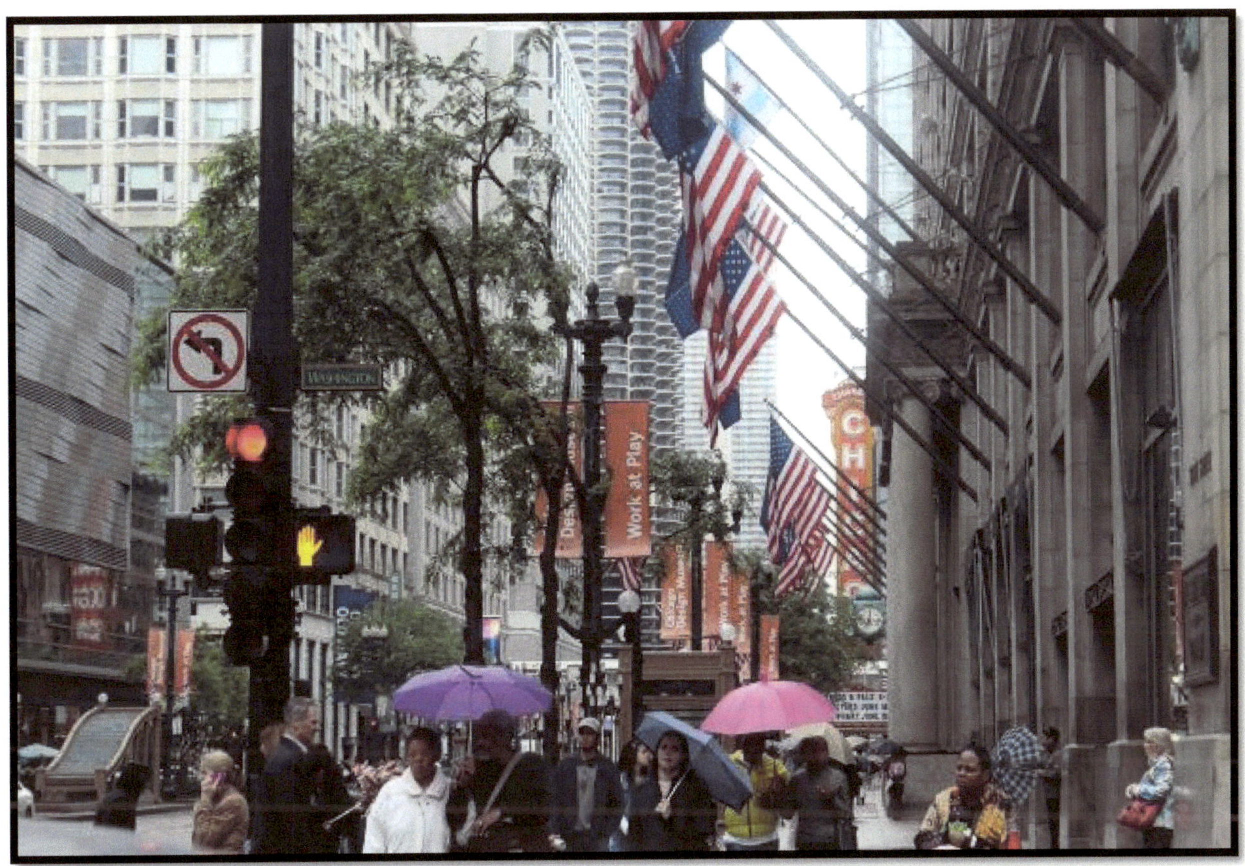

"The people of Chicago are a proud people - and for good reason." **Jane Byrne**

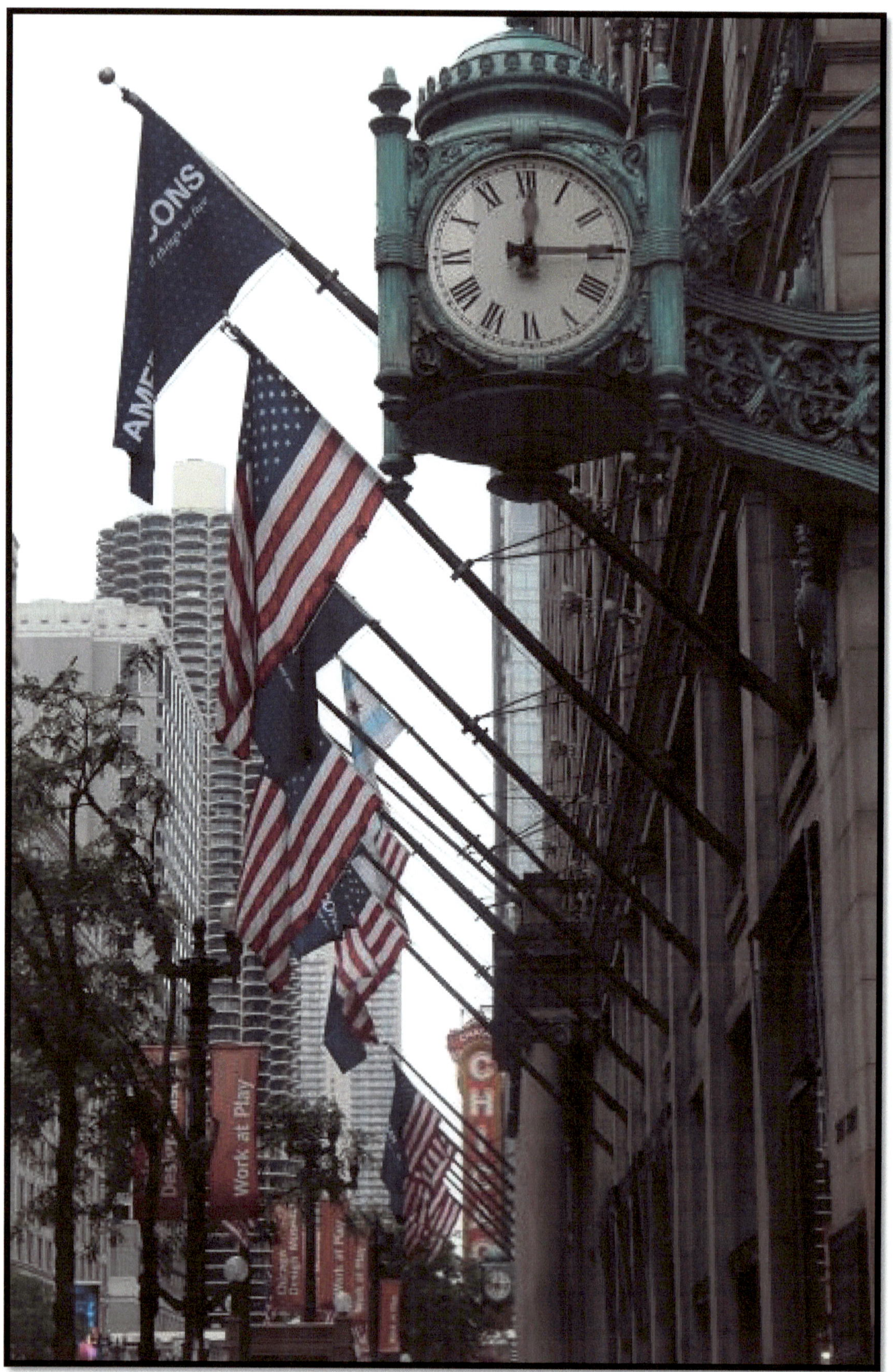
Work at Play

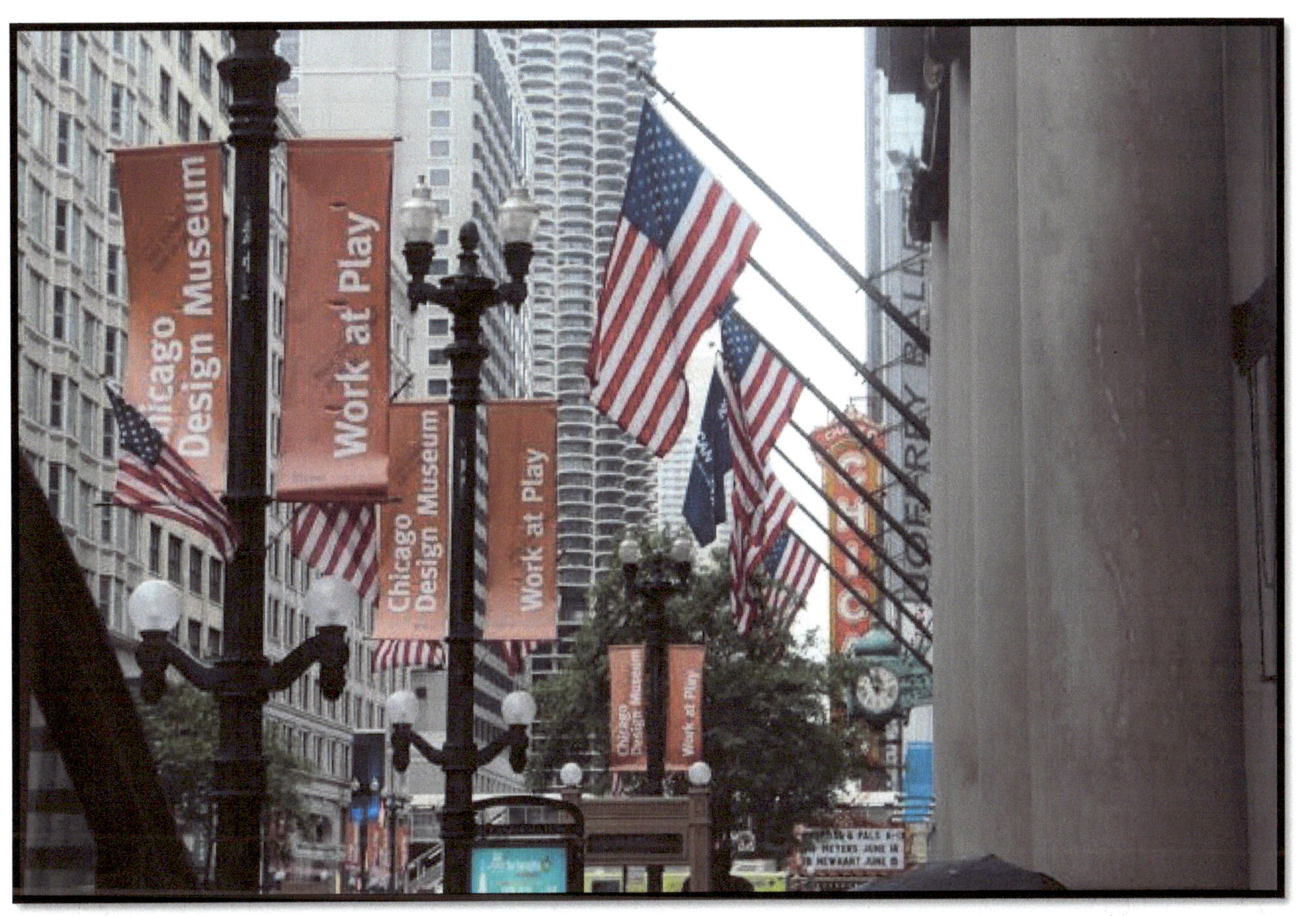

"Theater in Chicago will always be my first love." **William Petersen**

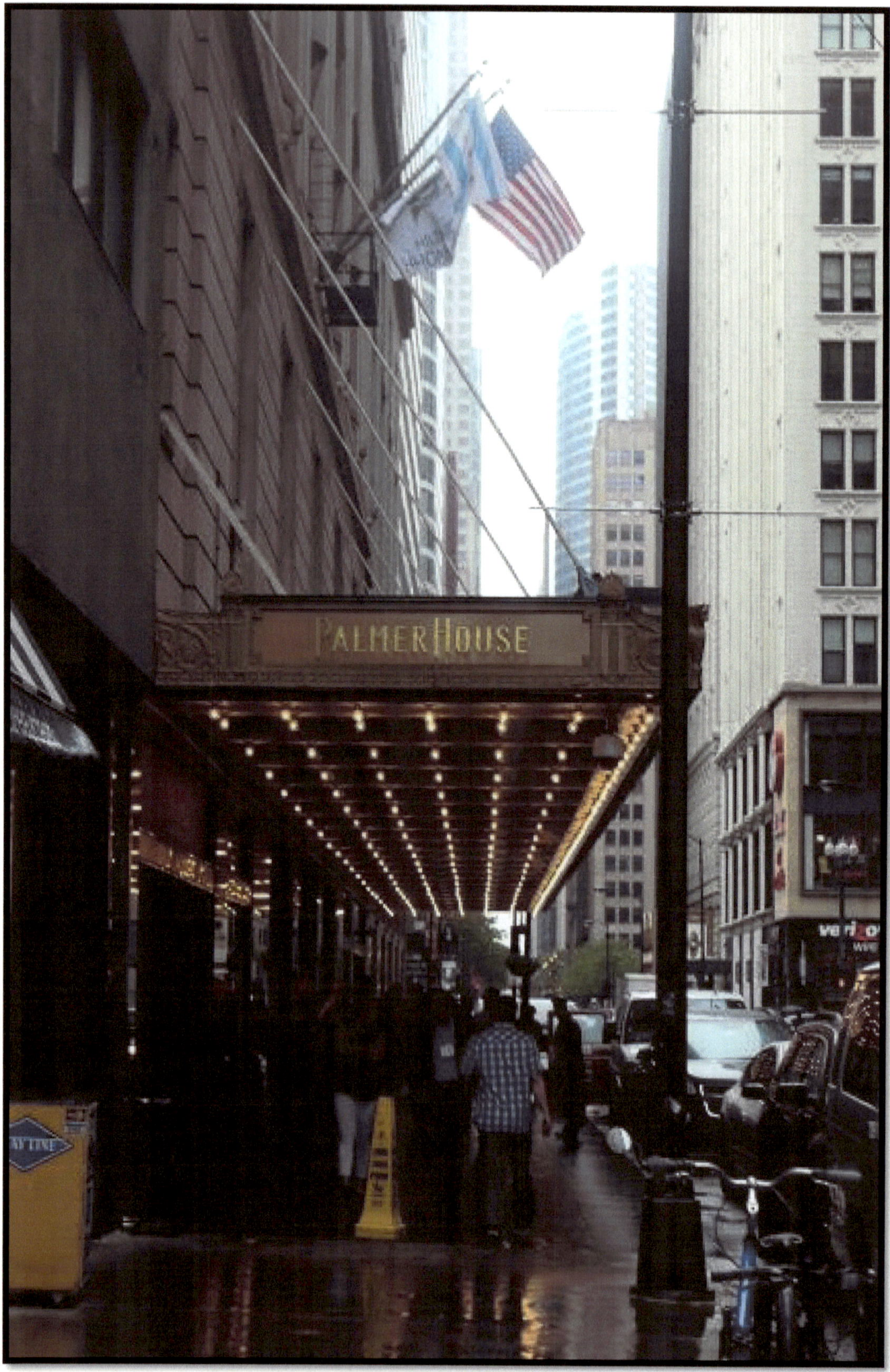
PALMER HOUSE

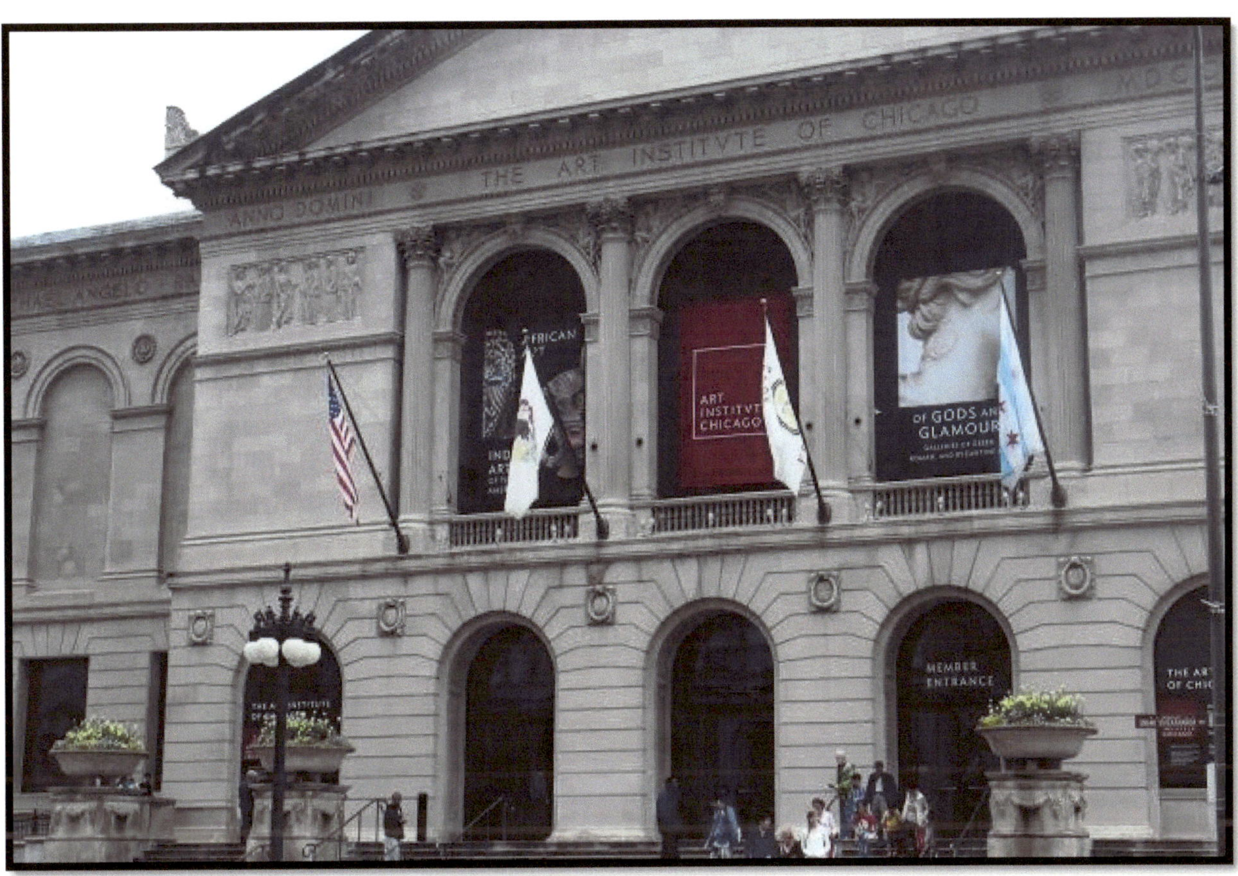

"I feel this is very important for us to have serene buildings because our civilization is chaotic as it is, you see; our whole machine age has brought about a chaos that has to be somehow counterbalanced" **Minoru Yamasaki**

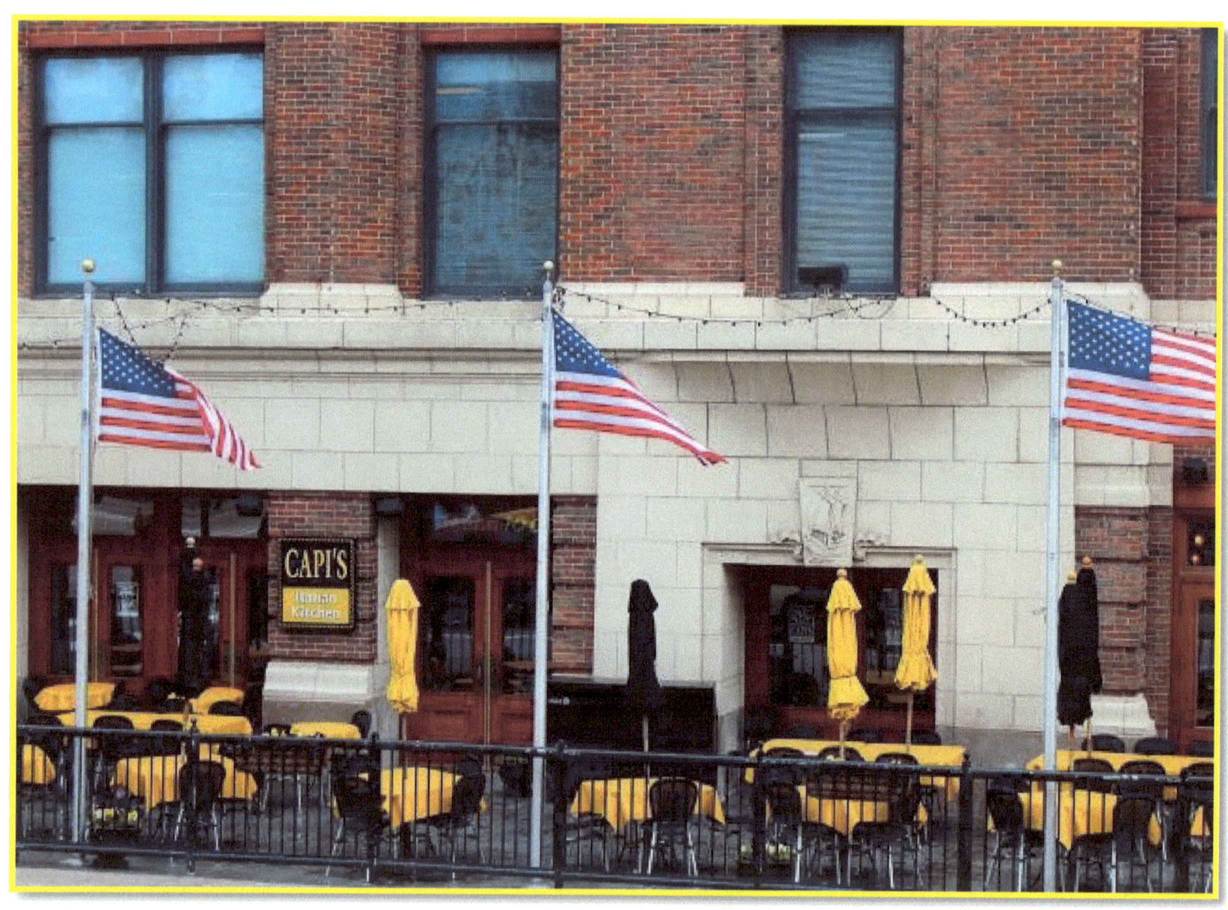

"Chicago sounds rough to the maker of verse. One comfort we have — Cincinnati sounds worse." **Oliver Wendell Holmes**

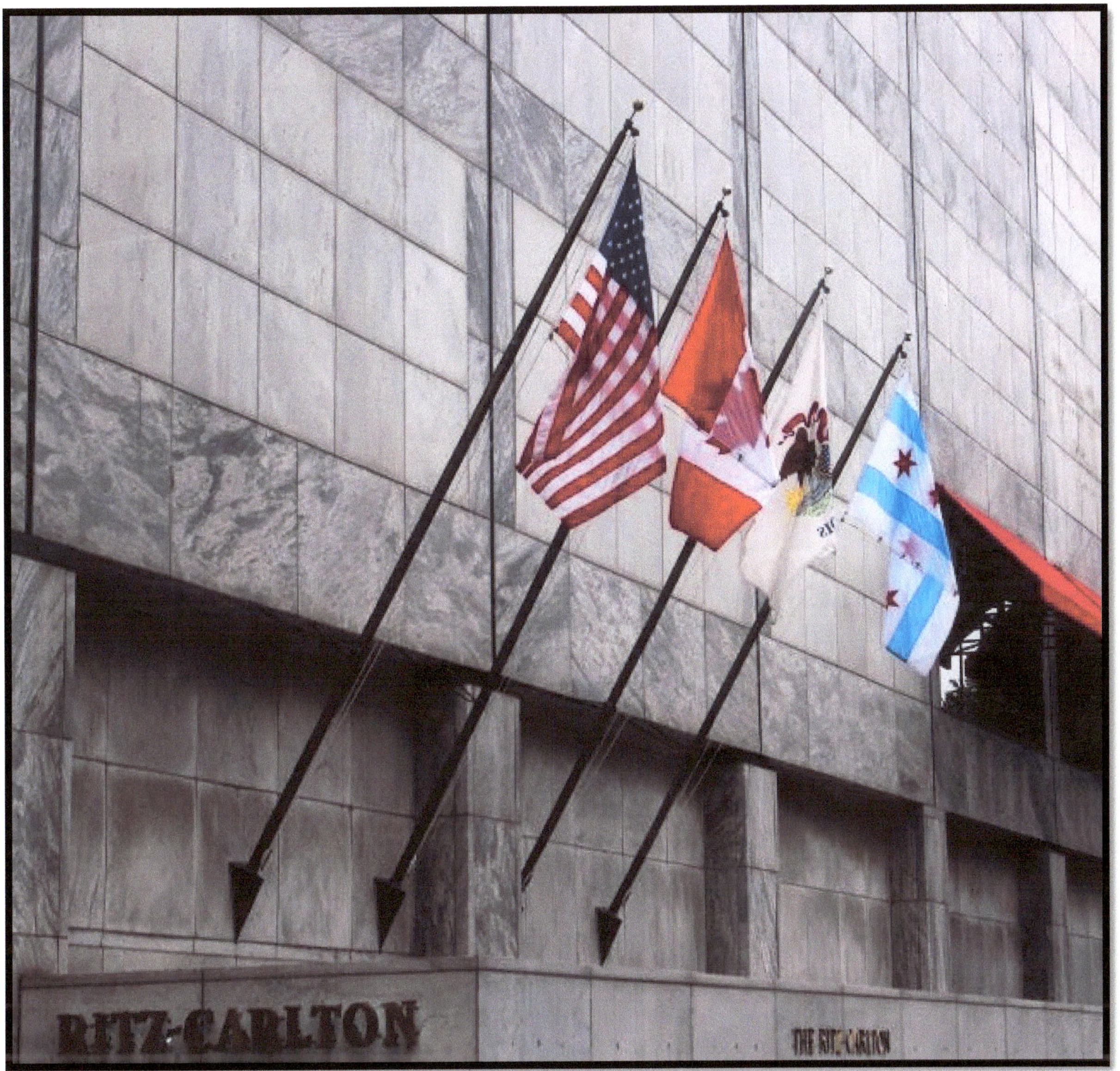

"Having spent a long time in open spaces, whether sea or desert, it is a luxury to be able to take refuge in towns with narrow streets which provide a fragile fortress against the assaults of the infinite. There is such a sense of security against the boundless there, even if the murmur of the wave or the silence of the sands still pursue one through tortuous corridors. The winds, despite their subtle spirits, are themselves lost in the vestibules of this labyrinth and, unable to find a way through, whistle and turn in turbulence like demented dervishes. They will not break through the walls of this den in which life still pulsates in the shadows of humanity's black sun." **Georges Limbour**

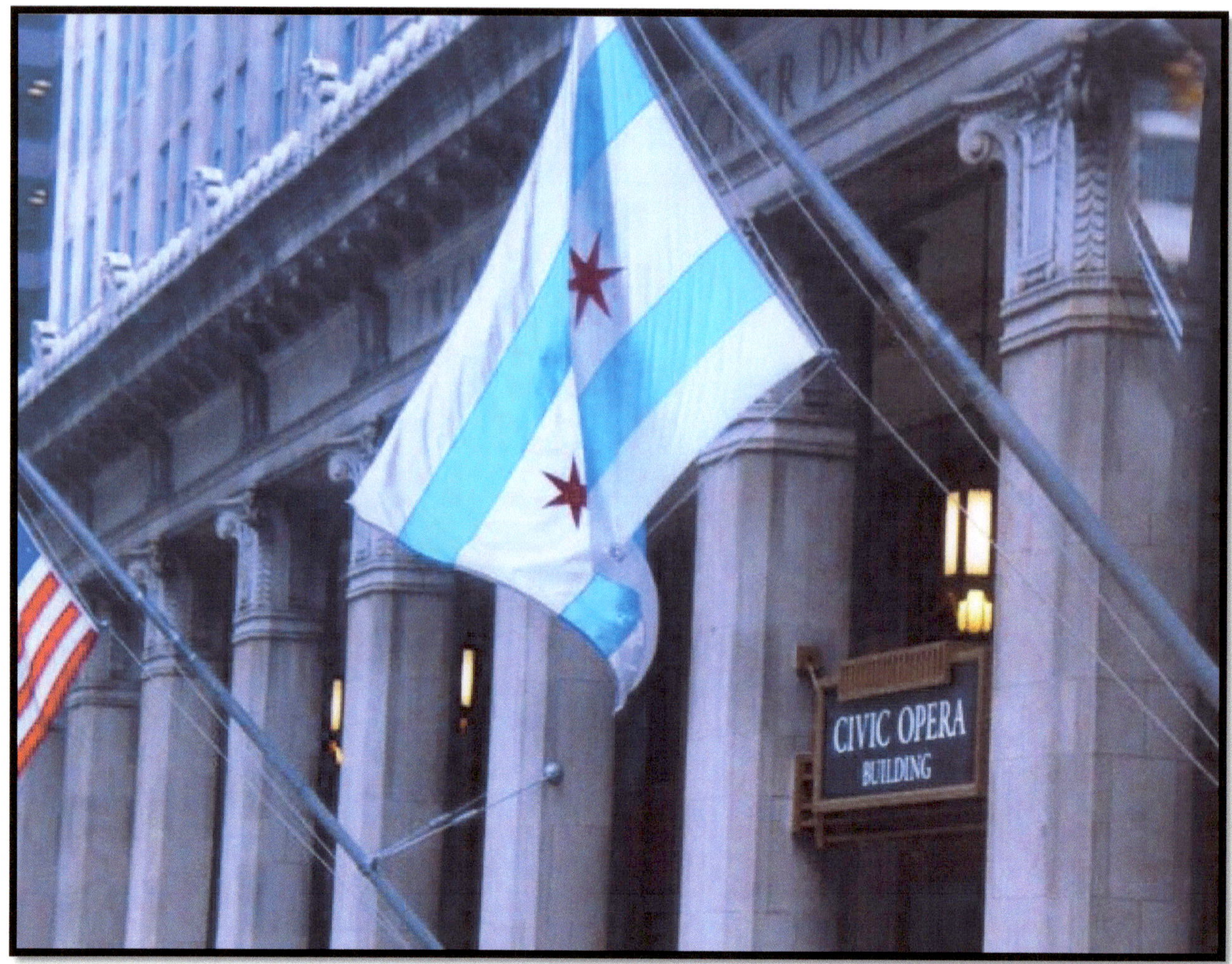

"I love Chicago; it is unique in the world. So much intellect, so many artistic voices - it has fantastic potential." **Jerome Sans**

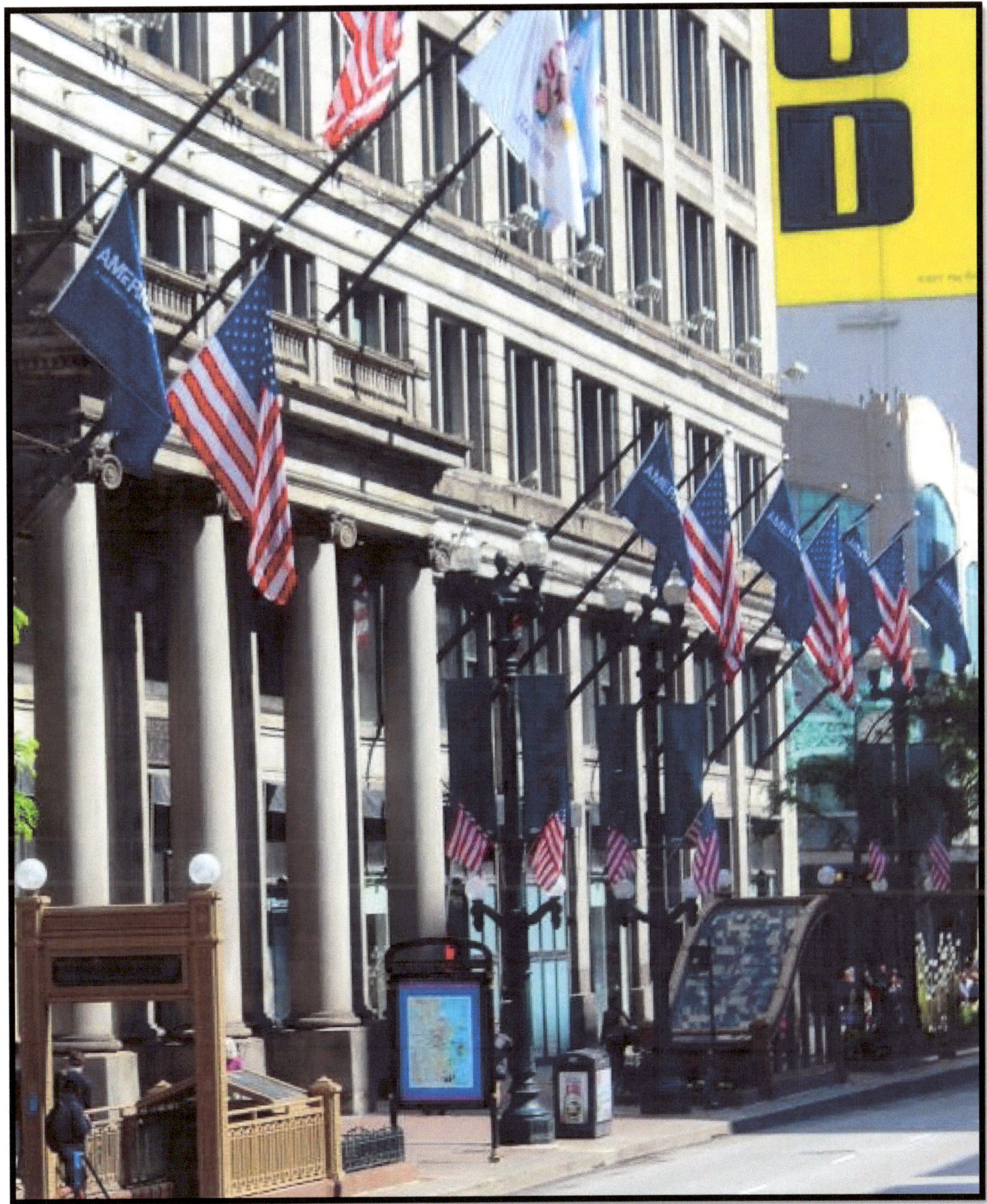

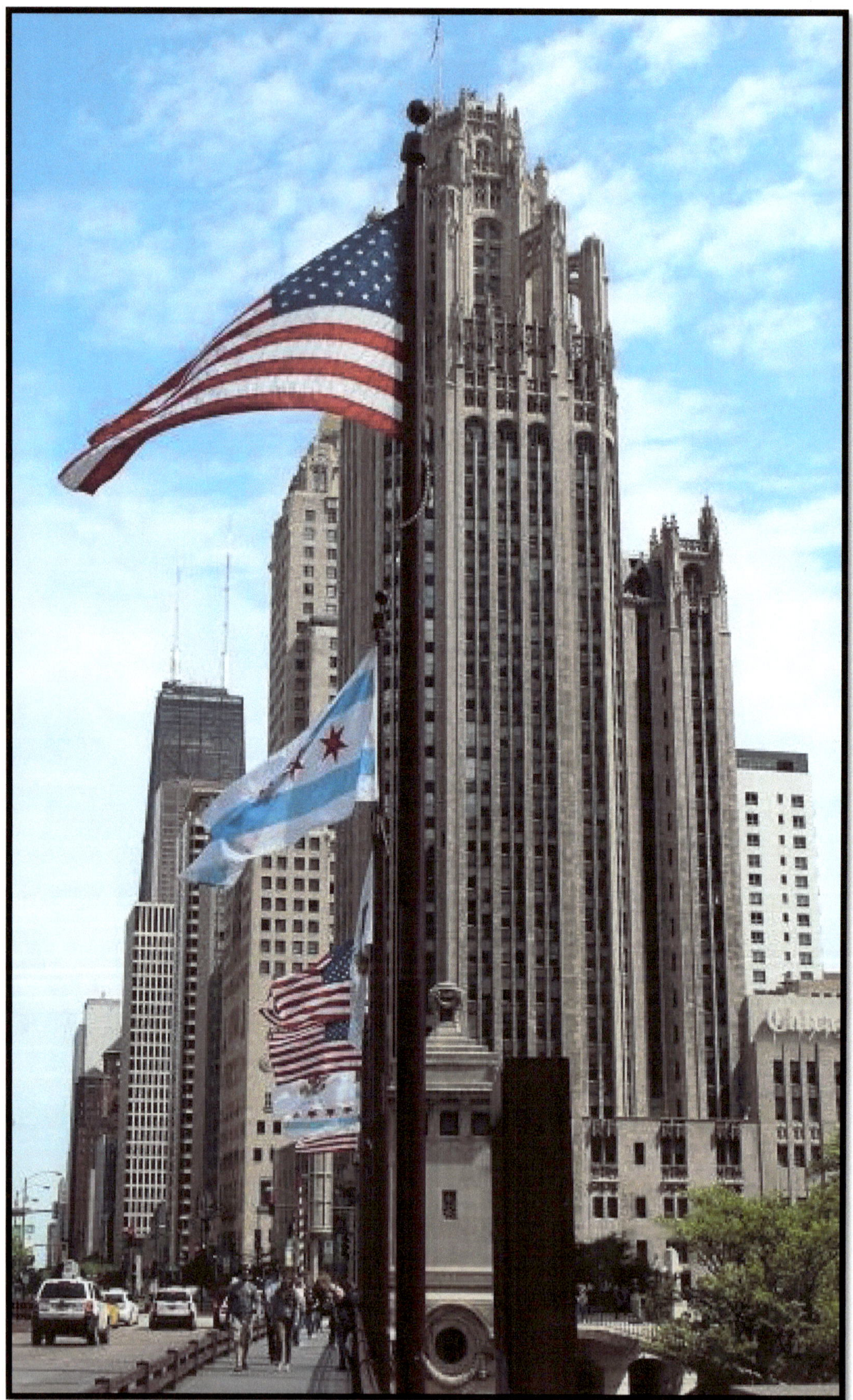

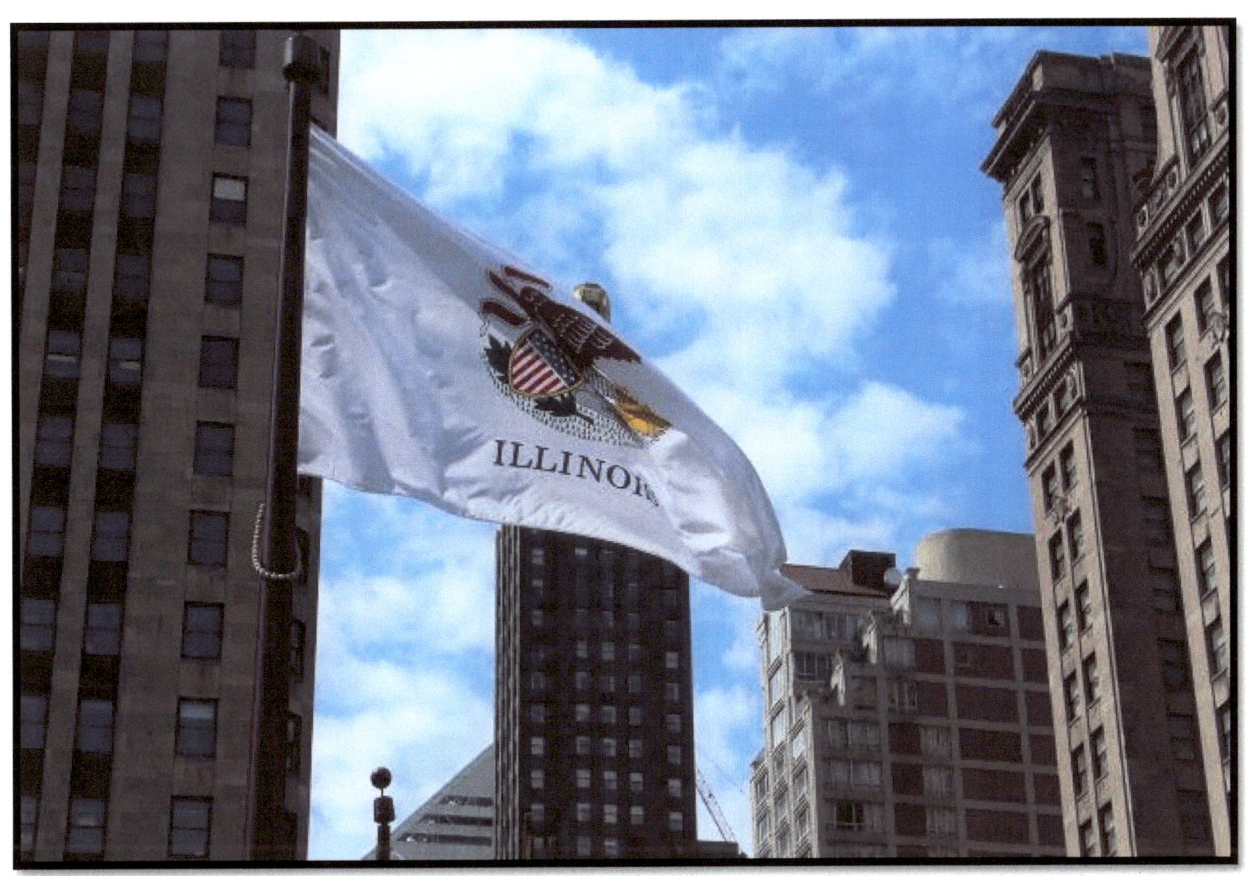

"Come and show me another city with lifted head singing so proud to be alive and coarse and strong and cunning...proud to be Hog Butcher, Tool Maker, Stacker of Wheat, Player with Railroads and Freight Handler to the Nation." — **Carl Sandburg**

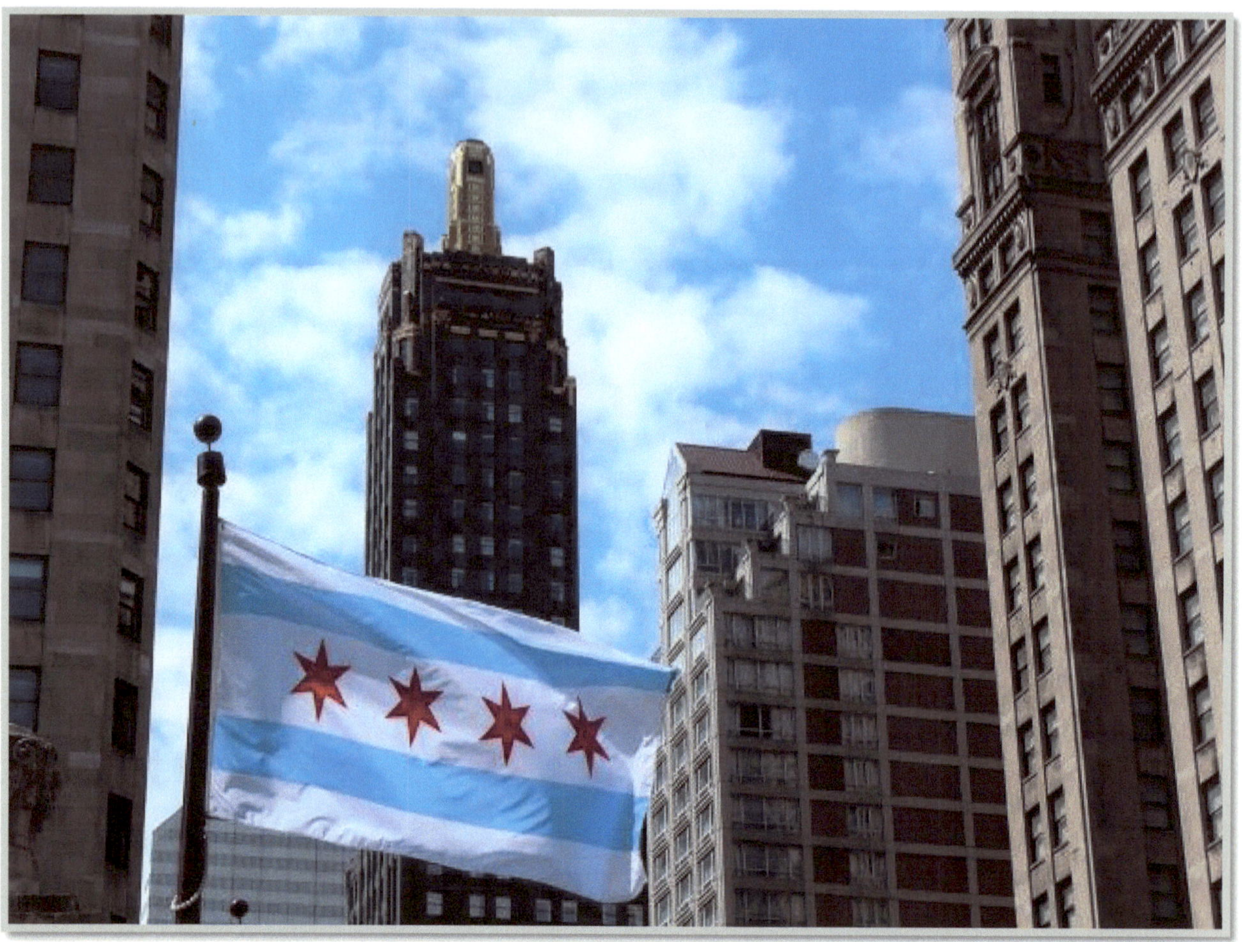

"Under the seeming disorder of the old city, wherever the old city is working successfully, is a marvelous order for maintaining the safety of the streets and the freedom of the city. It is a complex order. Its essence is intricacy of sidewalk use, bringing with it a constant succession of eyes. This order is all composed of movement and change, and although it is life, not art, we may fancifully call it the art form of the city and liken it to the dance — not to a simple-minded precision dance with everyone kicking up at the same time, twirling in unison and bowing off en masse, but to an intricate ballet in which the individual dancers and ensembles all have distinctive parts which miraculously reinforce each other and compose an orderly whole. The ballet of the good city sidewalk never repeats itself from place to place, and in any once place is always replete with new improvisations." **Jane Jacobs, The Death and Life of Great American Cities**

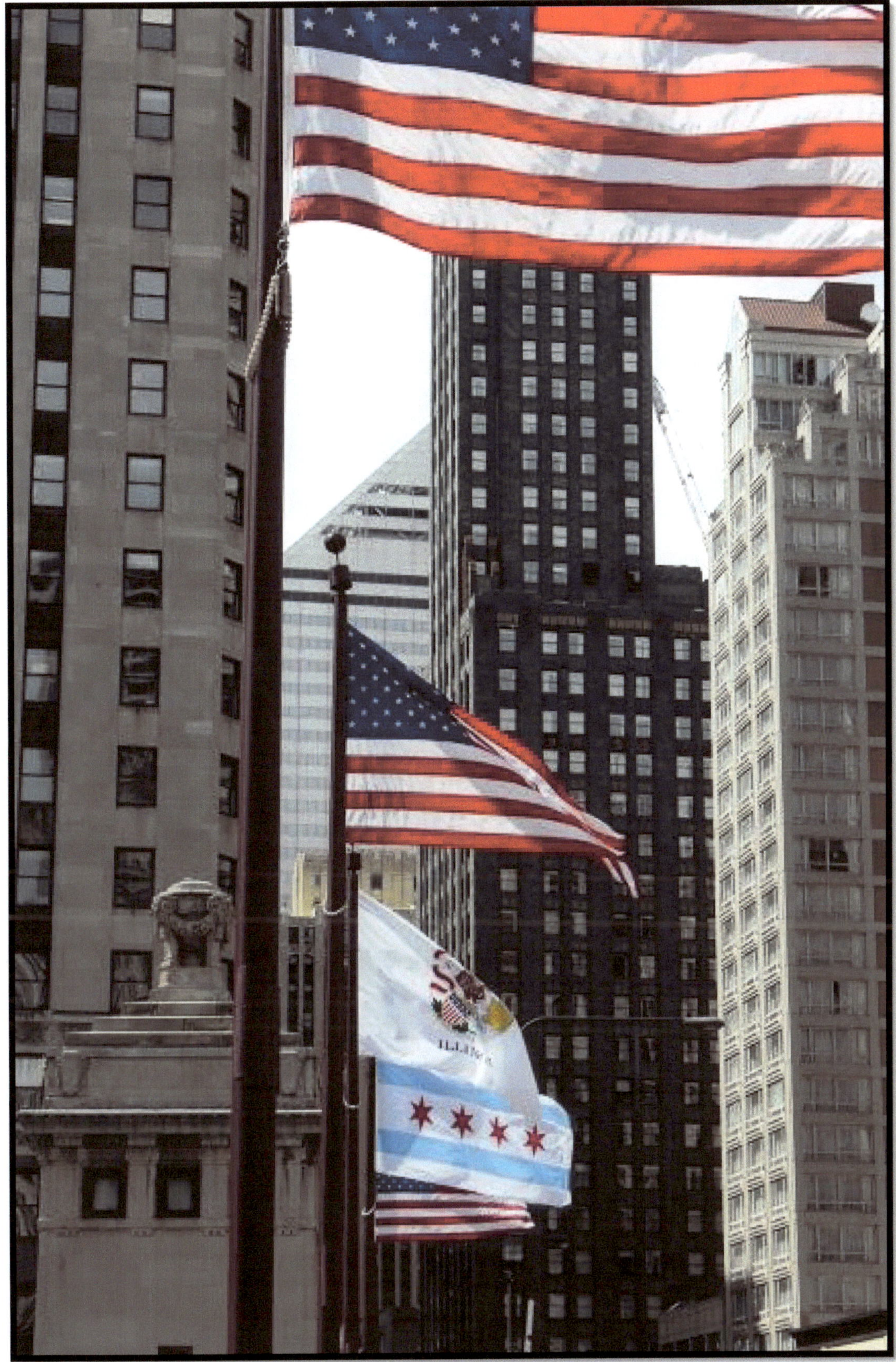

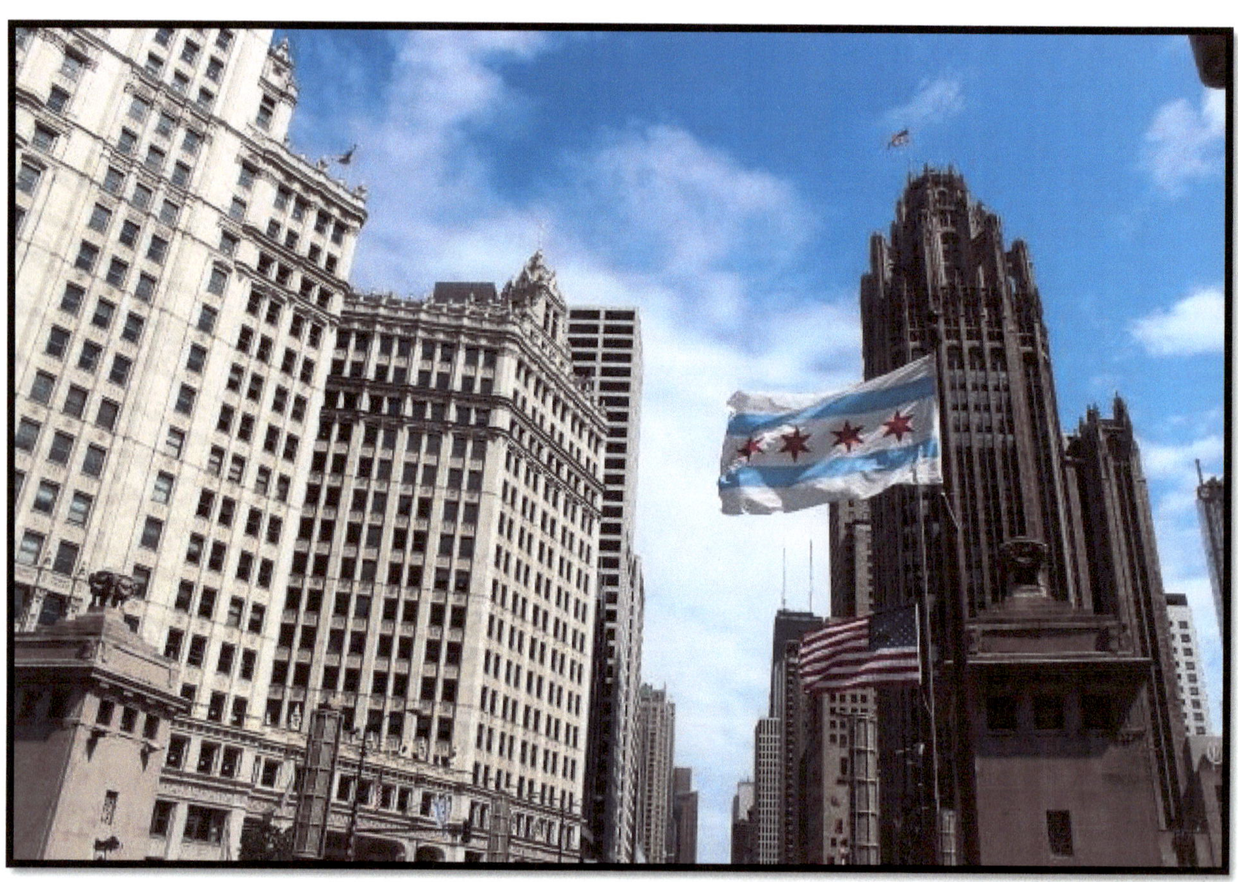

"Chicago's one of the rare places where architecture is more visible."

Frank Gehry.

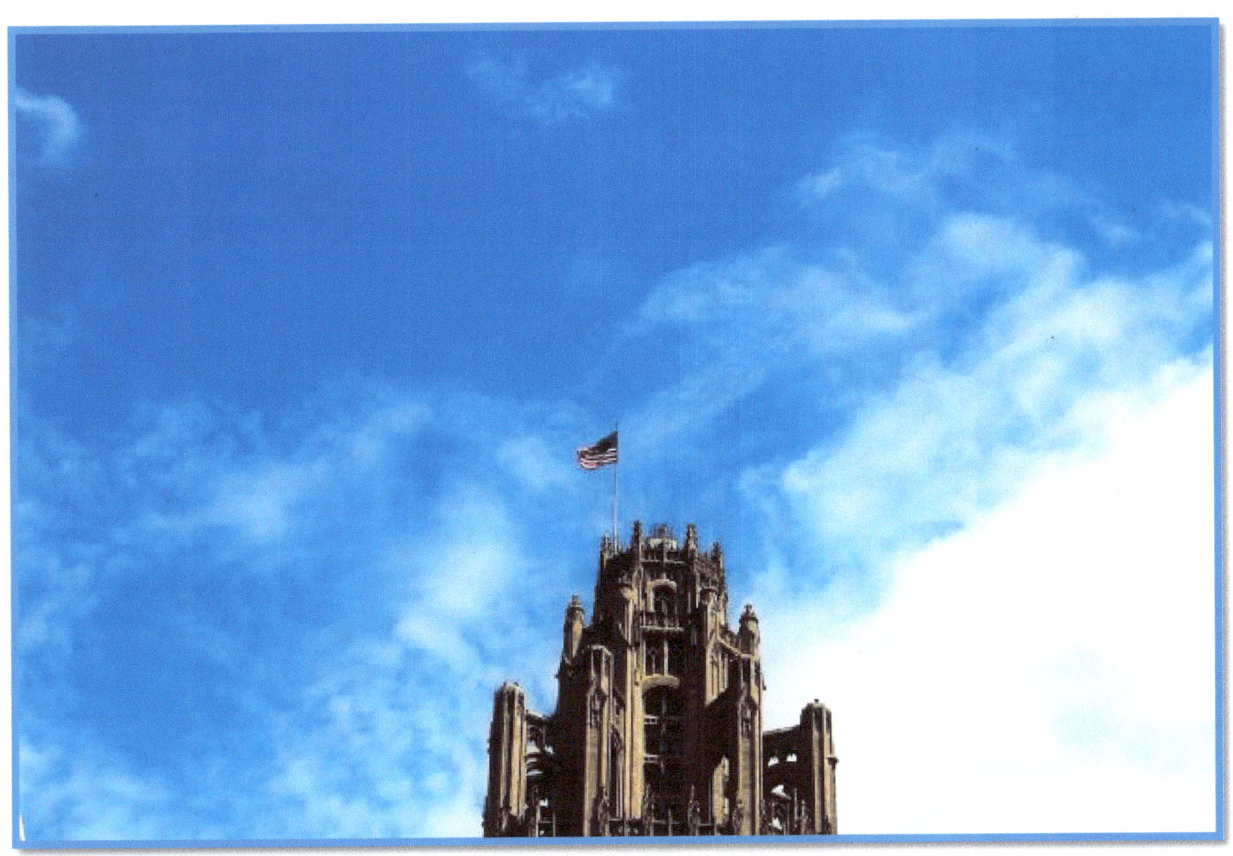

“We depend on our surroundings obliquely to embody the moods and ideas we respect and then to remind us of them. We look to our buildings to hold us, like a kind of psychological mould, to a helpful vision of ourselves. We arrange around us material forms which communicate to us what we need — but are at constant risk of forgetting what we need — within. We turn to wallpaper, benches, paintings and streets to staunch the disappearance of our true selves.” **Alain de Botton, The Architecture of Happiness**

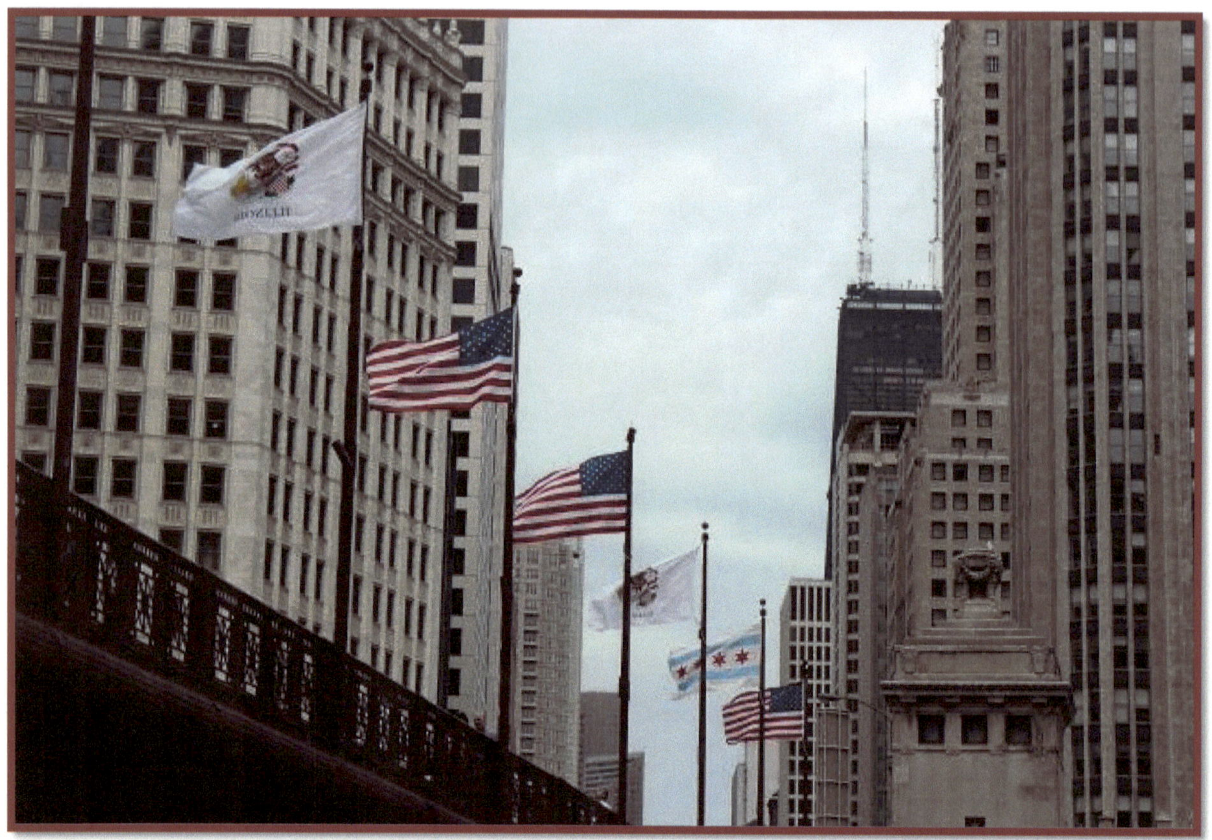

Chicago is the Great American City, and it was really great to live there during a time of economic expansion and opportunity and growth. I felt like I was living at the center of the world. **John Green**

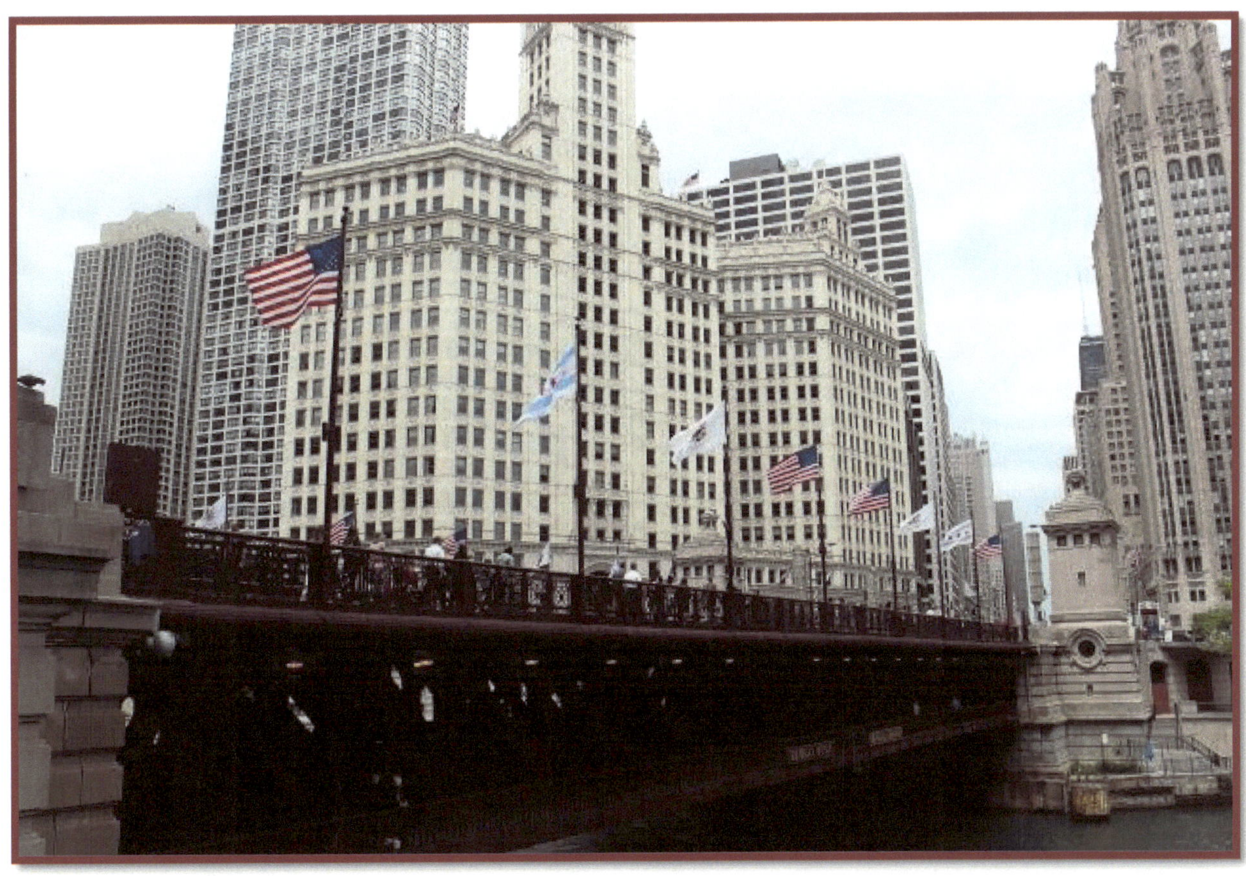

“So he bought tickets to the Greyhound and they climbed, painfully, inch by inch and with the knowledge that, once they reached the top, there would be one breath-taking moment when the car would tip precariously into space, over an incline six stories steep and then plunge, like a plunging plane. She buried her head against him, fearing to look at the park spread below. He forced himself to look: thousands of little people and hundreds of bright little stands, and over it all the coal-smoke pall of the river factories and railroad yards. He saw in that moment the whole dim-lit city on the last night of summer; the troubled streets that led to the abandoned beaches, the for-rent signs above overnight hotels and furnished basement rooms, moving trolleys and rising bridges: the cagework city, beneath a coalsmoke sky.” **Nelson Algren, Never Come Morning**

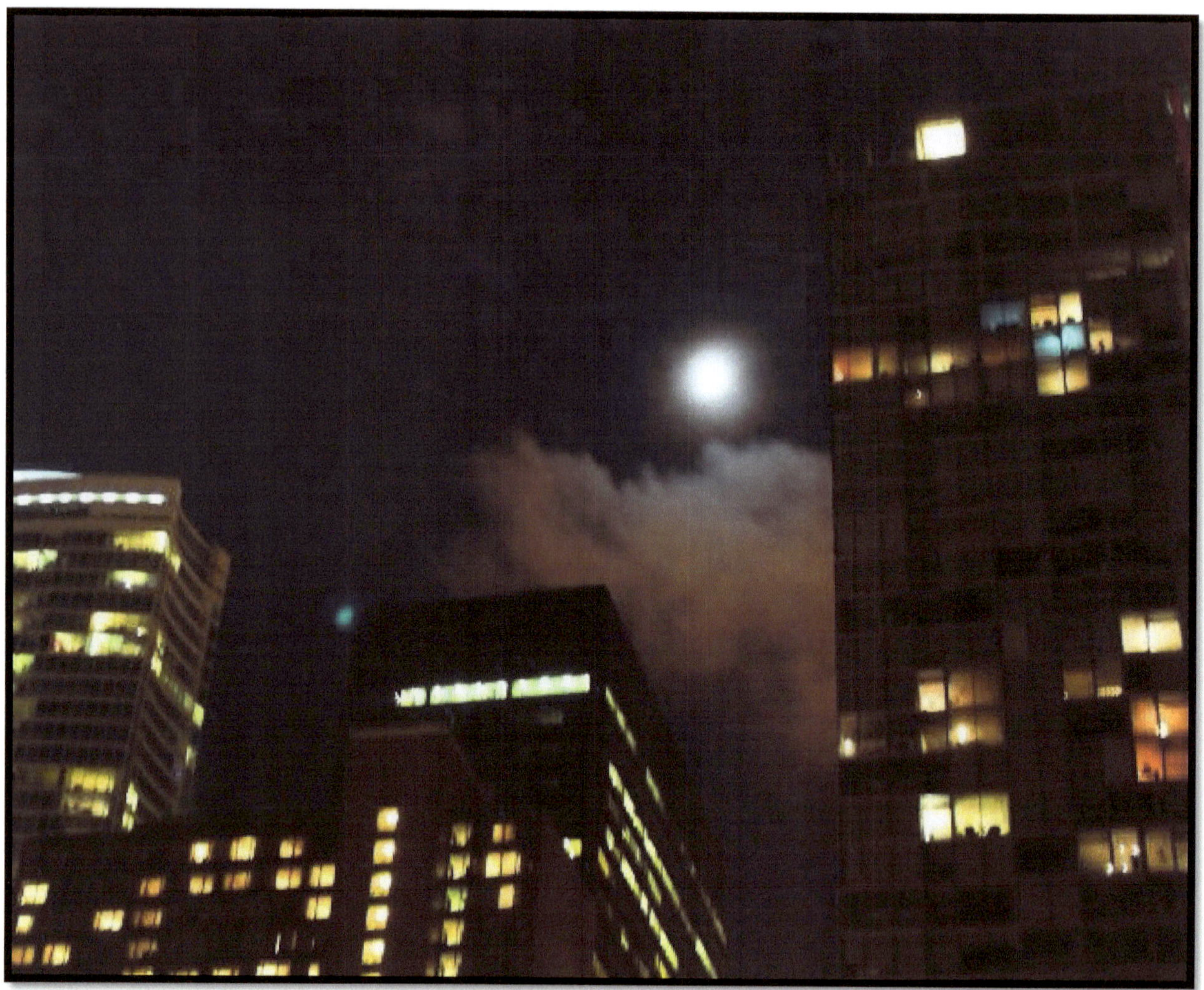

All cities are mad: but the madness is gallant. All cities are beautiful, but the beauty is grim. **Christopher Morley**

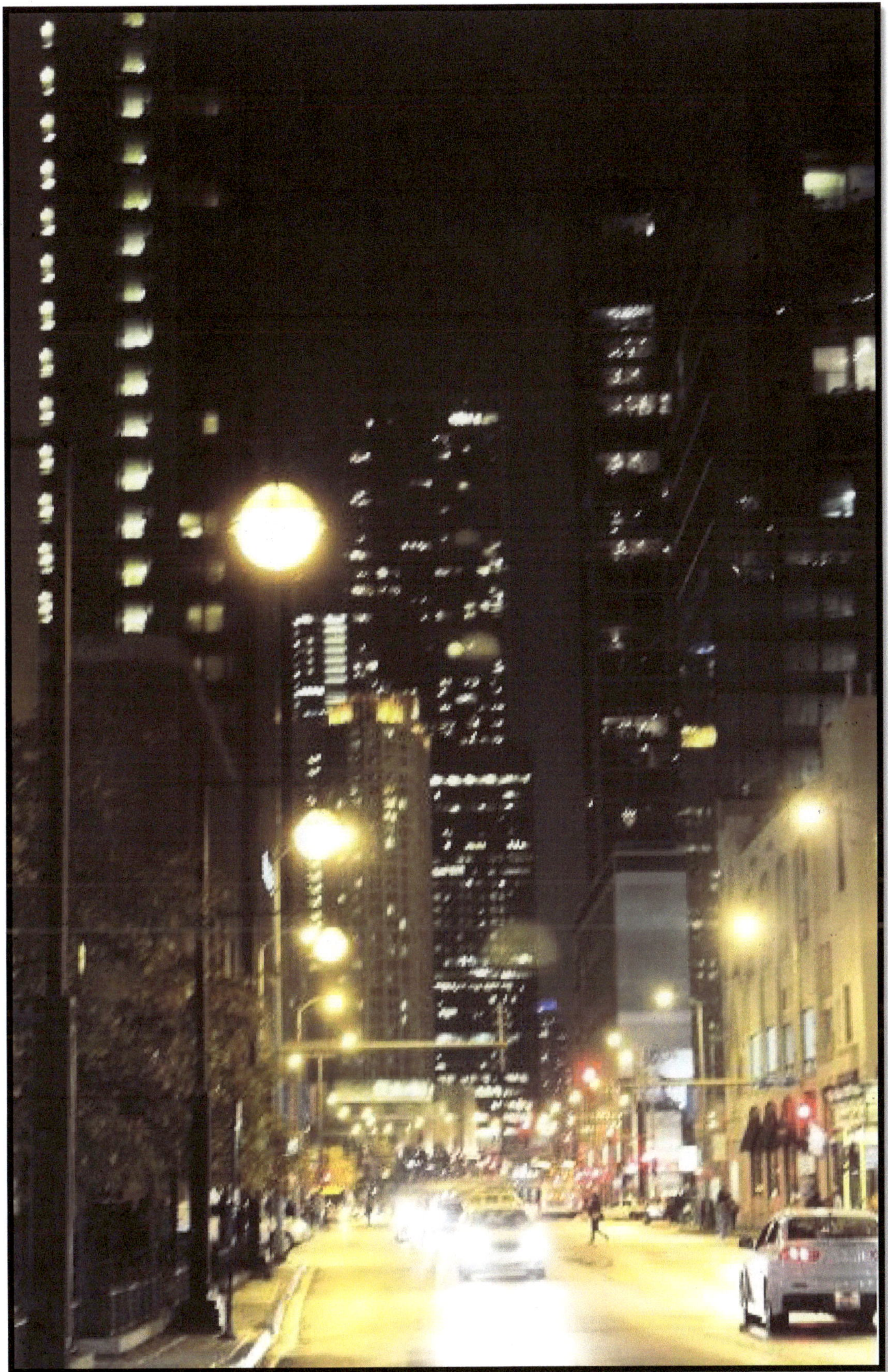

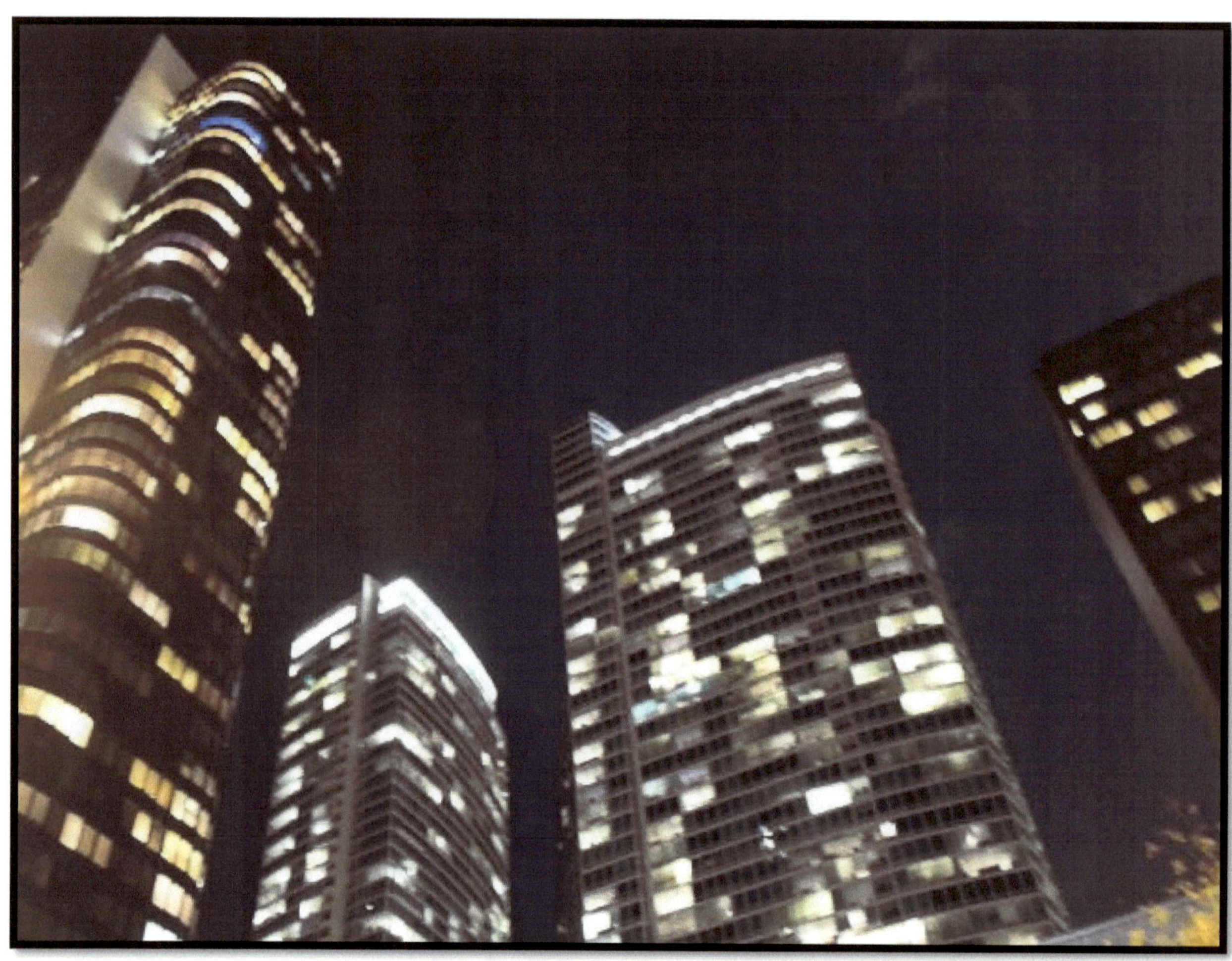

Towered cities please us then,
And the busy hum of men.
John Milton, L'Allegro.

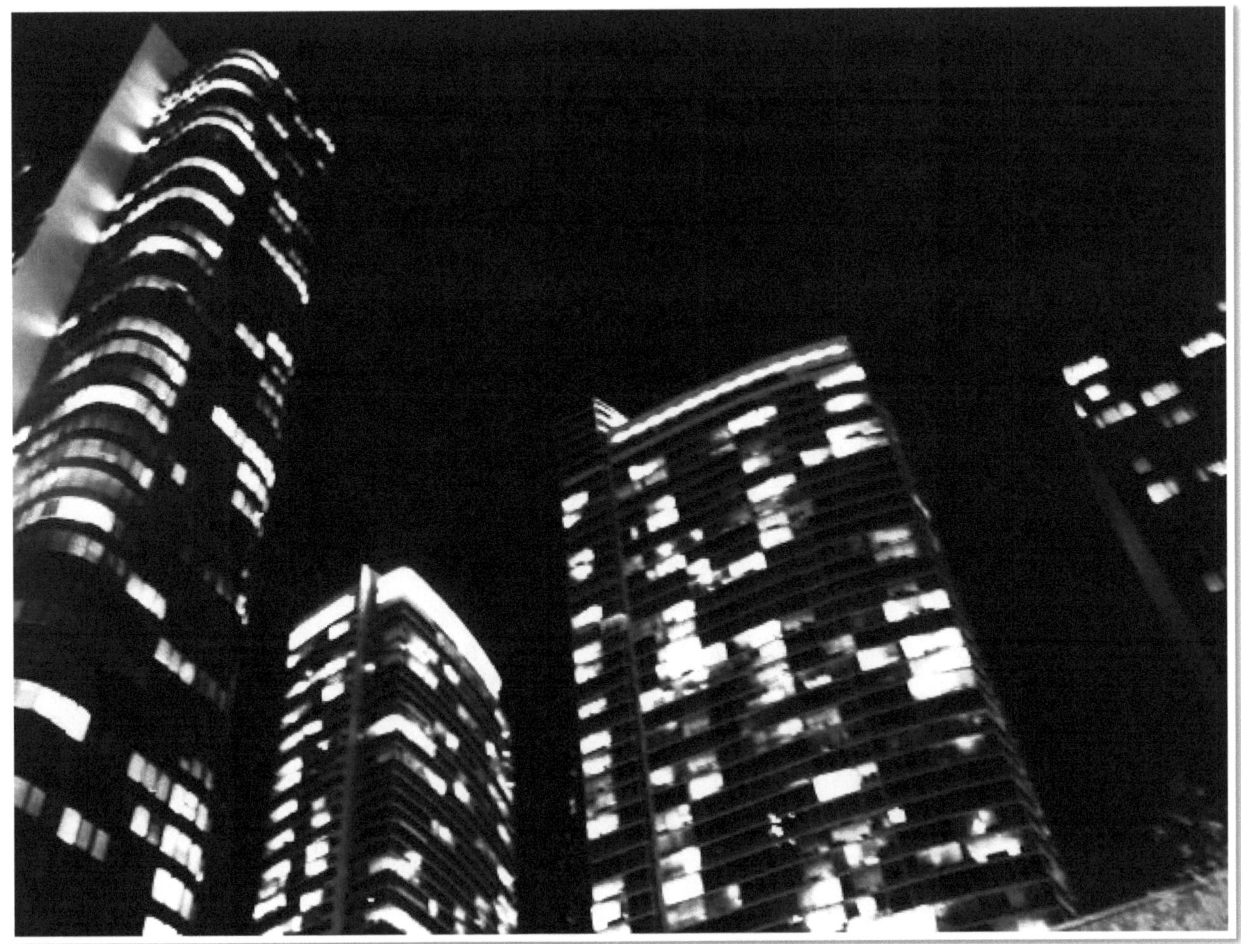

“In the Big City large and sudden things happen. You round a corner and thrust the rib of your umbrella into the eye of your old friend from Kootenai Falls. You stroll out to pluck a Sweet William in the park -- and lo! bandits attack you -- you are ambulanced to the hospital -- you marry your nurse; are divorced -- get squeezed while short on U. P. S. and D. O. W. N. S. -- stand in the bread line -- marry an heiress, take out your laundry and pay your club dues -- seemingly all in the wink of an eye.... The City is a sprightly youngster, and you are red paint upon its toy, and you get licked off.” **O. Henry, "The Complete Life of John Hopkins"**

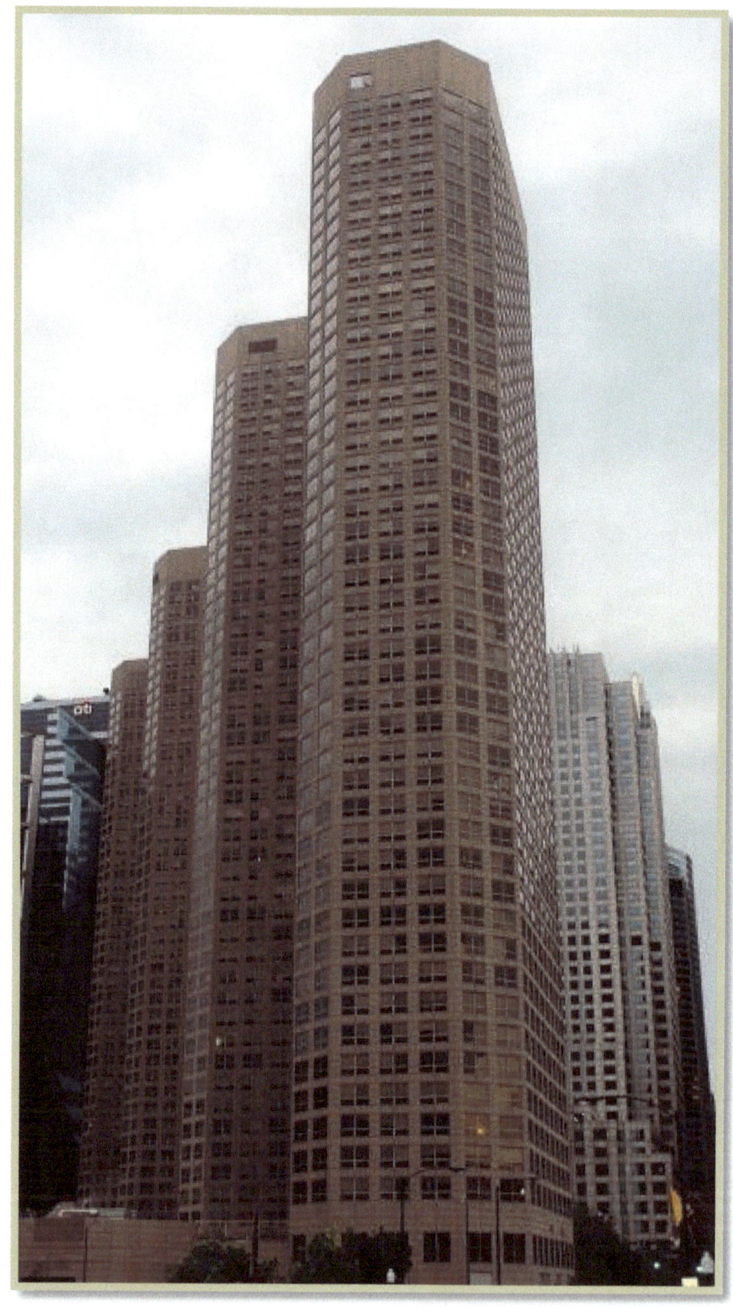

"At first I didn't cotton to Mies's Lake Shore Drive towers in Chicago, but when I went there and saw how they come down on the slab of one-and-seven-eighths-inch thick travertine, I turned around. I think that was an incredible statement of modesty and power…It was so subtle, understated and powerful as hell" **Frank Gehry**

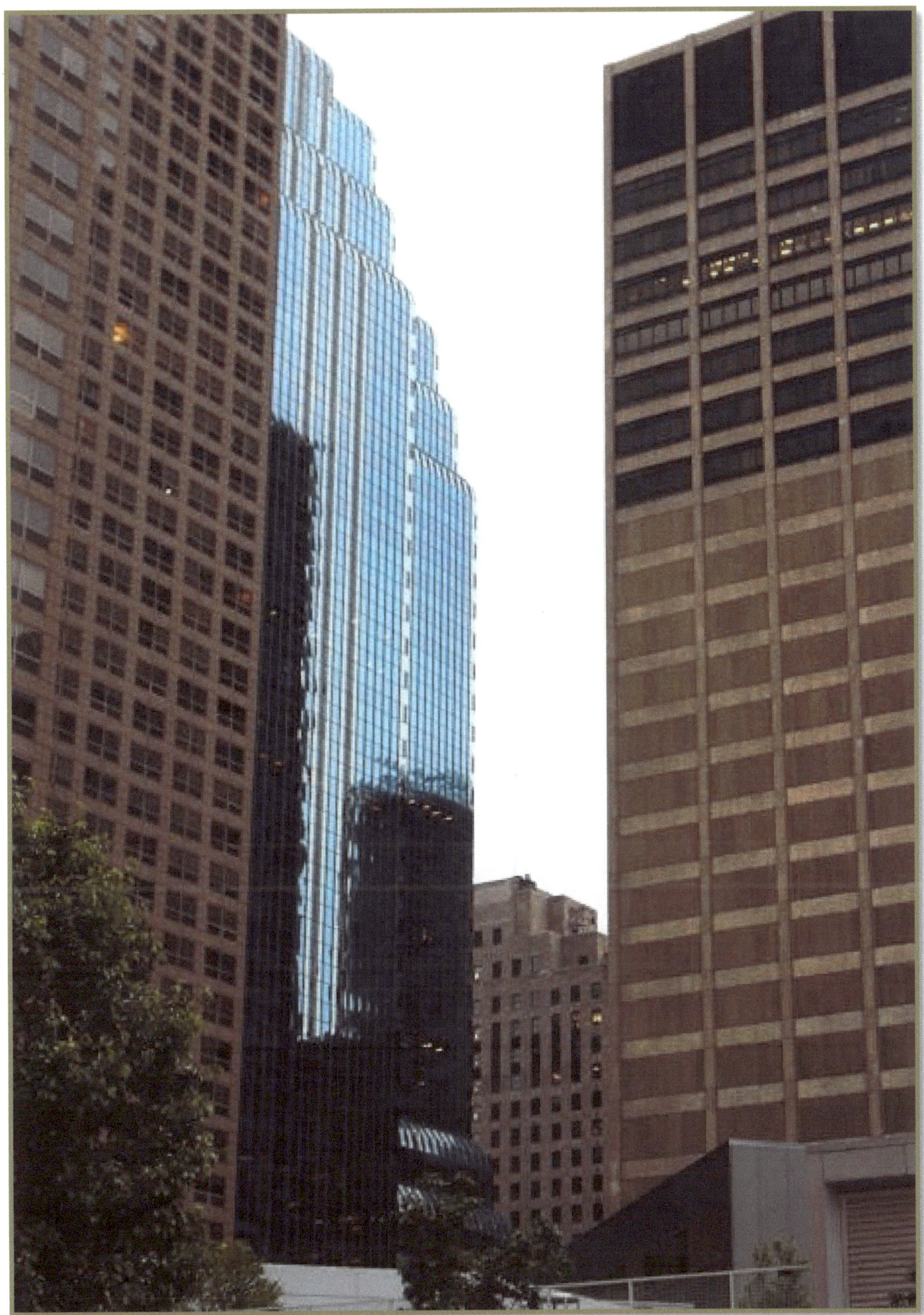

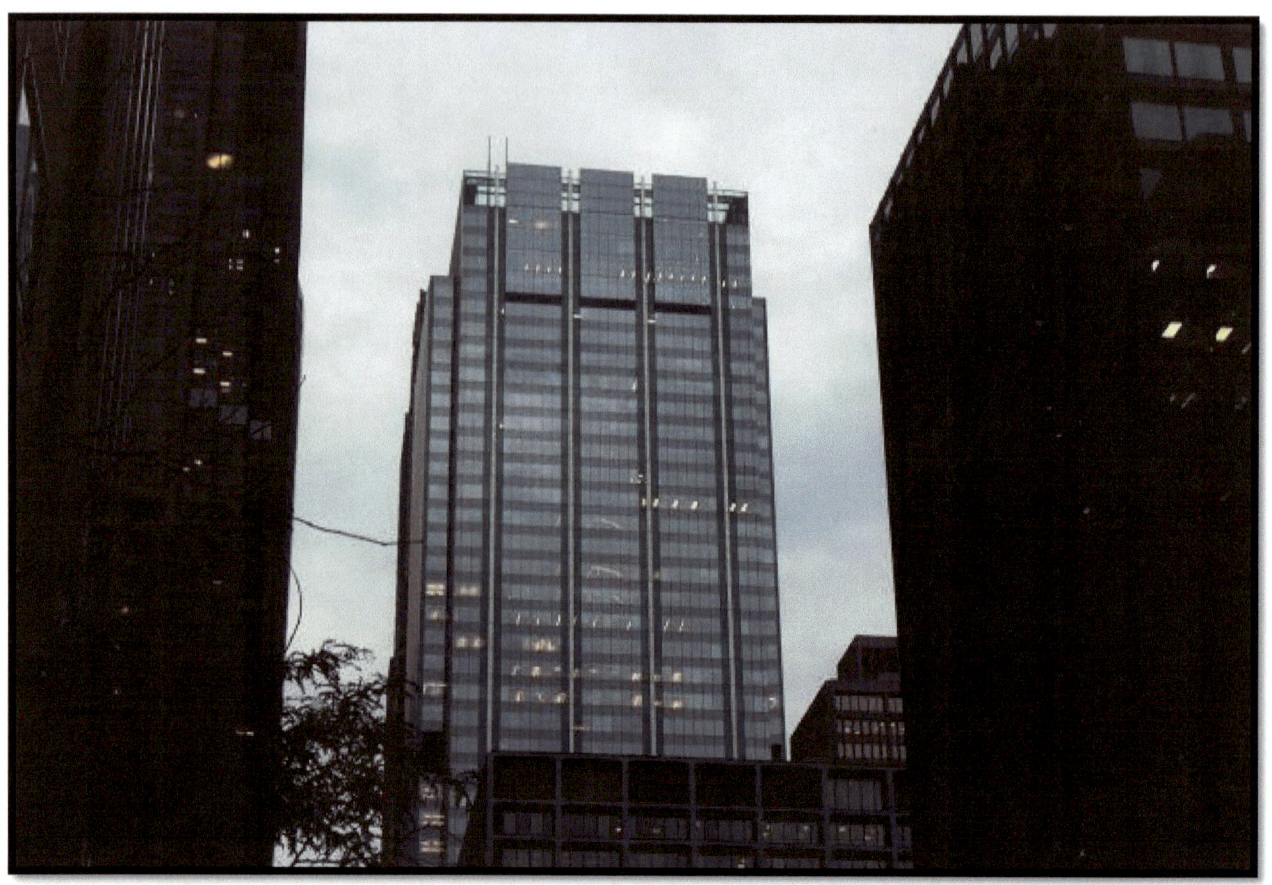

“The mother art is architecture. Without an architecture of our own we have no soul of our own civilization.” **Frank Lloyd , Oak Park.**

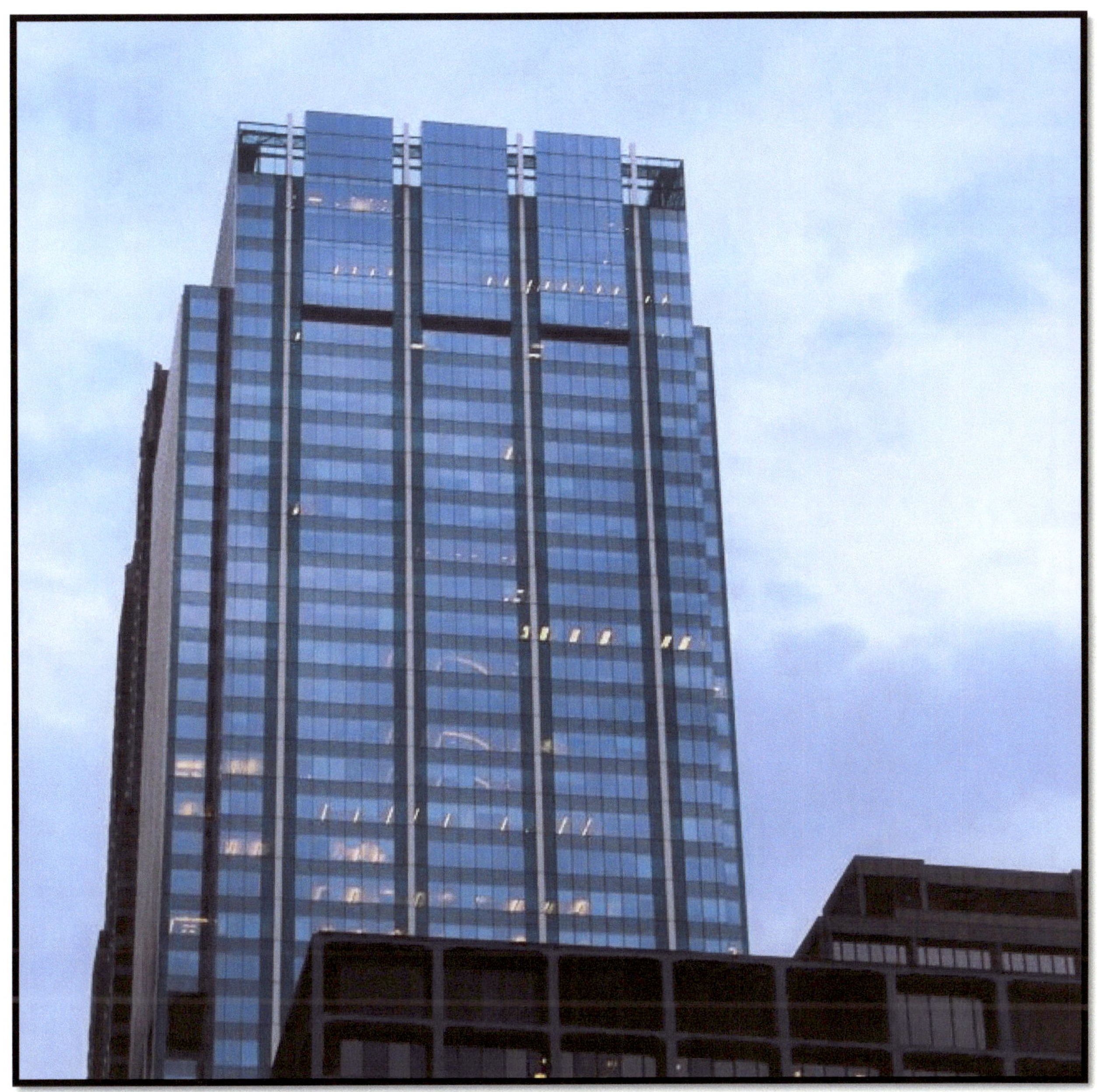

“I think there is a new awareness in this 21st century that design is as important to where and how we live as it is for museums, concert halls and civic buildings.” **Daniel Libeskind**

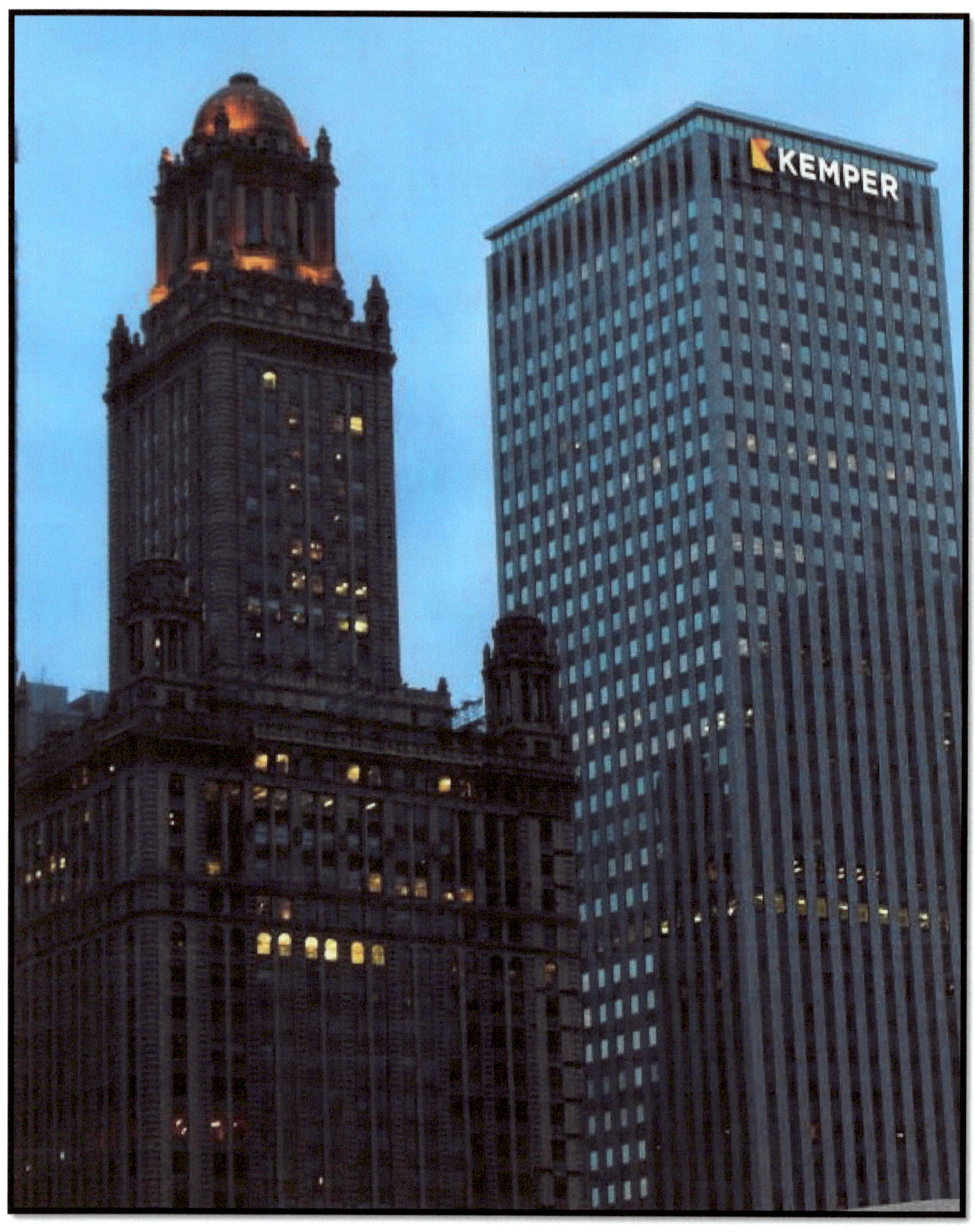

"The most beautiful modern city in the world is Chicago."

Nicola Bulgari

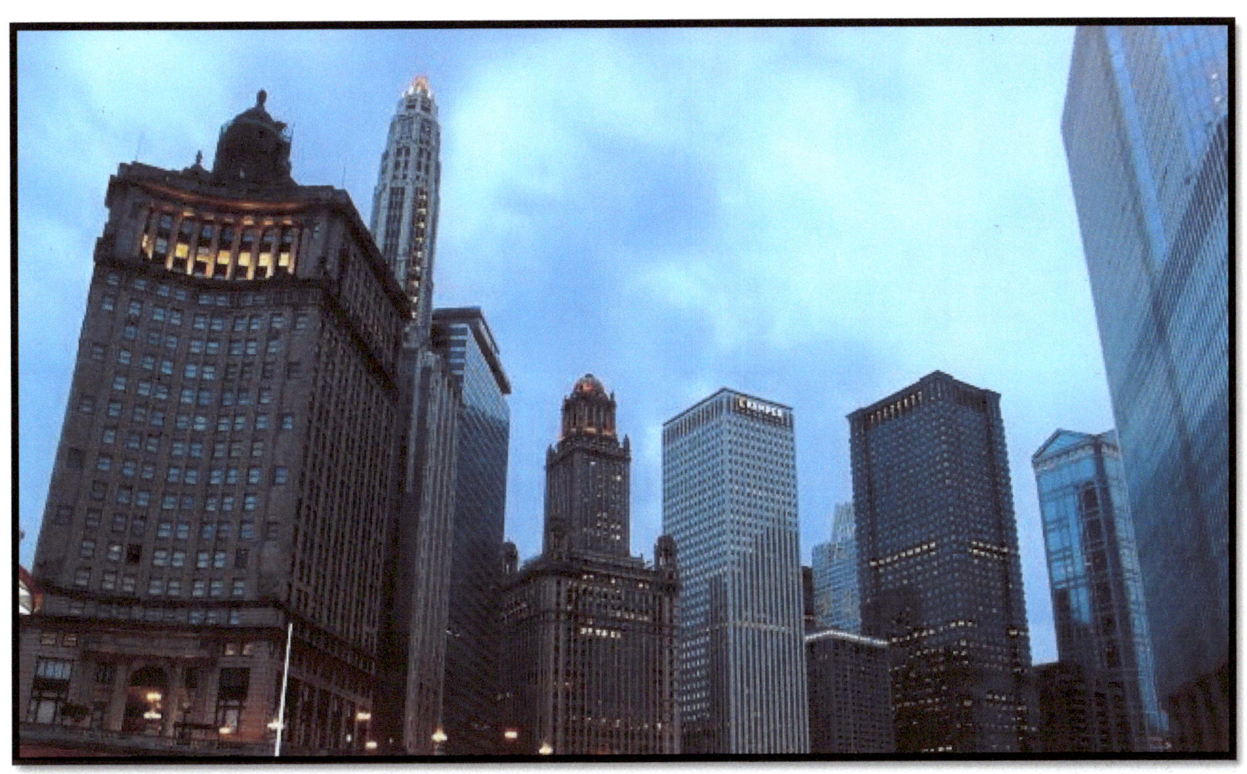

"I give you Chicago. It is not London and Harvard. It is not Paris and buttermilk. It is American in every chitling and sparerib. It is alive from snout to tail." **H. L. Mencken**

"Here is the difference between Dante, Milton, and me. They wrote about hell and never saw the place. I wrote about Chicago after looking the town over for years and years." **Carl Sandburg**

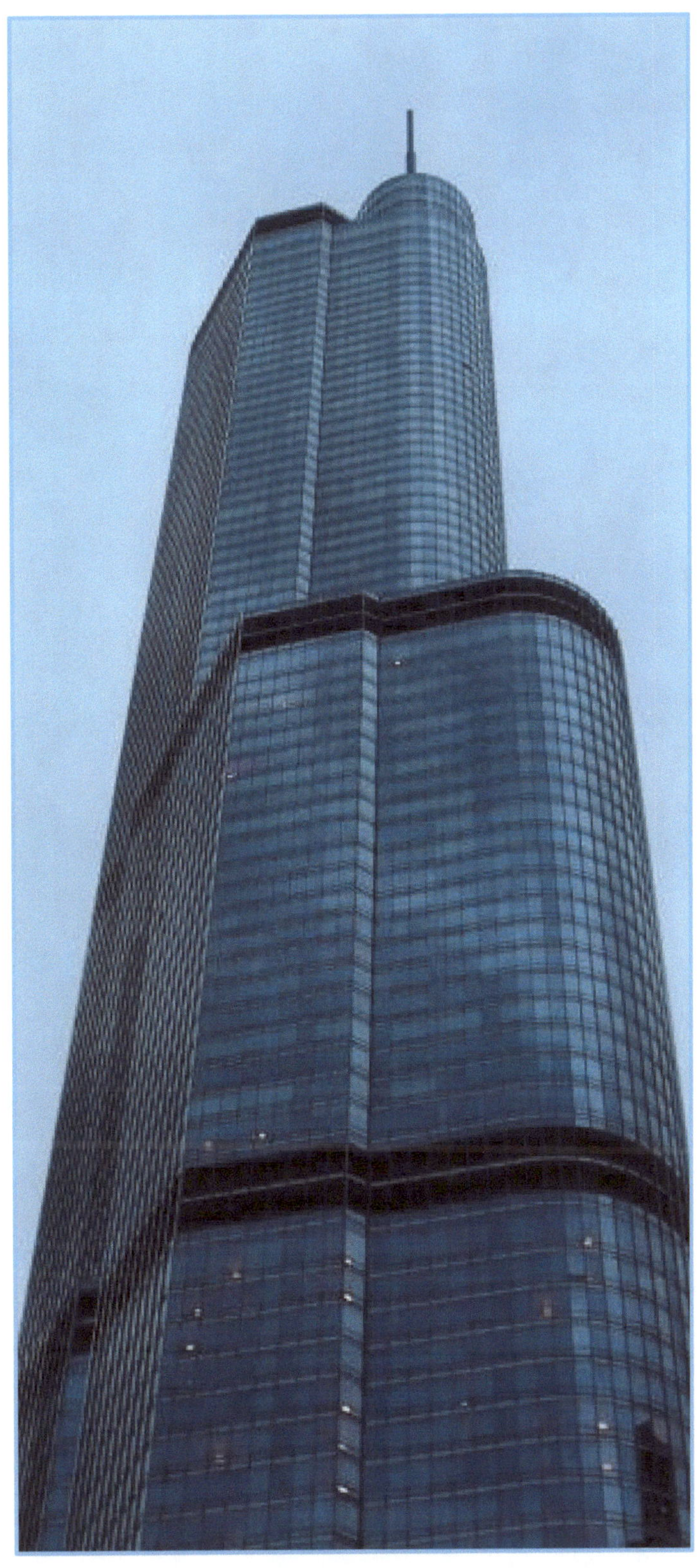

The American attitude towards efficiency and execution should always underlie architecture." **Helmut Jahn, Chicagoan**

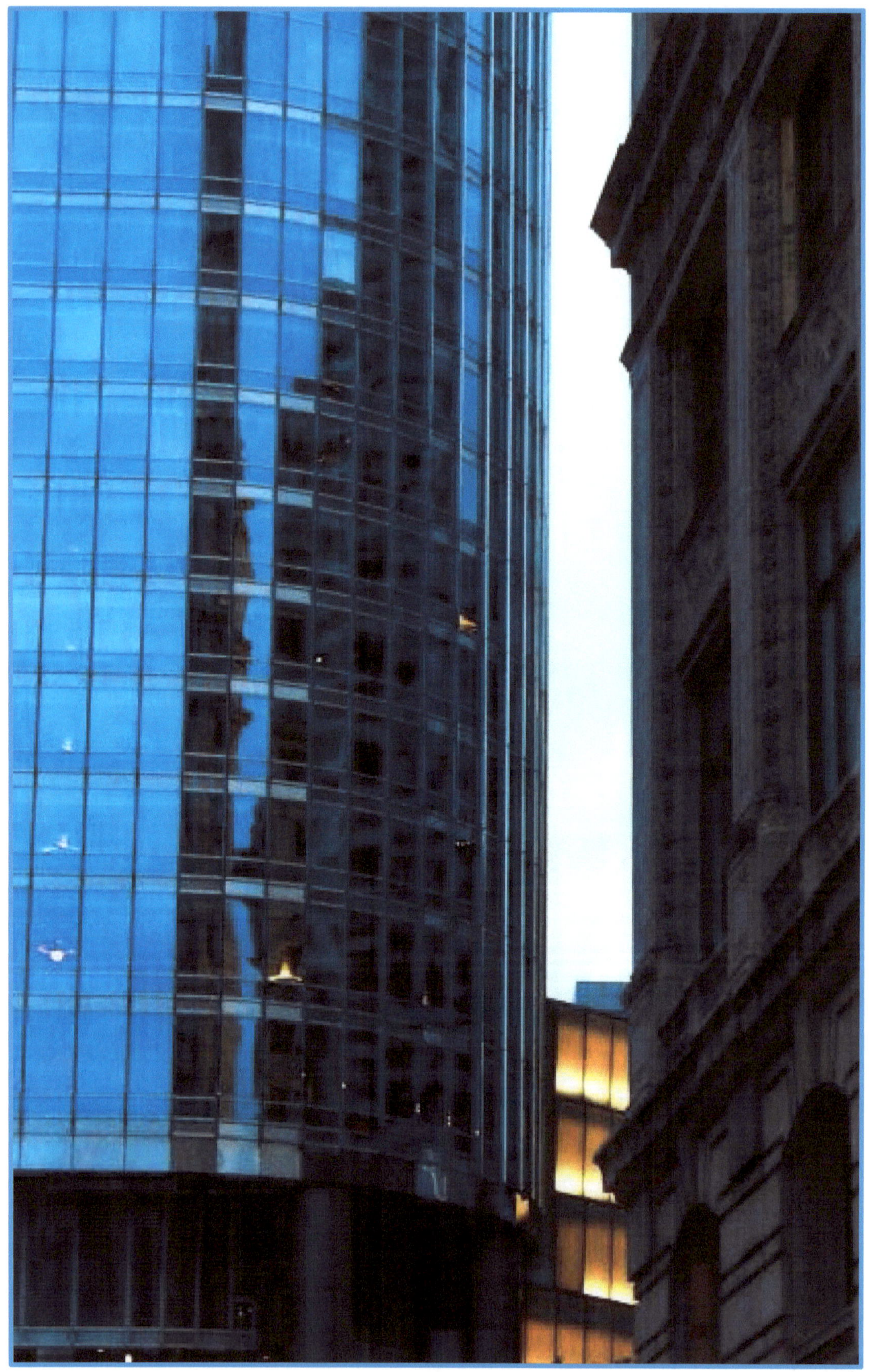

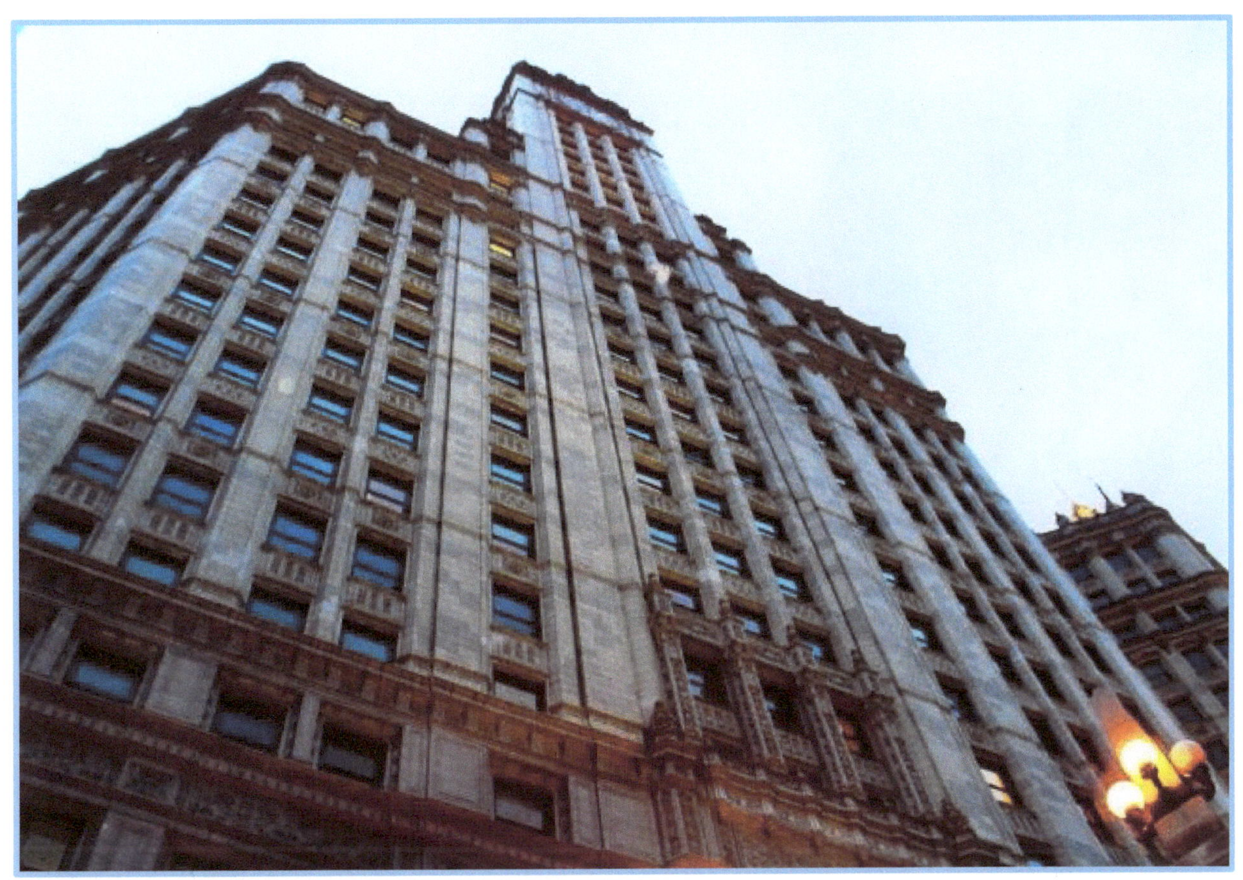

“A great building must begin with the unmeasurable, must go through measurable means when it is being designed and in the end must be unmeasurable.” **Louis Kahn**

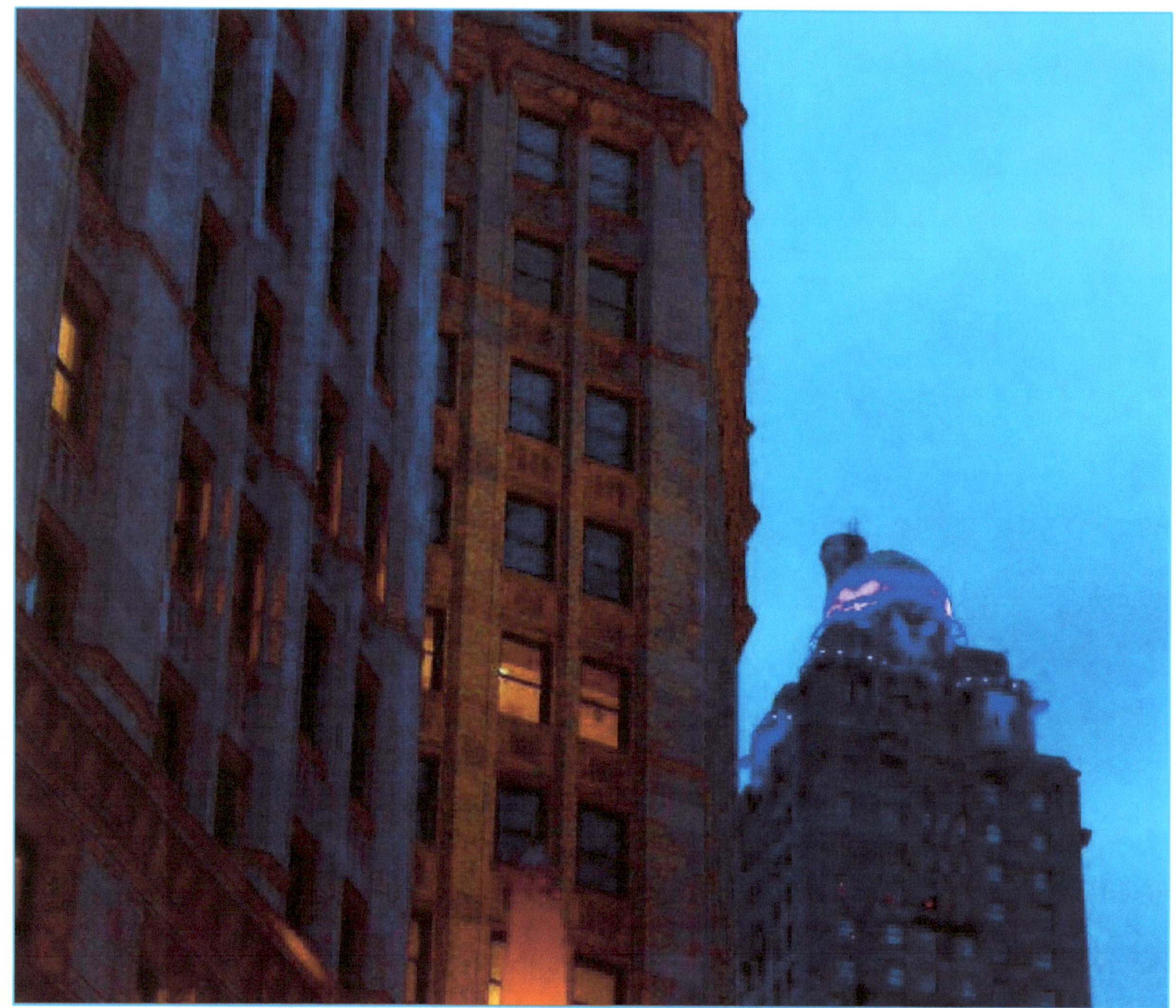

"The greatest products of architecture are less the works of individuals than of society; rather the offspring of a nation's effort, than the inspired flash of a man of genius..." **Victor Hugo, The Hunchback of Notre-Dame**

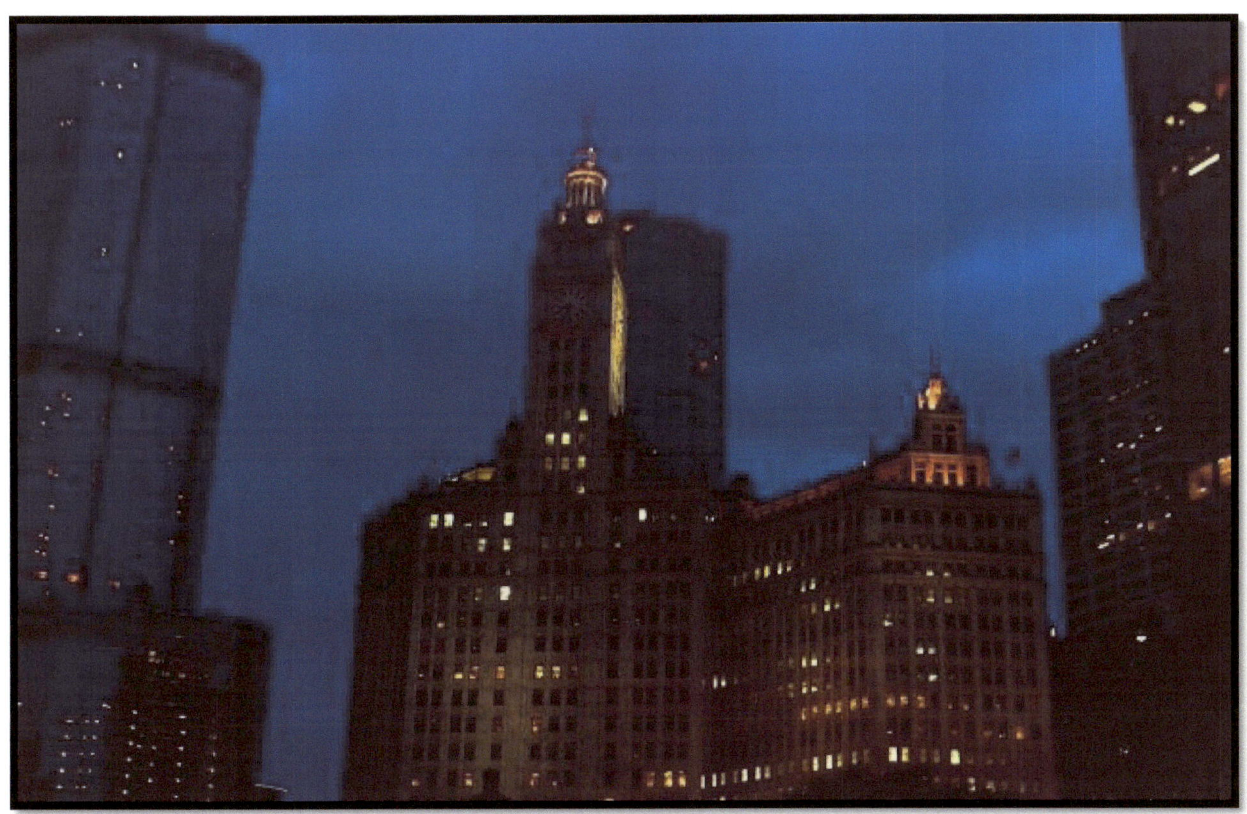

“All architecture is great architecture after sunset; perhaps architecture is really a nocturnal art, like the art of fireworks.” **Gilbert K. Chesterton**

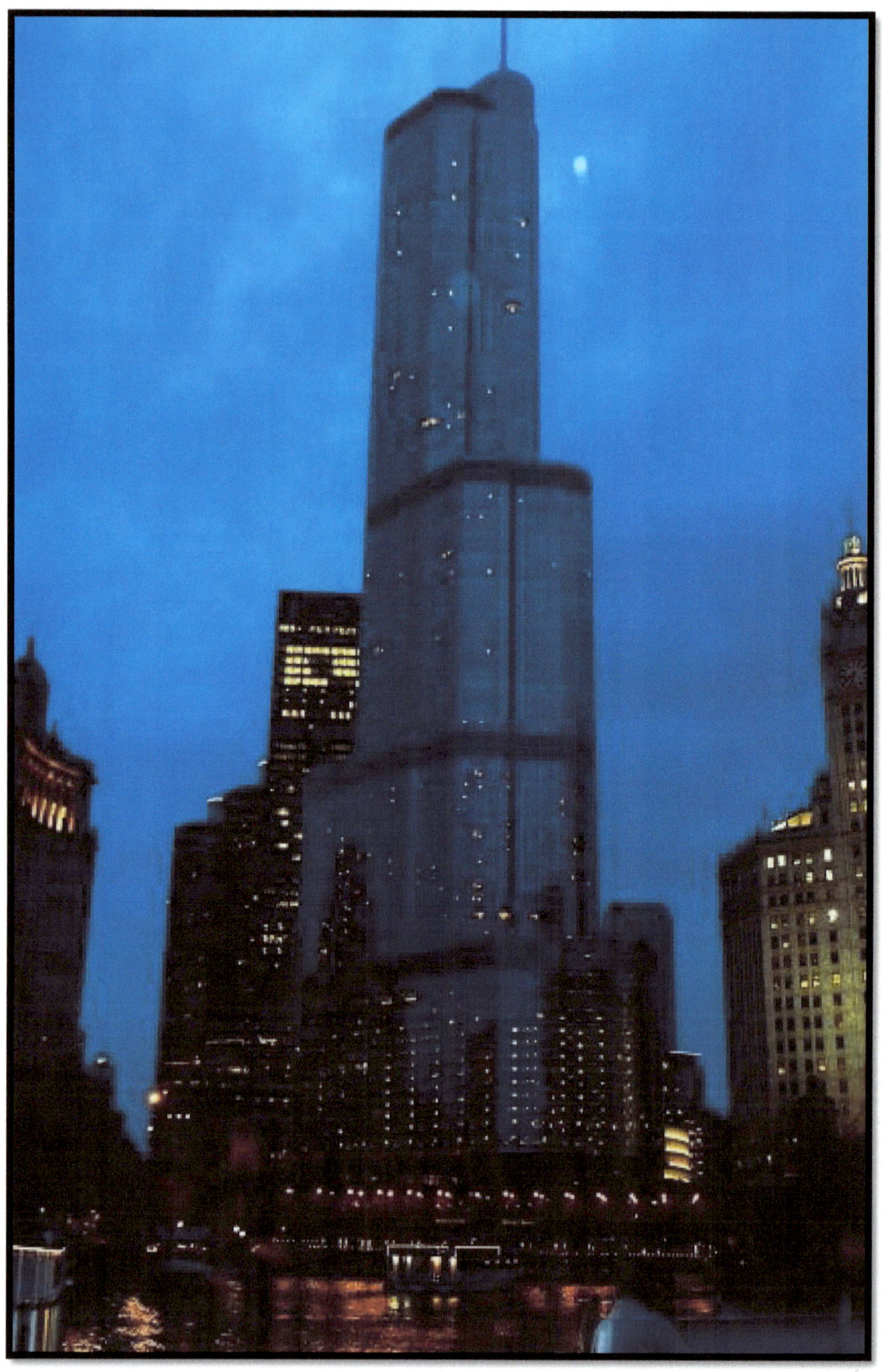

"I love Chicago. I lived there briefly for three months and kept a boat under one of those space-age buildings. It was very Jetsons." **Candace Bushnell**

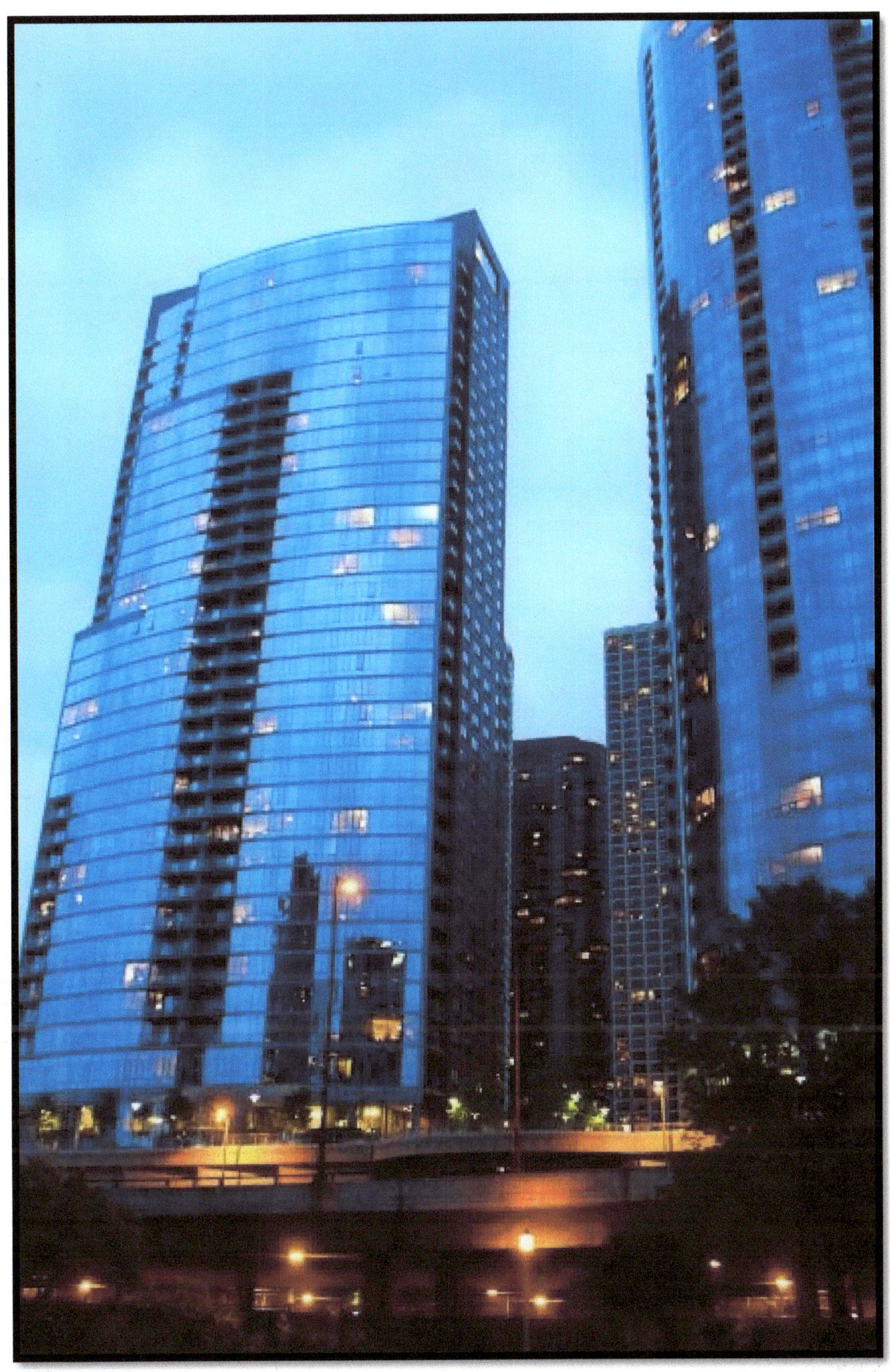

"Maybe we can show government how to operate better as a result of better architecture. Eventually, I think Chicago will be the most beautiful great city left in the world." **Frank Lloyd Wright**

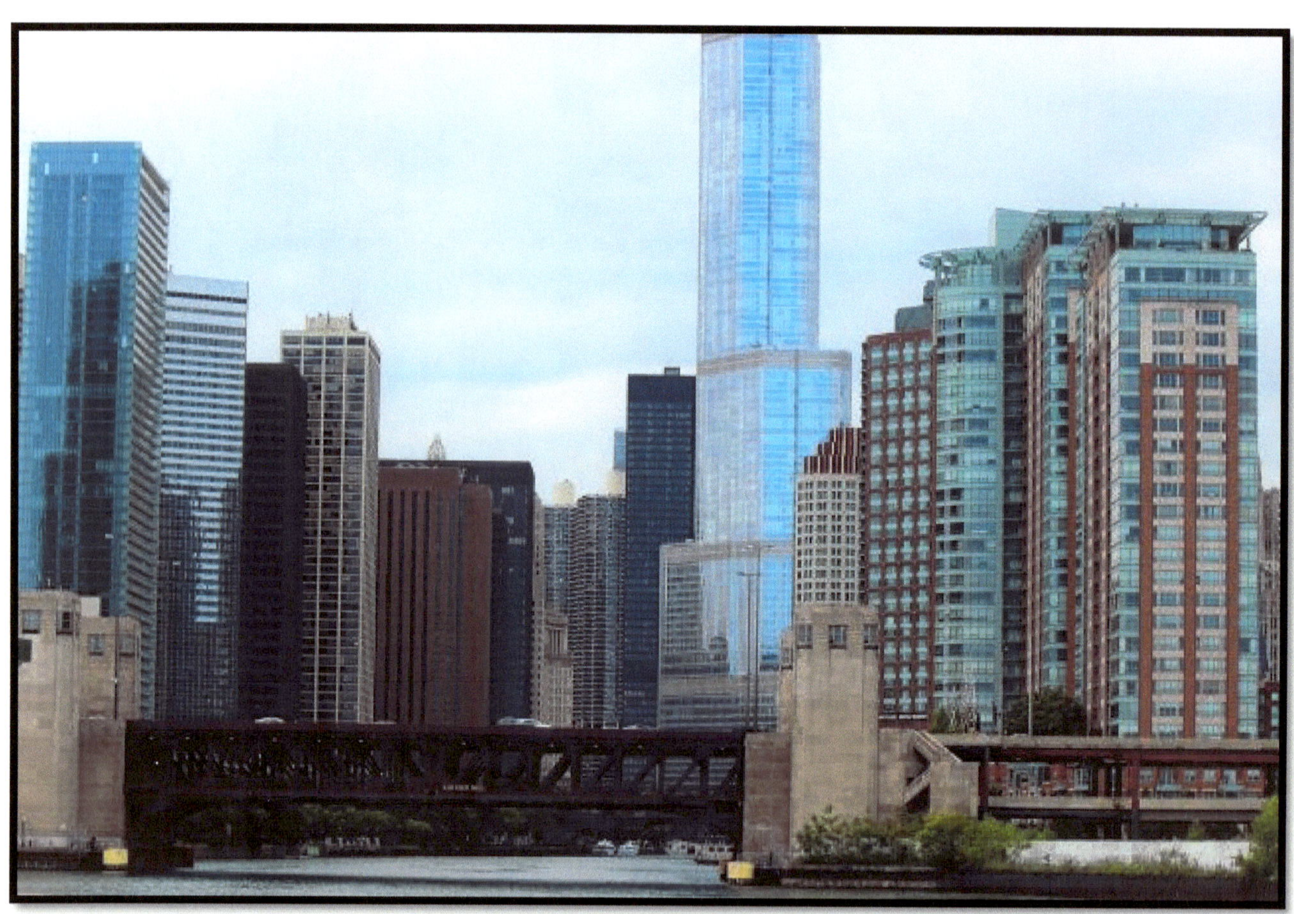

"I warn you, Jedediah, you're not going to like it in Chicago. The wind comes howling in off the lake and gosh only knows if they ever heard of lobster Newburg." **Orson Welles as *Citizen Kane***

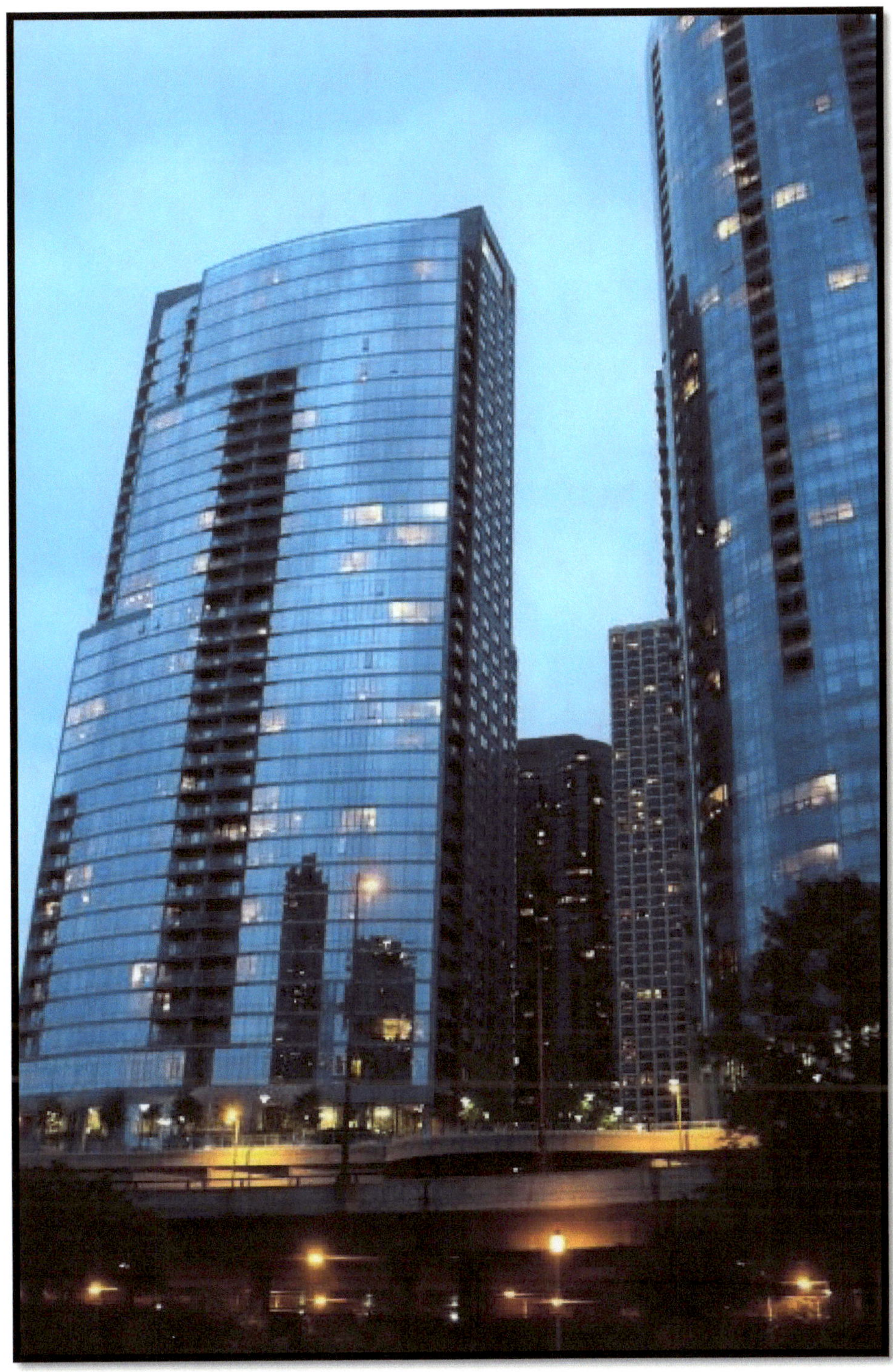

“When there were fears about the future of this nation’s older cities… when a few of the cities teetered on the brink of bankruptcy, all eyes were focused on Chicago for contrast." **Mayor Jane Byrne**

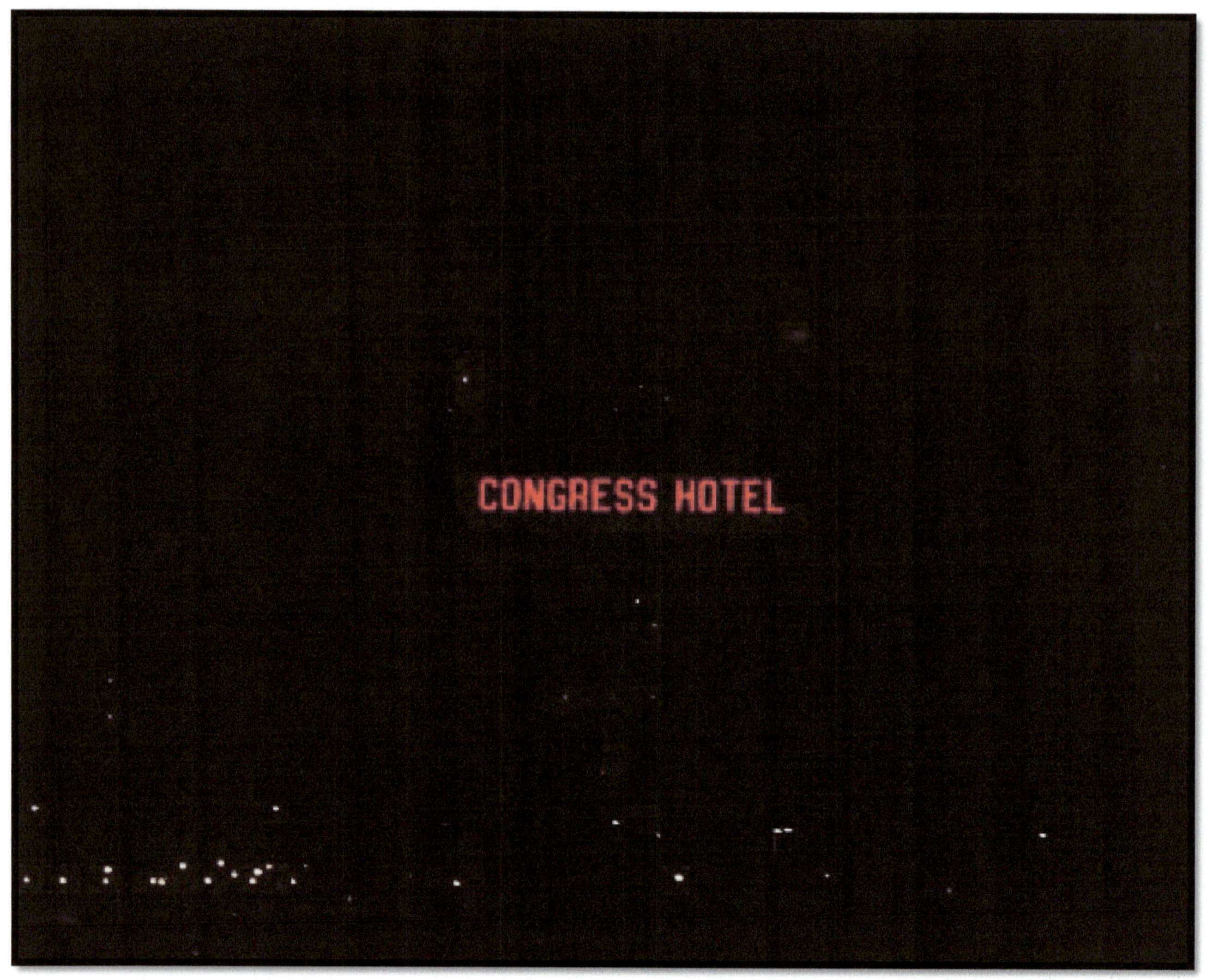

“How soon country people forget. When they fall in love with a city it is forever, and it is like forever. As though there never was a time when they didn't love it. The minute they arrive at the train station or get off the ferry and glimpse the wide streets and the wasteful lamps lighting them, they know they are born for it. There, in a city, they are not so much new as themselves: their stronger, riskier selves.”

Toni Morrison, Jazz

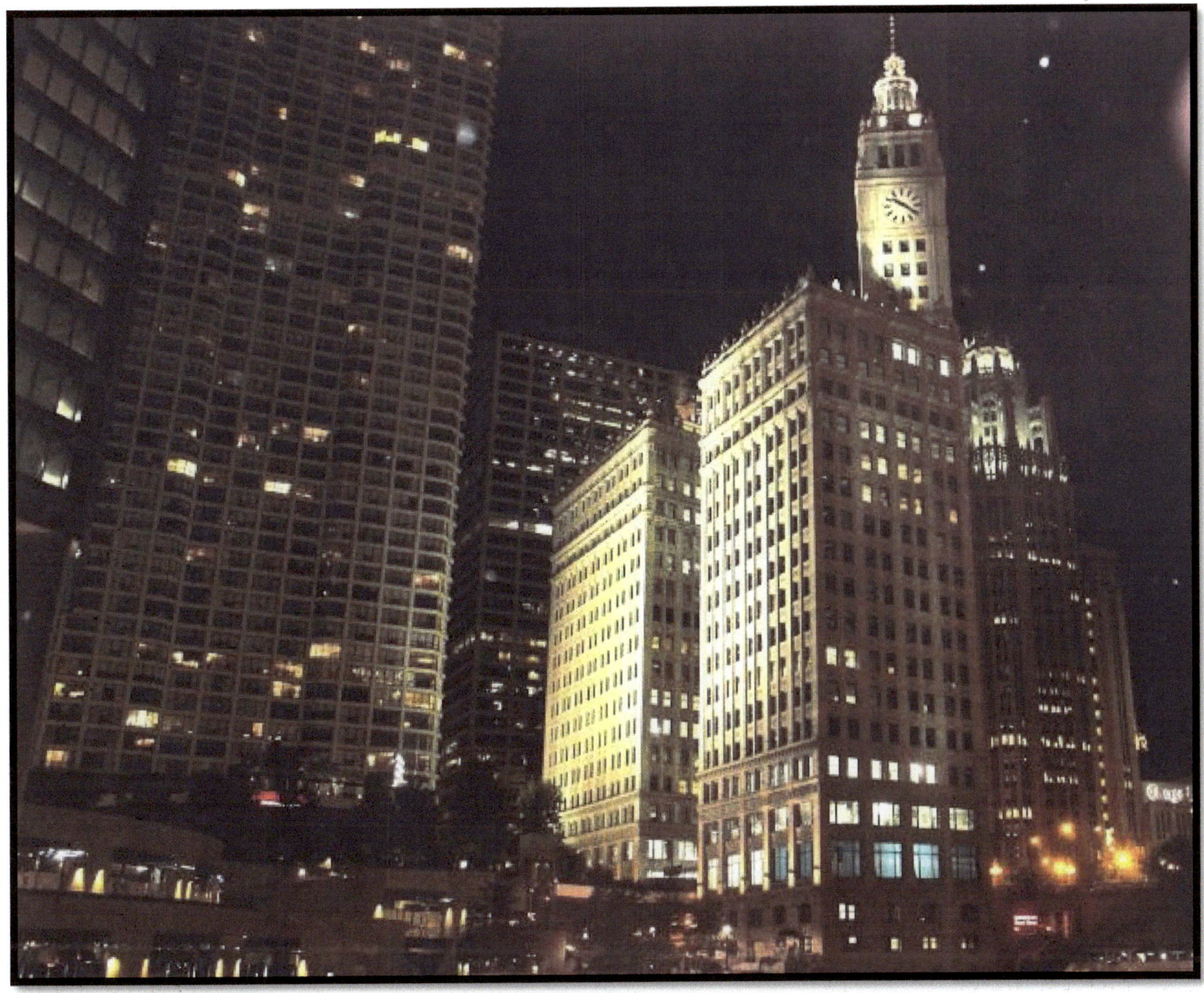

"It is the pervading law of all things organic, and inorganic, of all things physical and metaphysical, of all things human and all things super-human, of all true manifestations of the head, of the heart, of the soul, that the life is recognizable in its expression, that form ever follows function. This is the law."—**1896 essay "The Tall Office Building Artistically Considered" Louis Sullivan, Chicagoan**

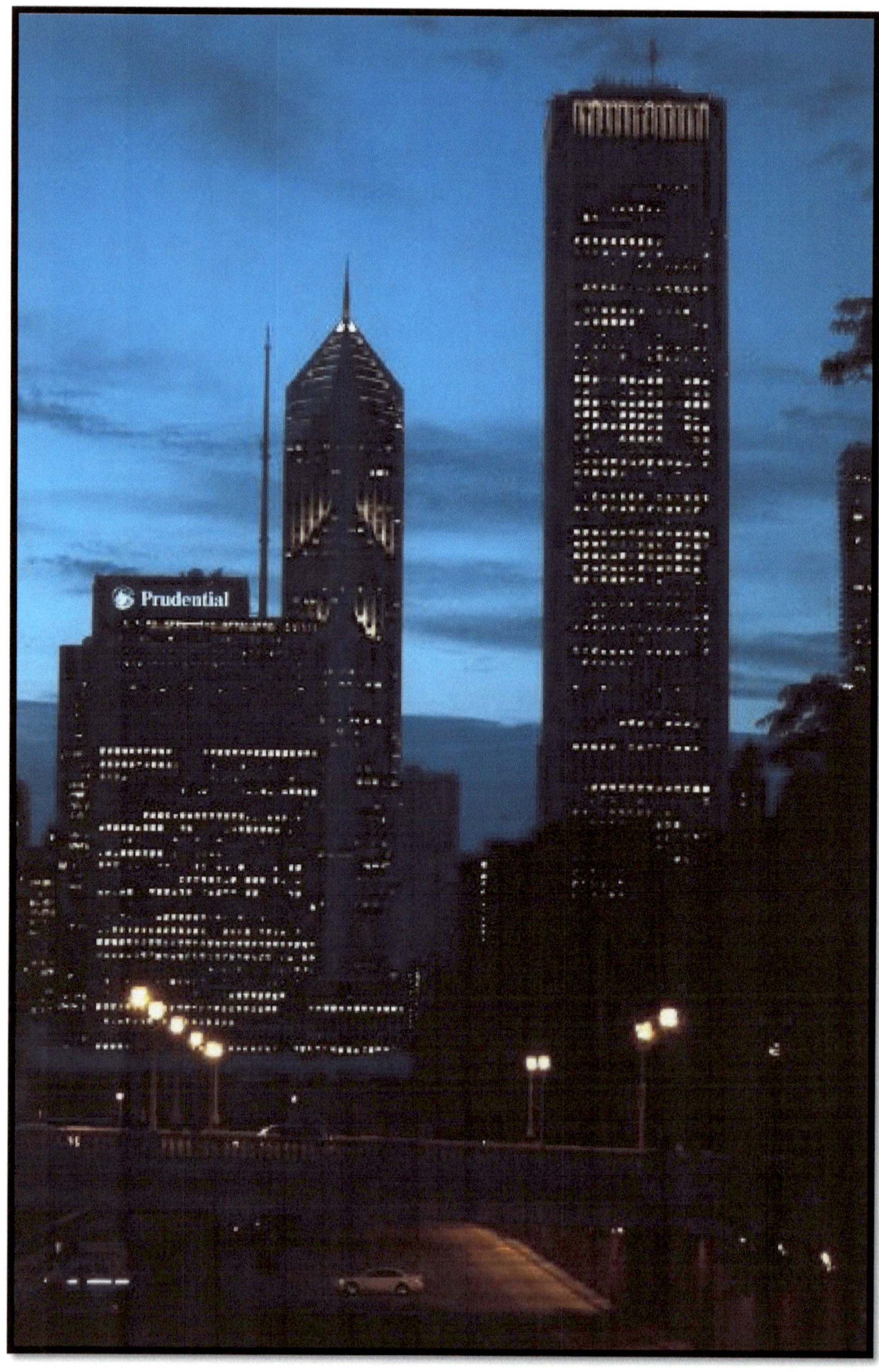

"Every building is a prototype. No two are alike." **Helmut Jahn, Chicagoan**

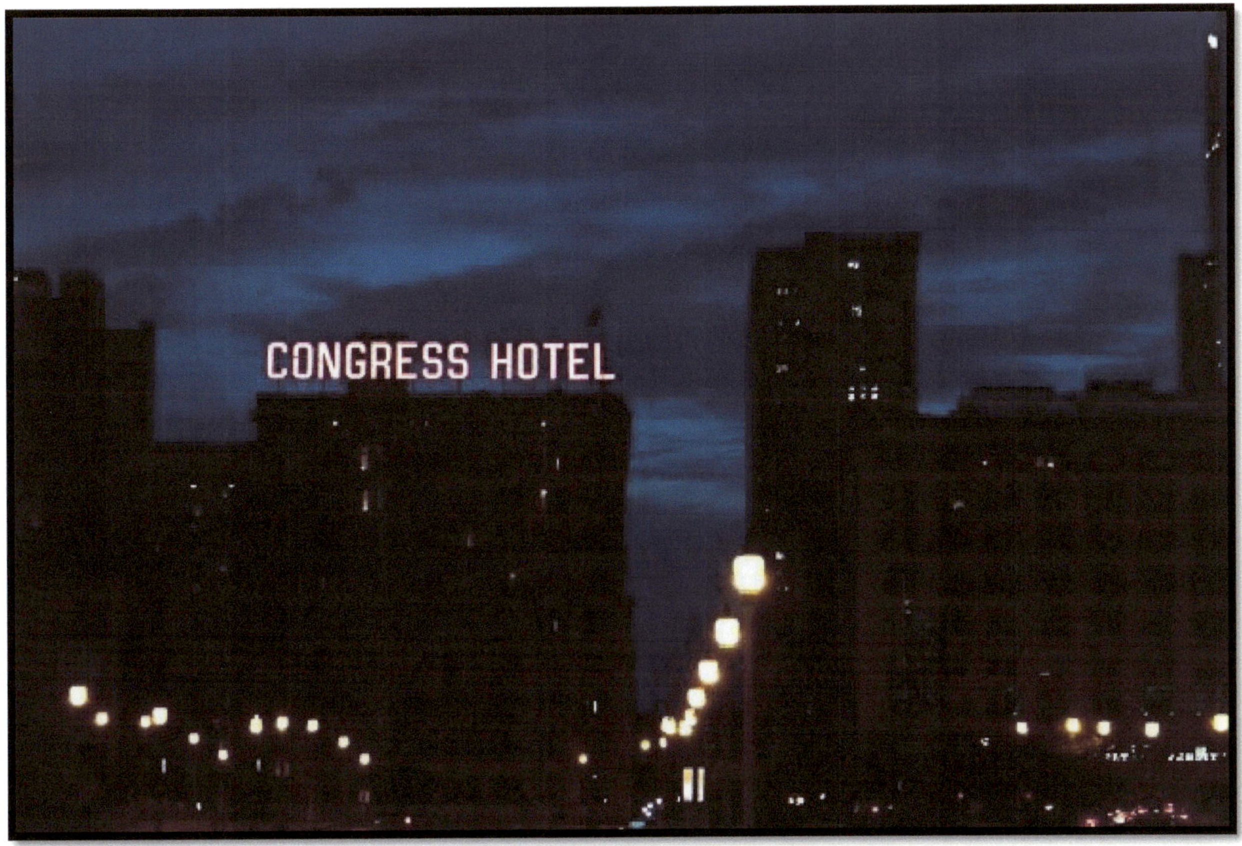

Flinging magnetic curses amid the toil of piling job on job, here is a tall bold slugger set vivid against the little soft cities;
Fierce as a dog with tongue lapping for action, cunning as a savage pitted against the wilderness,
    Bareheaded,
    Shoveling,
    Wrecking,
    Planning,
    Building, breaking, rebuilding,
Under the smoke, dust all over his mouth, laughing with white teeth,
Under the terrible burden of destiny laughing as a young man laughs,
Laughing even as an ignorant fighter laughs who has never lost a battle,
Bragging and laughing that under his wrist is the pulse. and under his ribs the heart of the people,
        Laughing!

Carl Sandburg, Chicago

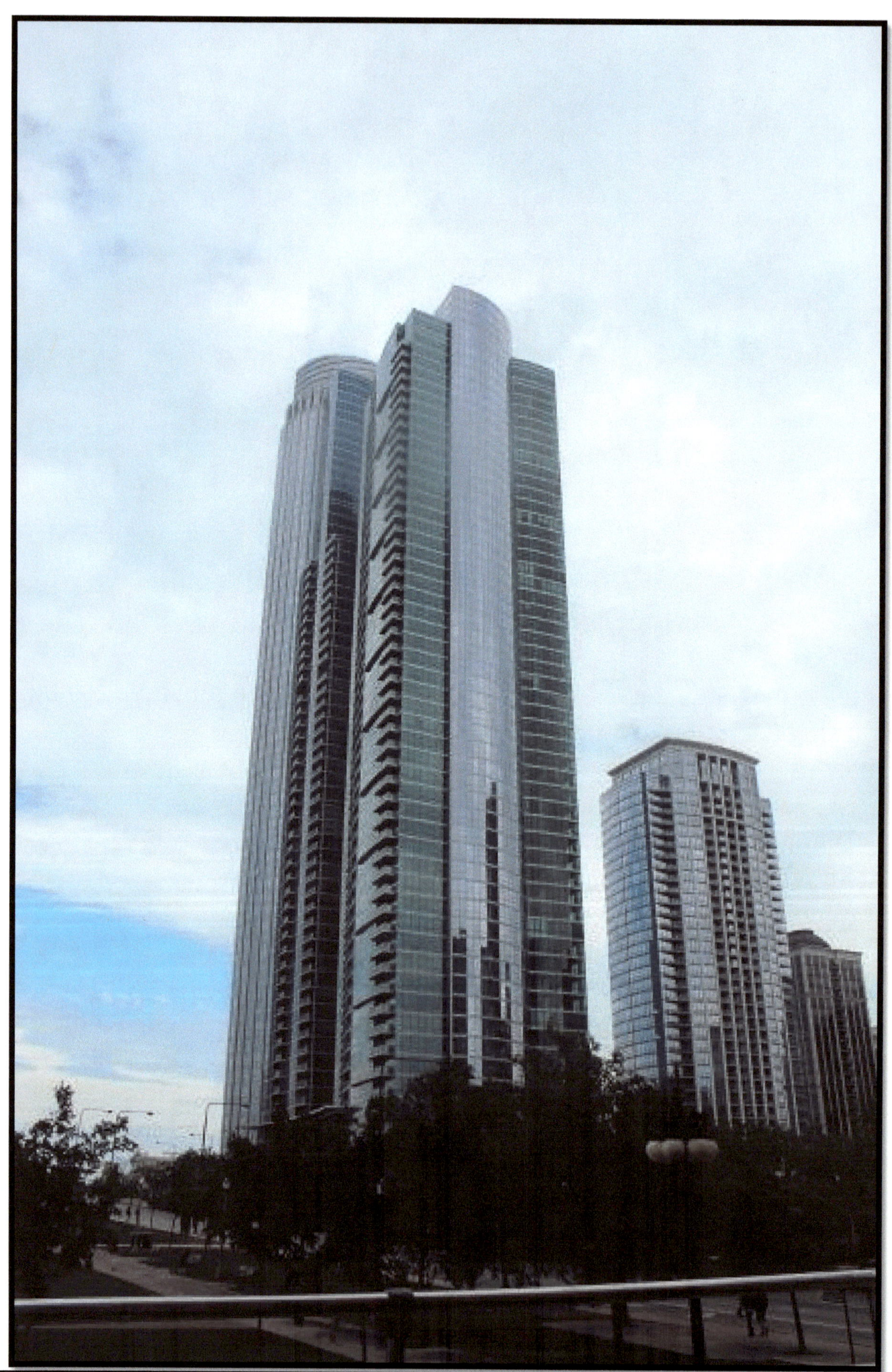

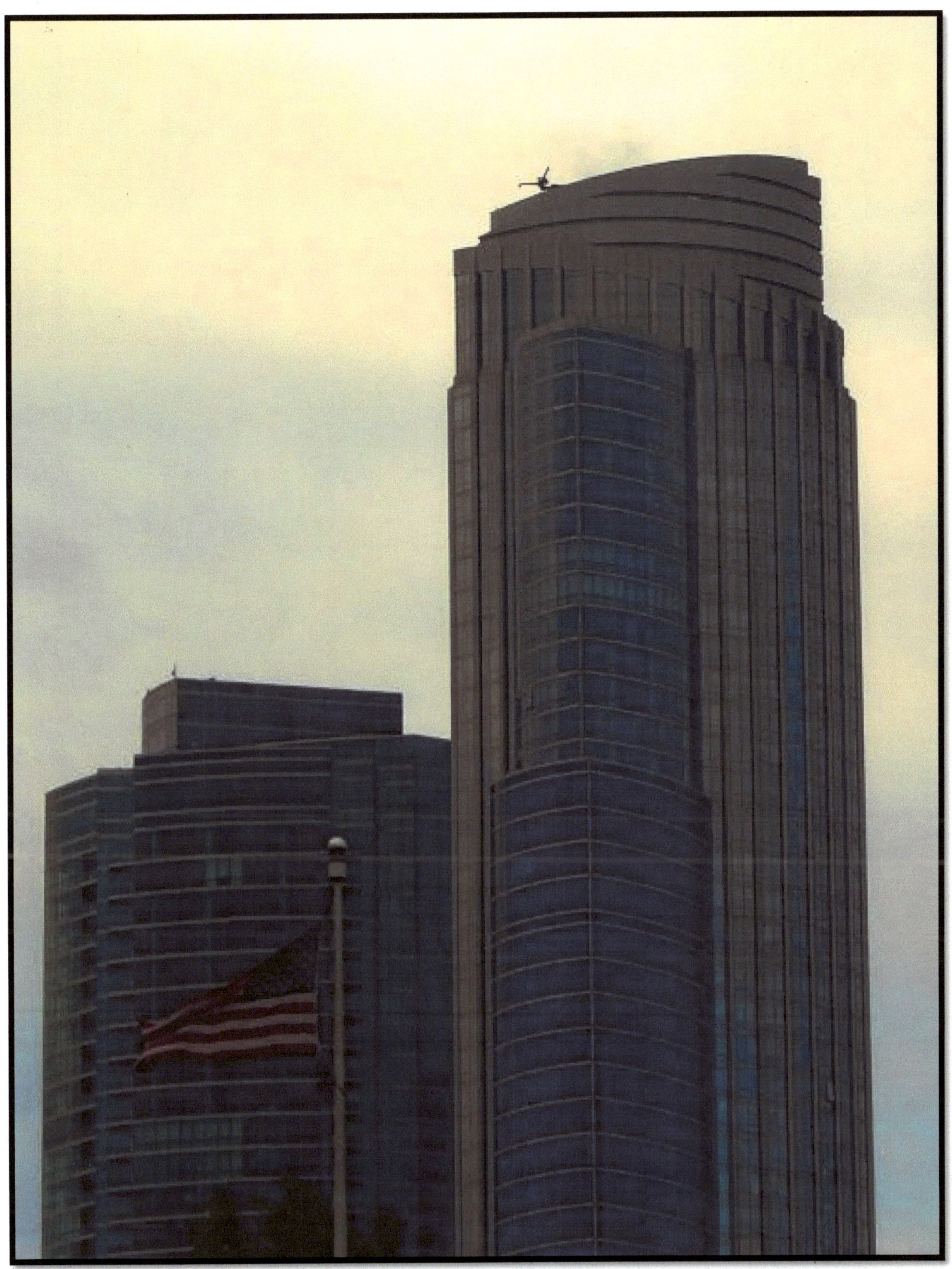

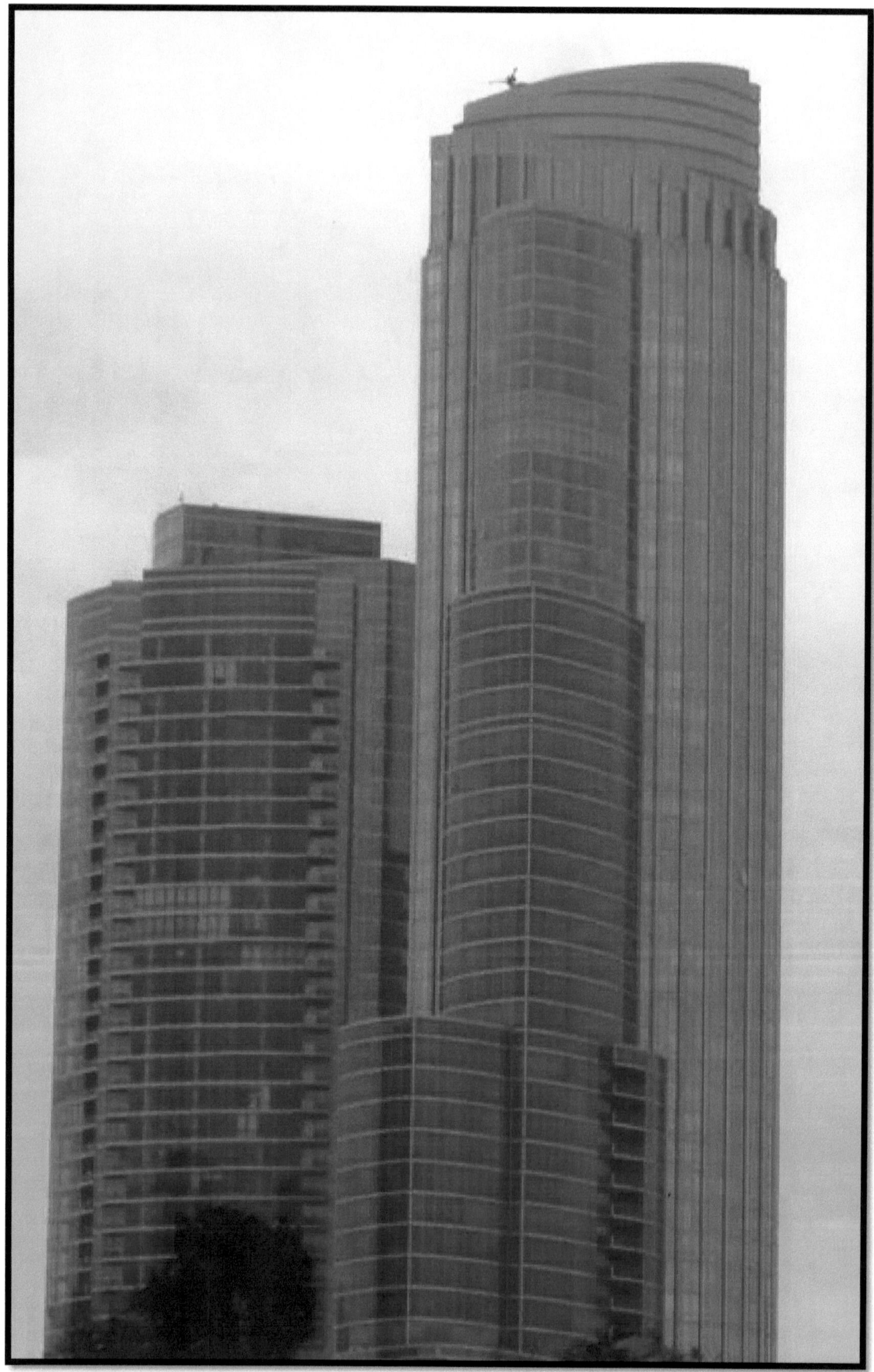

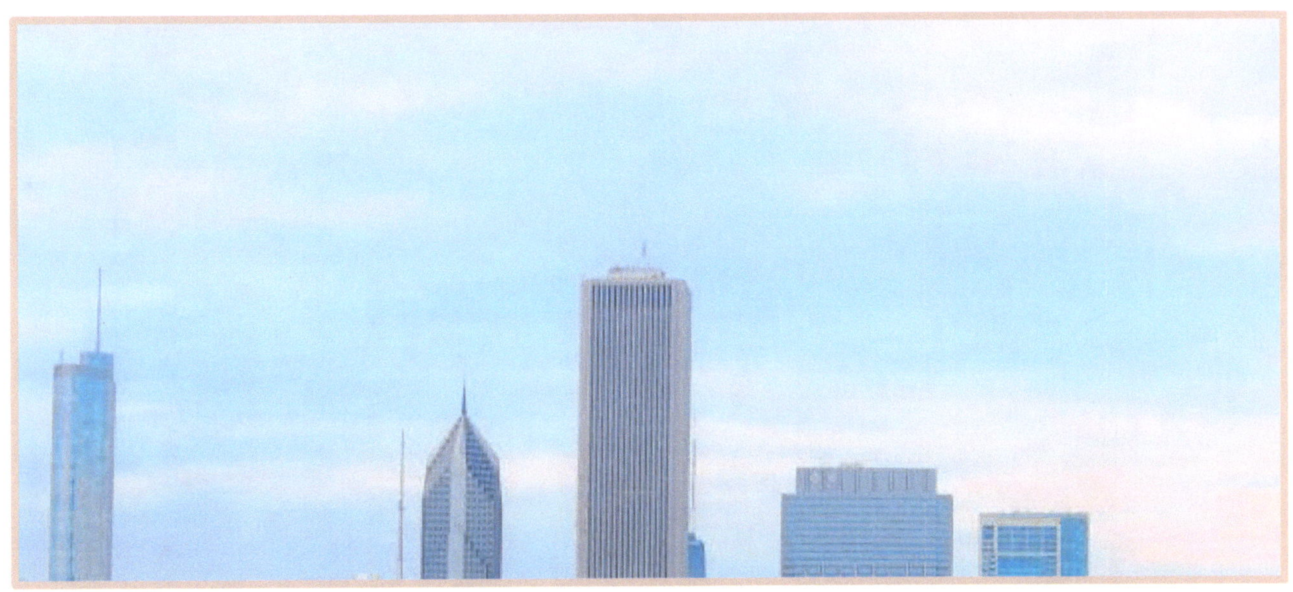

"Cities are never random. No matter how chaotic they might seem, everything about them grows out of a need to solve a problem. In fact, a city is nothing more than a solution to a problem, that in turn creates more problems that need more solutions, until towers rise, roads widen, bridges are built, and millions of people are caught up in a mad race to feed the problem-solving, problem-creating frenzy." **Neal Shusterman, Downsiders**

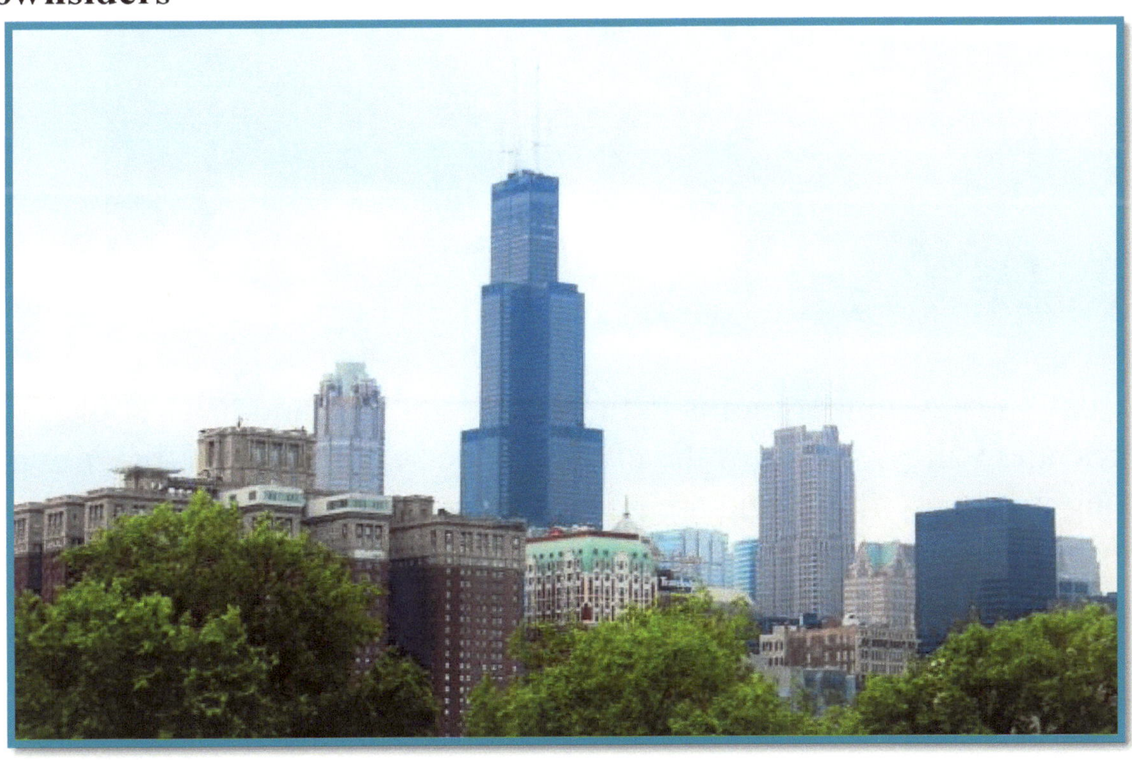

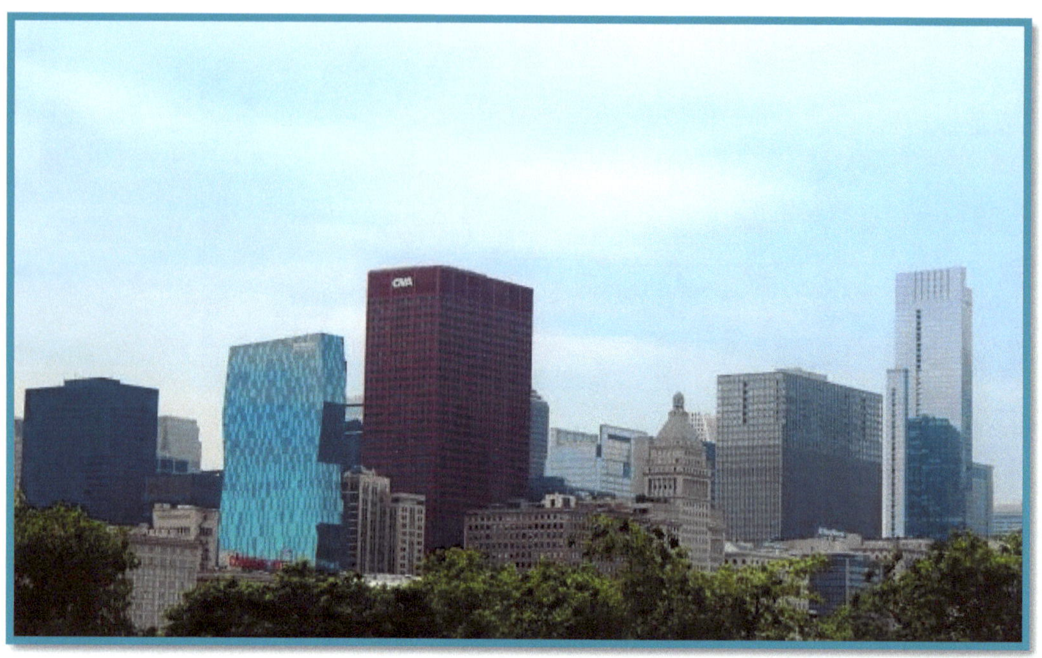

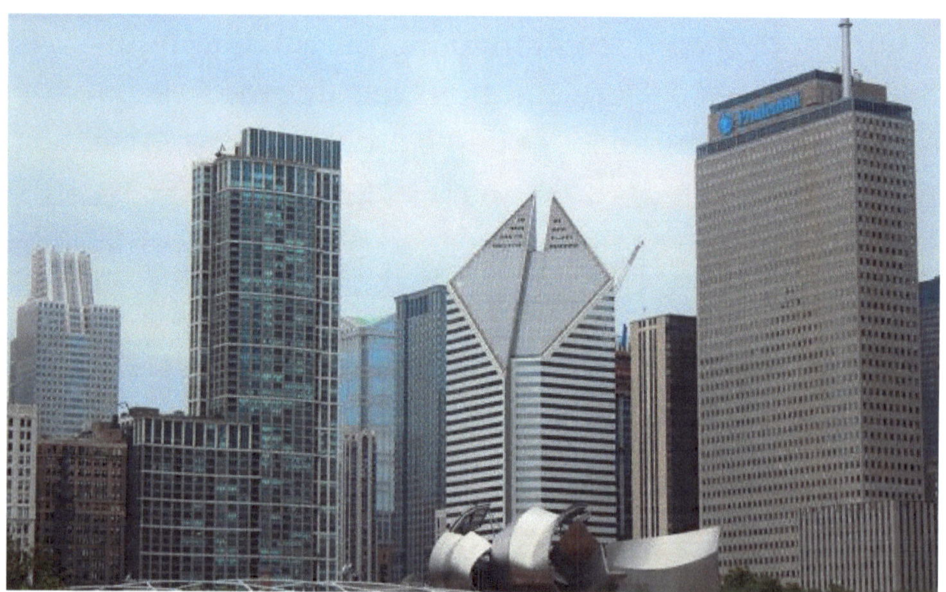

"By day the skyscraper looms in the smoke and sun and has a soul. Prairie and valley, streets of the city, pour people into it and they mingle among its twenty floors and are poured out again back to the streets, prairies and valleys. It is the men and women, boys and girls so poured in and out all day that give the building a soul of dreams and thoughts and memories." ***Skyscraper*, Carl Sandburg, *Chicago Poems*.**

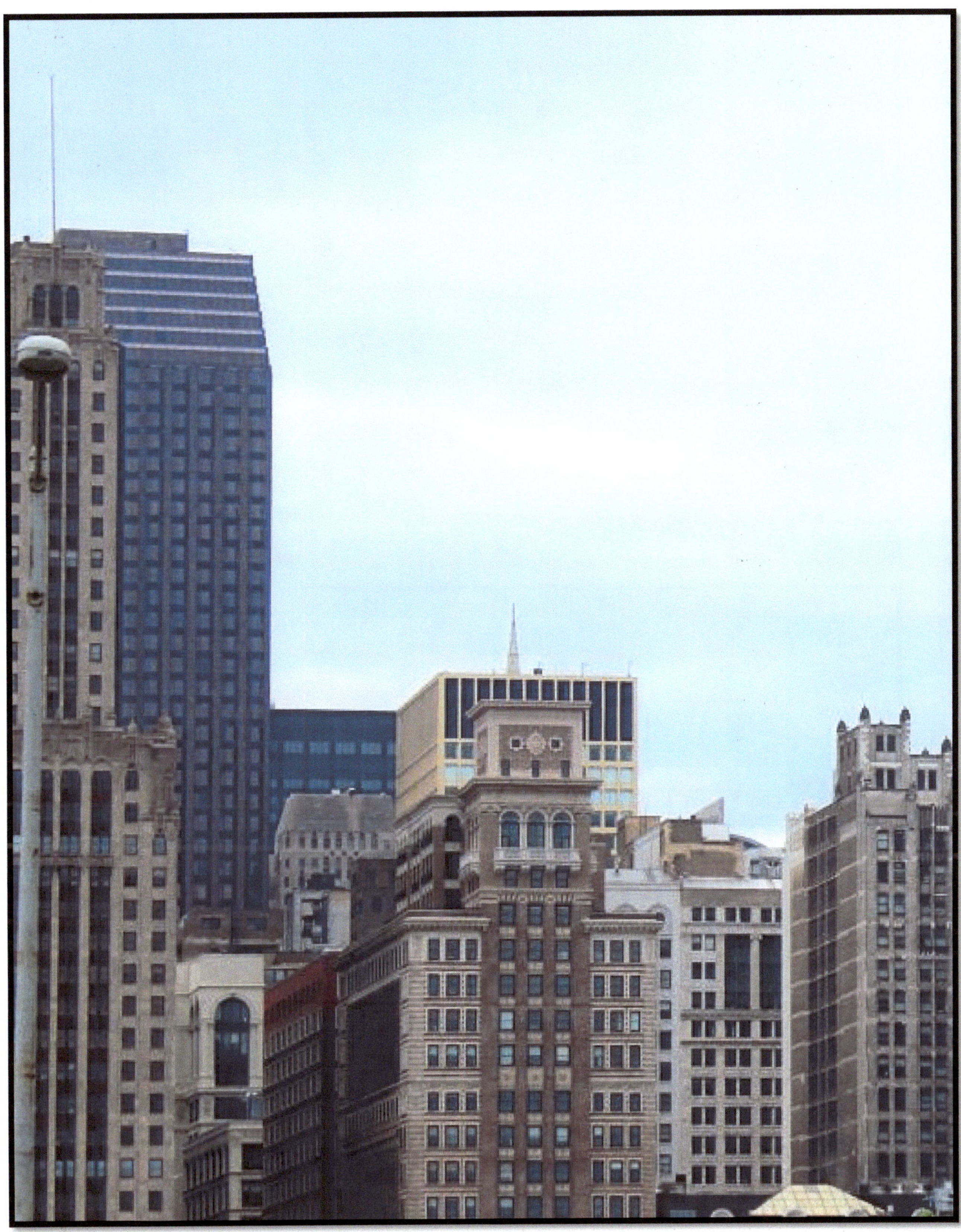

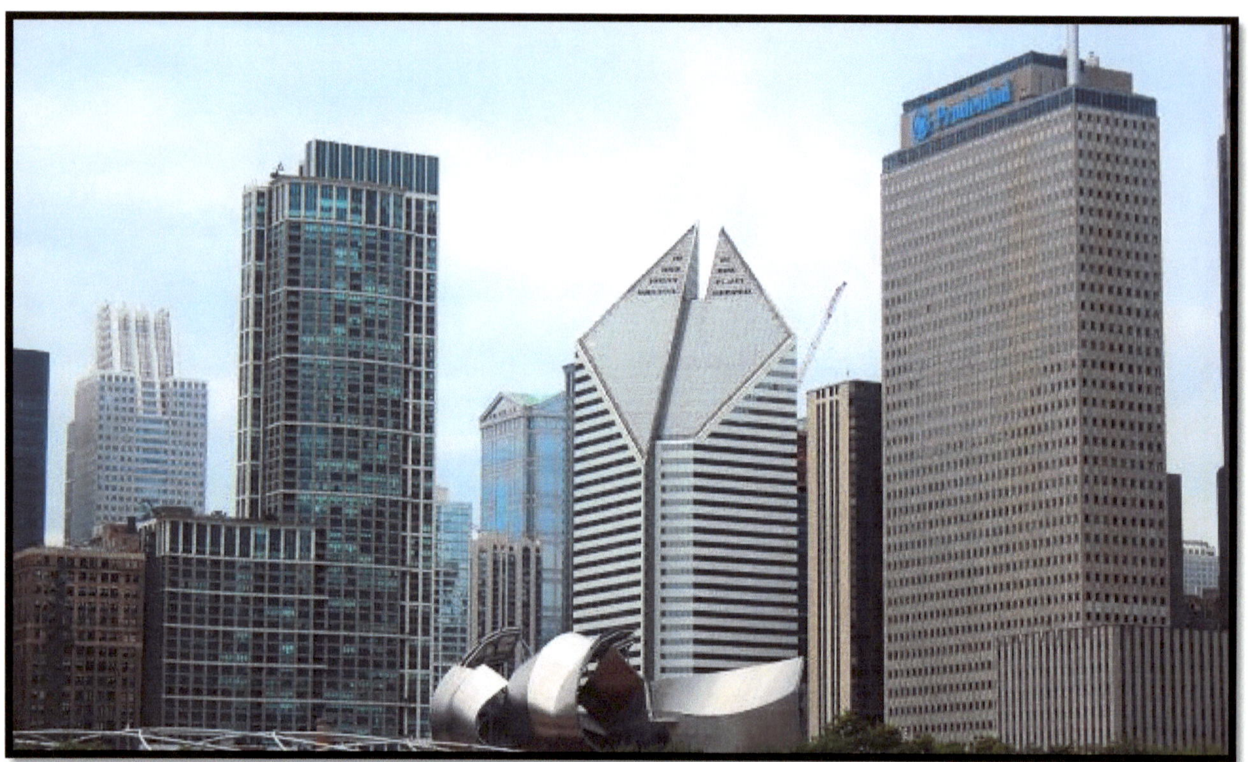
Prudential

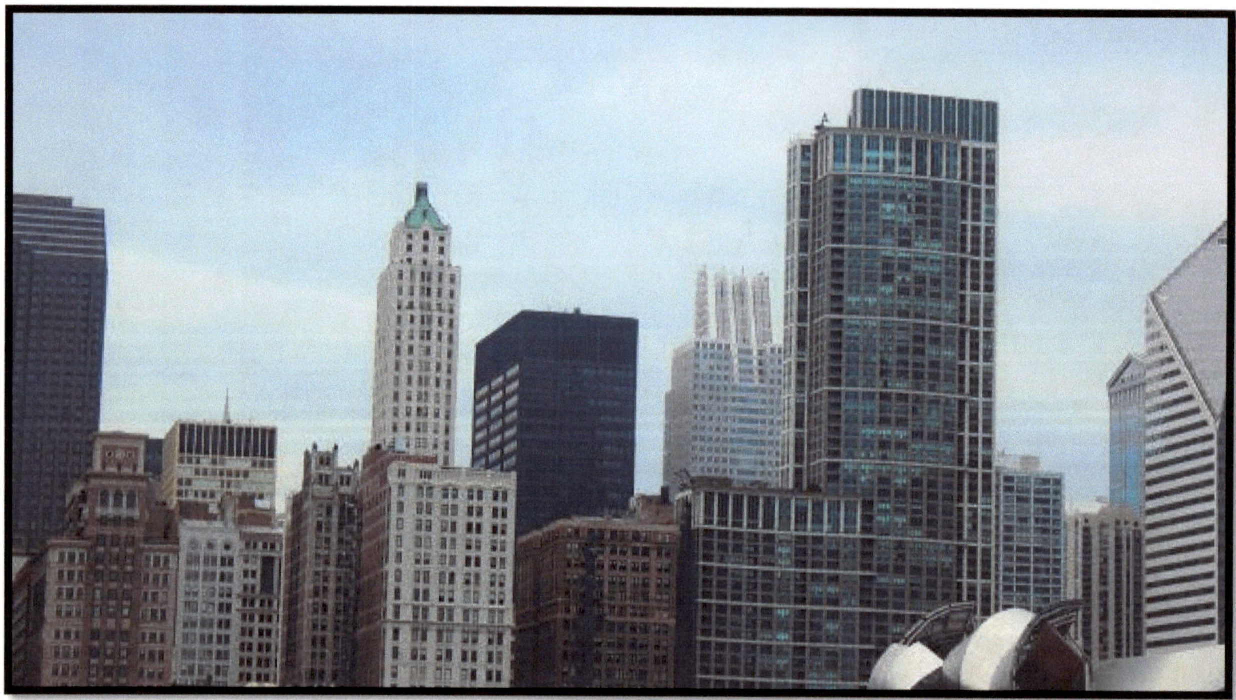

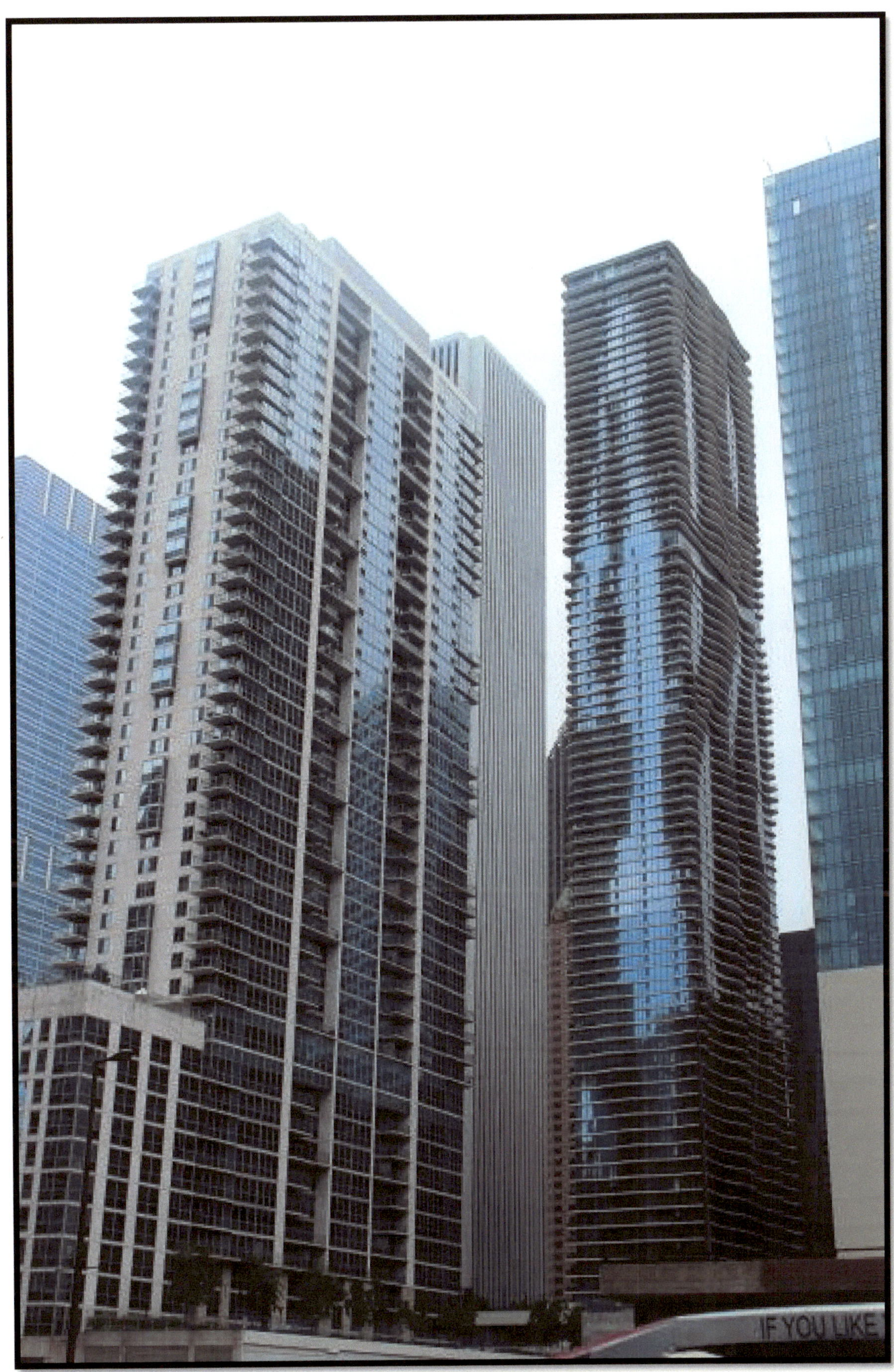
IF YOU LIKE

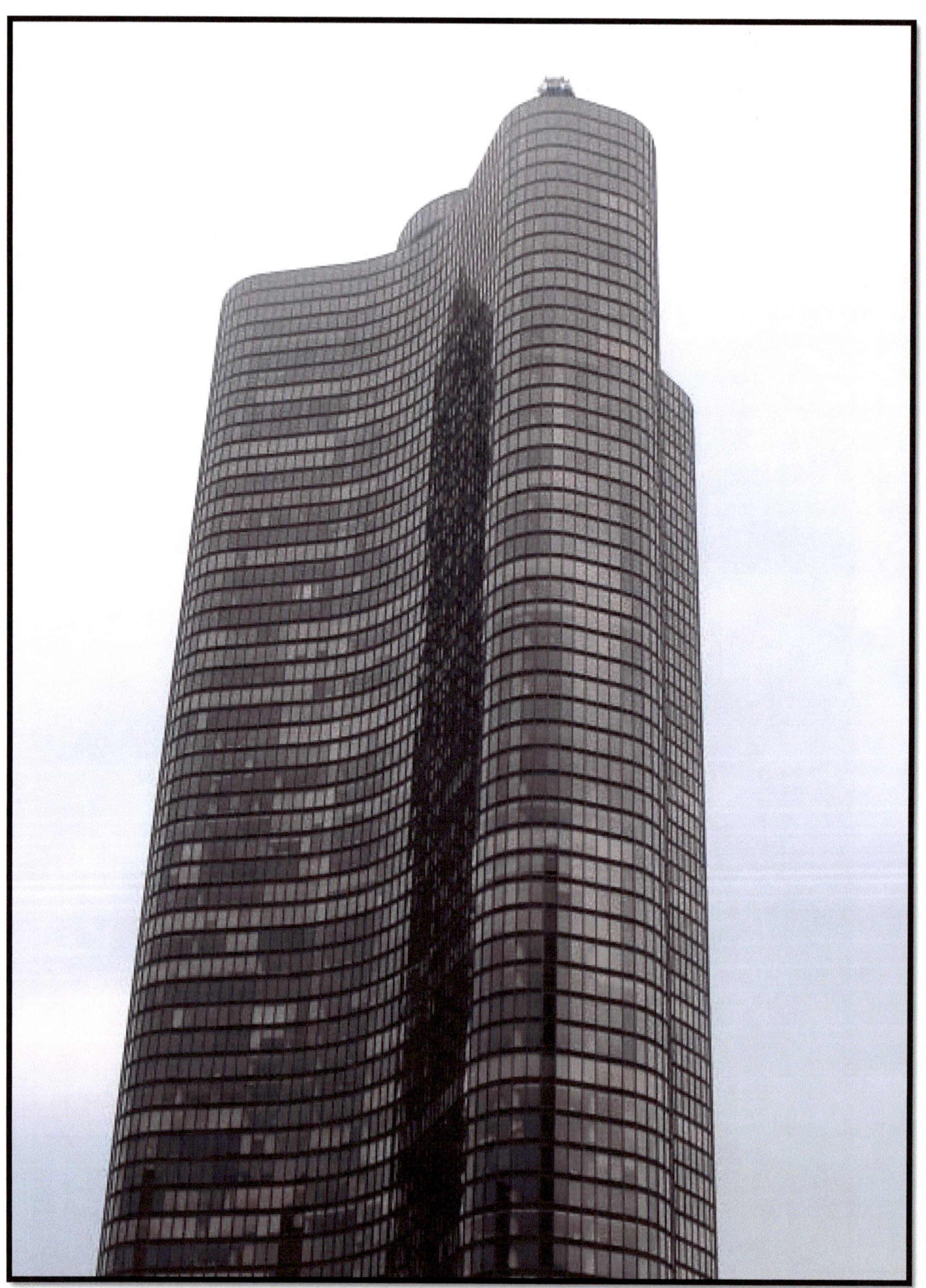

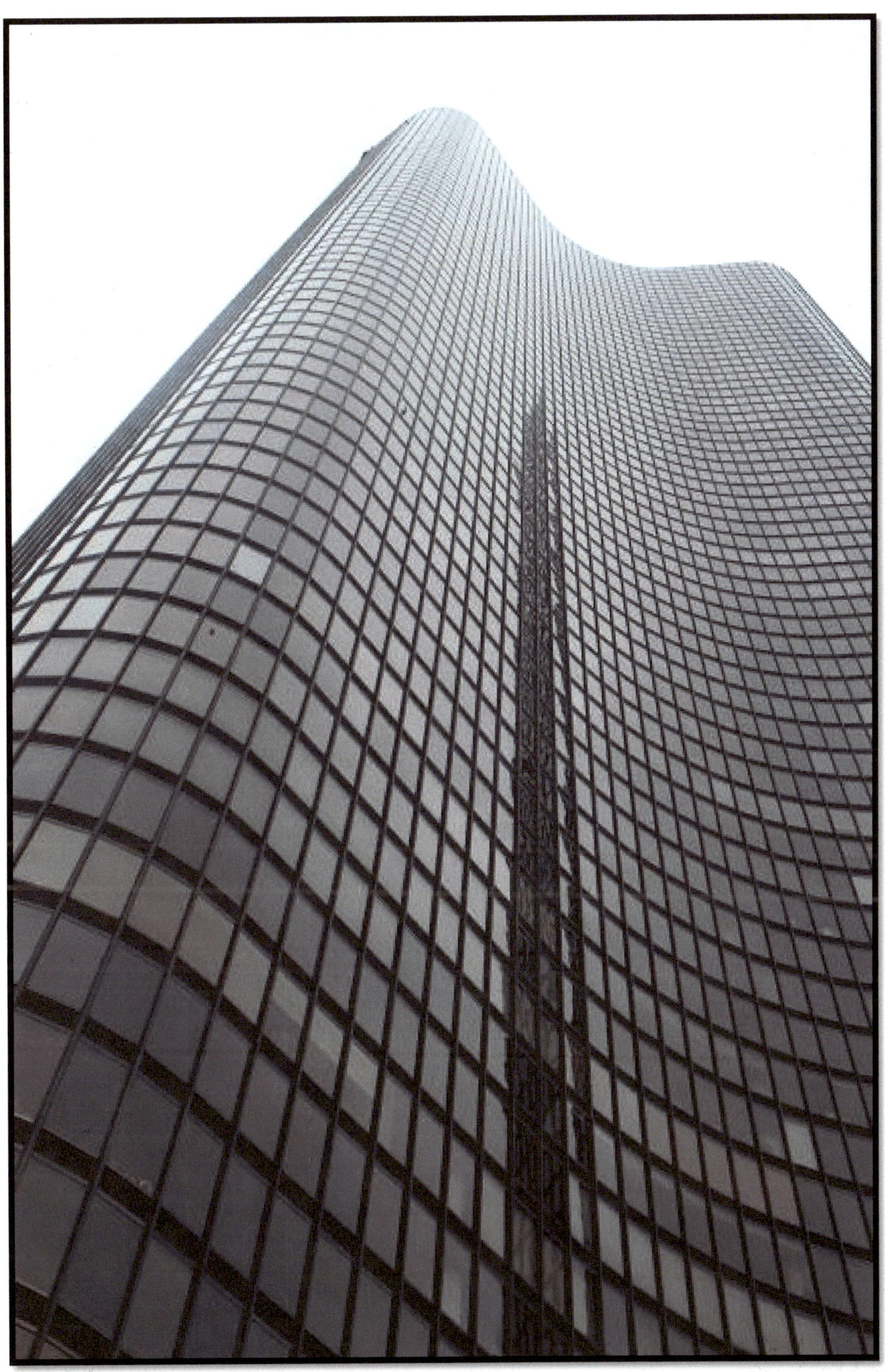

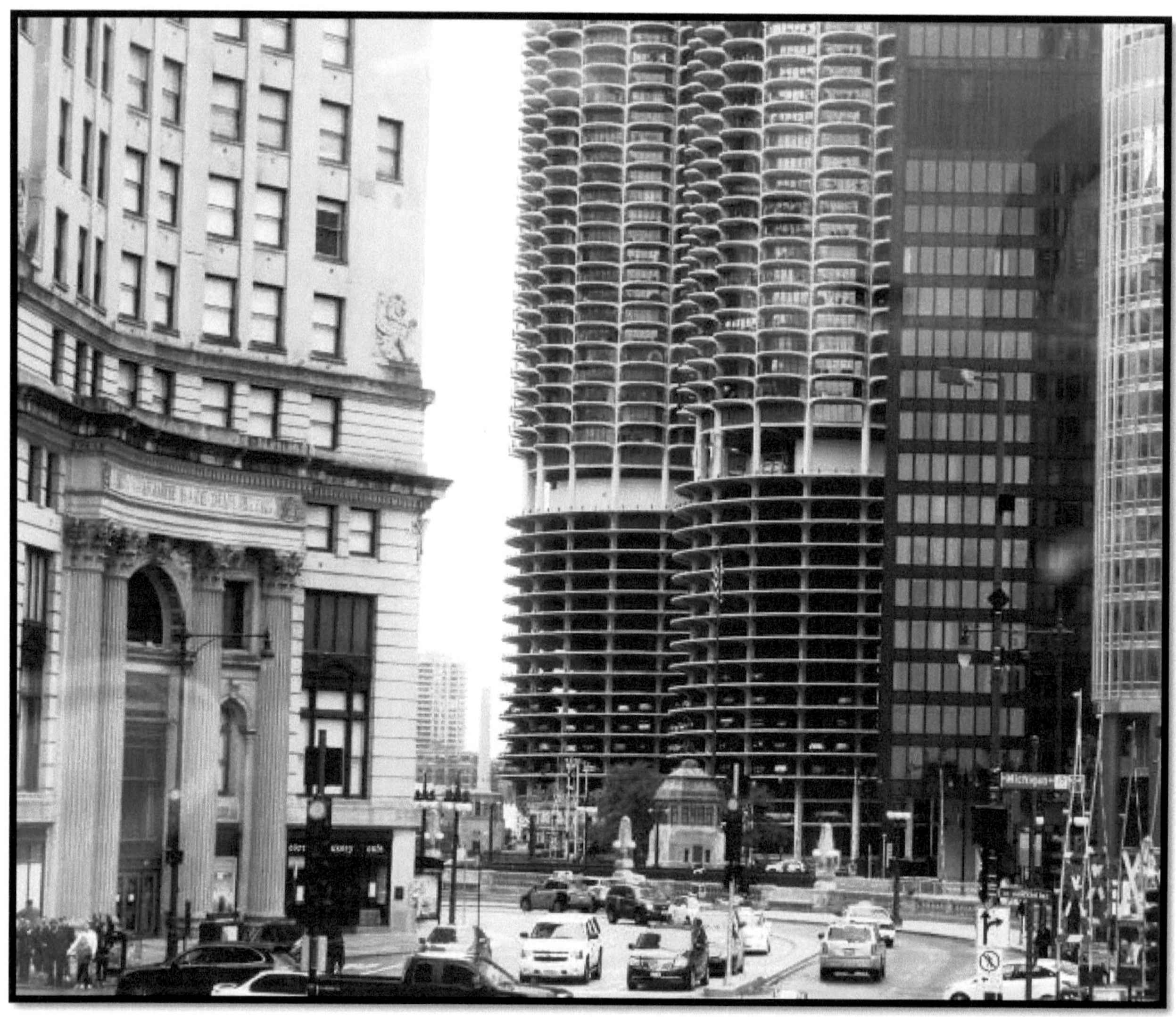

"A facade of skyscrapers facing a lake and behind the facade, every type of dubiousness." E. M. Forster

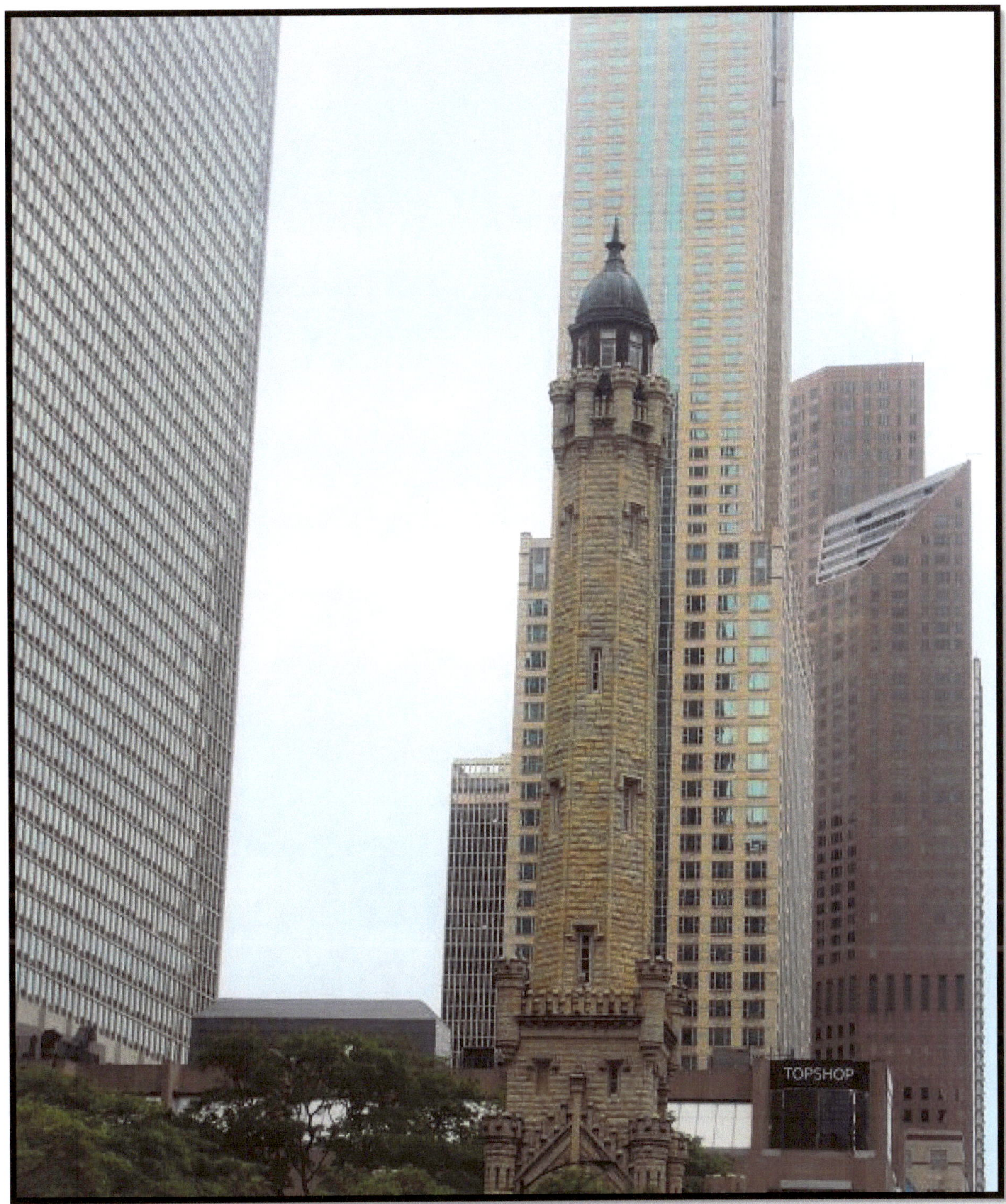
TOPSHOP

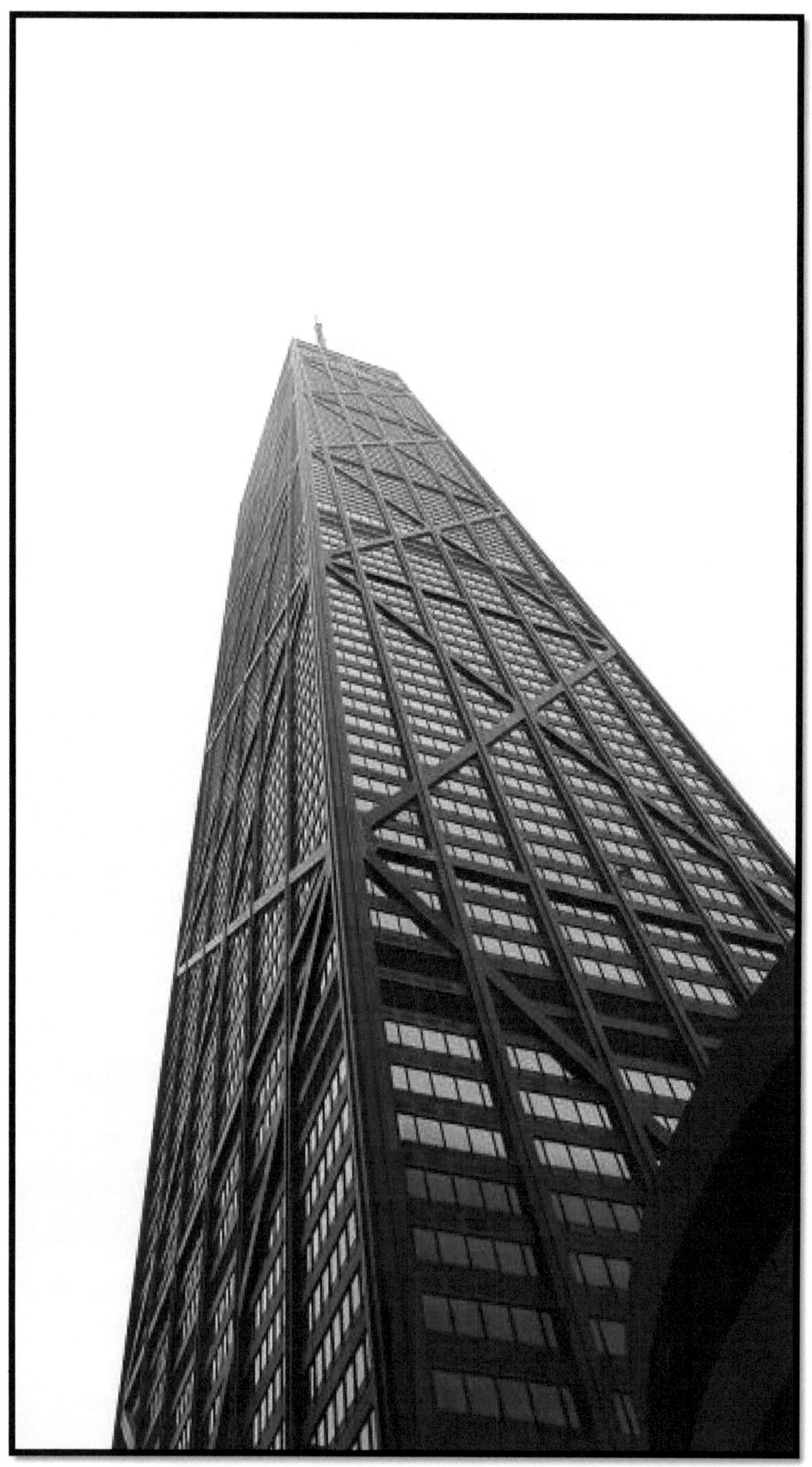

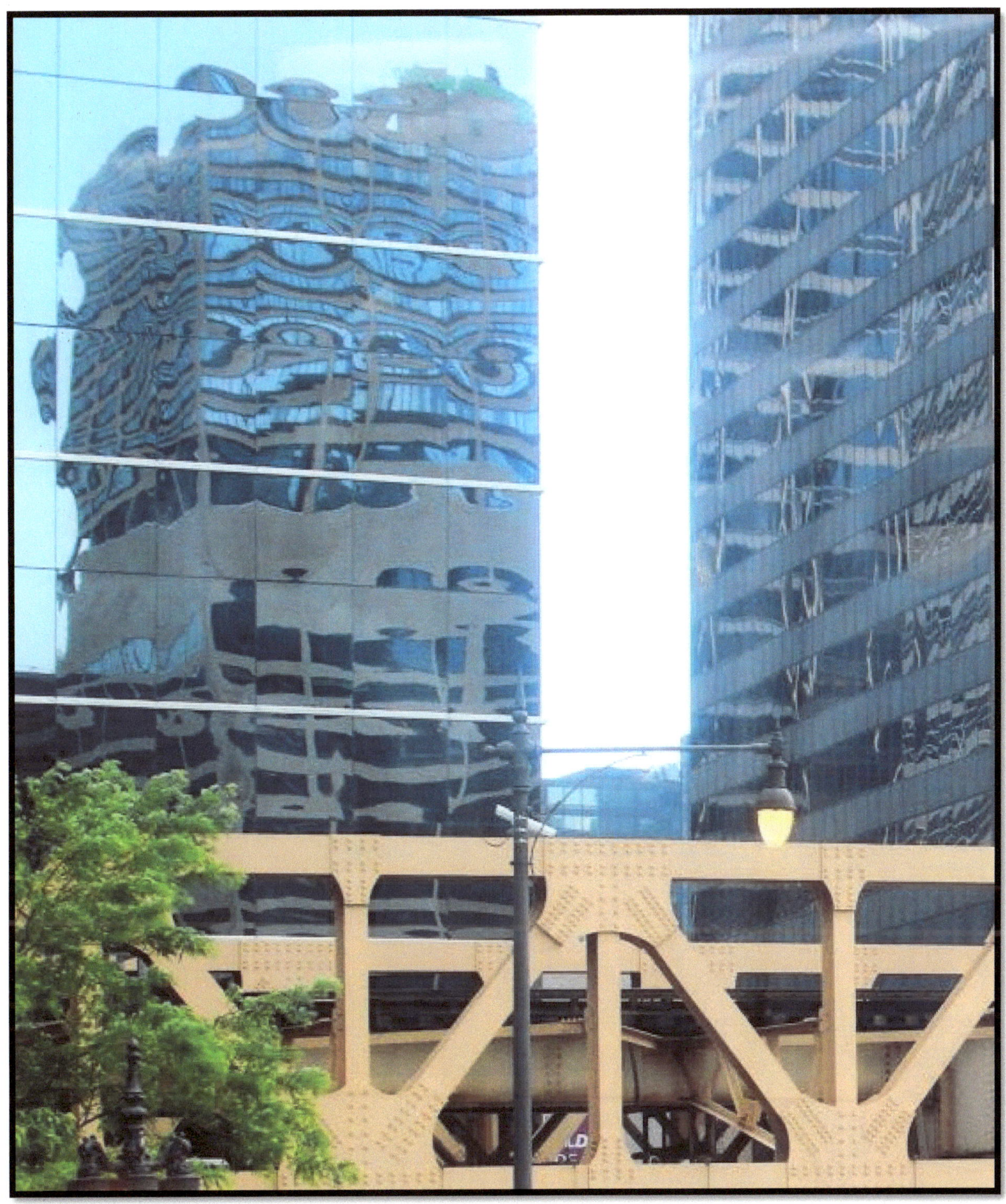

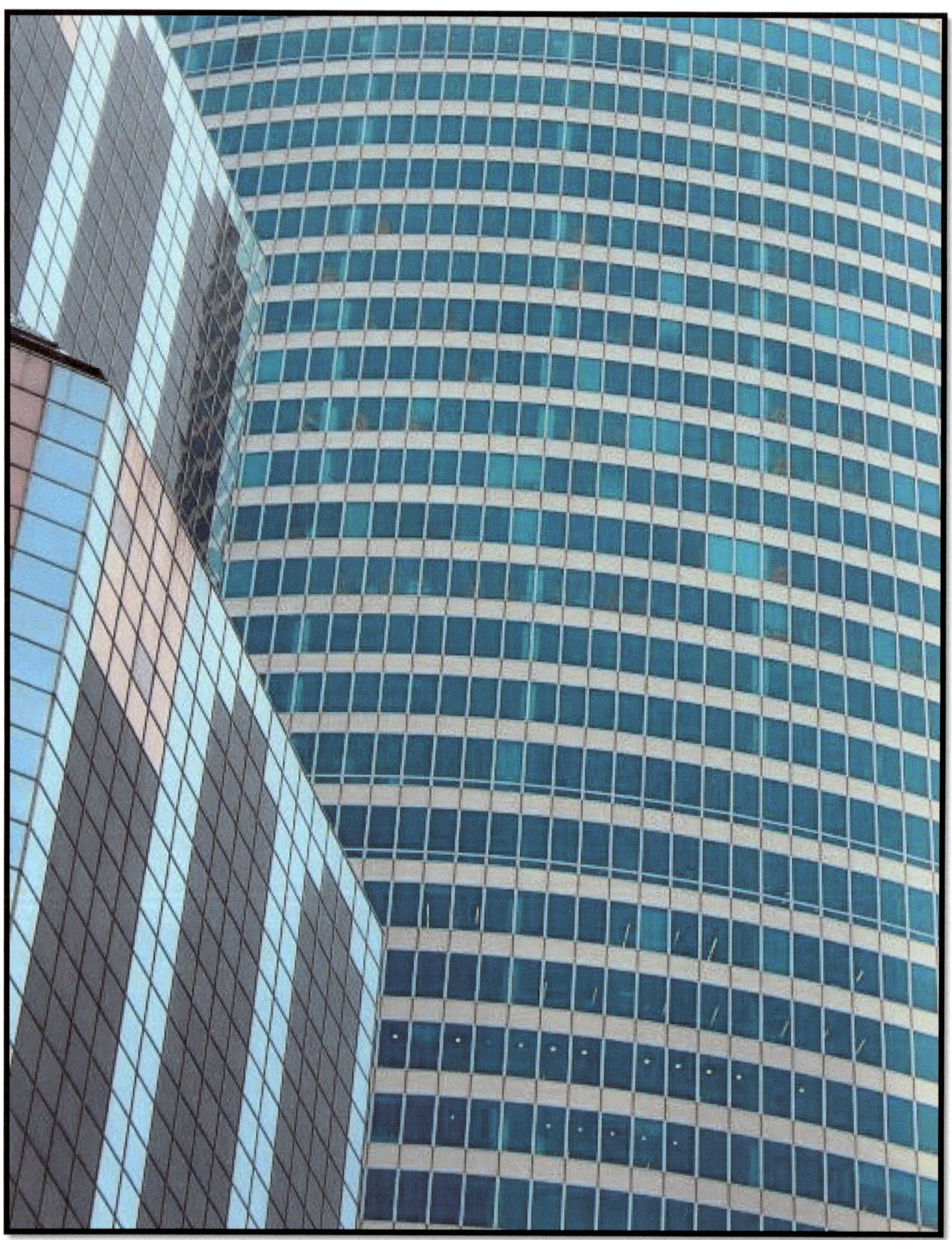

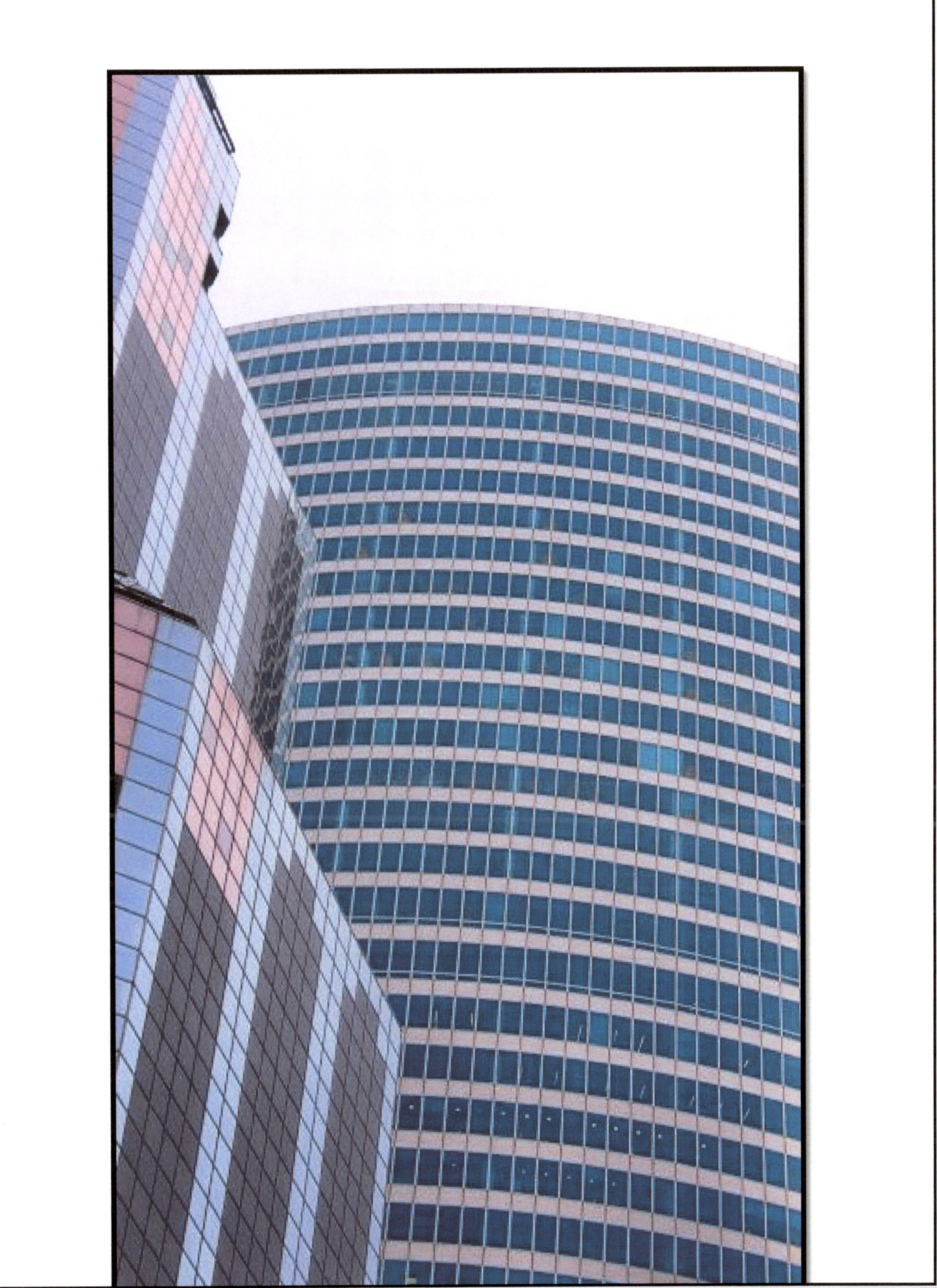

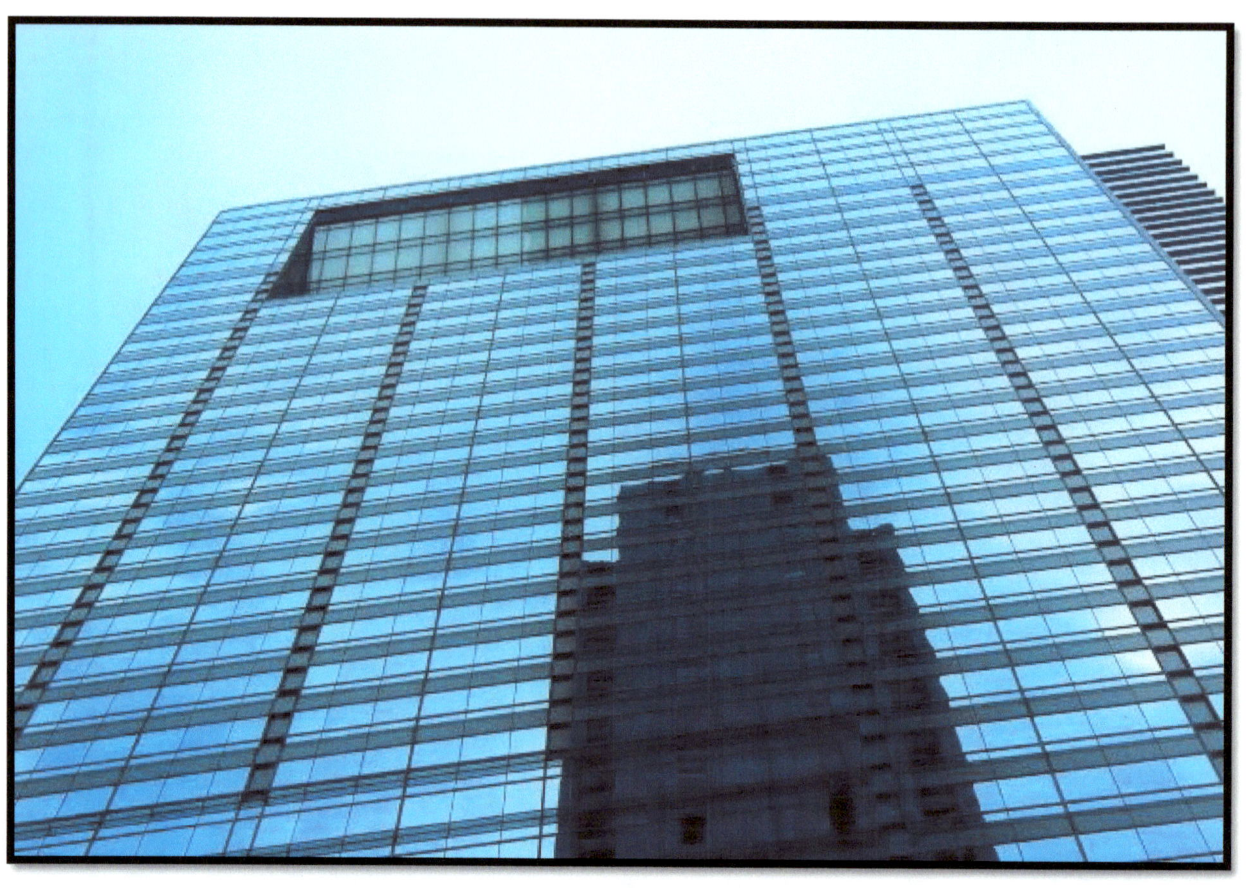

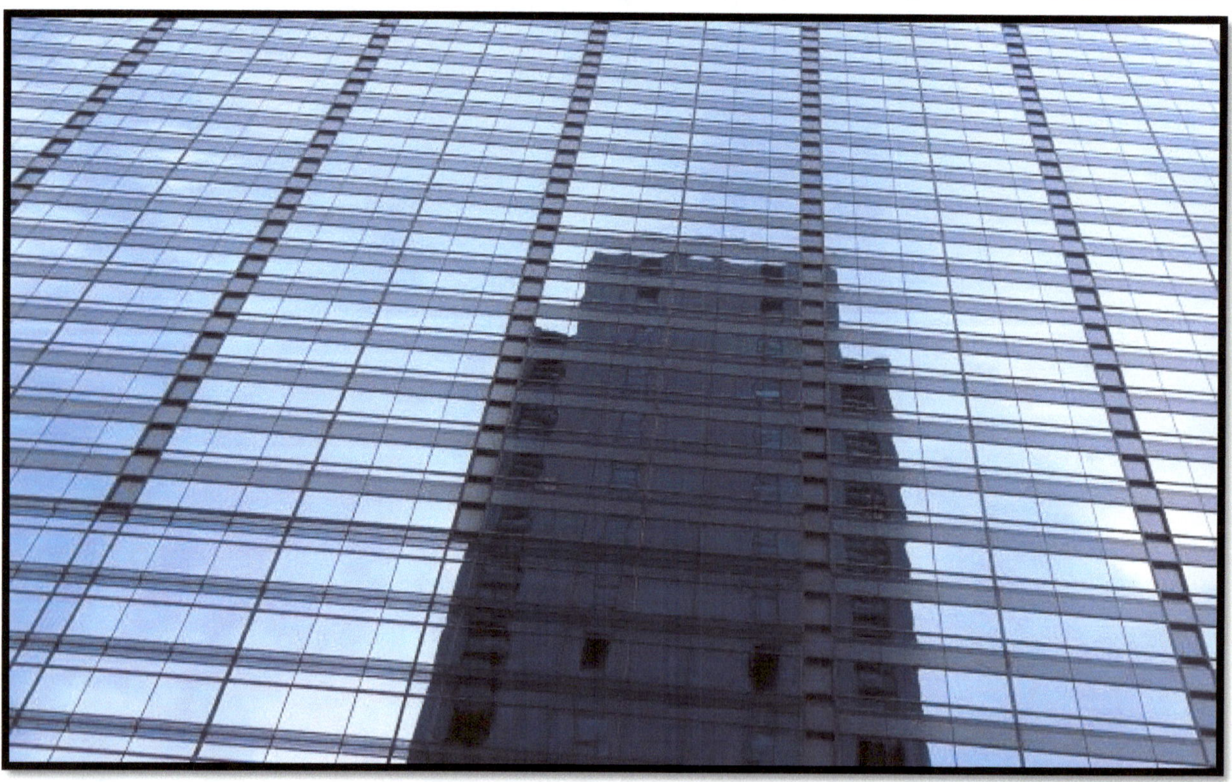

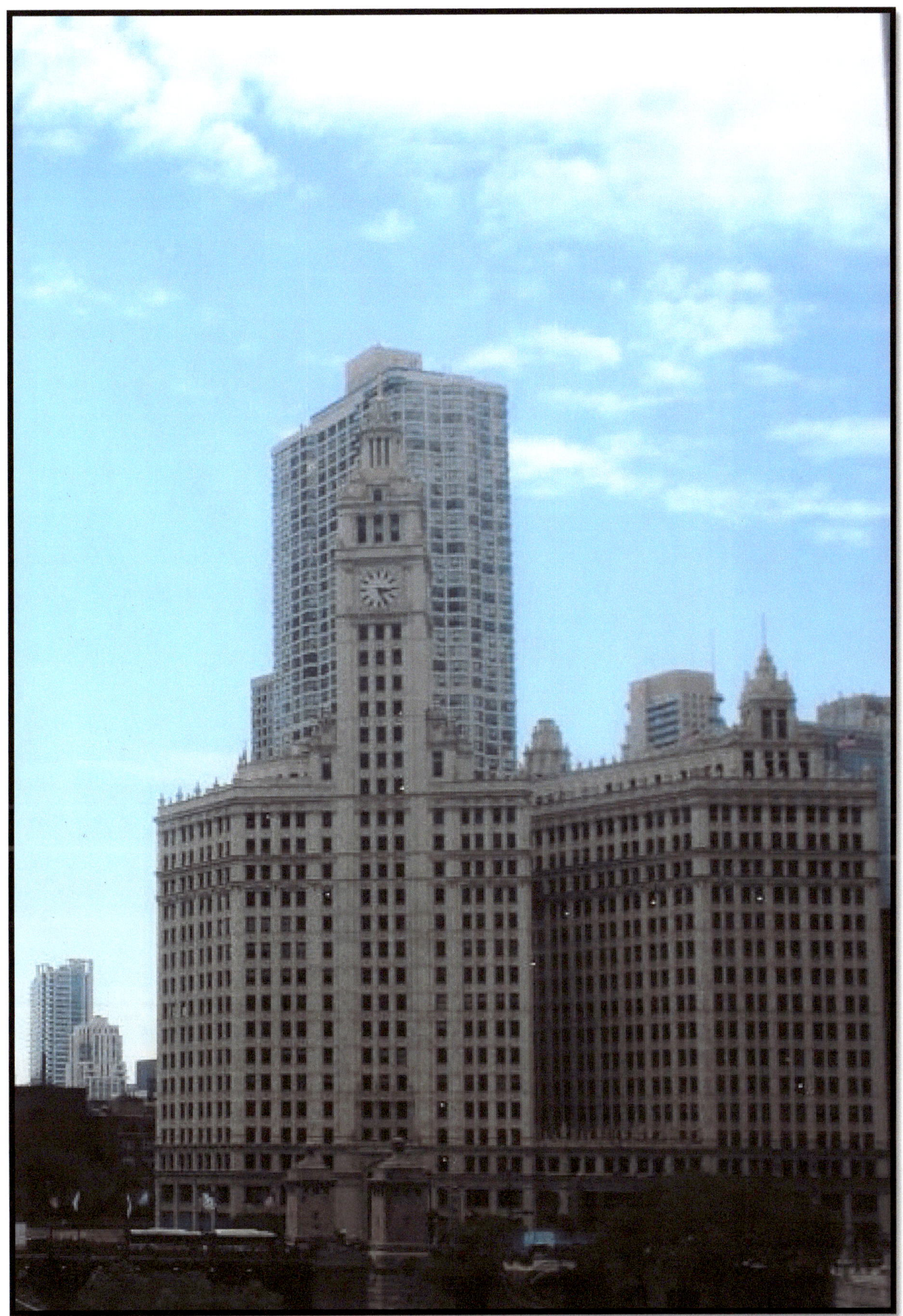

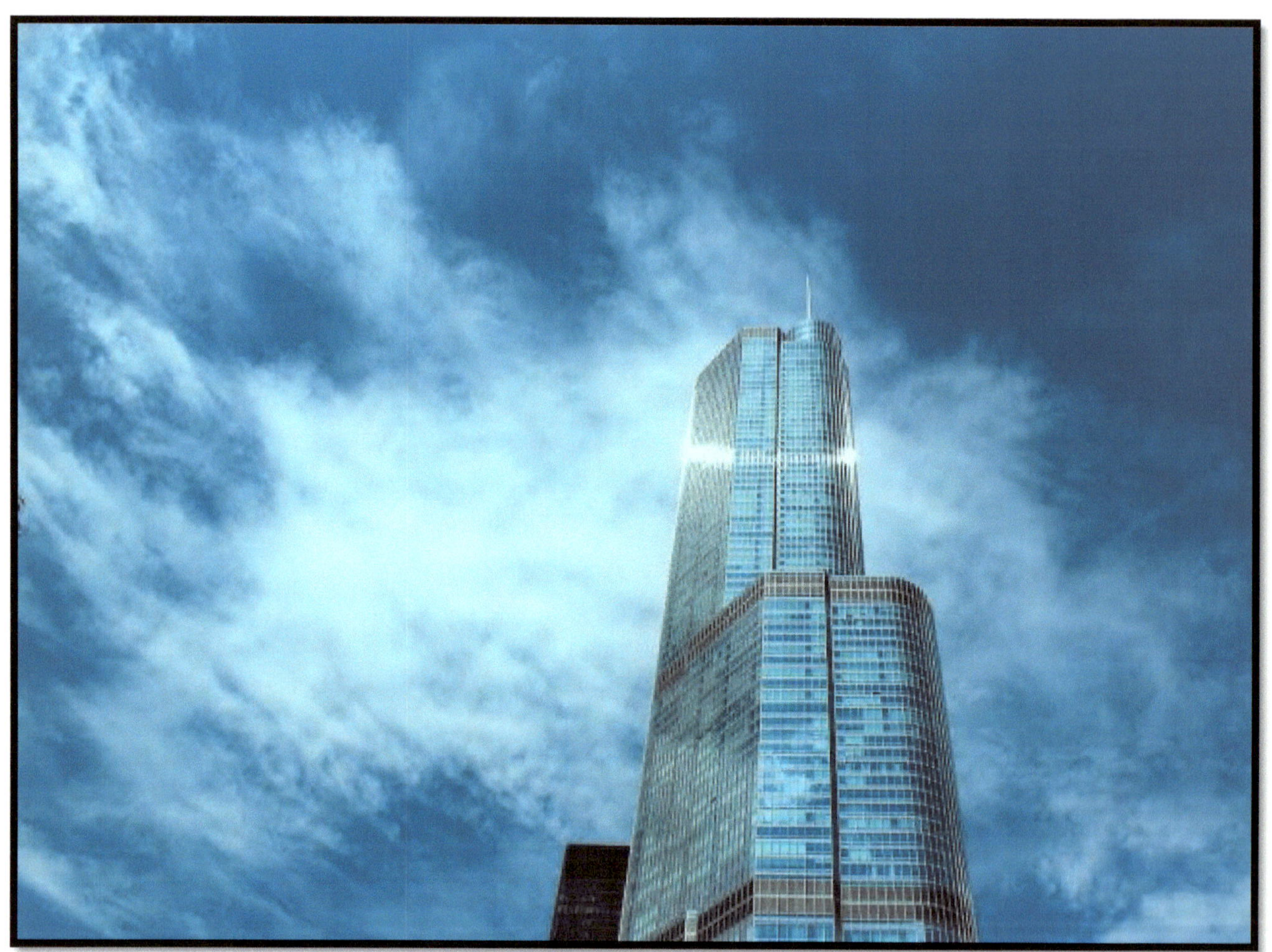

“Great buildings that move the spirit have always been rare. In every case they are unique, poetic, products of the heart.” **Arthur Erickson**

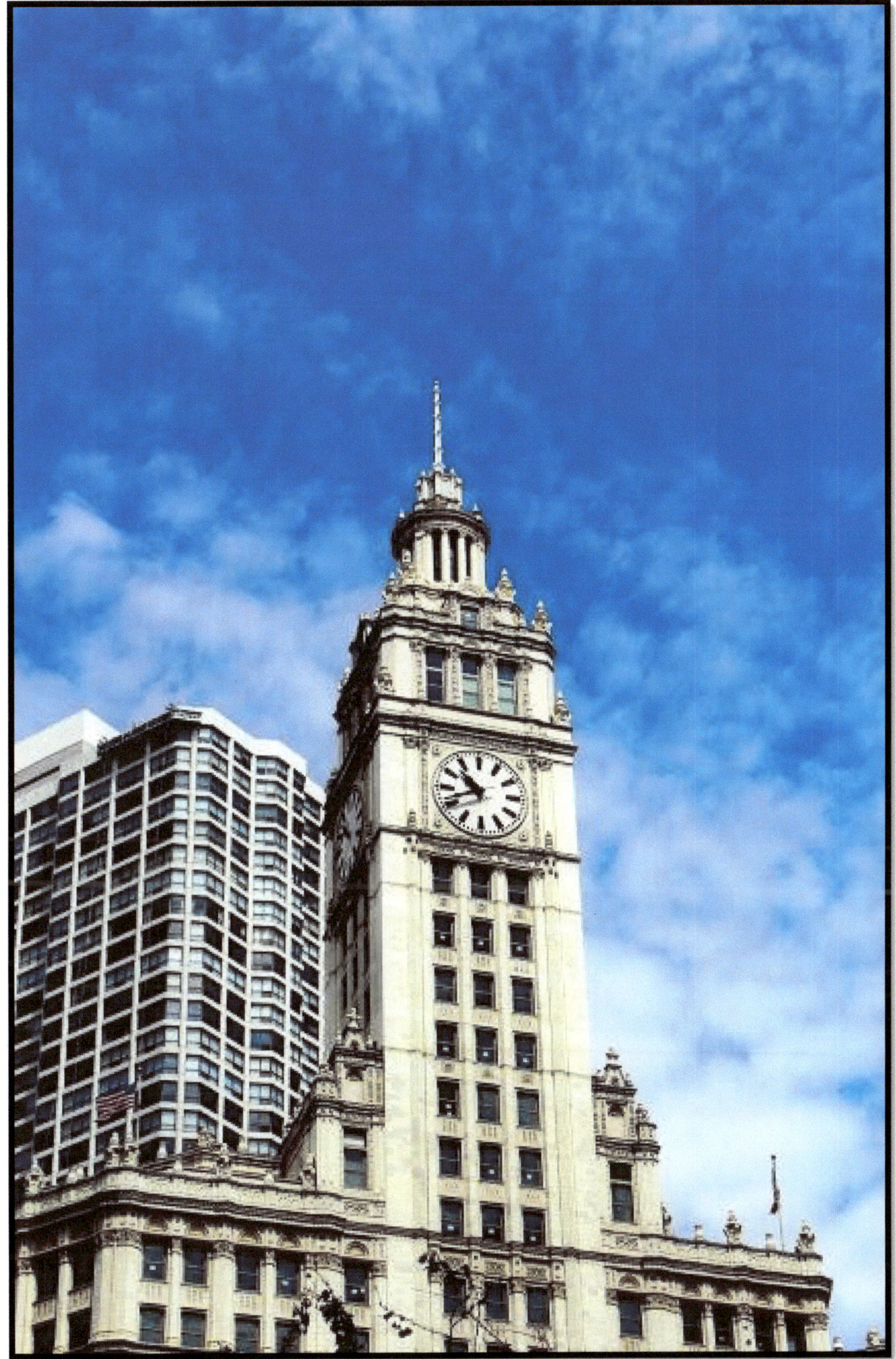

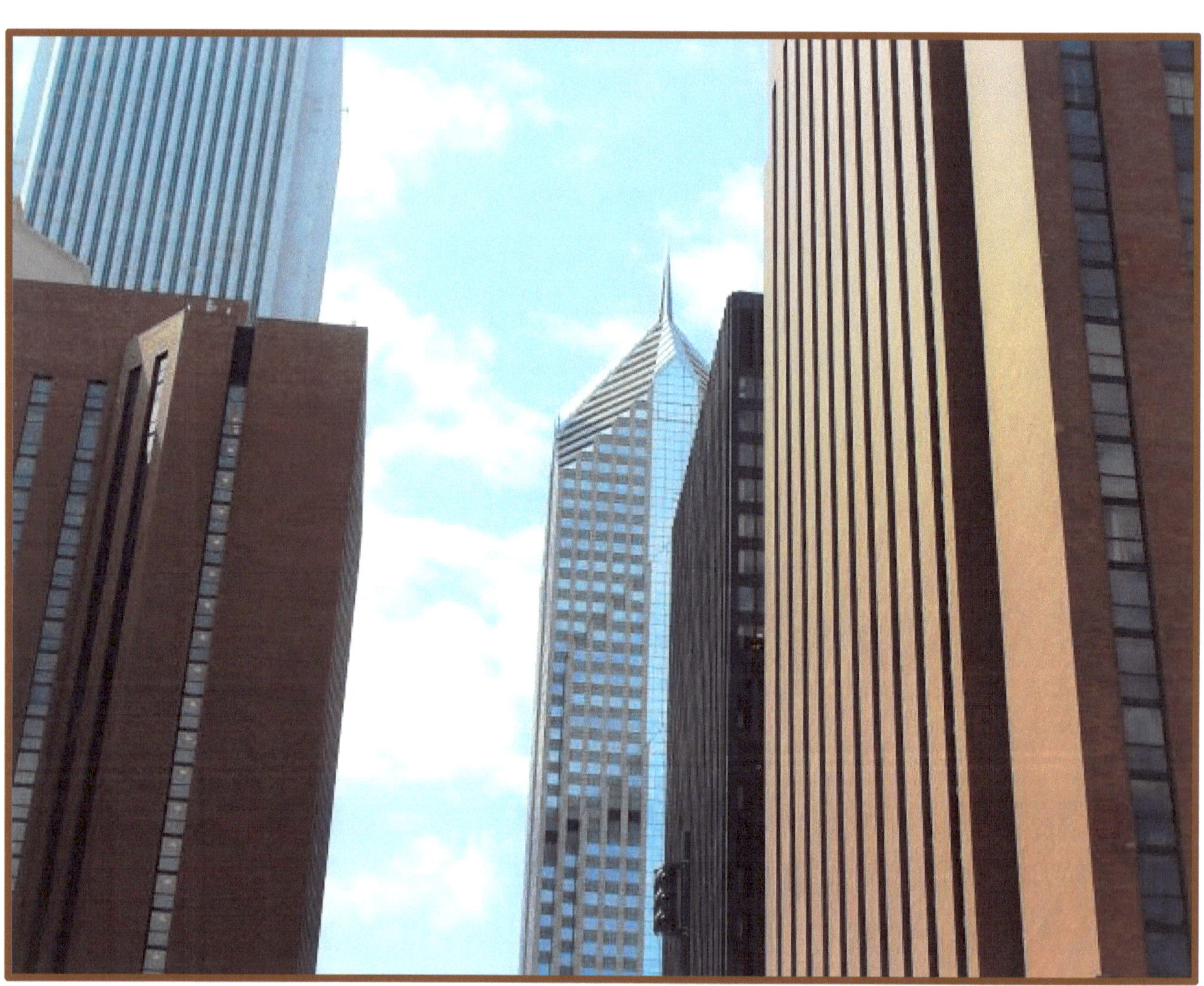

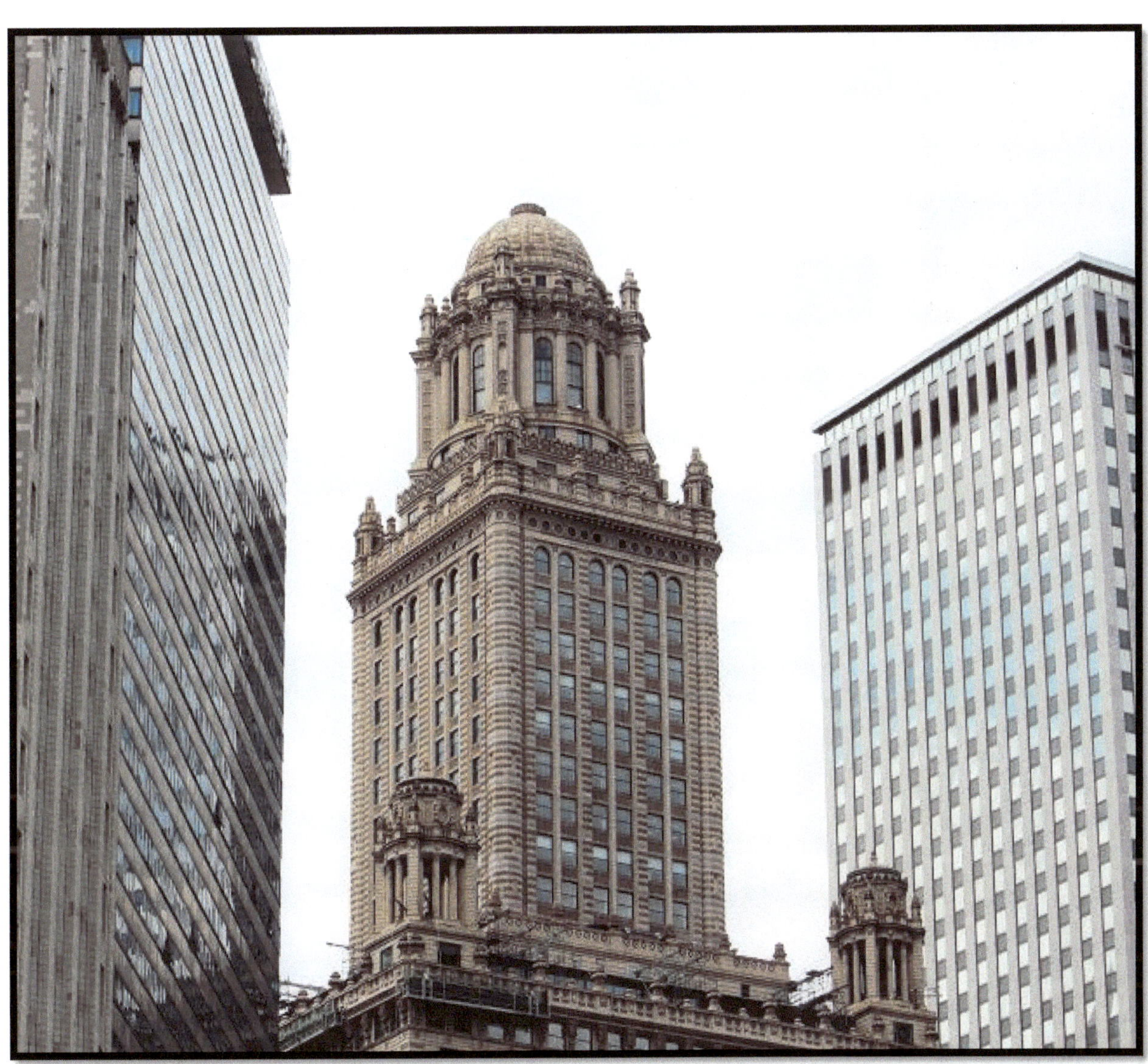

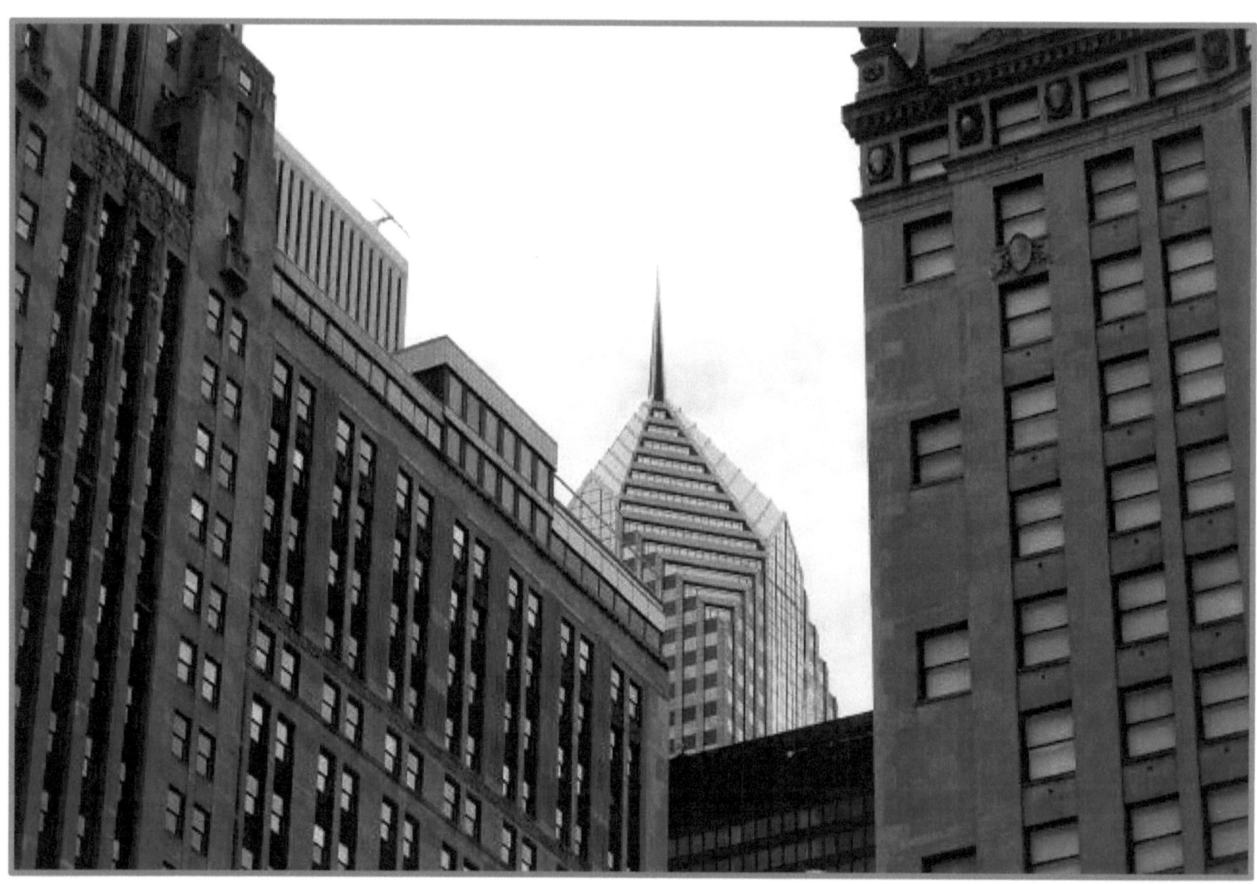

"Chicago seems a big city instead of merely a large place." **A. J. Liebling, first to designate Chicago "*The Second City,*" *1949***

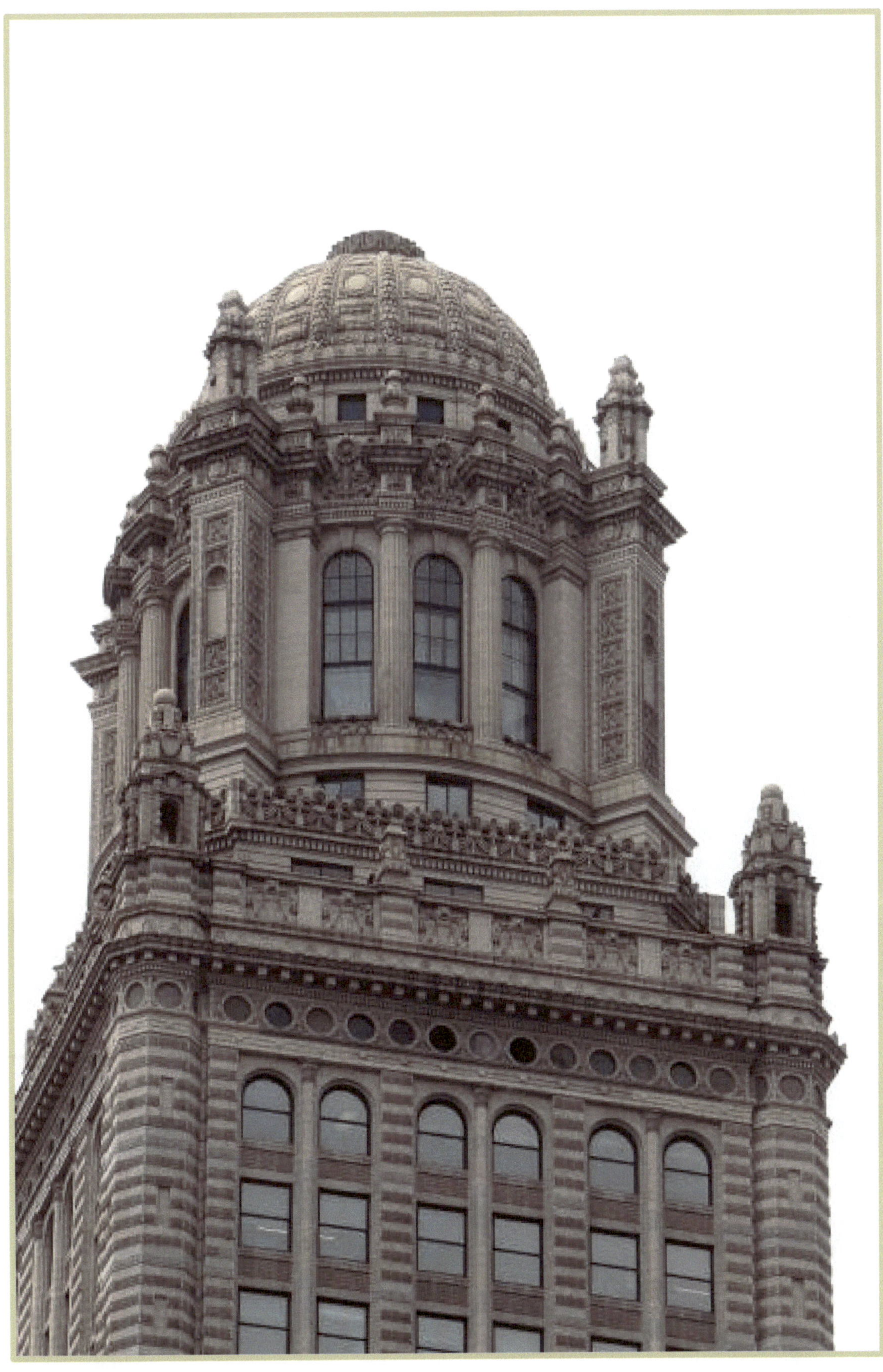

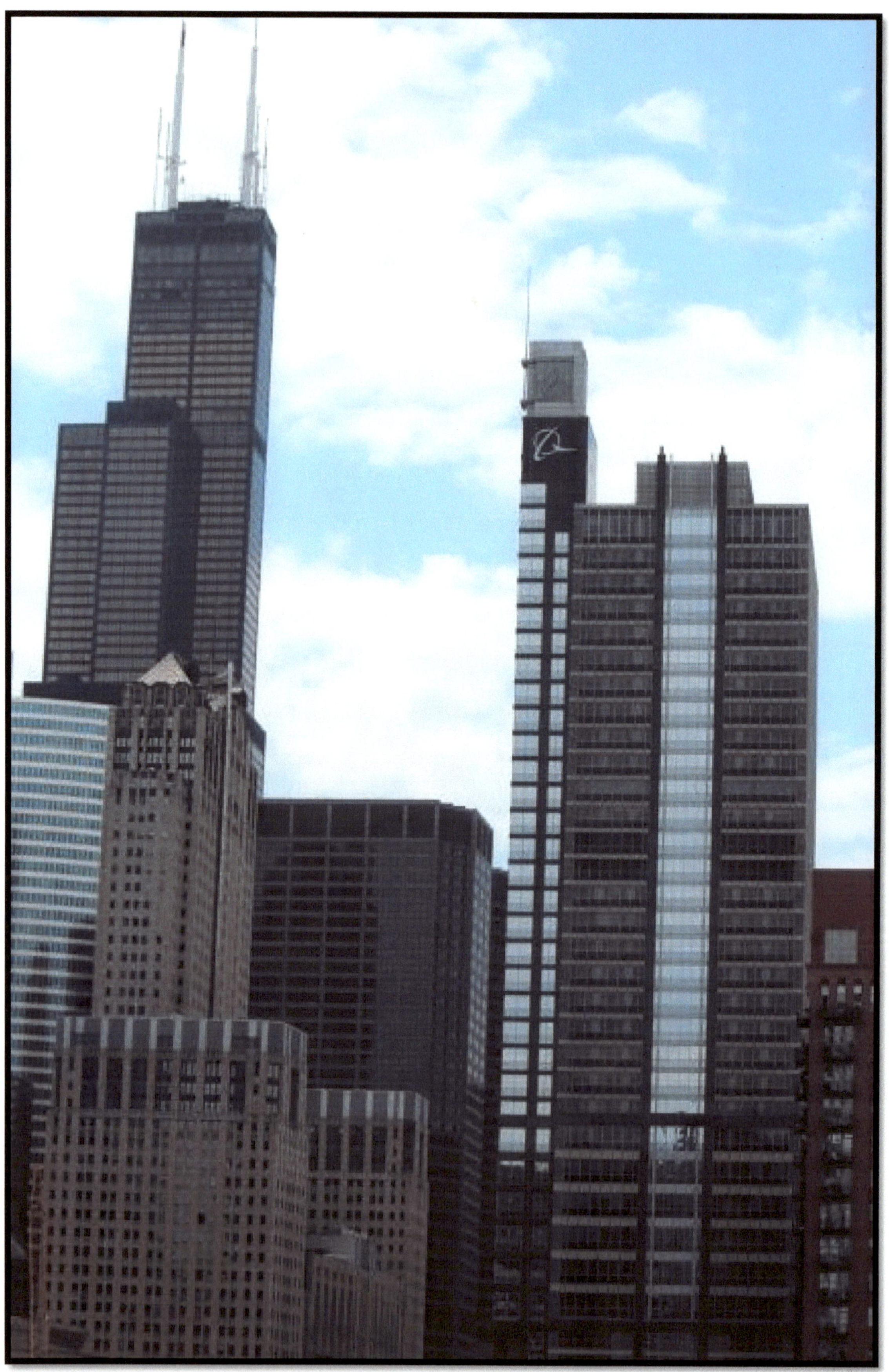

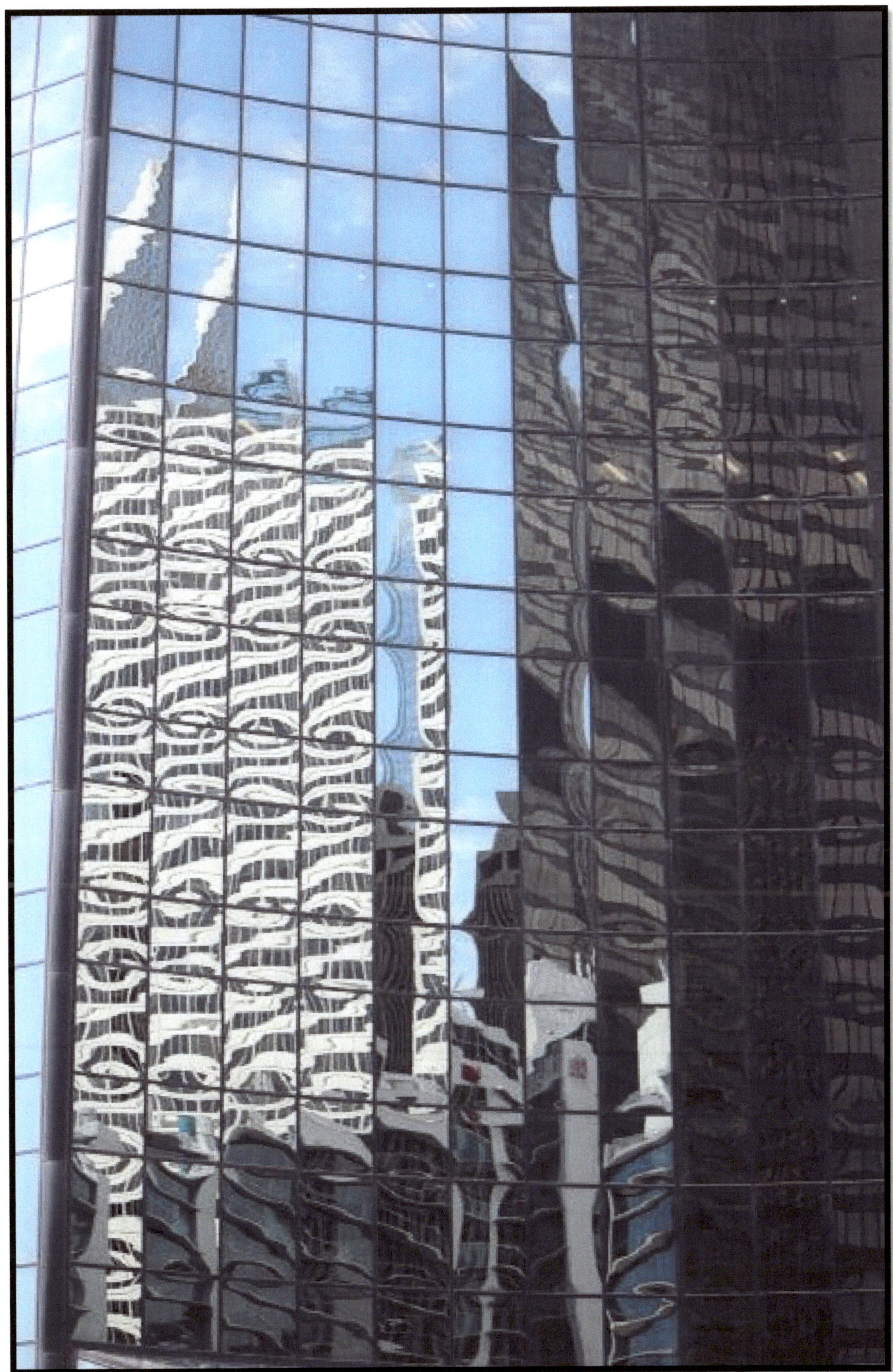

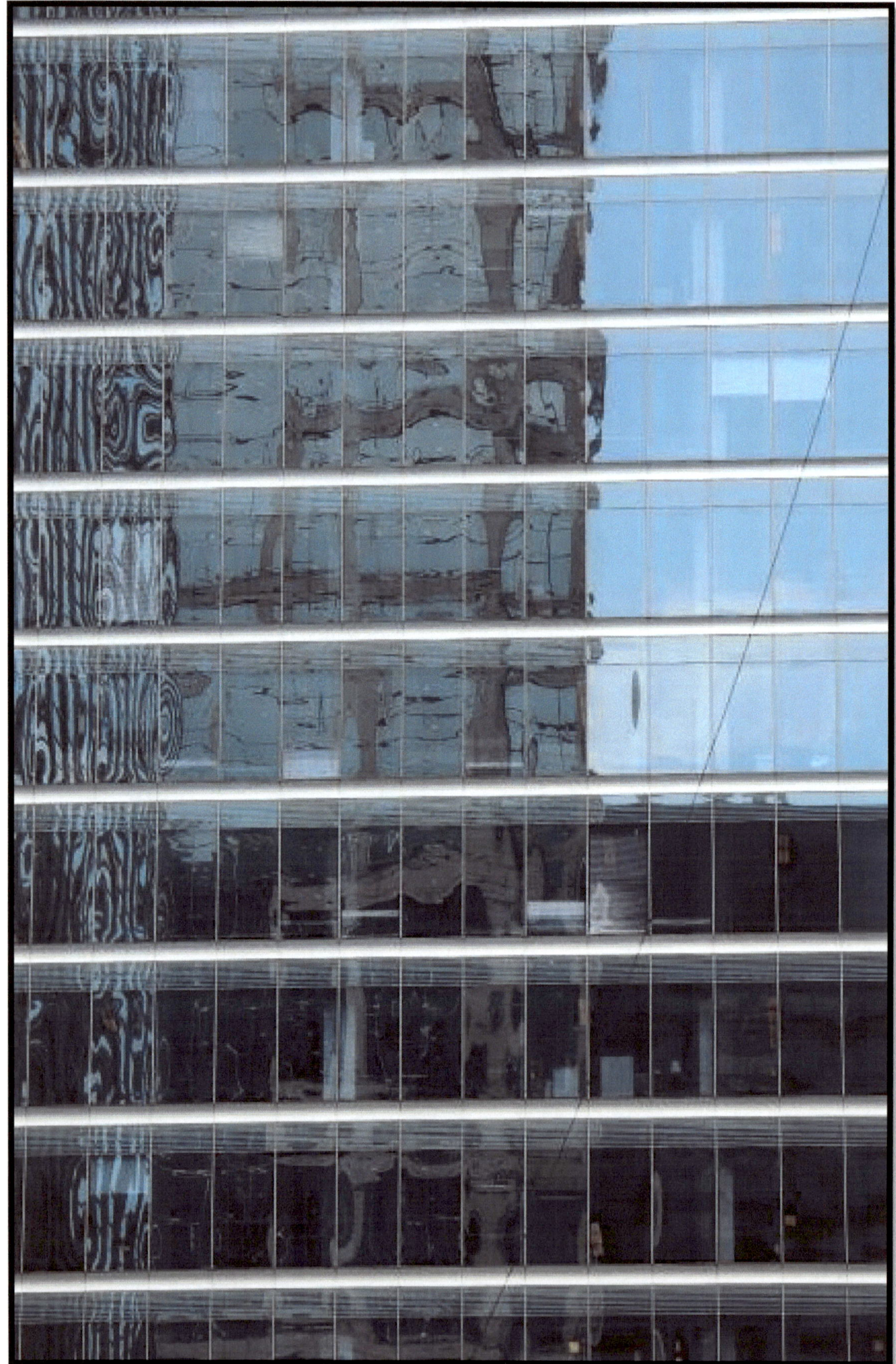

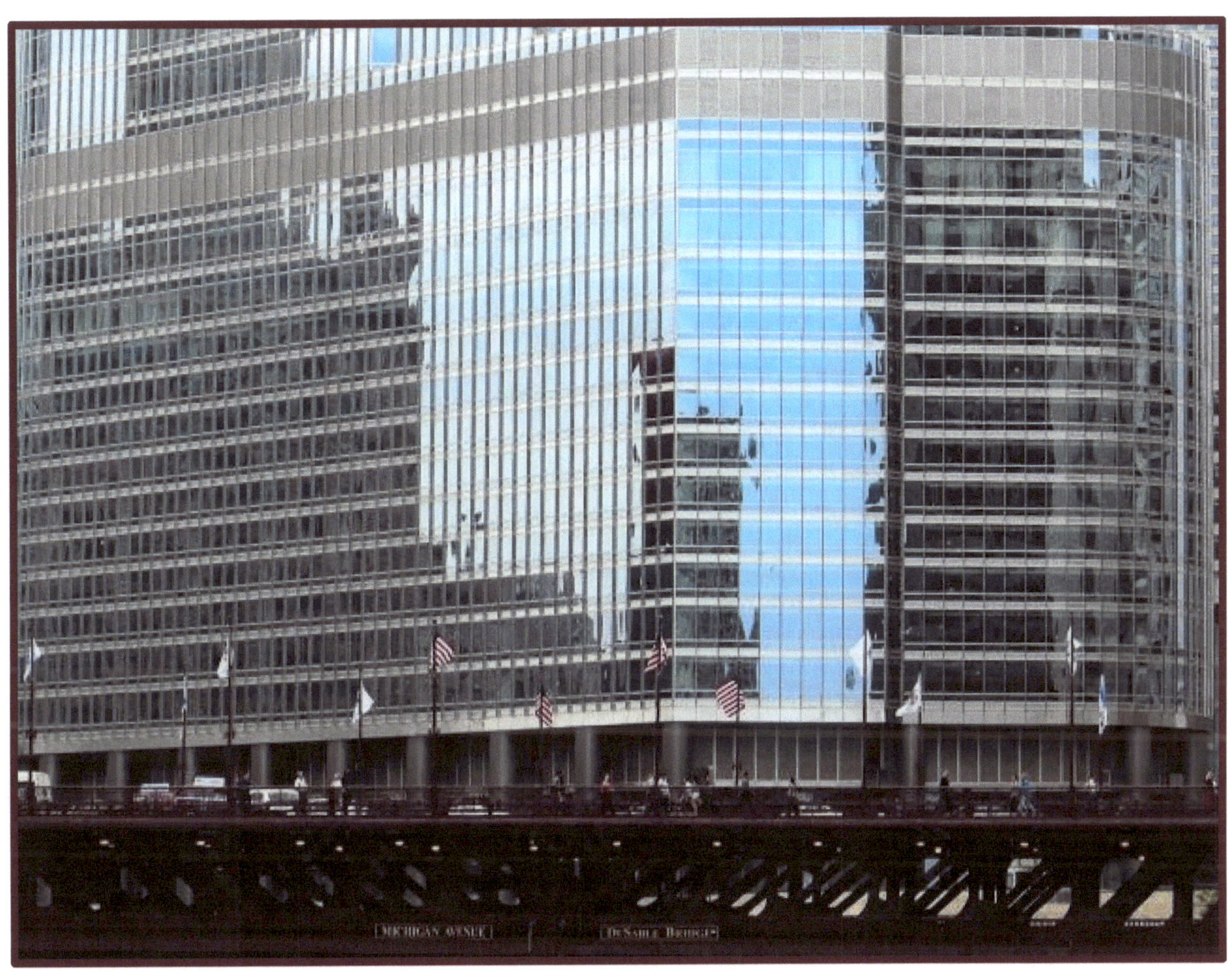

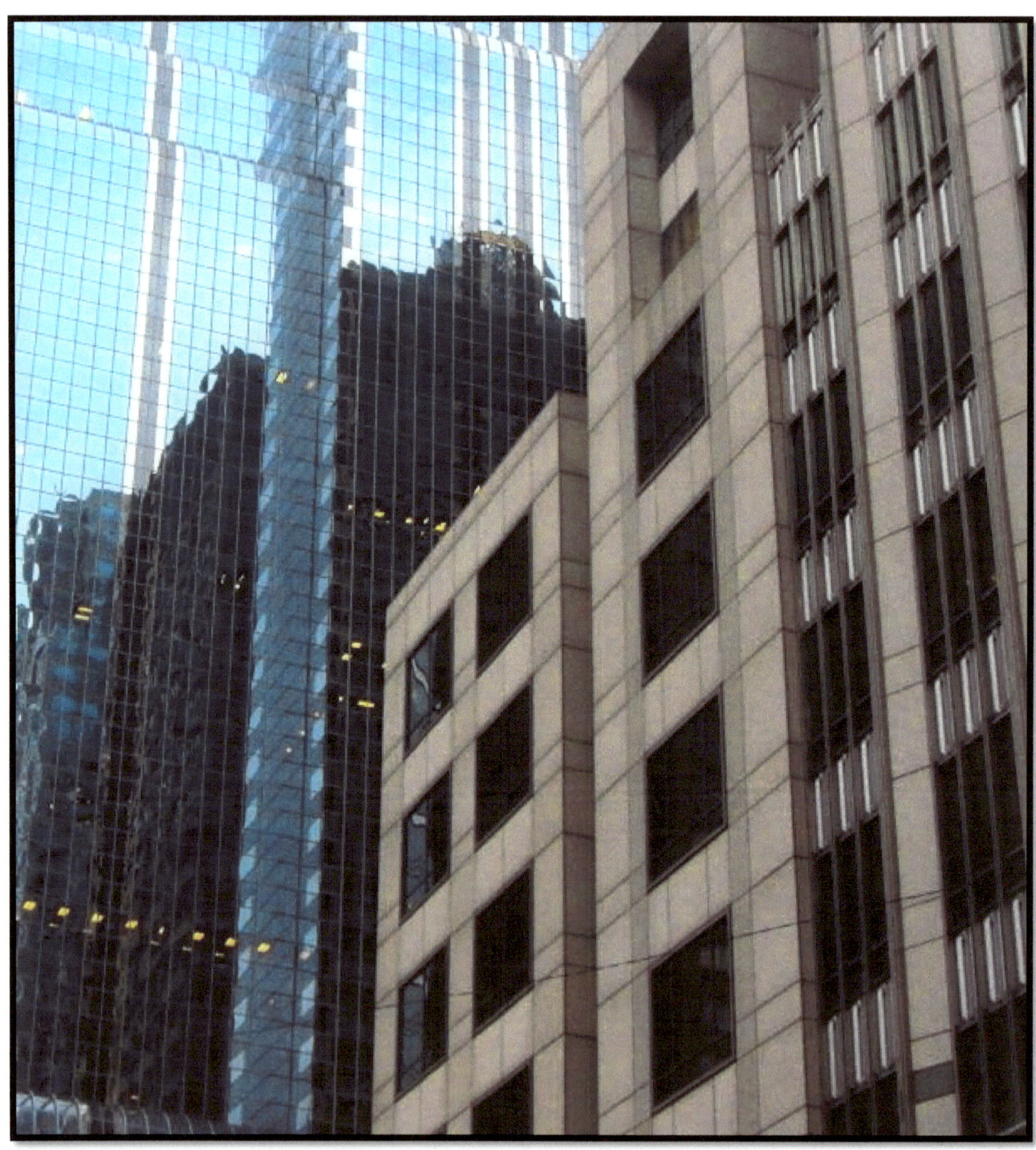

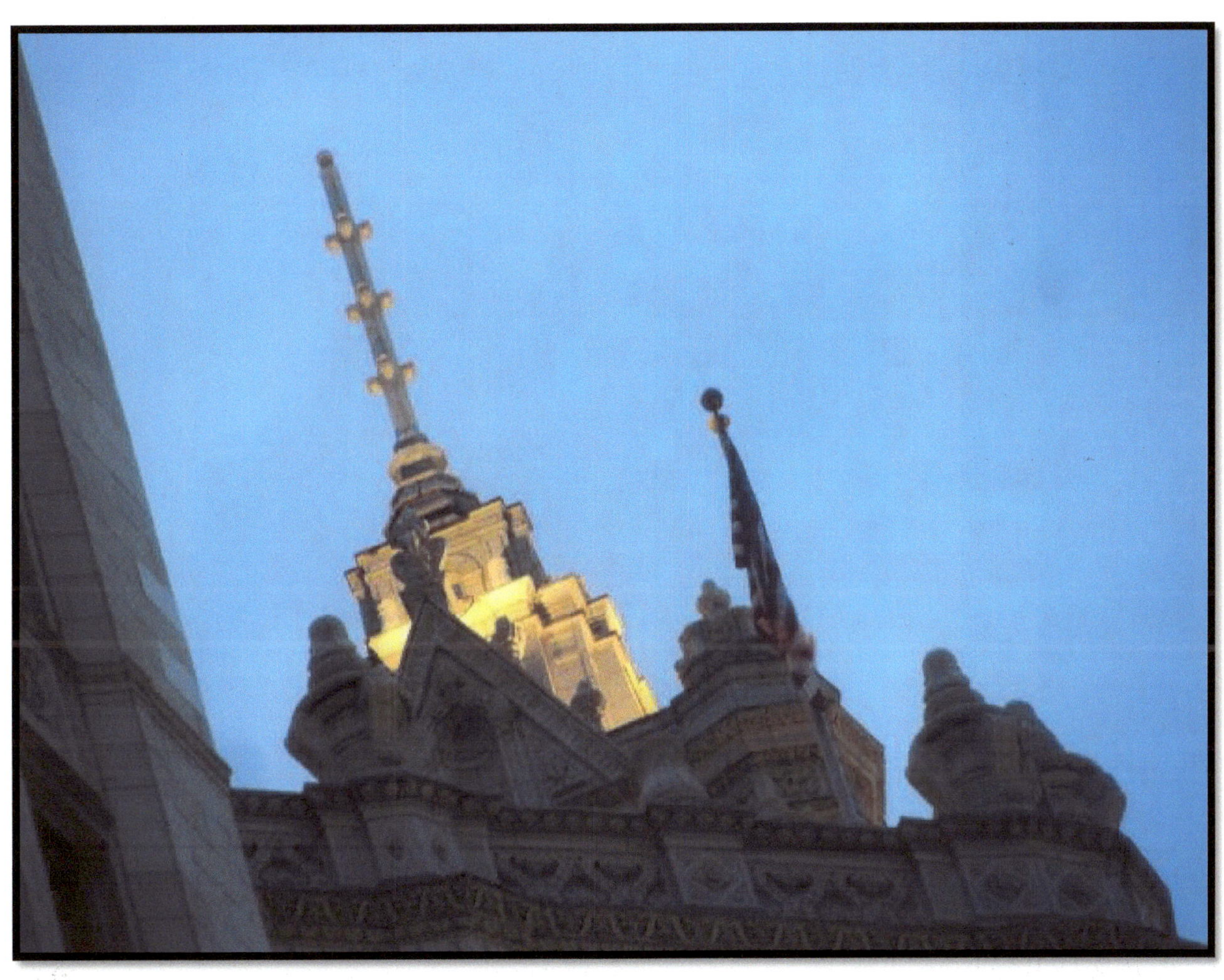

"In the twilight, it was a vision of power." **Upton Sinclair, *The Jungle***

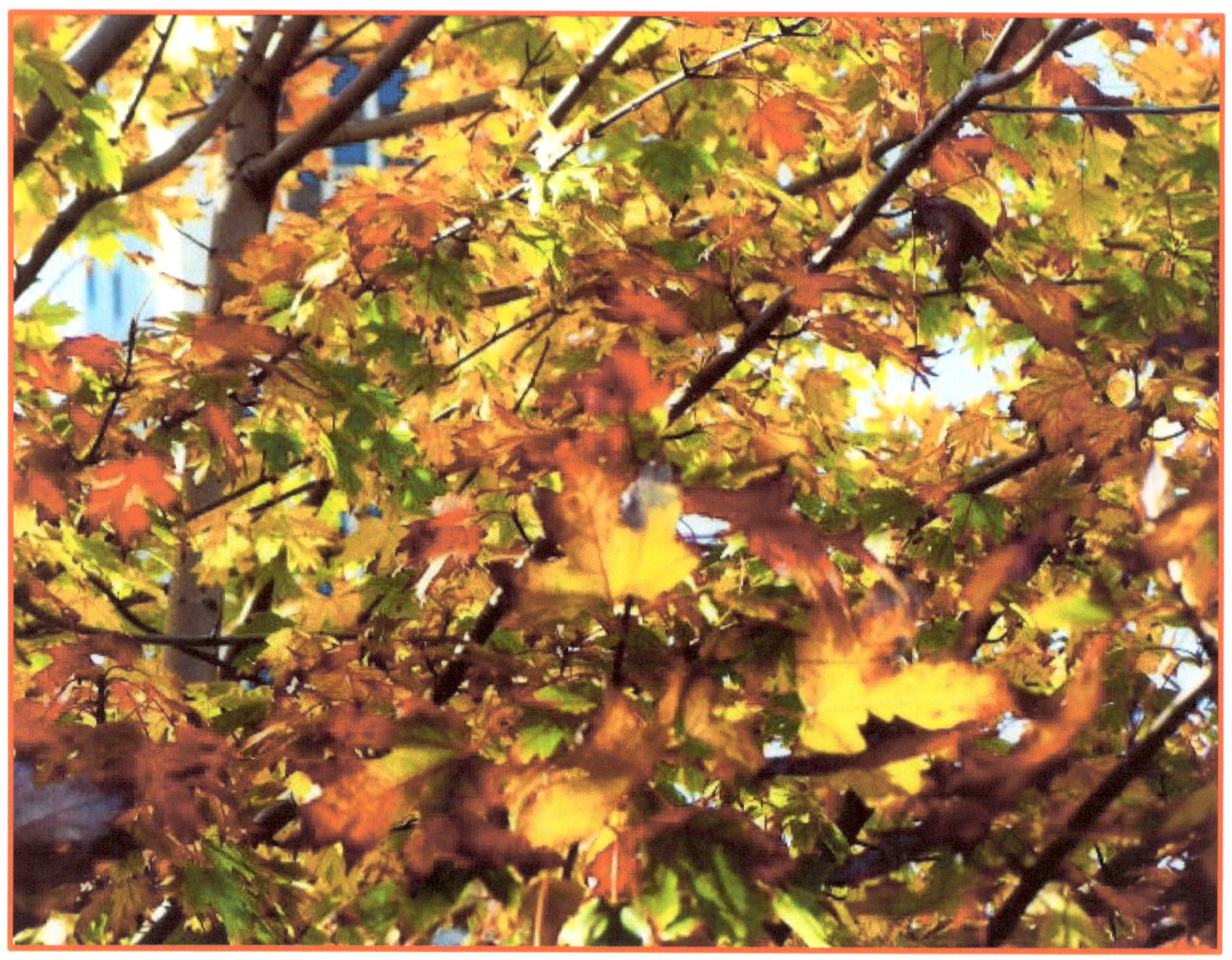

"Imagine what a harmonious world it could be if every single person, both young and old shared a little of what he is good at doing."

Quincy Jones, Chicagoan

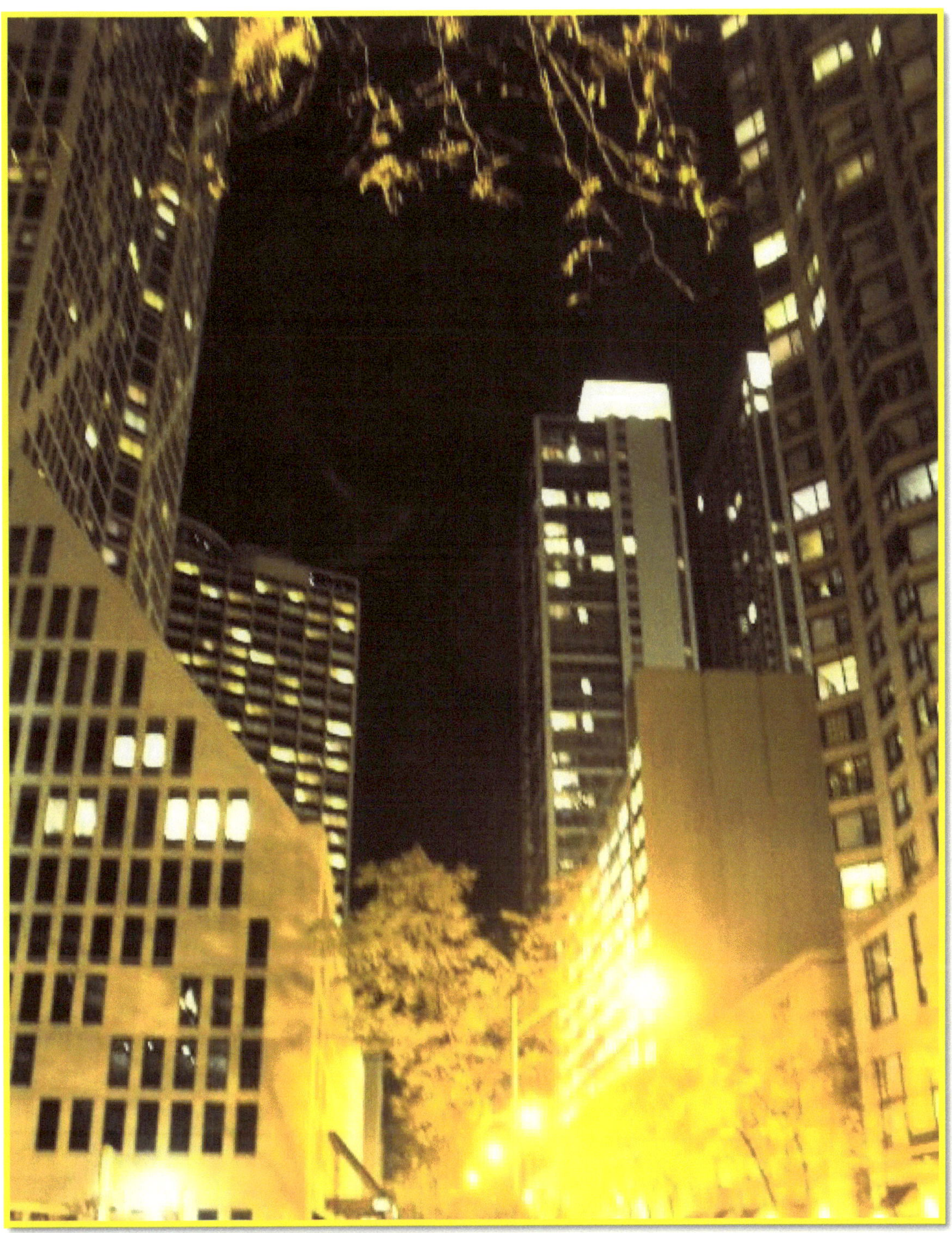

Spelled in electric fire on the roof are words telling miles of houses and people where to buy a thing for money. The sign speaks till midnight.

Sandburg

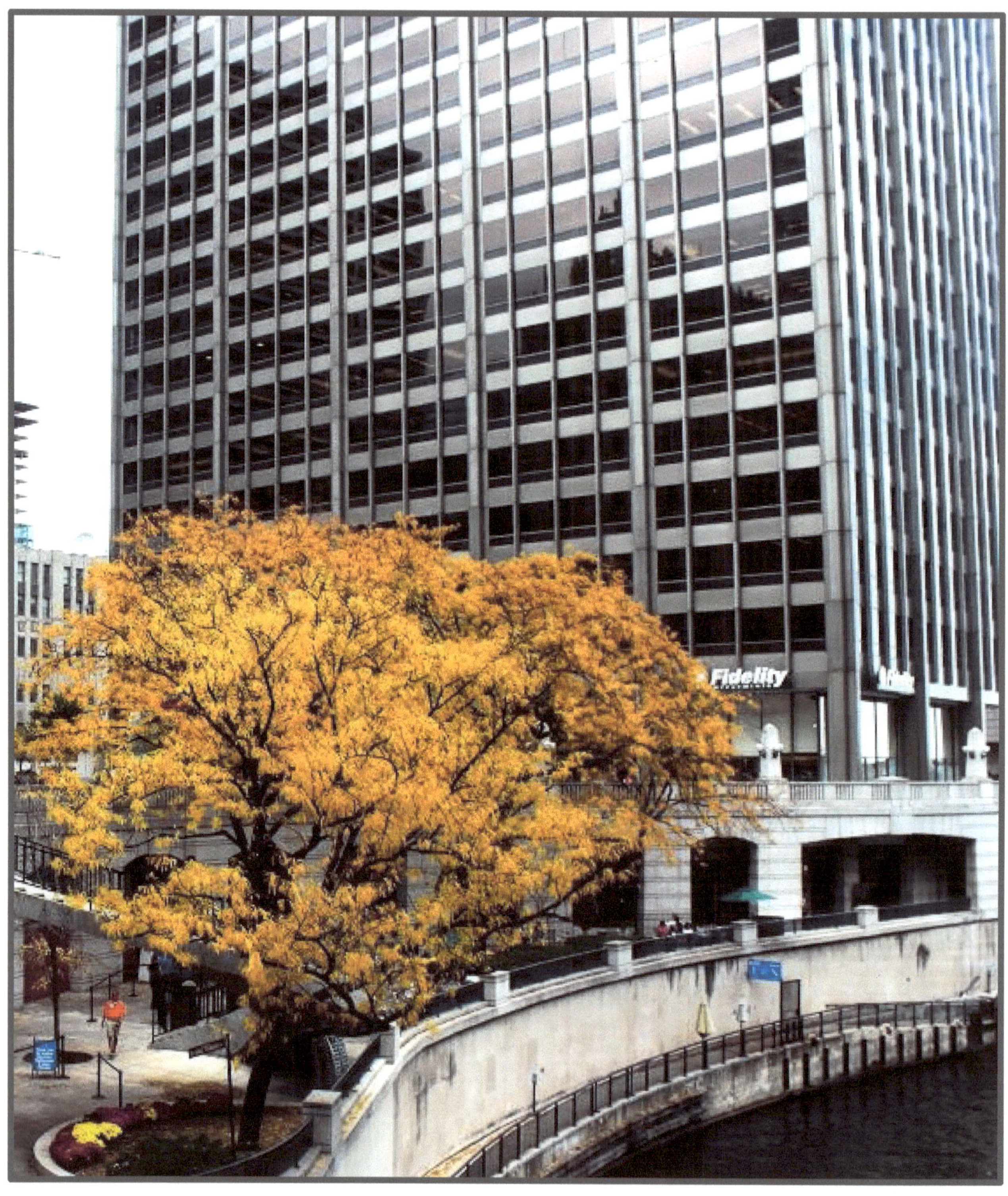

"Every city is a living body." **St. Augustine, City of God.**

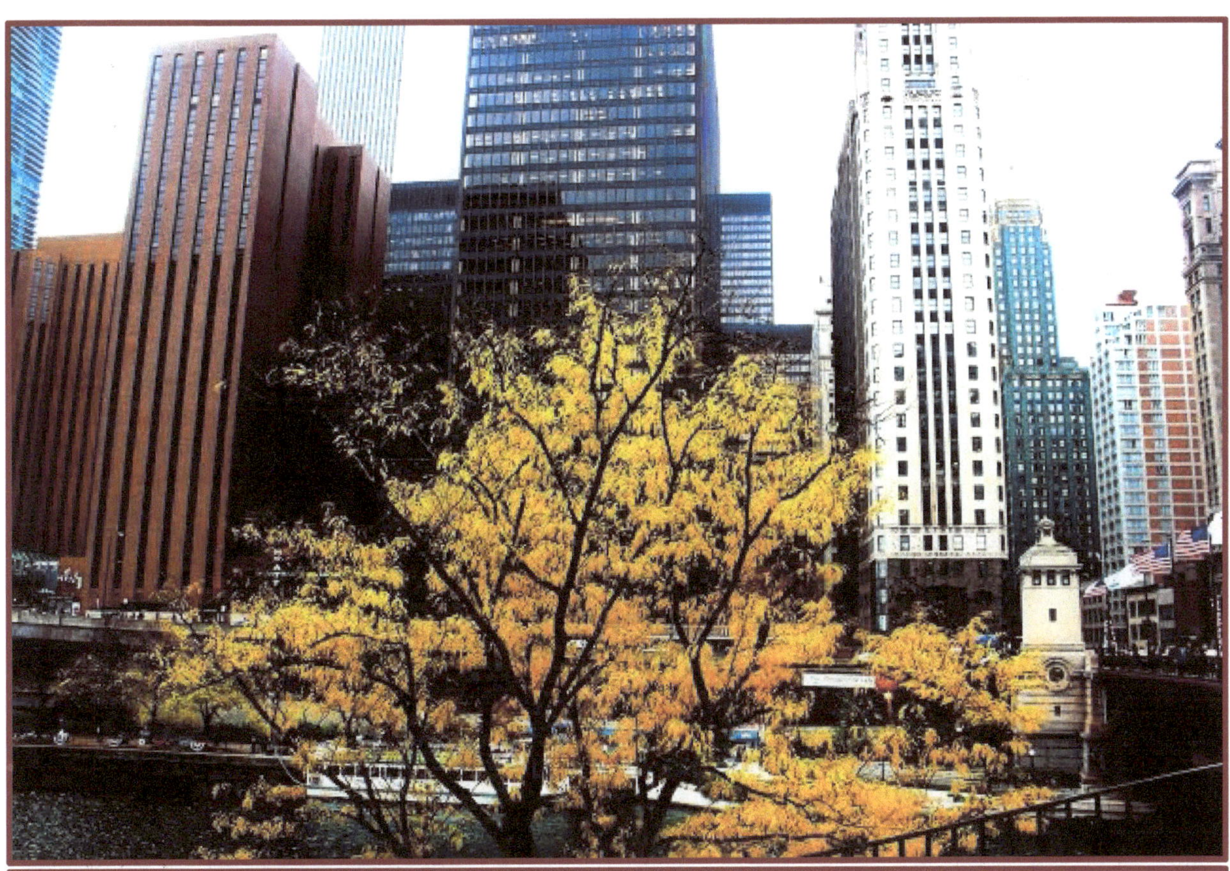

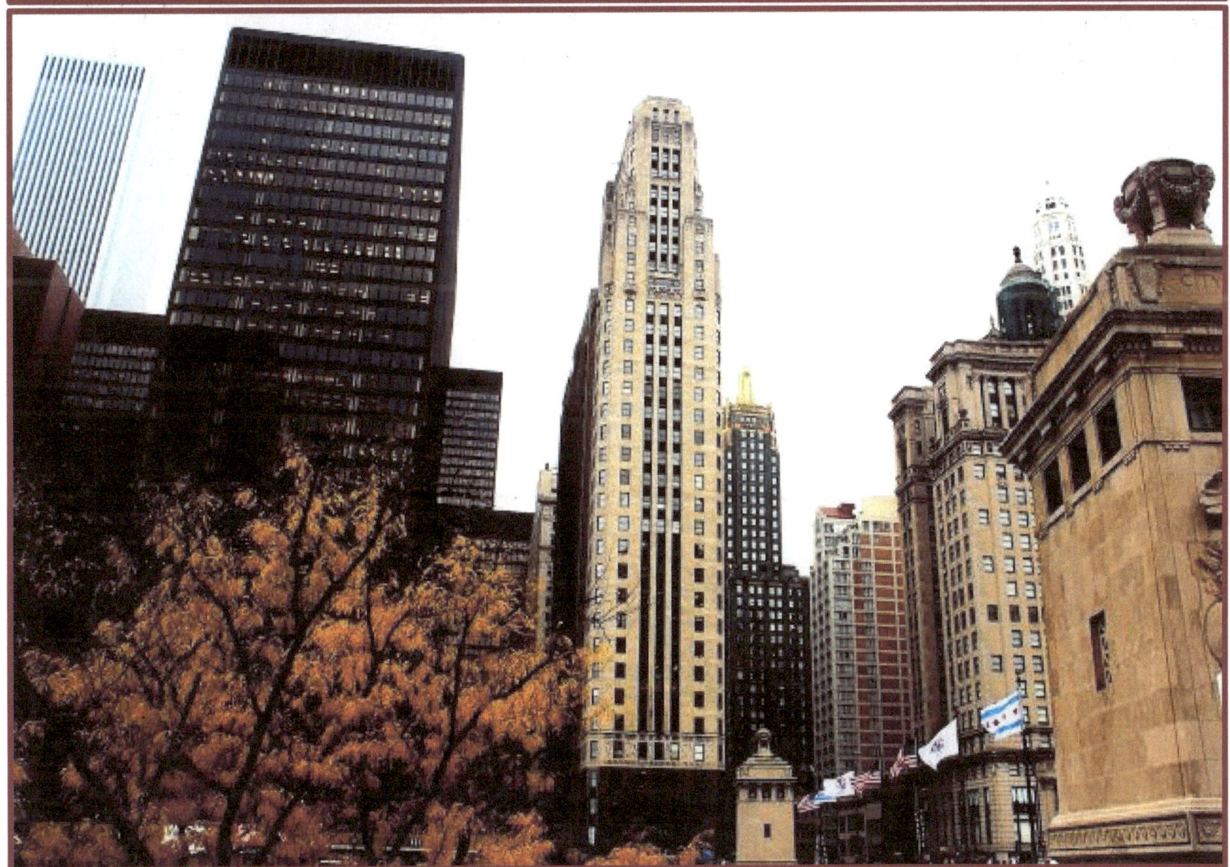

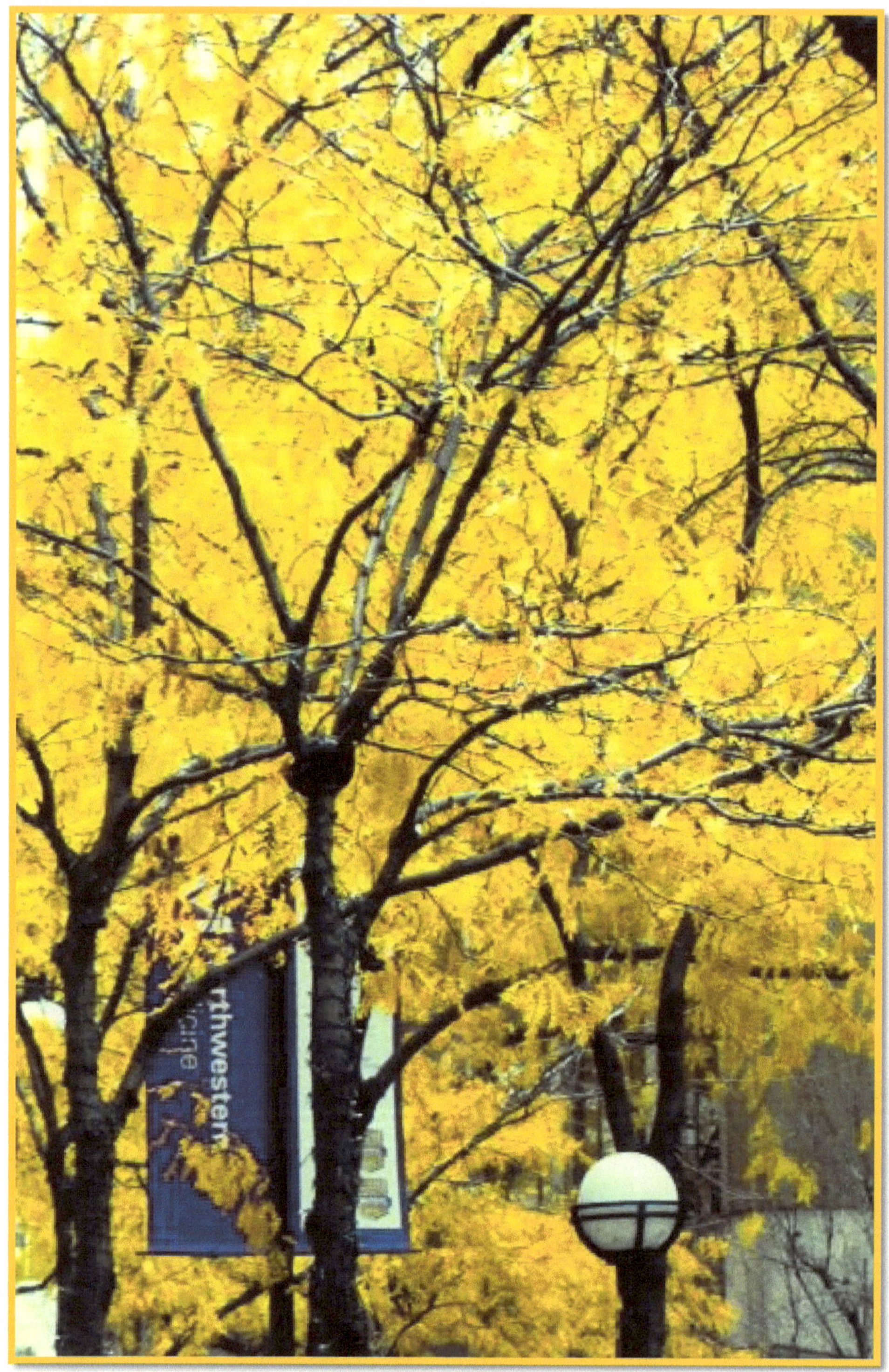

"...a city that was to live by night after the wilderness had passed. A city that was to forge out of steel and blood-red neon its own peculiar wilderness." **Nelson Algren, Chicago: City on the Make**

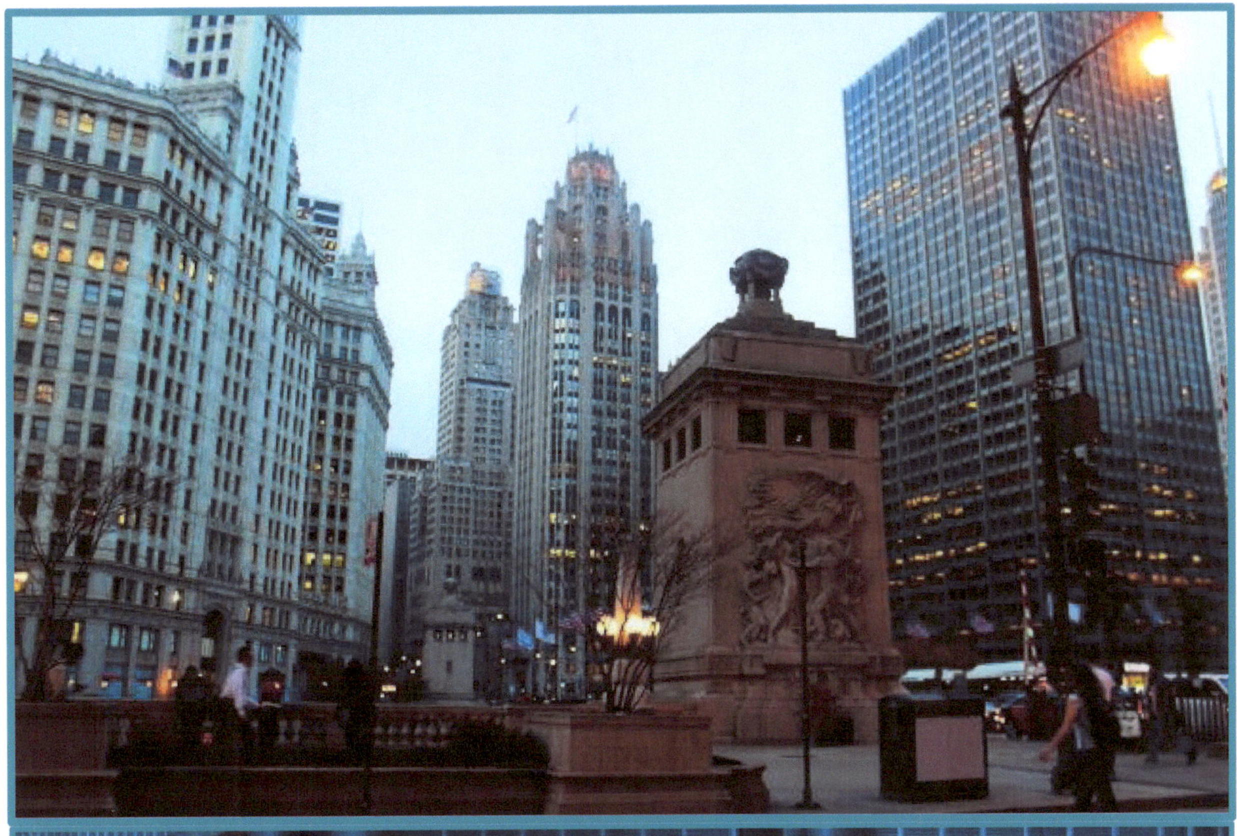

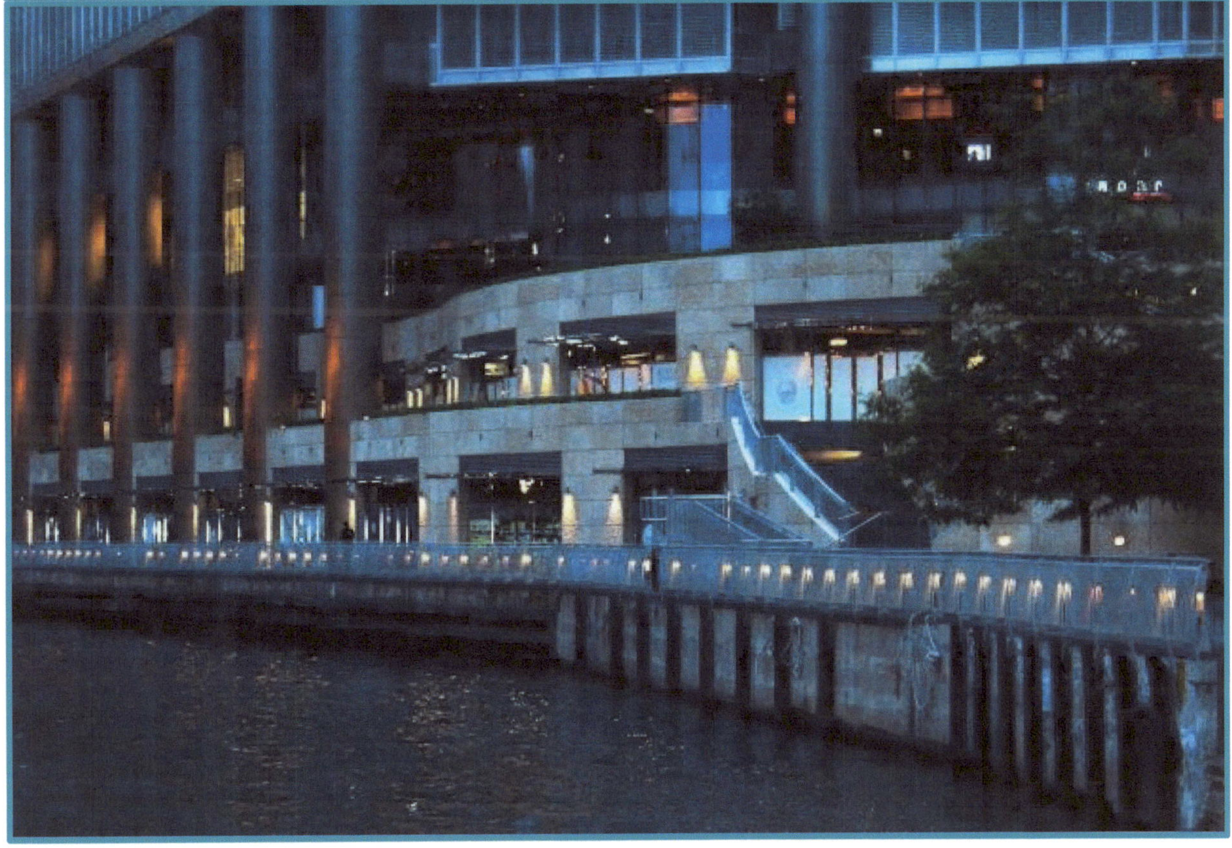

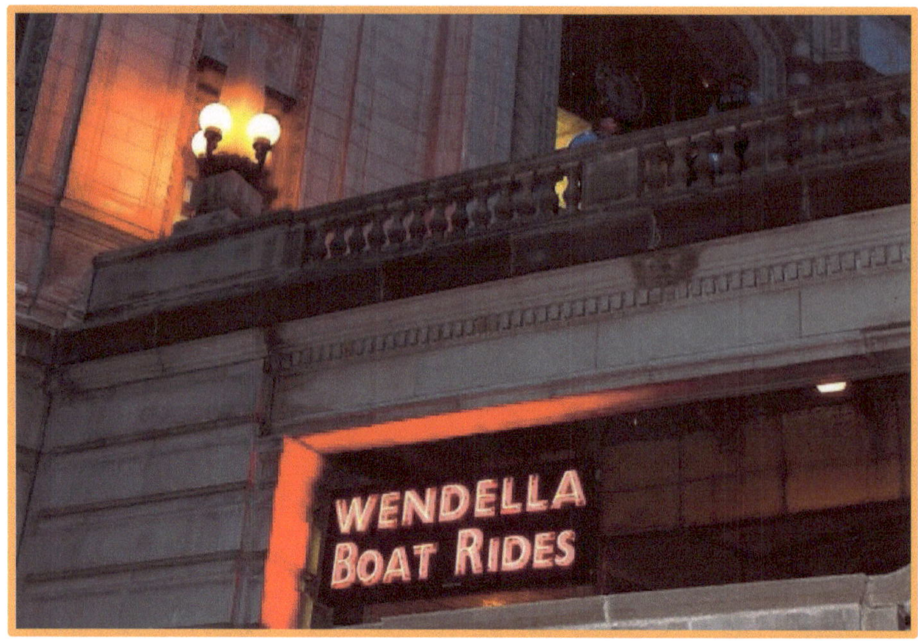

"If I could just go for a walk. If I could just look at buildings again, and smell that Lake Michigan, I'd give a million." **Al Capone from prison.**

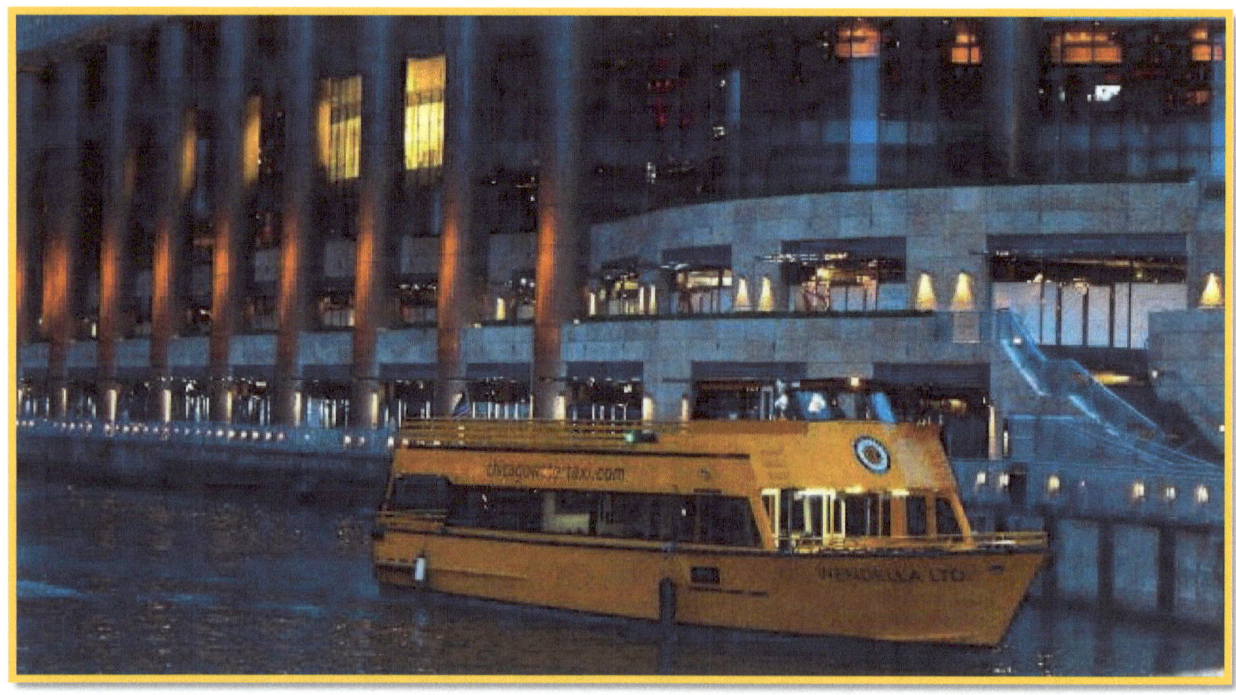

"Architecture is about public space held by buildings." **Richard Rogers.**

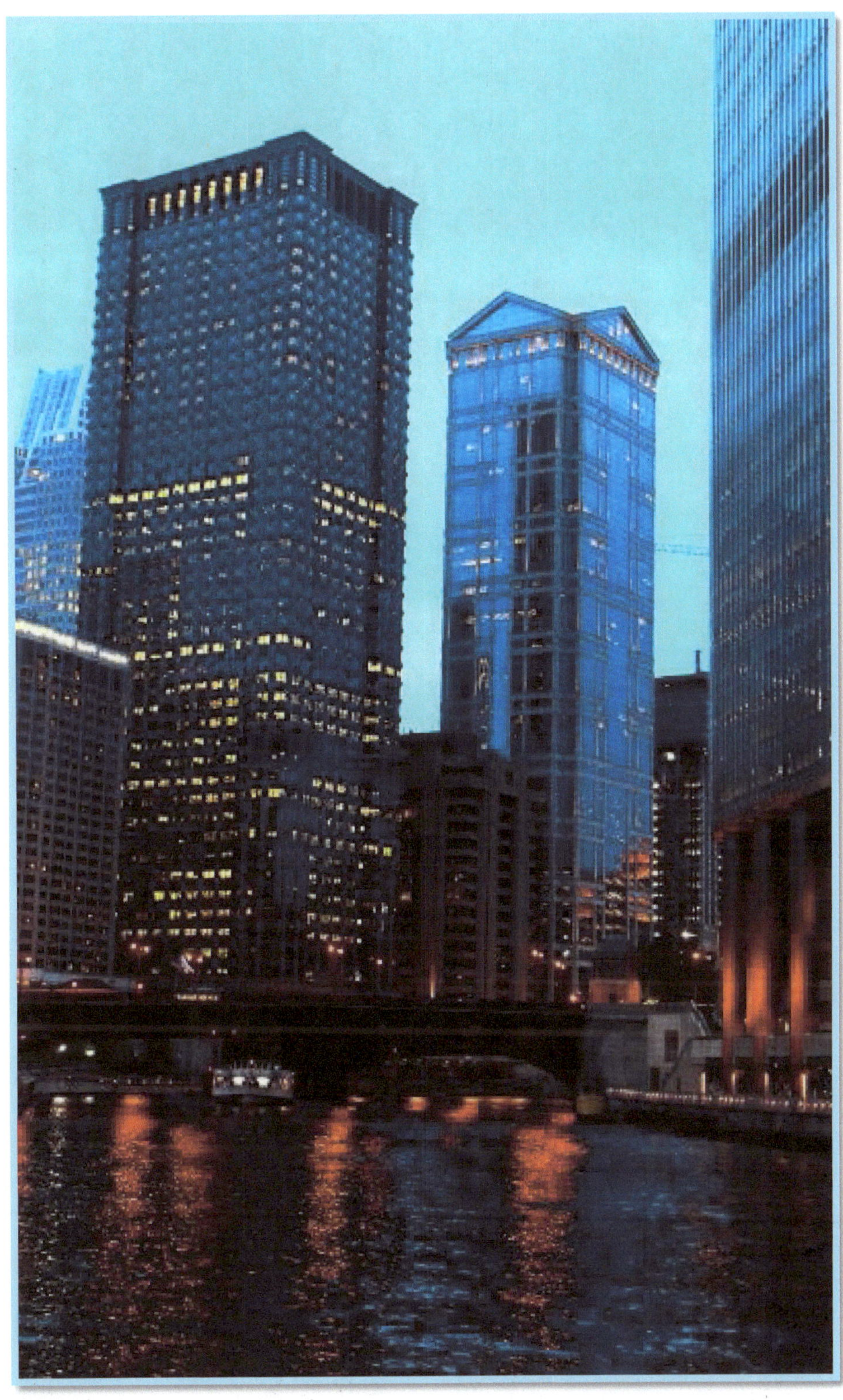

"Going to Chicago was like going out of the world…" **Muddy Waters**

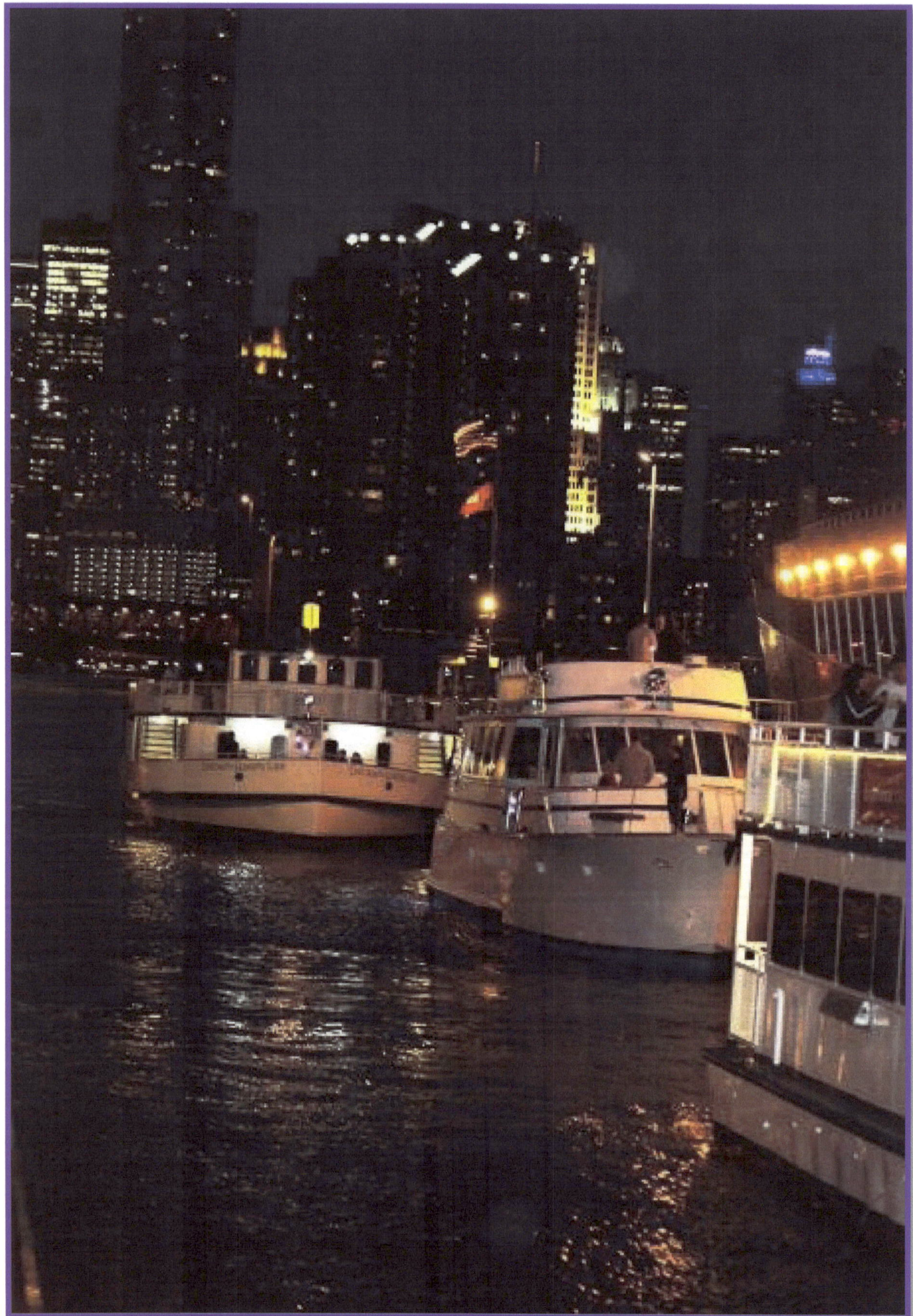

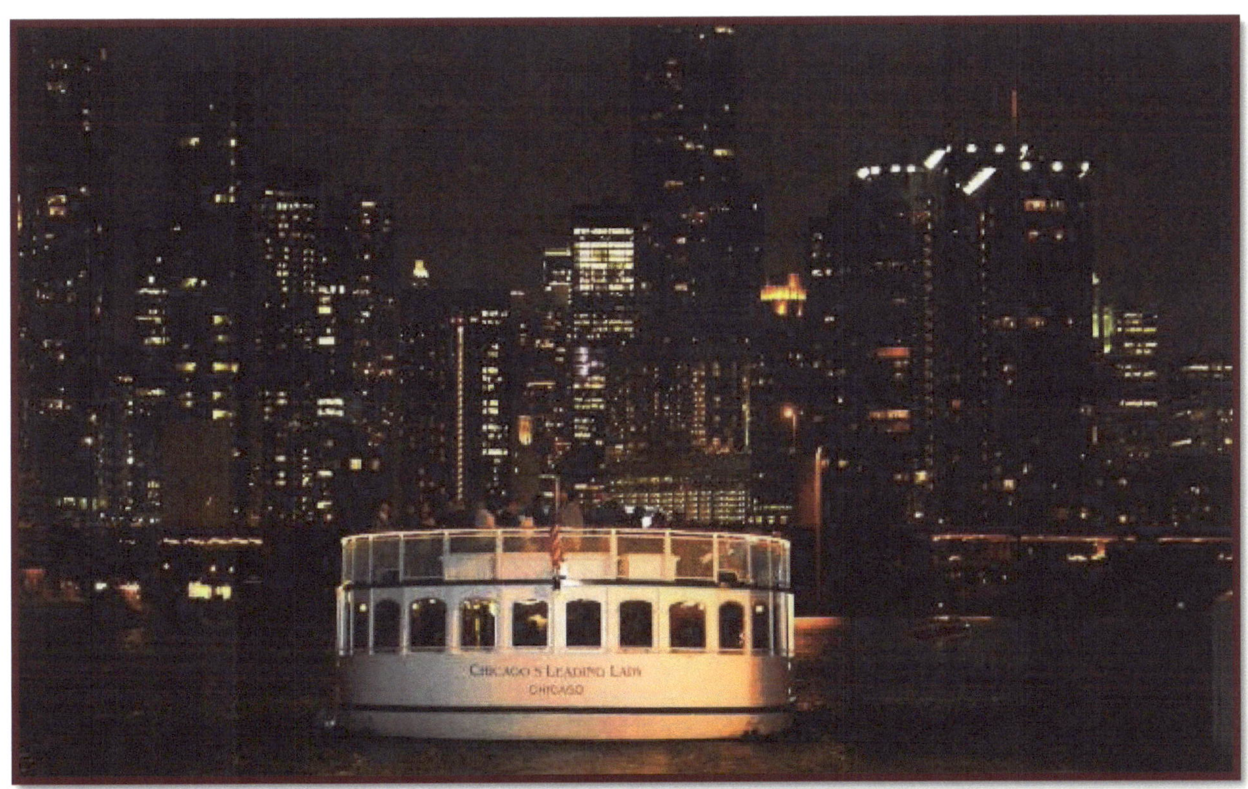
CHICAGO'S LEADING LADY
CHICAGO

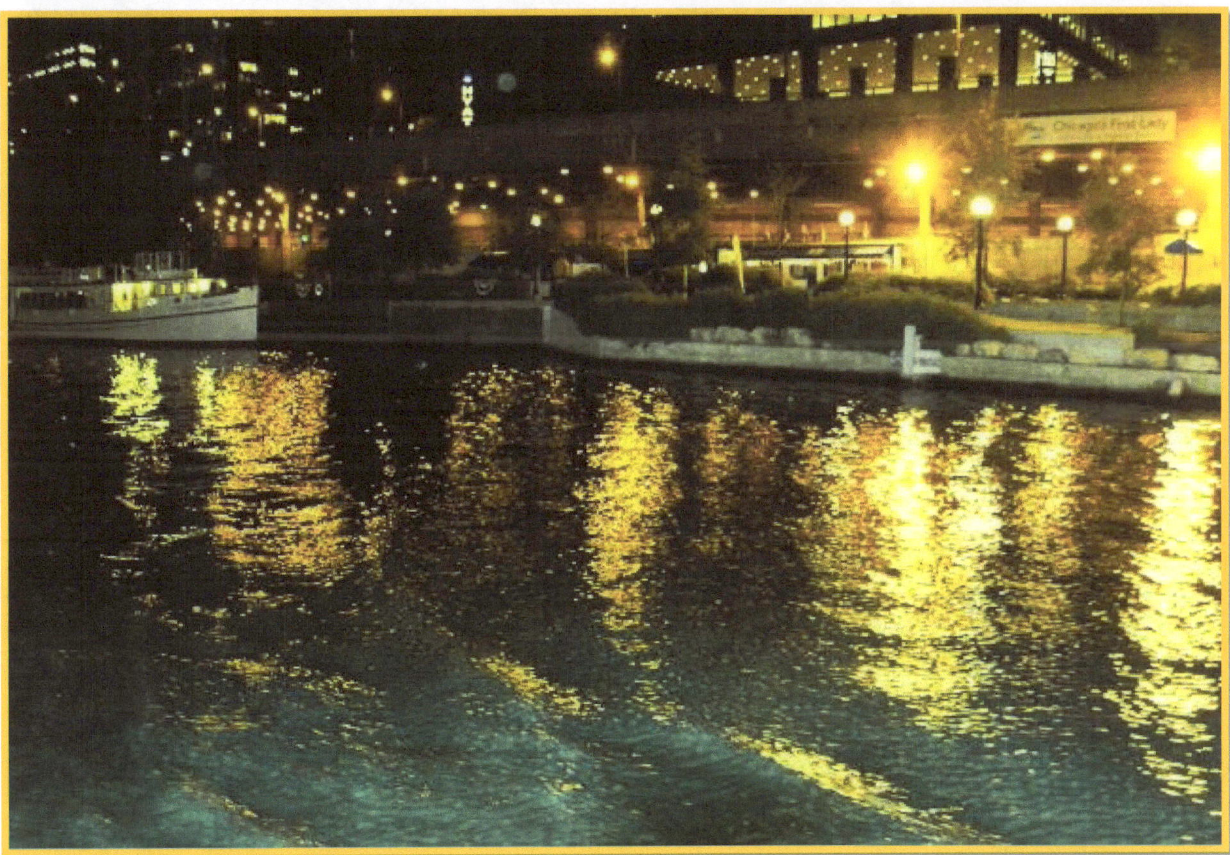

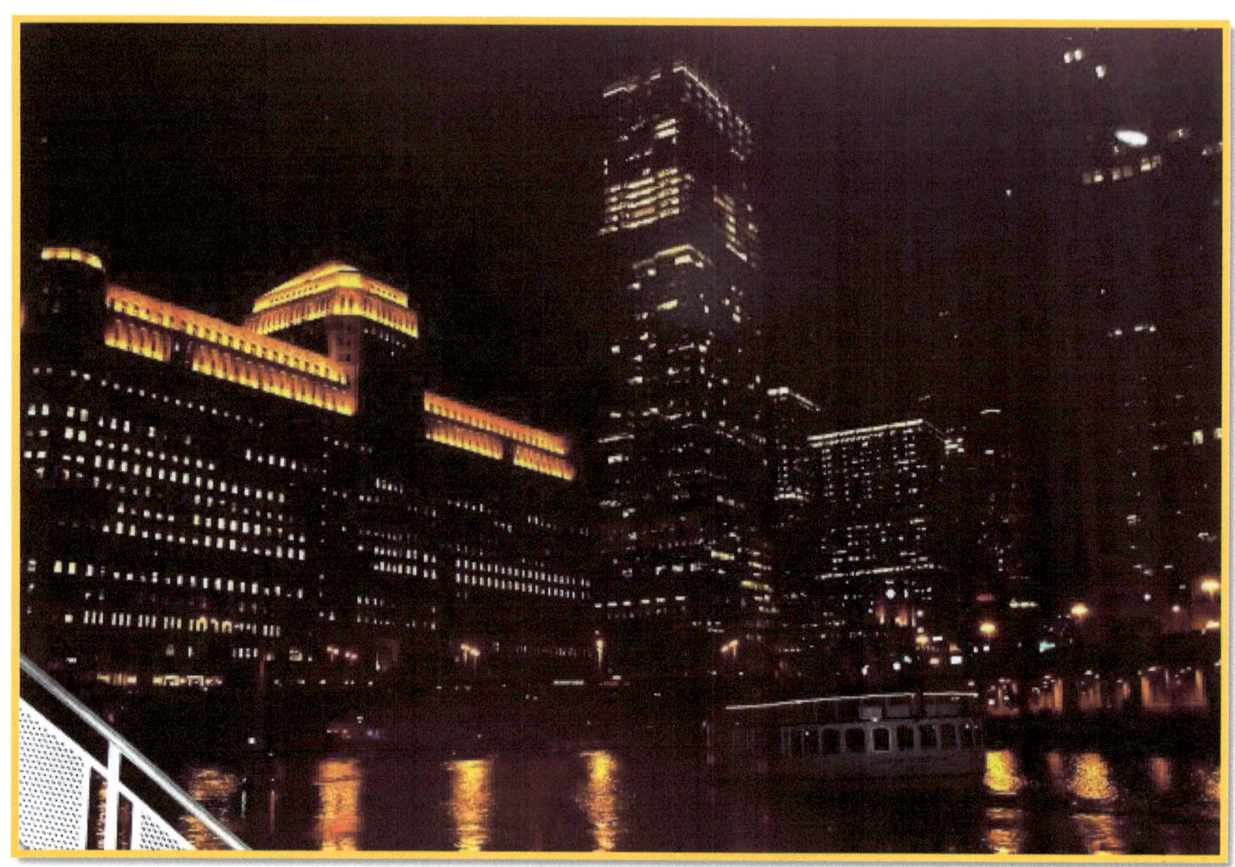

"The mother art is architecture. Without an architecture of our own we have no soul of our own civilization." **Frank Lloyd Wright**

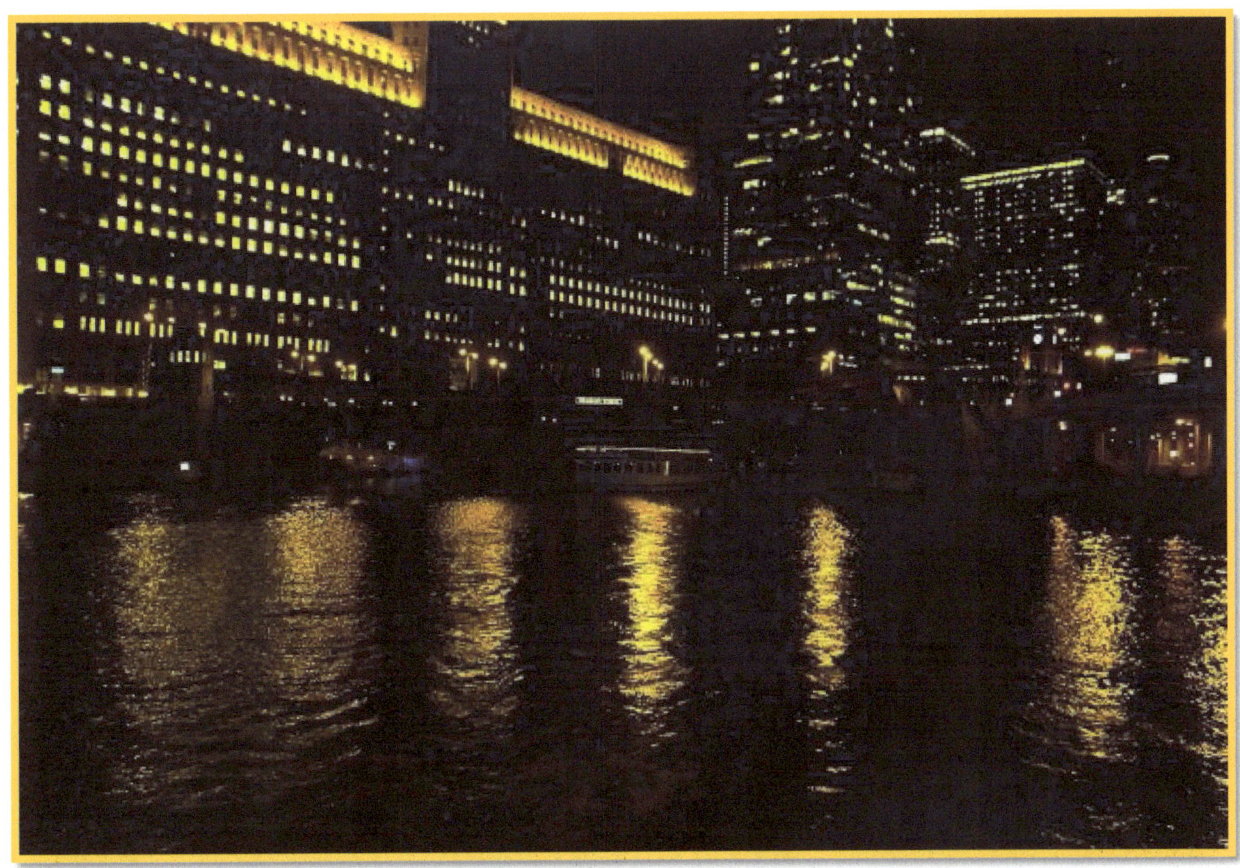

"The city as a center where, any day in any year, there may be a fresh encounter with a new talent, a keen mind or a gifted specialist-this is essential to the life of a country. To play this role in our lives a city must have a soul-a university, a great art or music school, a cathedral or a great mosque or temple, a great laboratory or scientific center, as well as the libraries and museums and galleries that bring past and present together. A city must be a place where groups of women and men are seeking and developing the highest things they know." **Margaret Mead**

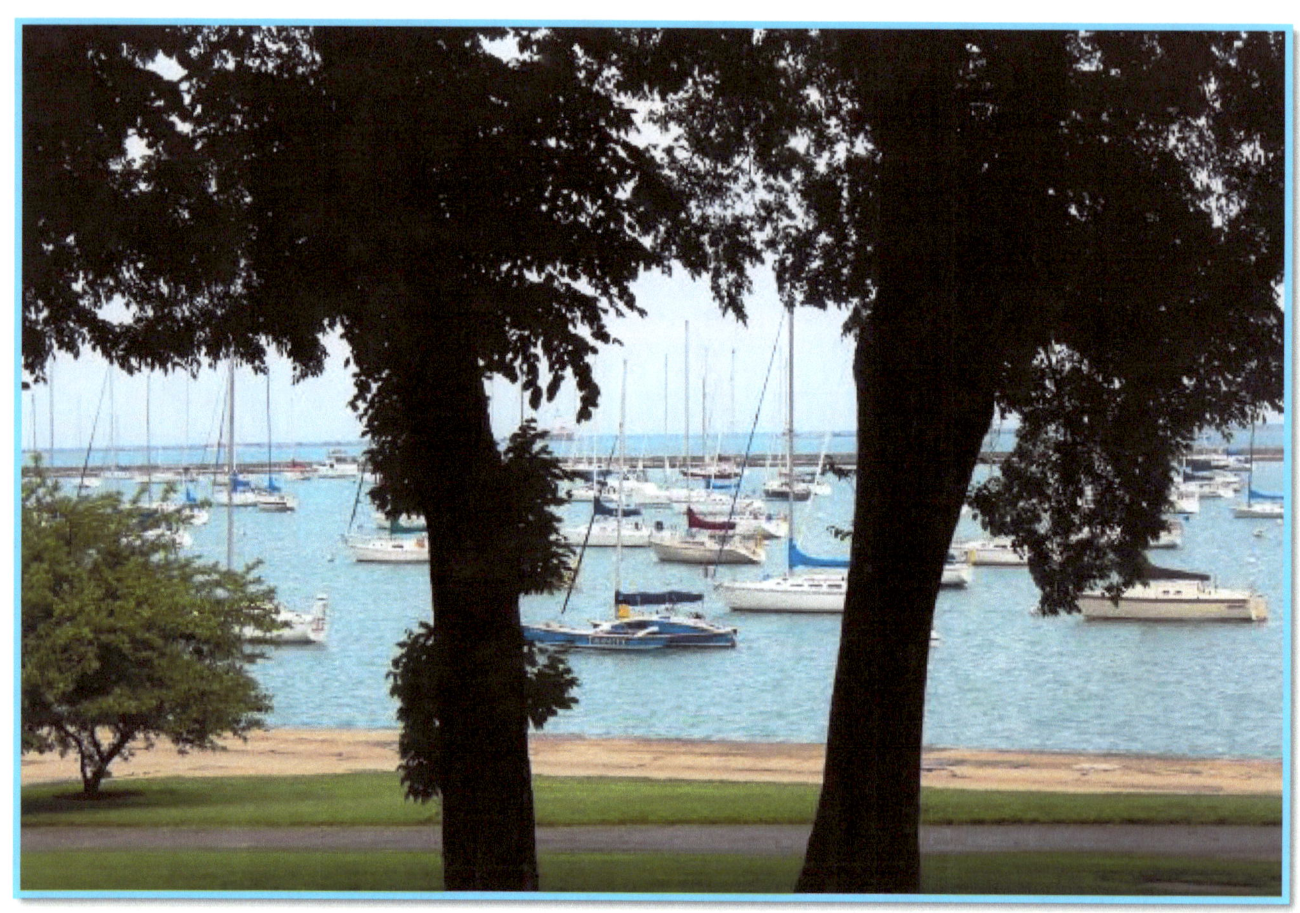

"I came sudden, at the city's edge,
On a blue burst of lake,
Long lake waves breaking under the sun
On a spray-flung curve of shore;
And a fluttering storm of gulls,
Masses of great gray wings
And flying white bellies
Veering and wheeling free in the open. "
The Harbor, Carl Sandburg Chicago Poems.

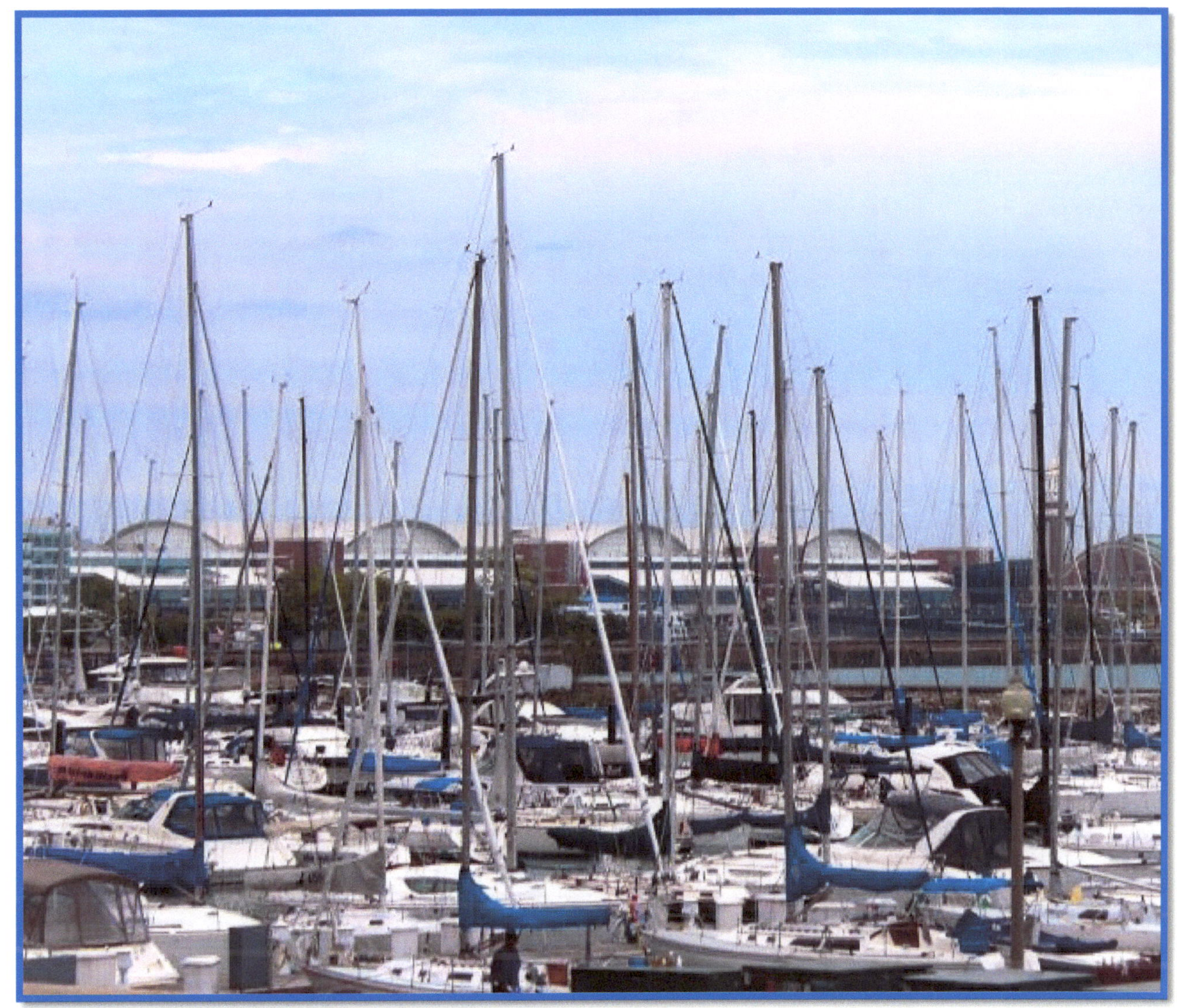

“The more successfully a city mingles everyday diversity of uses and users in its everyday streets, the more successfully, casually (and economically) its people thereby enliven and support well-located parks that can thus give back grace and delight to their neighborhoods instead of vacuity.” **Jane Jacobs, The Death and Life of Great American Cities**

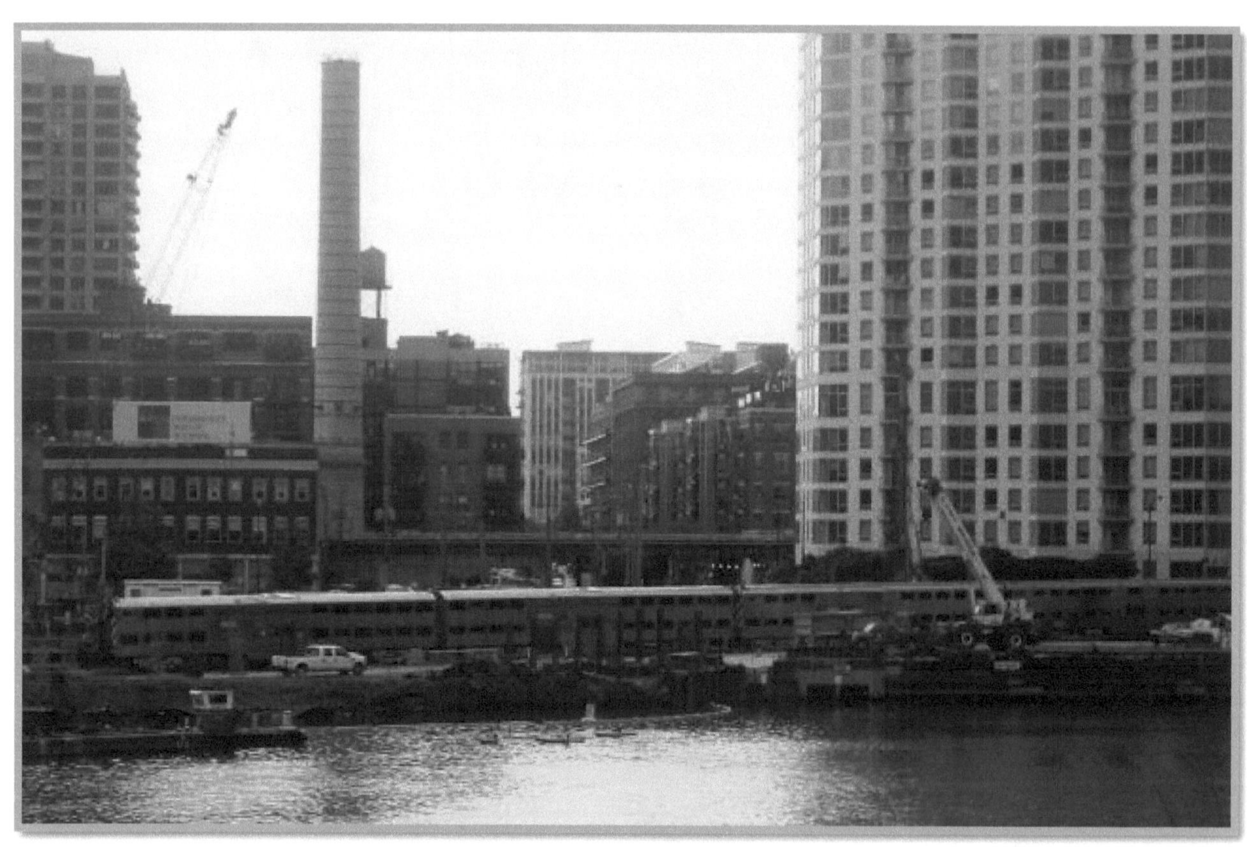

"Chicago ain't no sissy town." **Michael Hinky Dink Kenna**

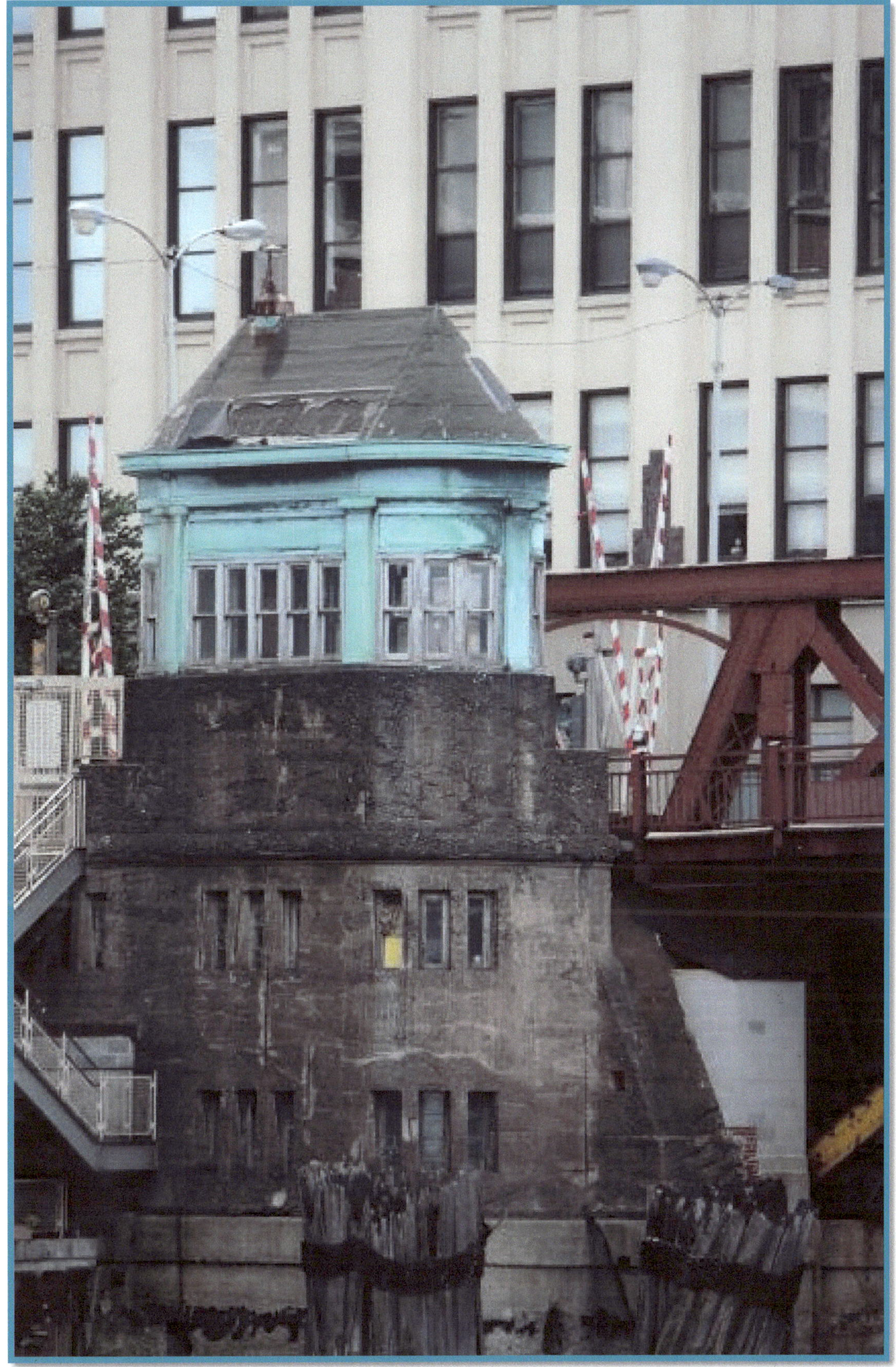

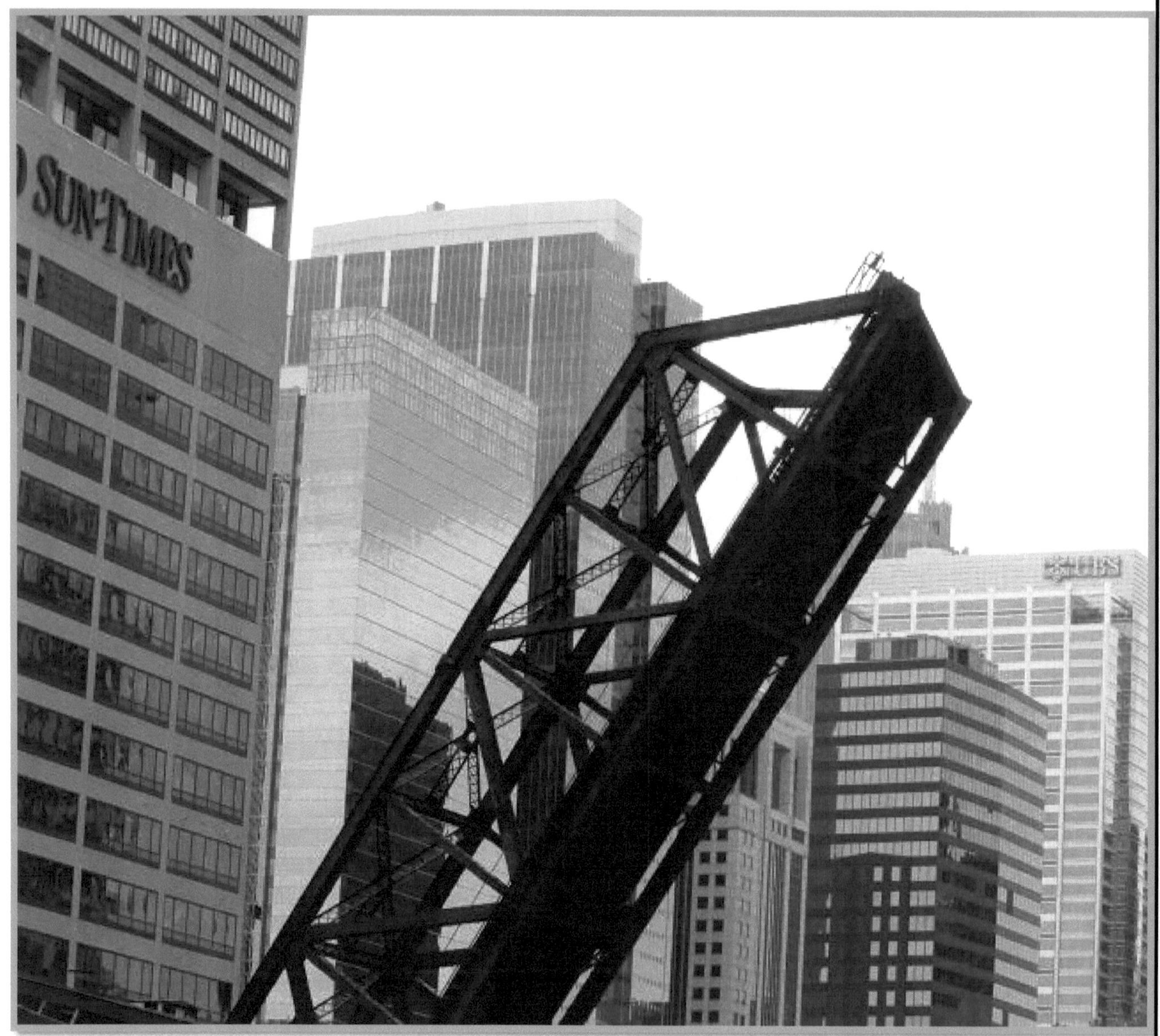

"Why do people resist [engines, bridges, and cities] so? They are symbols and products of the imagination, which is the force that ensures justice and historical momentum in an imperfect world, because without imagination we would not have the wherewithal to challenge certainty, and we could never rise above ourselves." **Mark Helprin, Winter's Tale**

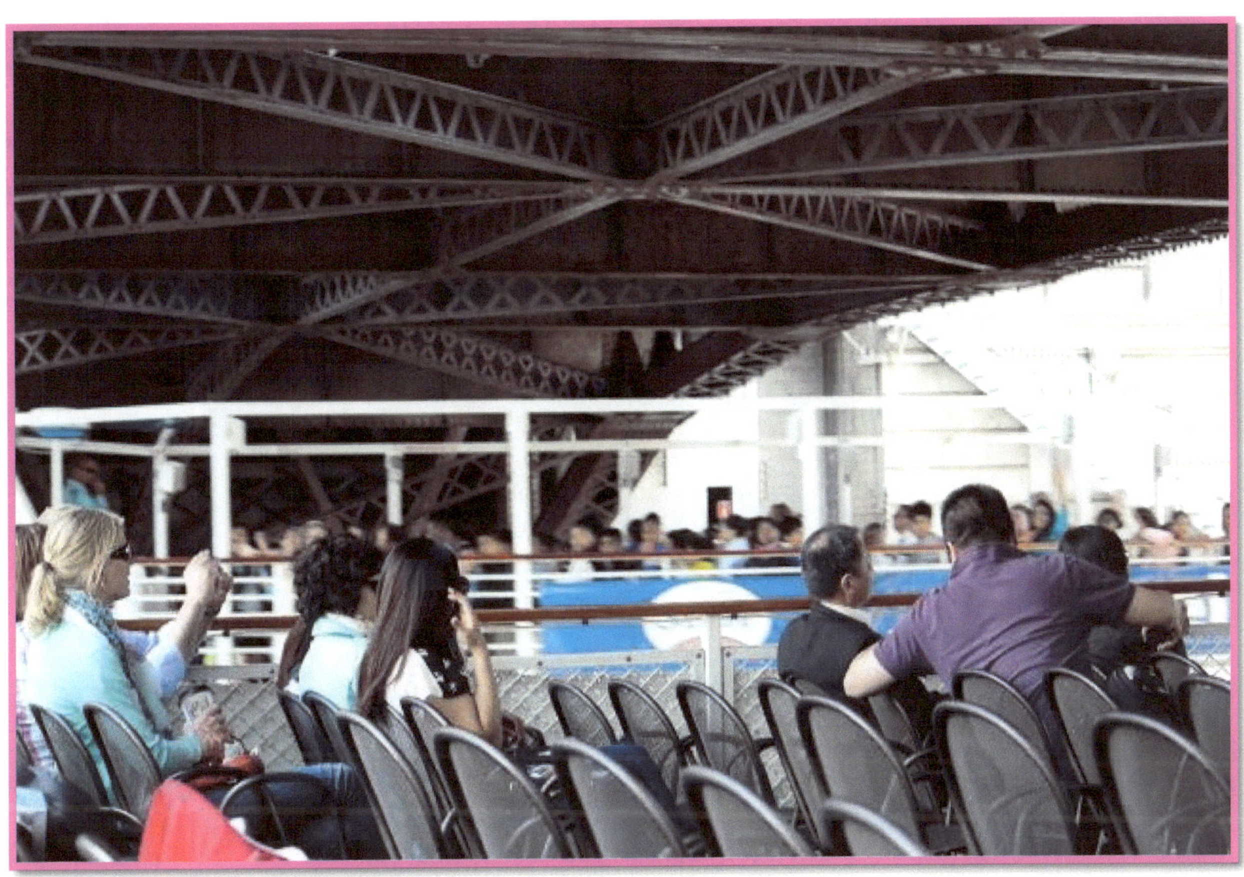

“Cities have always offered anonymity, variety, and conjunction, qualities best basked in by walking: one does not have to go into the bakery or the fortune-teller's, only to know that one might. A city always contains more than any inhabitant can know, and a great city always makes the unknown and the possible spurs to the imagination.” **Rebecca Solnit, Wanderlust: A History of Walking**

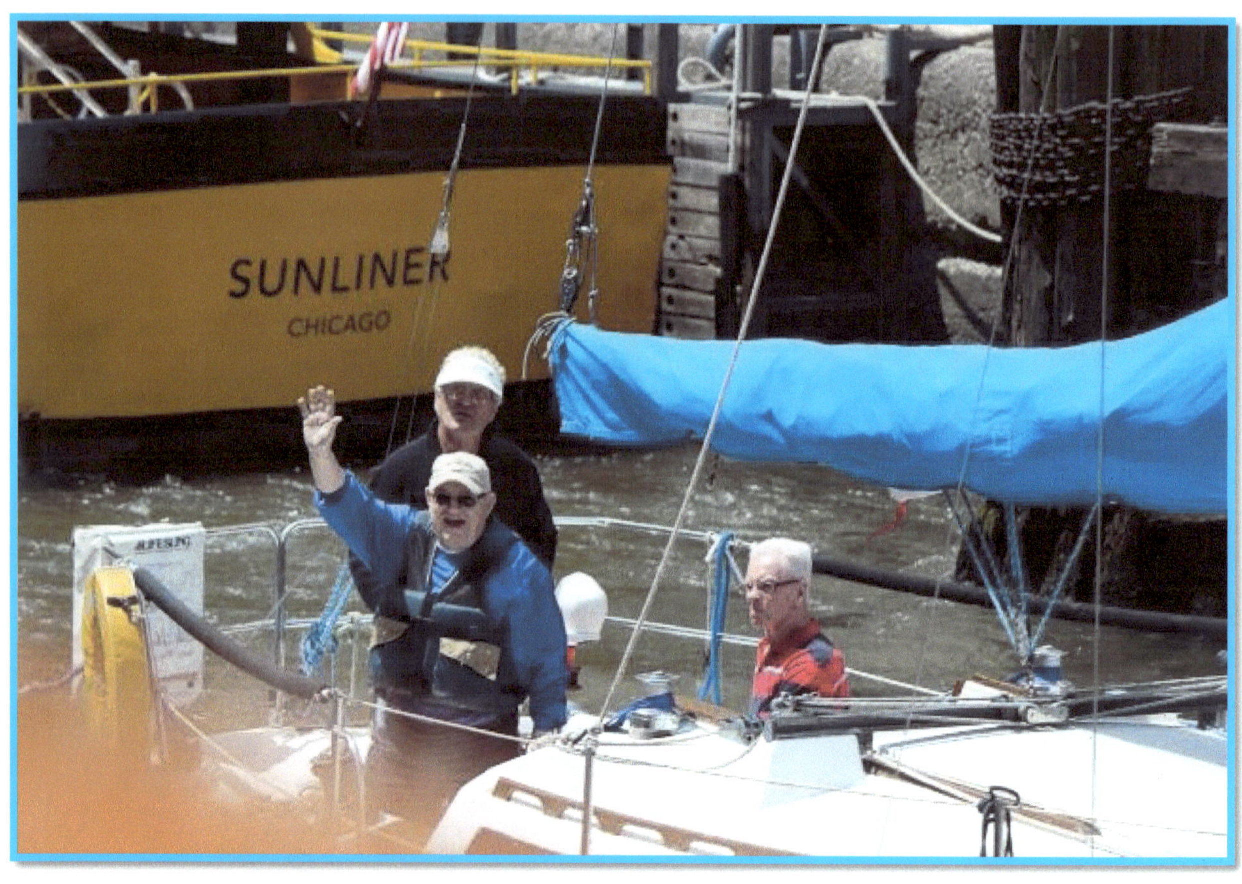

"Chicago, mistress of the lakes,
Controller of our inland trade,
The freest city of our states,
What wondrous strides thy fame has made!"
Charles Frederick White *To Chicago*

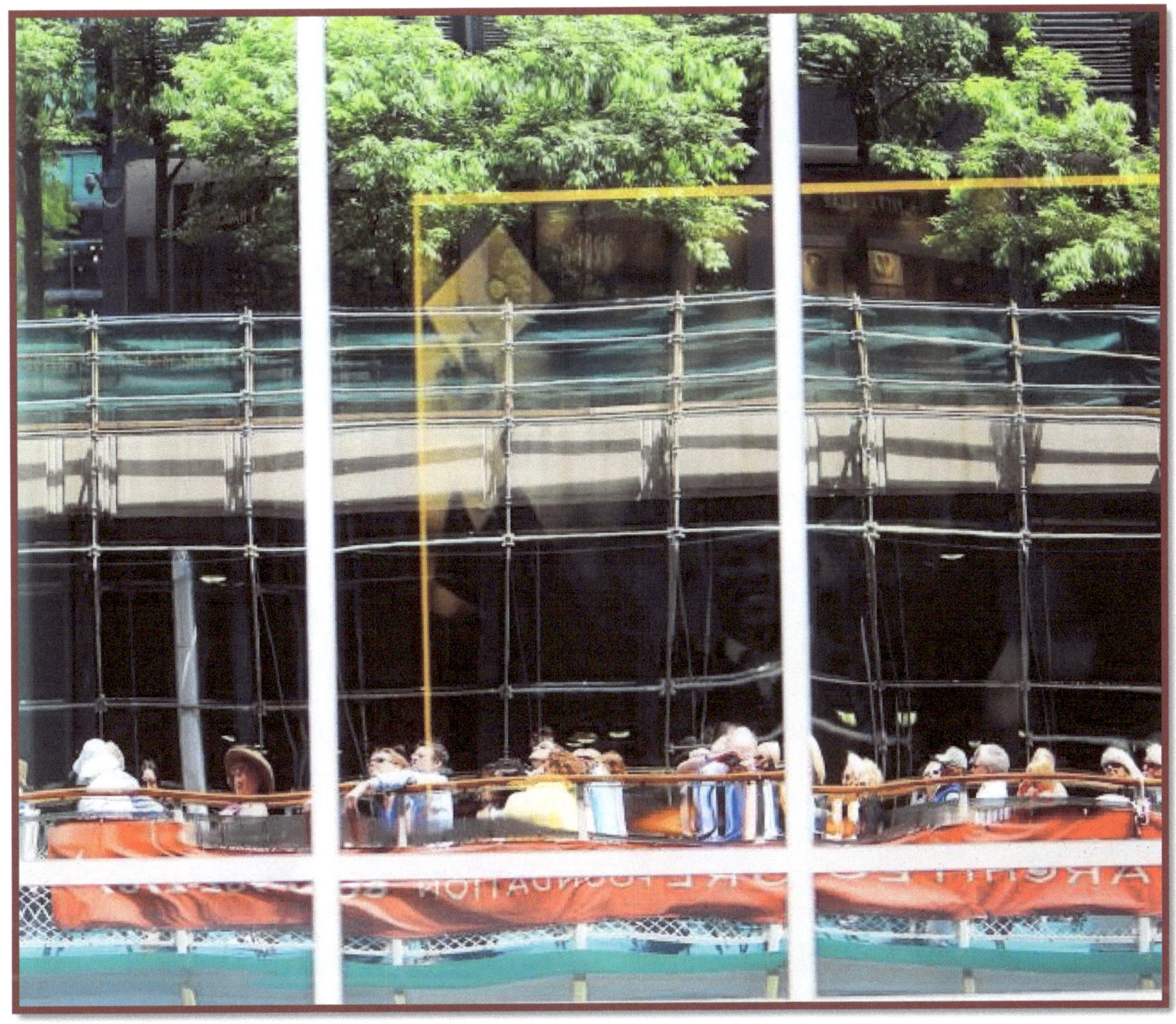

"Buildings, too, are children of Earth and Sun." **Frank Lloyd Wright**

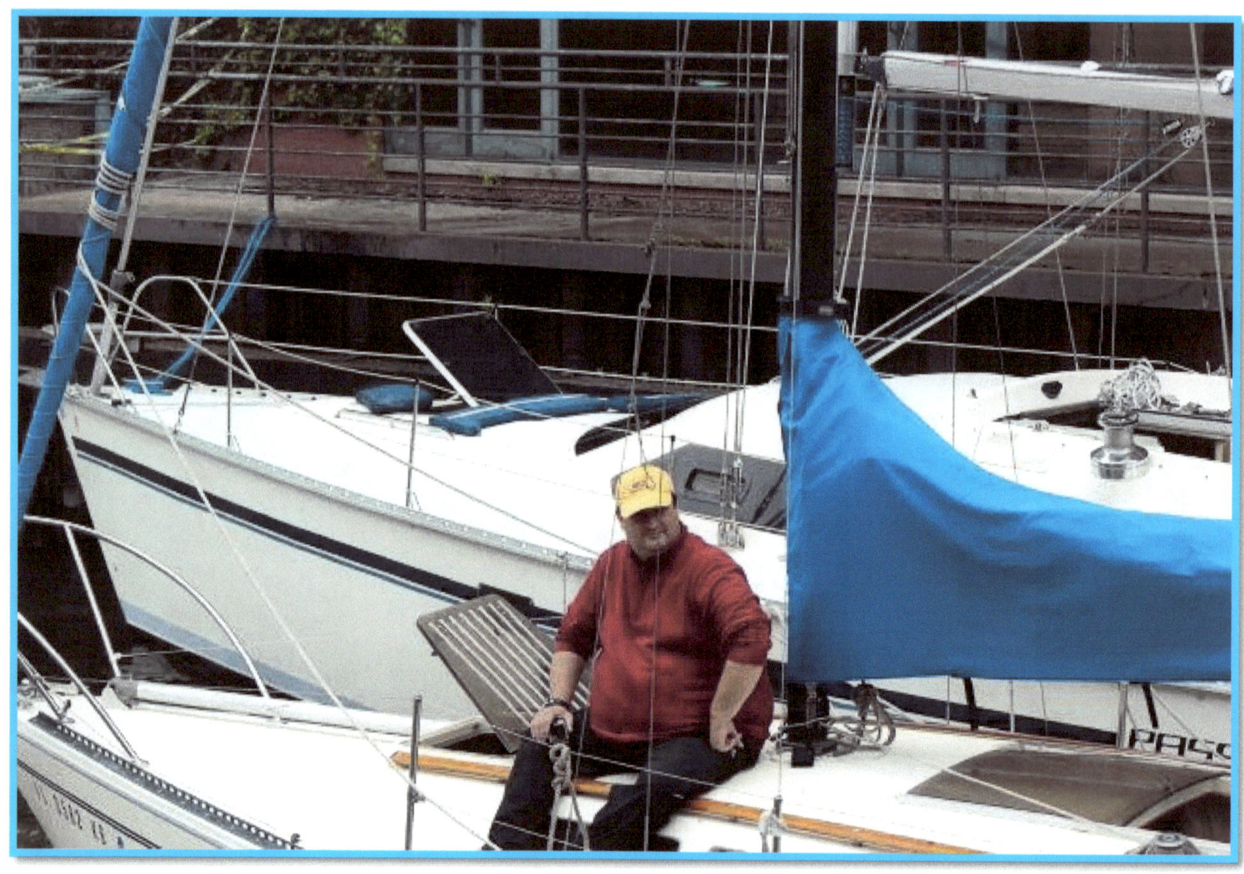

"(Chicago) is the most perfect presentation of individualistic industrialism I have ever seen.."**H. G. Wells**

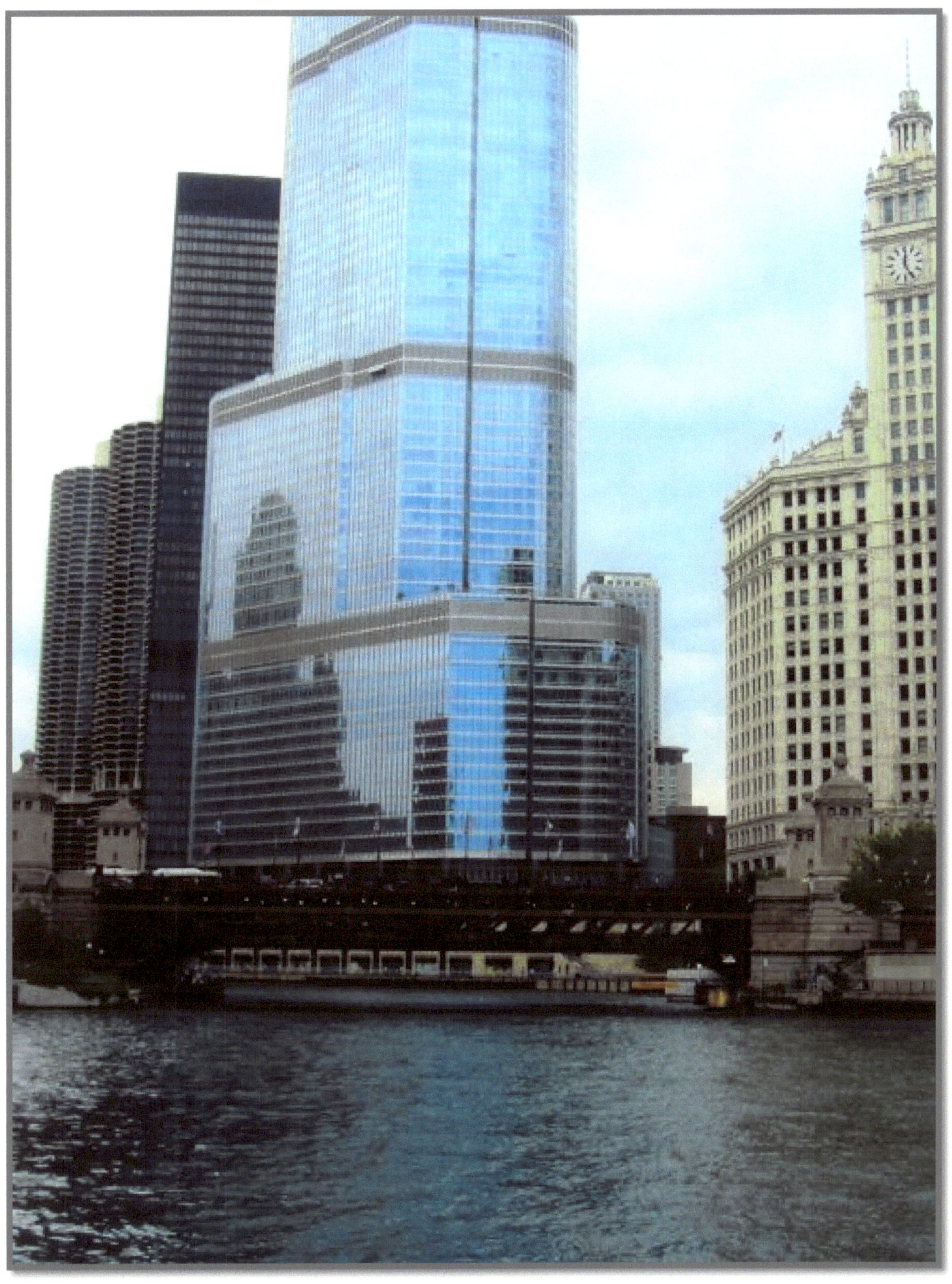

"You feel like an ant contemplating Chicago." **Robert Fulghum**

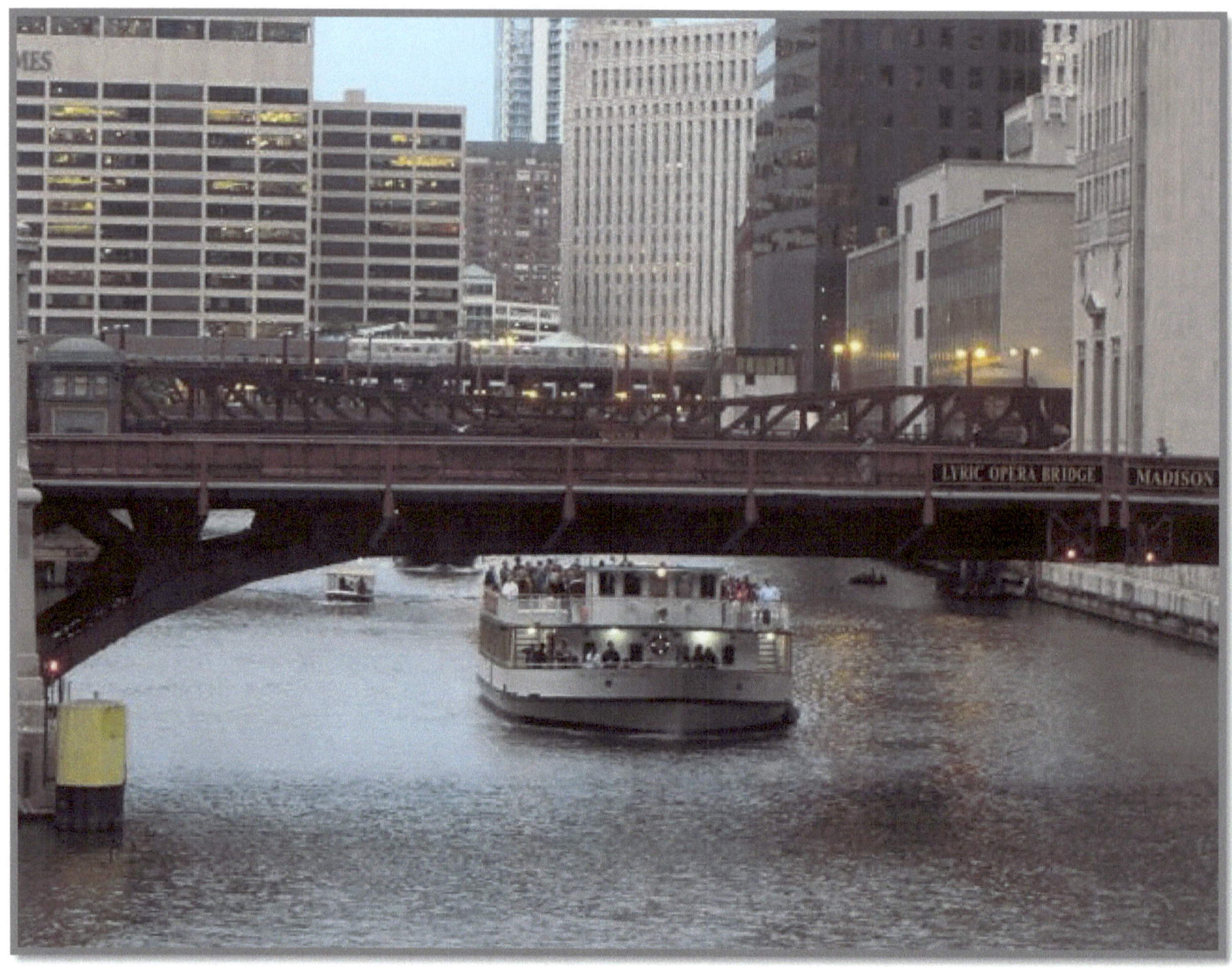

"We're Chicago - we can do anything, damn it." **Elva Rupio, Gensler Chicago**

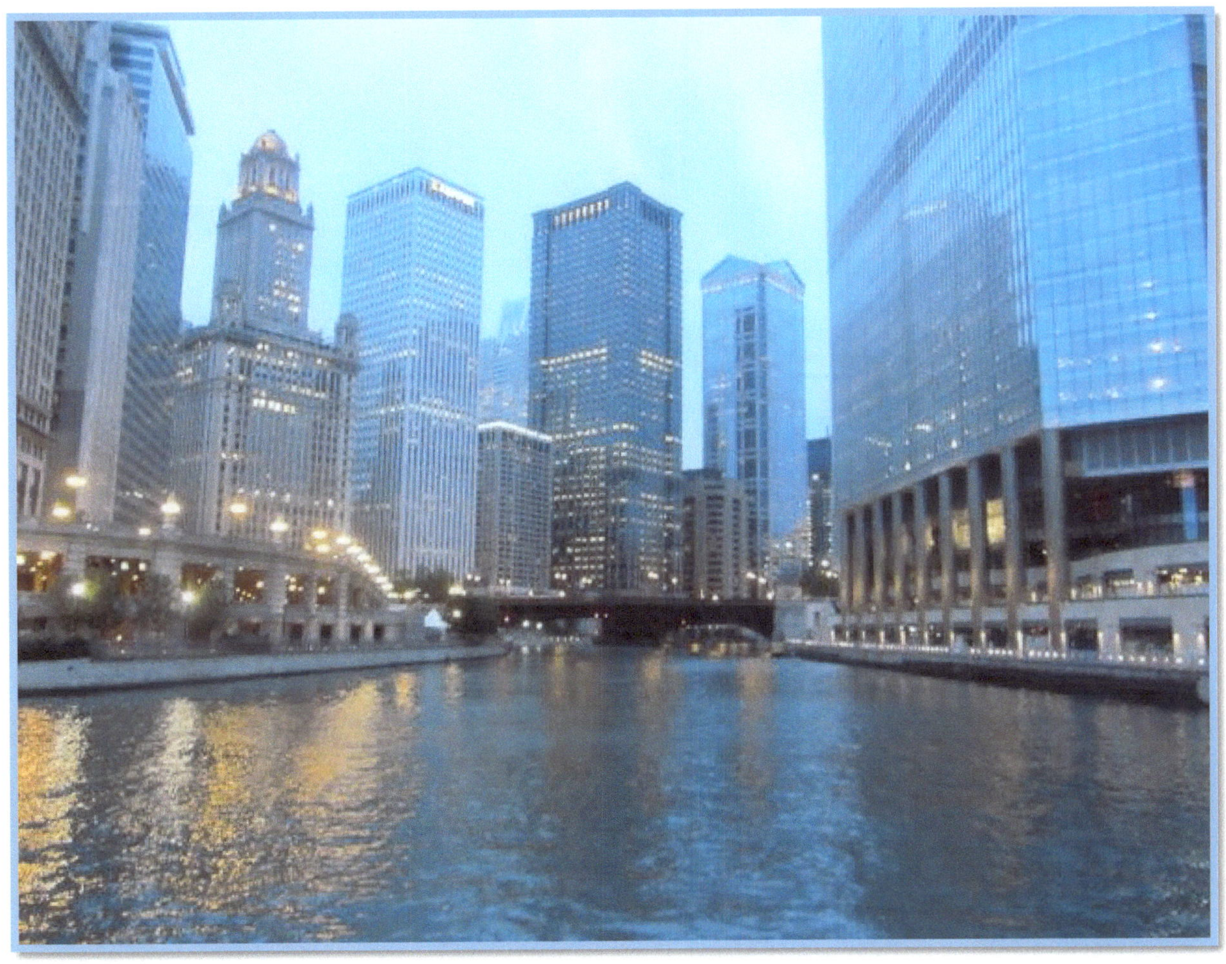

A young watchman leans at a window and sees the lights of barges butting their way across a harbor, nets of red and white lanterns in a railroad yard, and a span of glooms splashed with lines of white and blurs of crosses and clusters over the sleeping city. By night the skyscraper looms in the smoke and the stars and has a soul.

Carl Sandburg Chicago Poems.

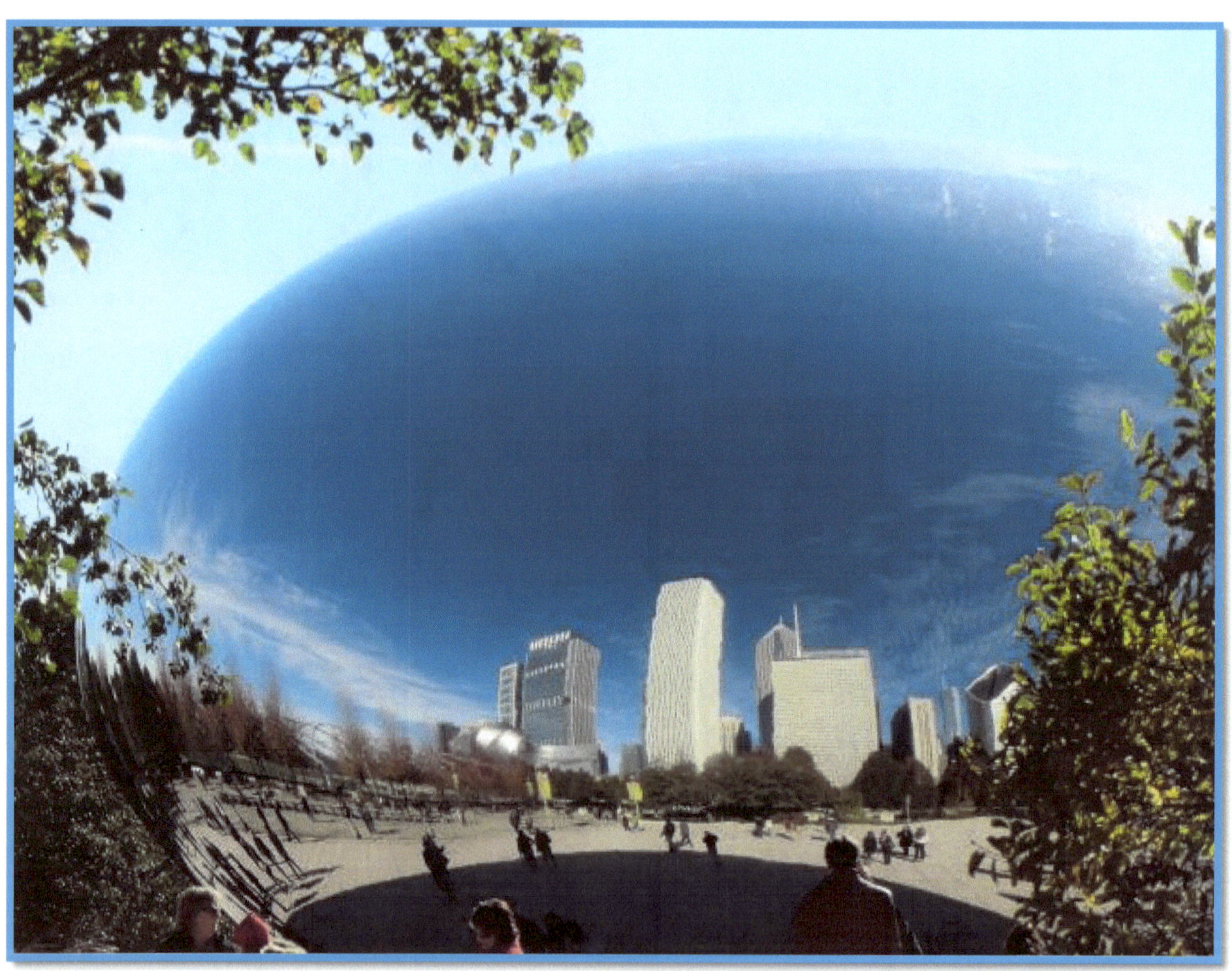

“We require from buildings two kinds of goodness: first, the doing their practical duty well: then that they be graceful and pleasing in doing it.”

John Ruskin

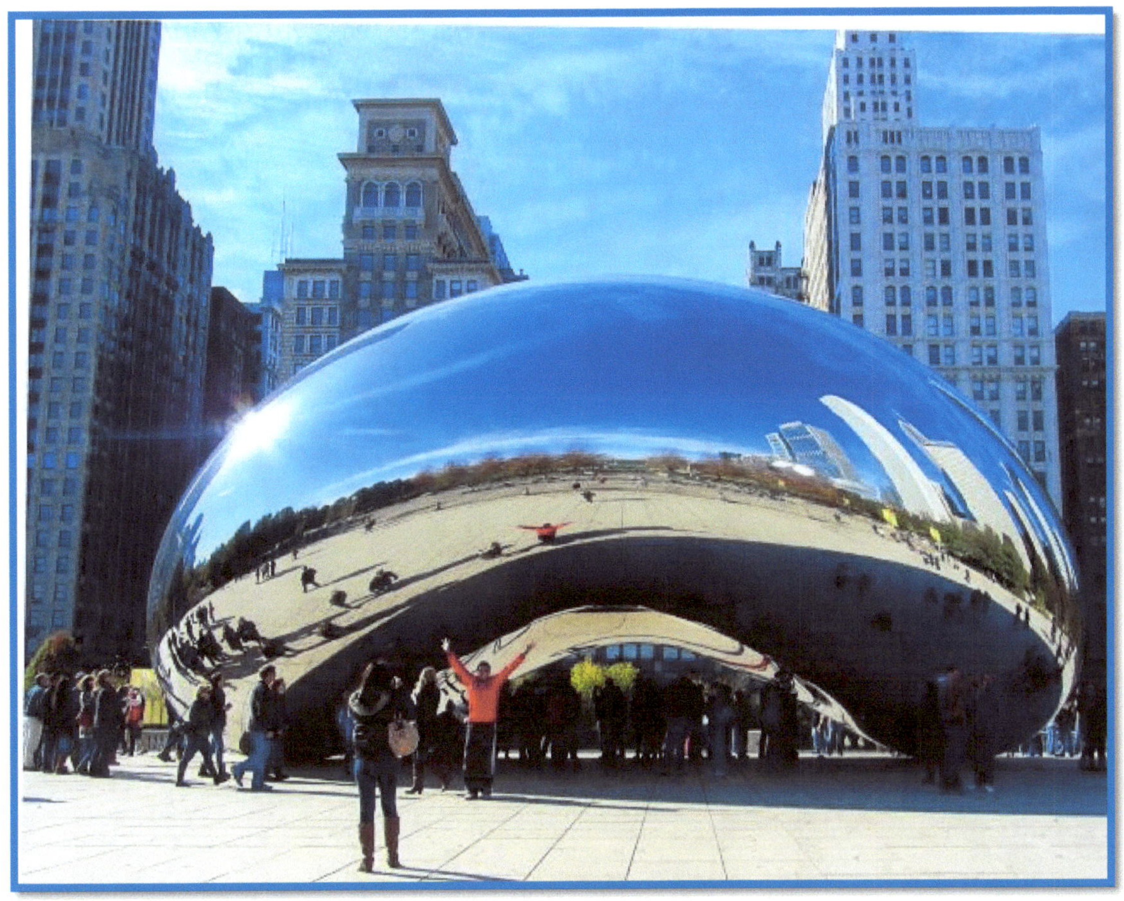

"One thing I carried my whole life, especially from my grandparents in Chicago, was a huge idealism for the world." **Abigail Washburn**

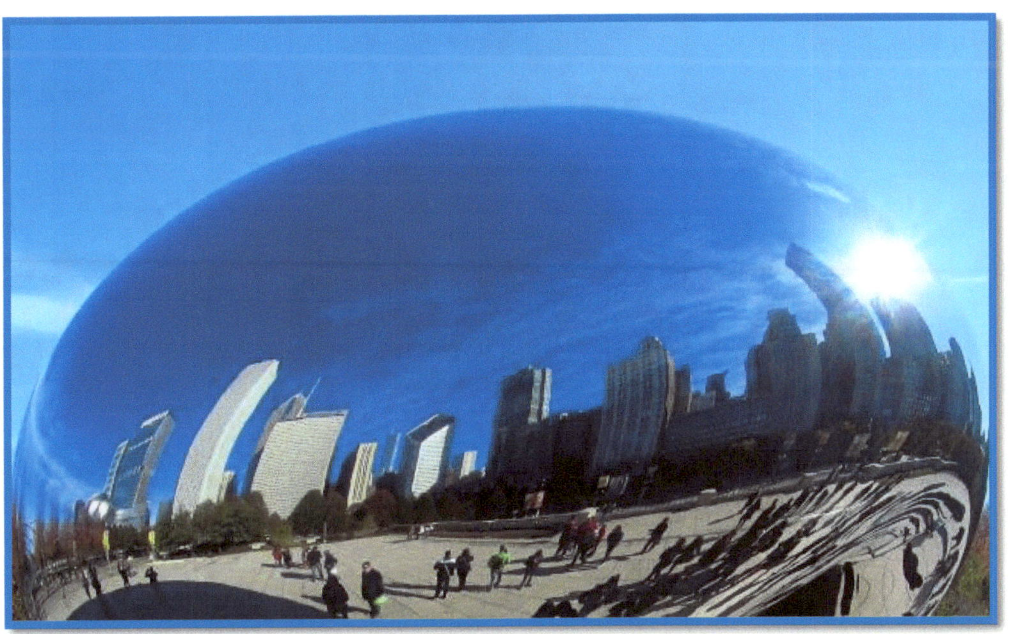

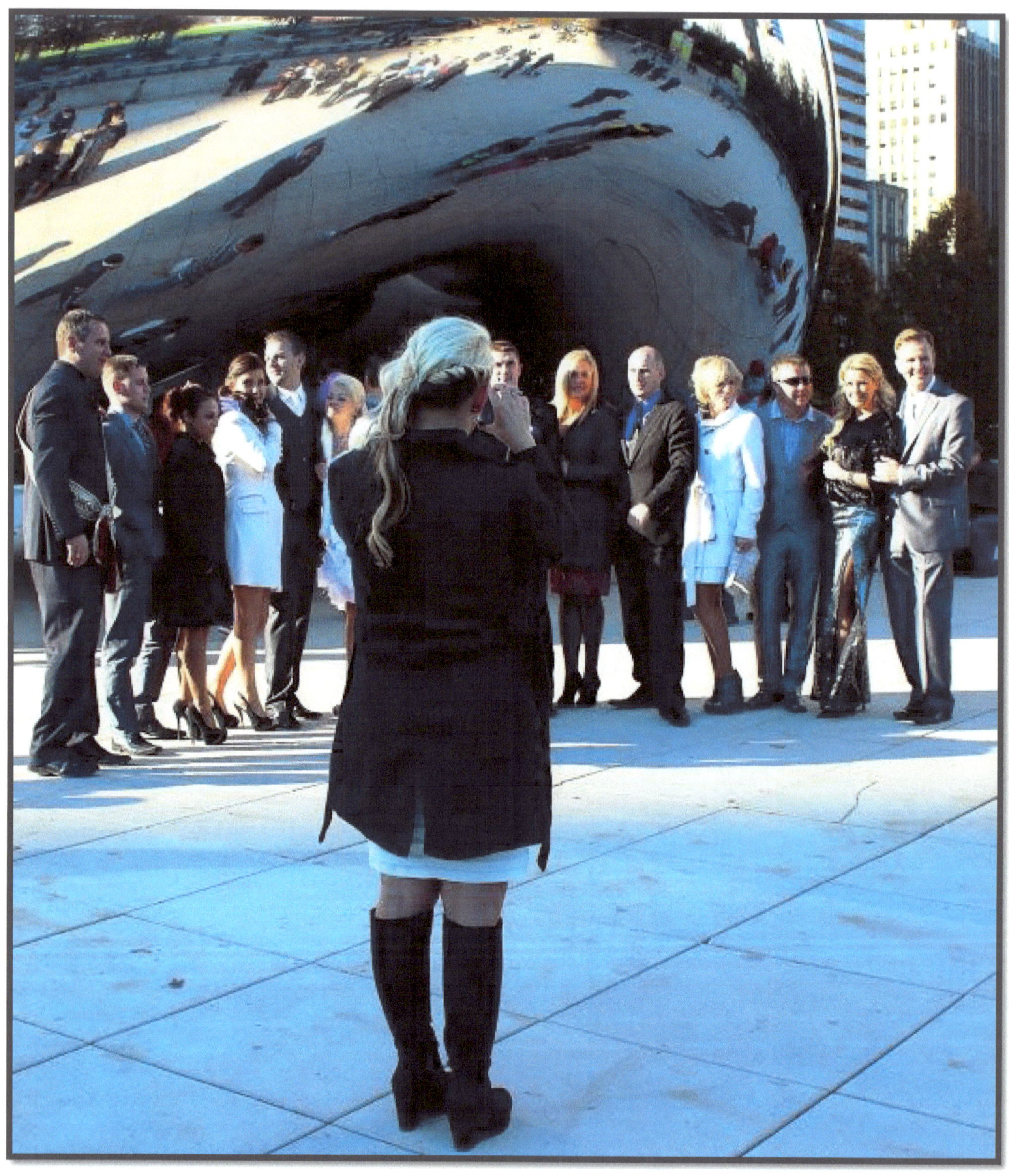

“Love wishes to perpetuate itself. Love wishes for immortality.”
Mortimer Adler , Chicagoan

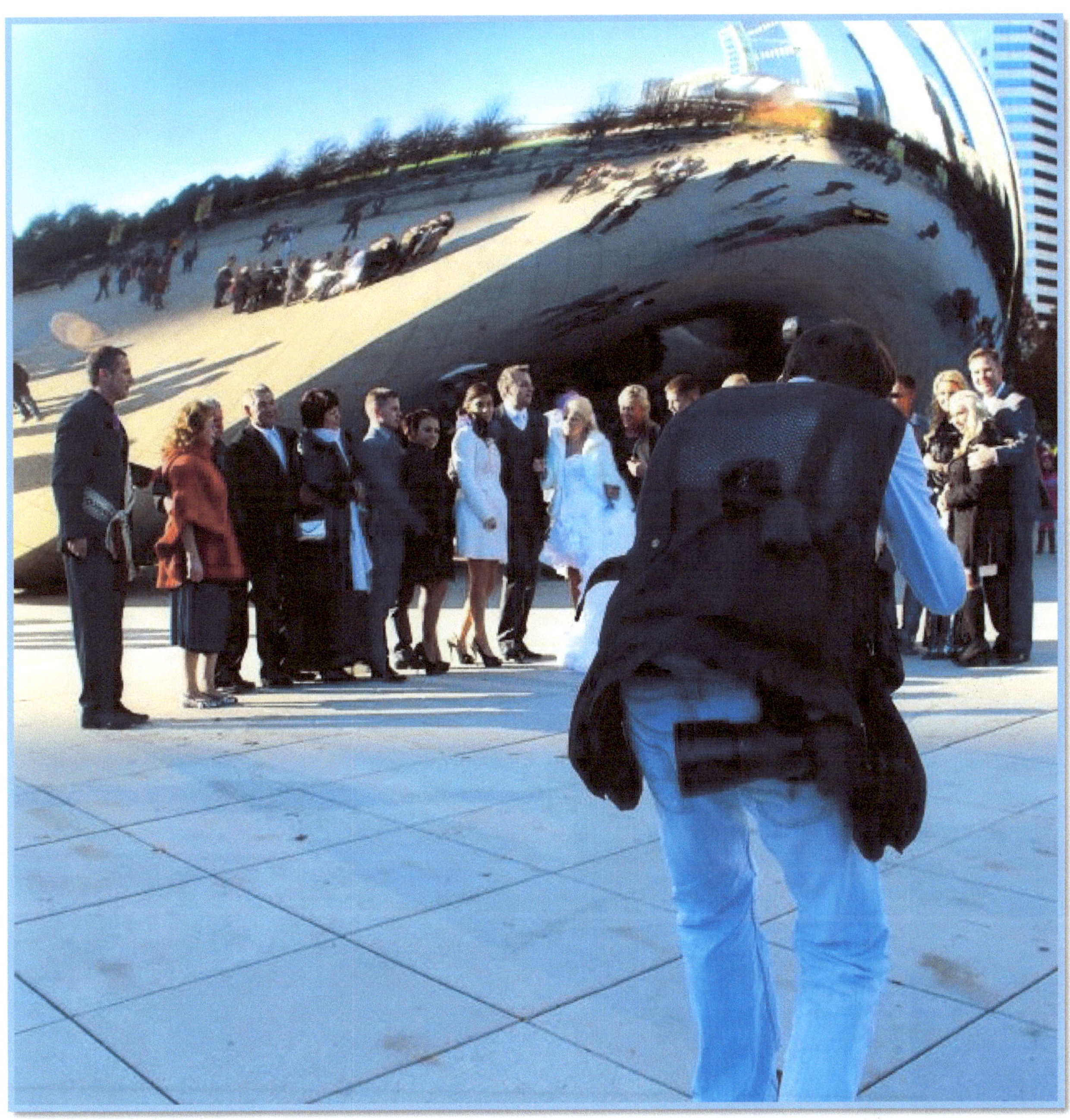

"We all become great explorers during our first few days in a new city, or a new love affair". **Mignon McLaughlin**

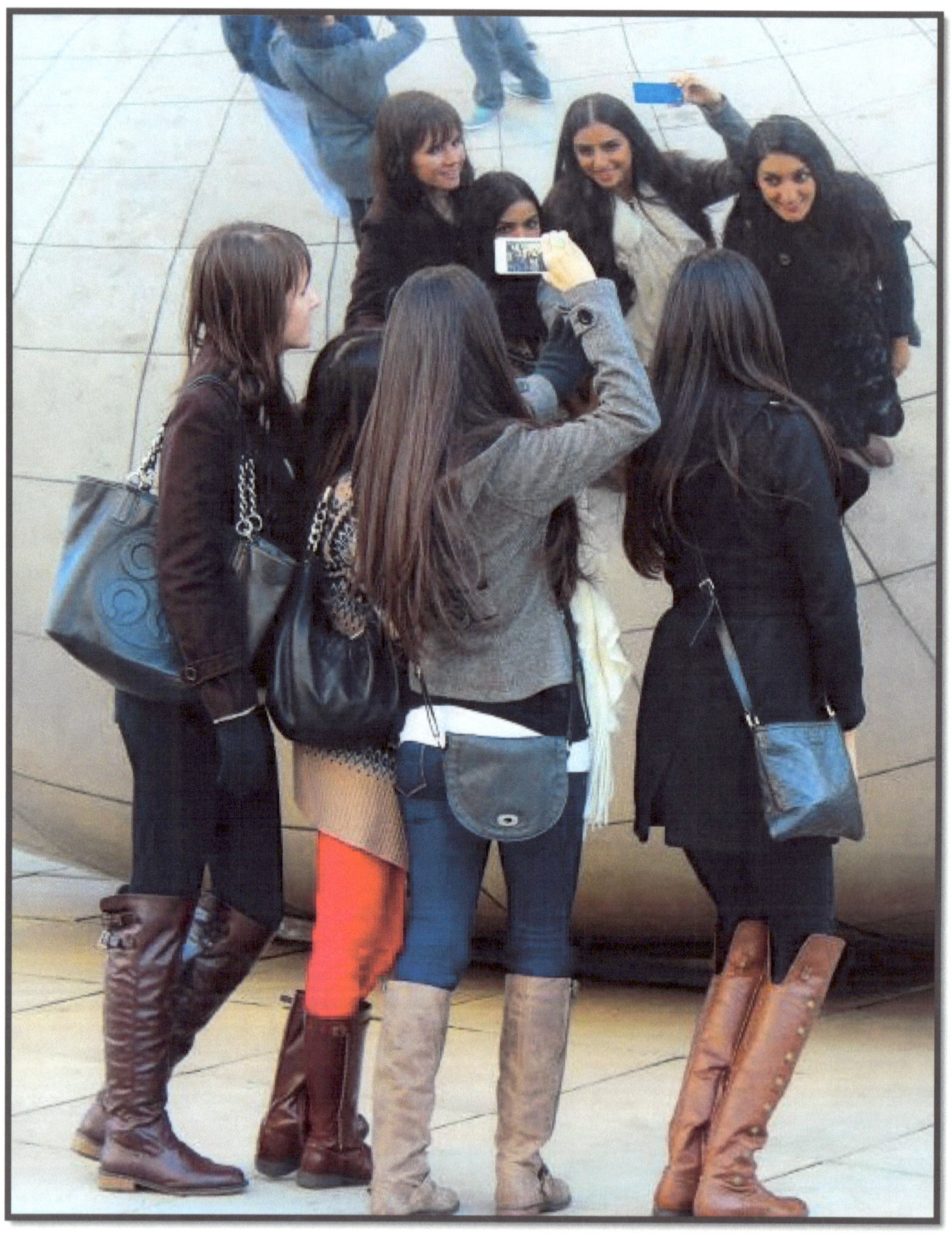

“Cities have the capability of providing something for everybody, only because, and only when, they are created by everybody.” **Jane Jacobs, The Death and Life of Great American Cities**

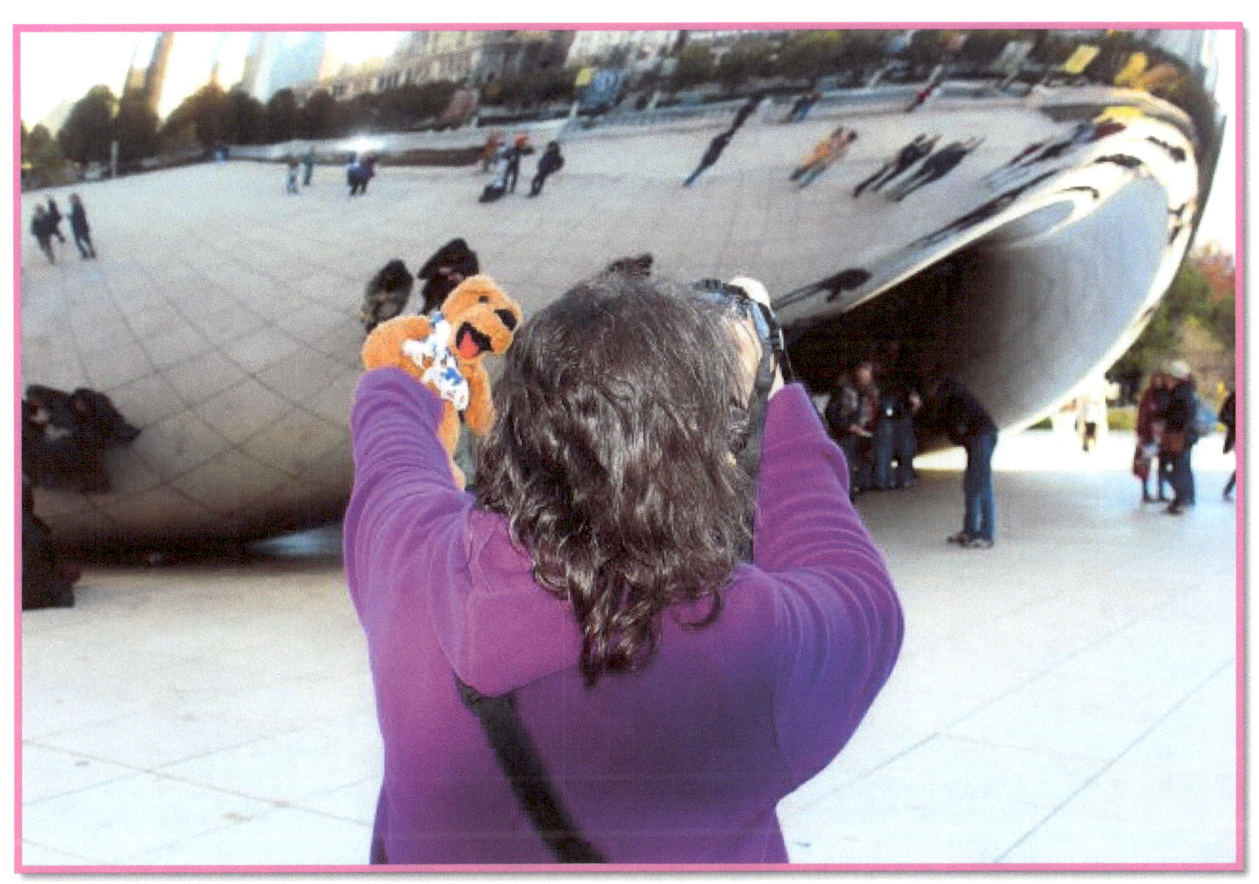

"Architecture is a visual art, and the buildings speak for themselves."

Julia Morgan

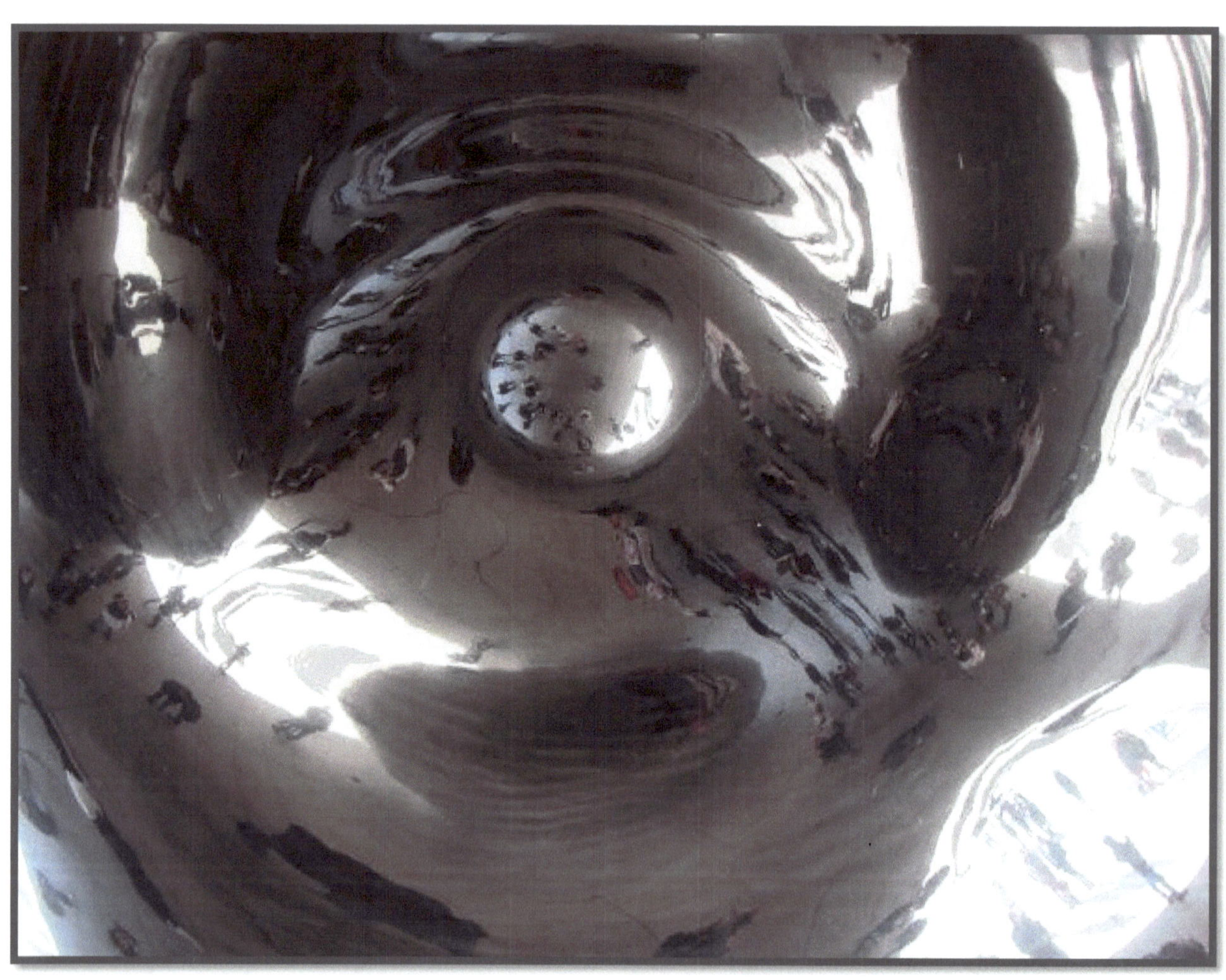

"Architecture is the will of an epoch translated into space."

Ludwig Mies van der Rohe

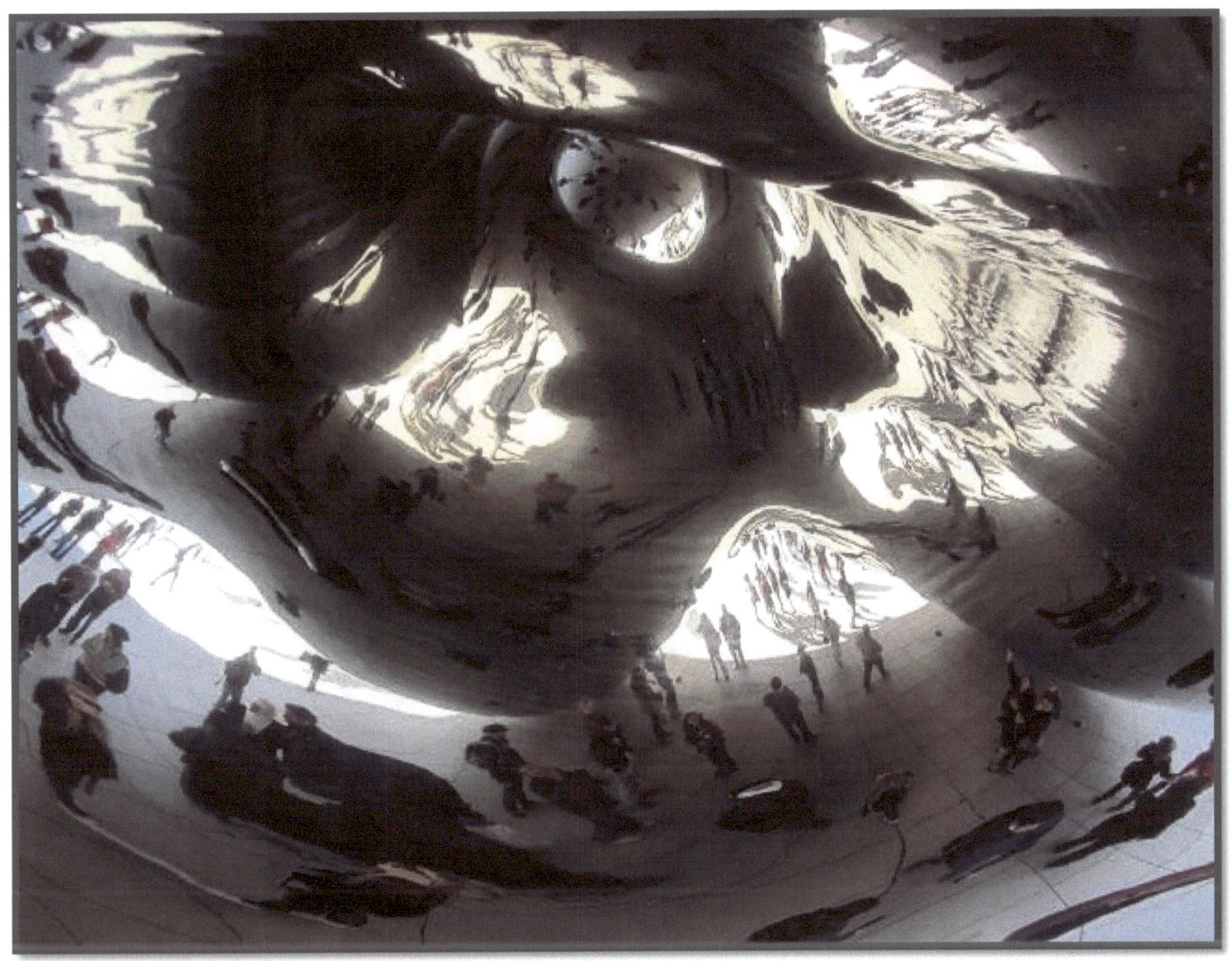

"There is no society ever discovered in the remotest corner of the world that has not had something that we would consider the arts. Visual arts - decoration of surfaces and bodies - appears to be a human universal."

Steven Pinker

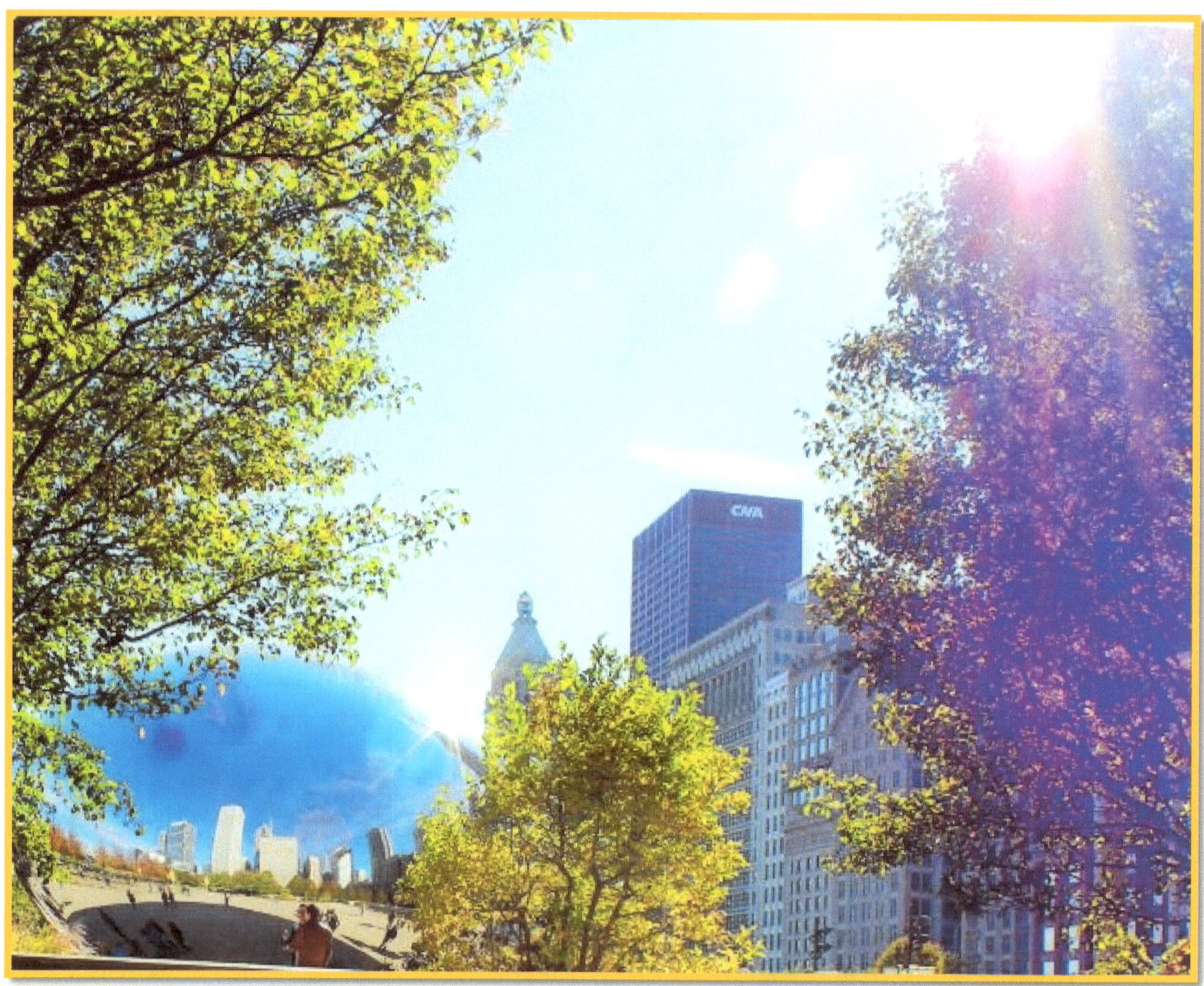

"… with visual arts, you have some really cool, wonderful striking images that make you think and then again you have wonderful striking images that just take you away from the existing world for a second. And I like the latter a bit more." **Ville Valo.**

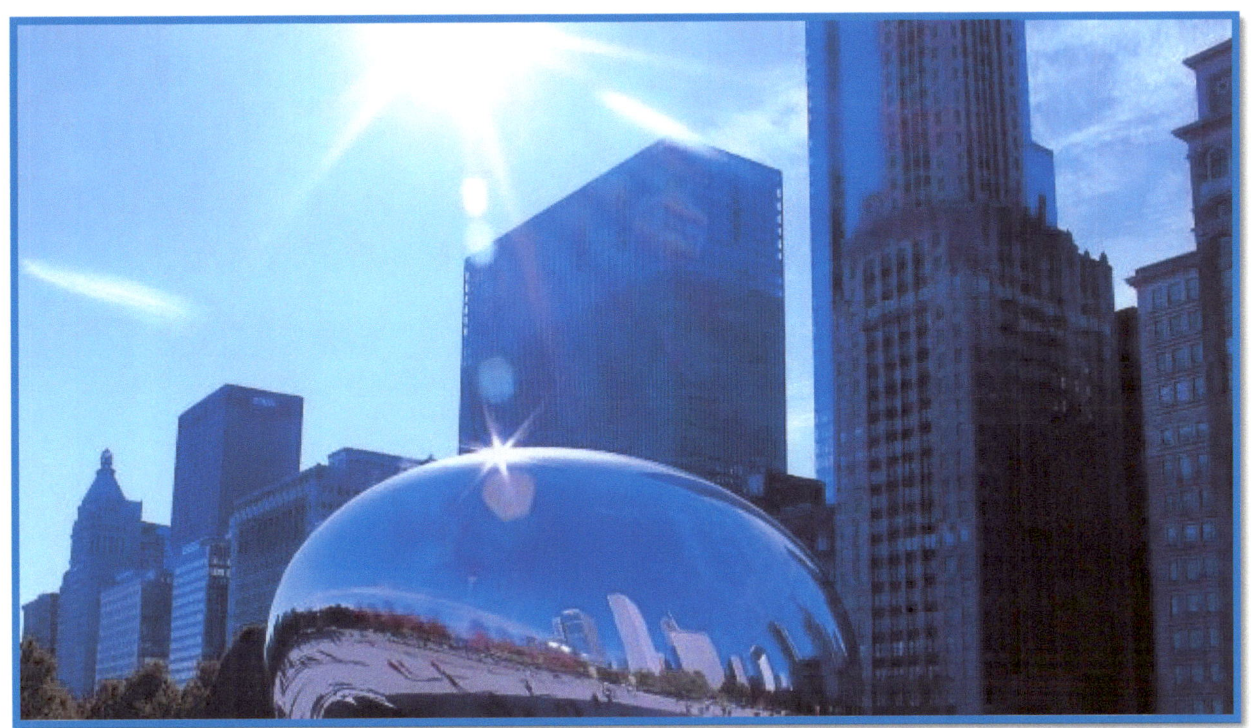

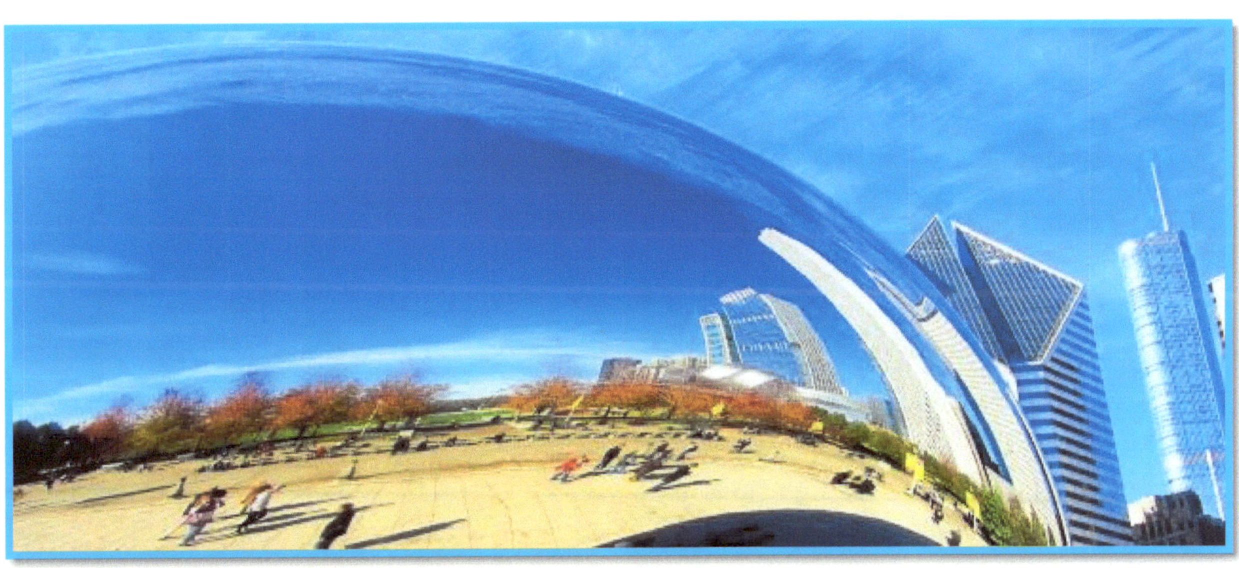

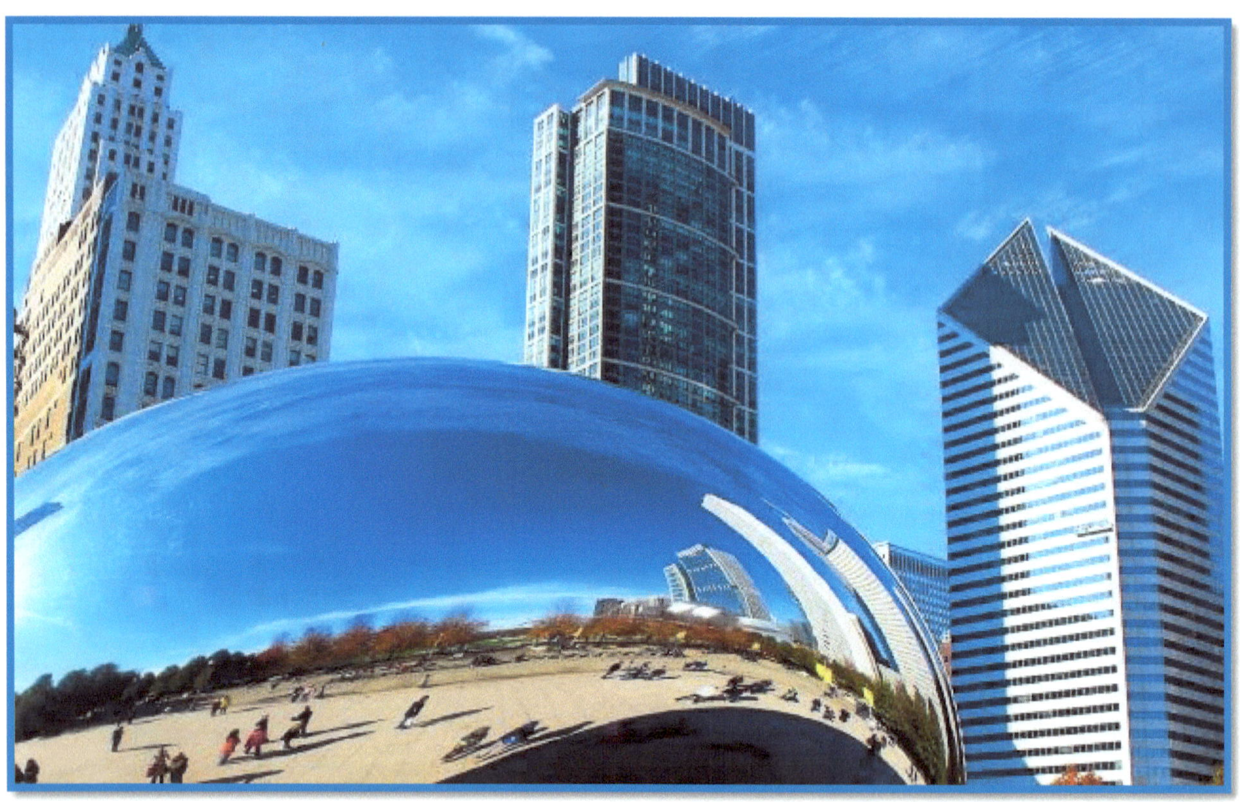

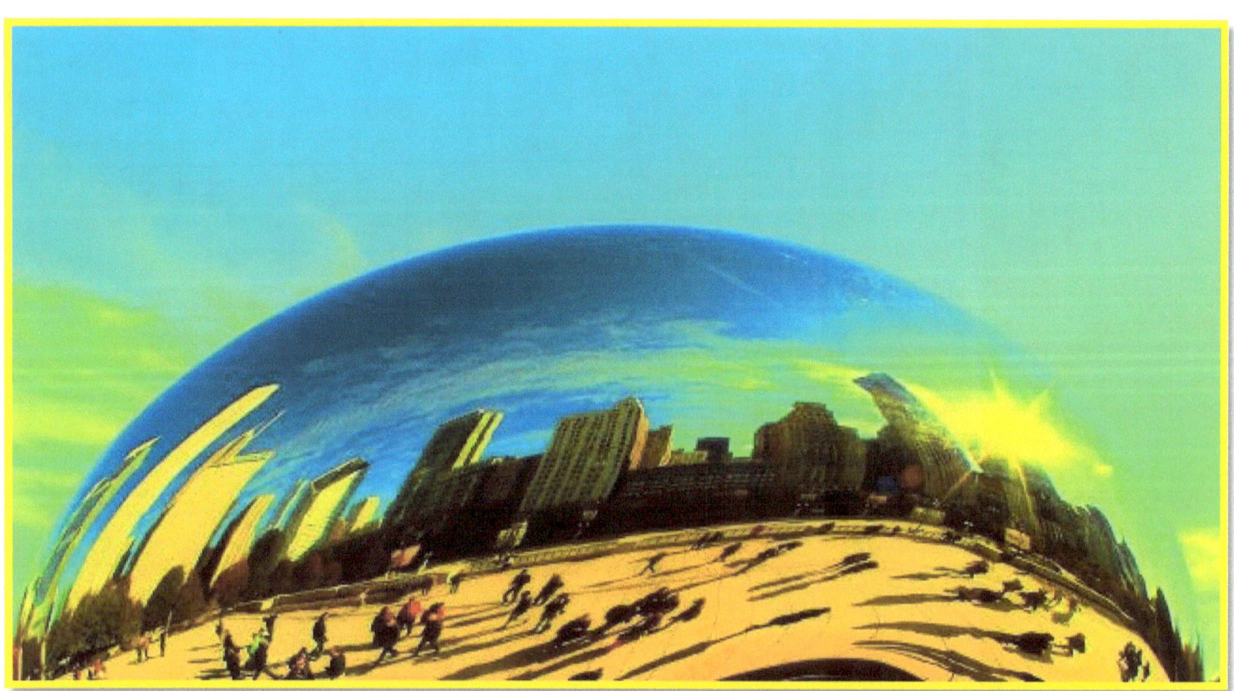

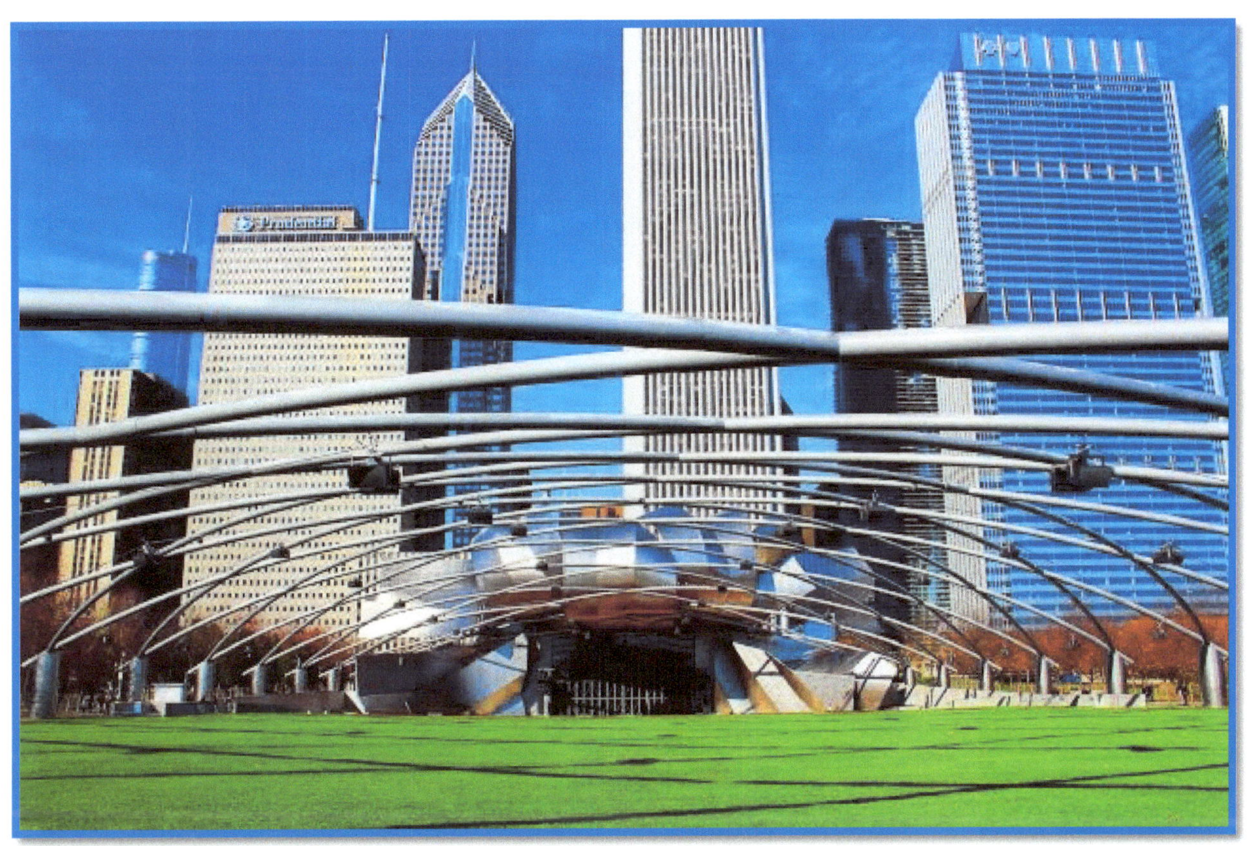

"What is one to think of those fools who tell one that the artist is always subordinate to nature? Art is in harmony parallel with nature."

Paul Cezanne

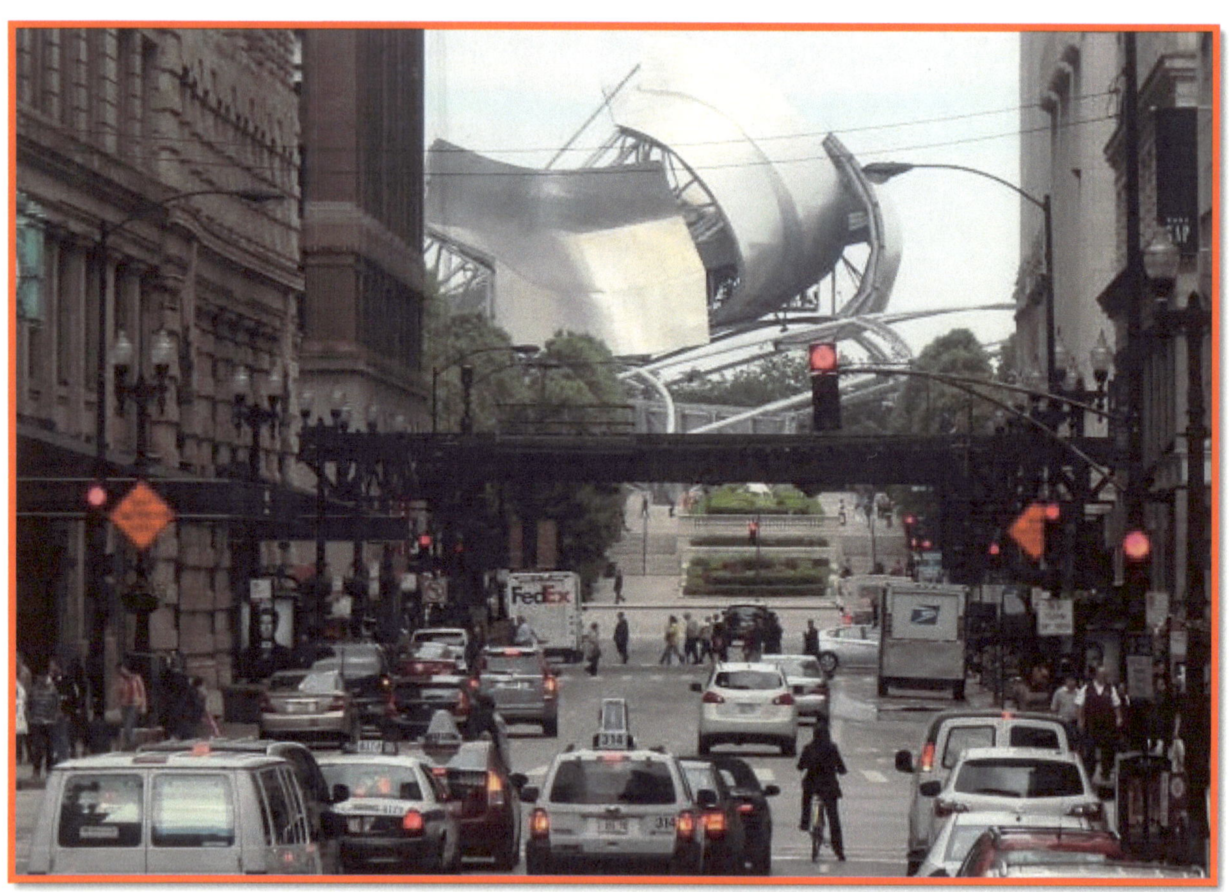

"The object of art is not to reproduce reality, but to create a reality of the same intensity."**Alberto Giacometti**

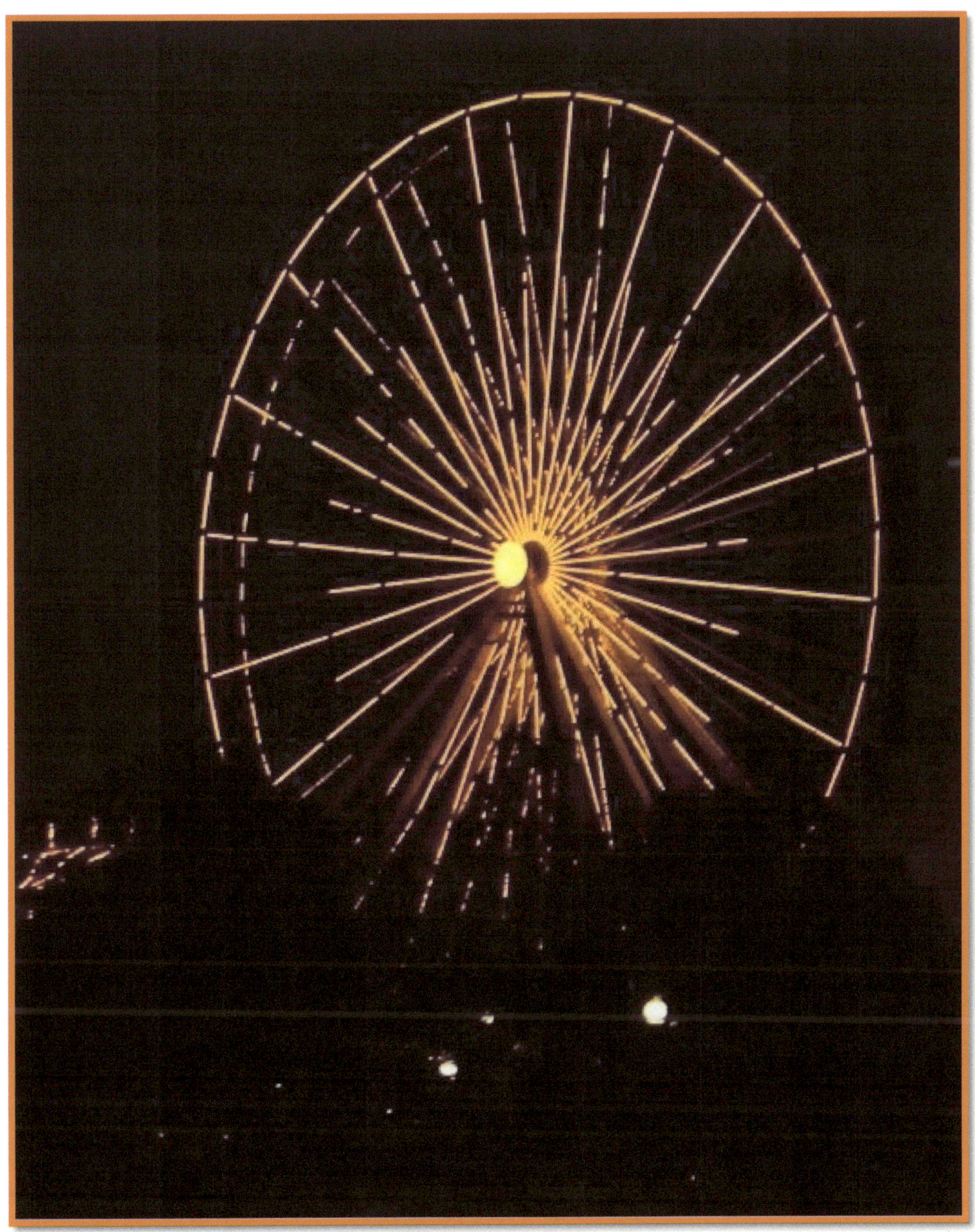

"...a city that was to live by night after the wilderness had passed. A city that was to forge out of steel and blood-red neon its own peculiar wilderness." — **Nelson Algren, *Chicago: City on the Make***

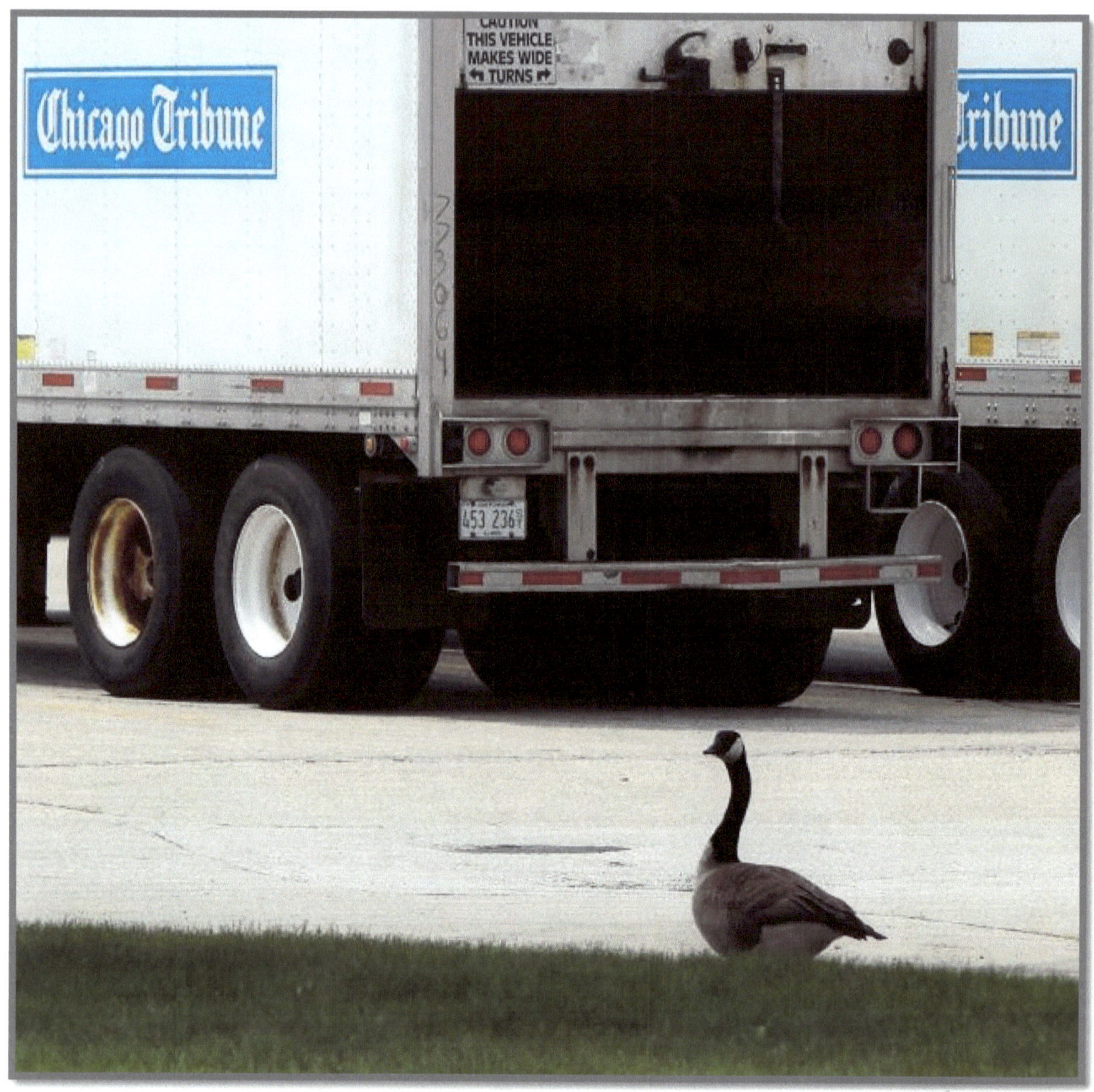

"Chicago is a city of contradictions, of private visions haphazardly overlaid and linked together. If the city was unhappy with itself yesterday-and invariably it was-it will reinvent itself today." **Pat Colander *A Metropolis of No Little Plans***

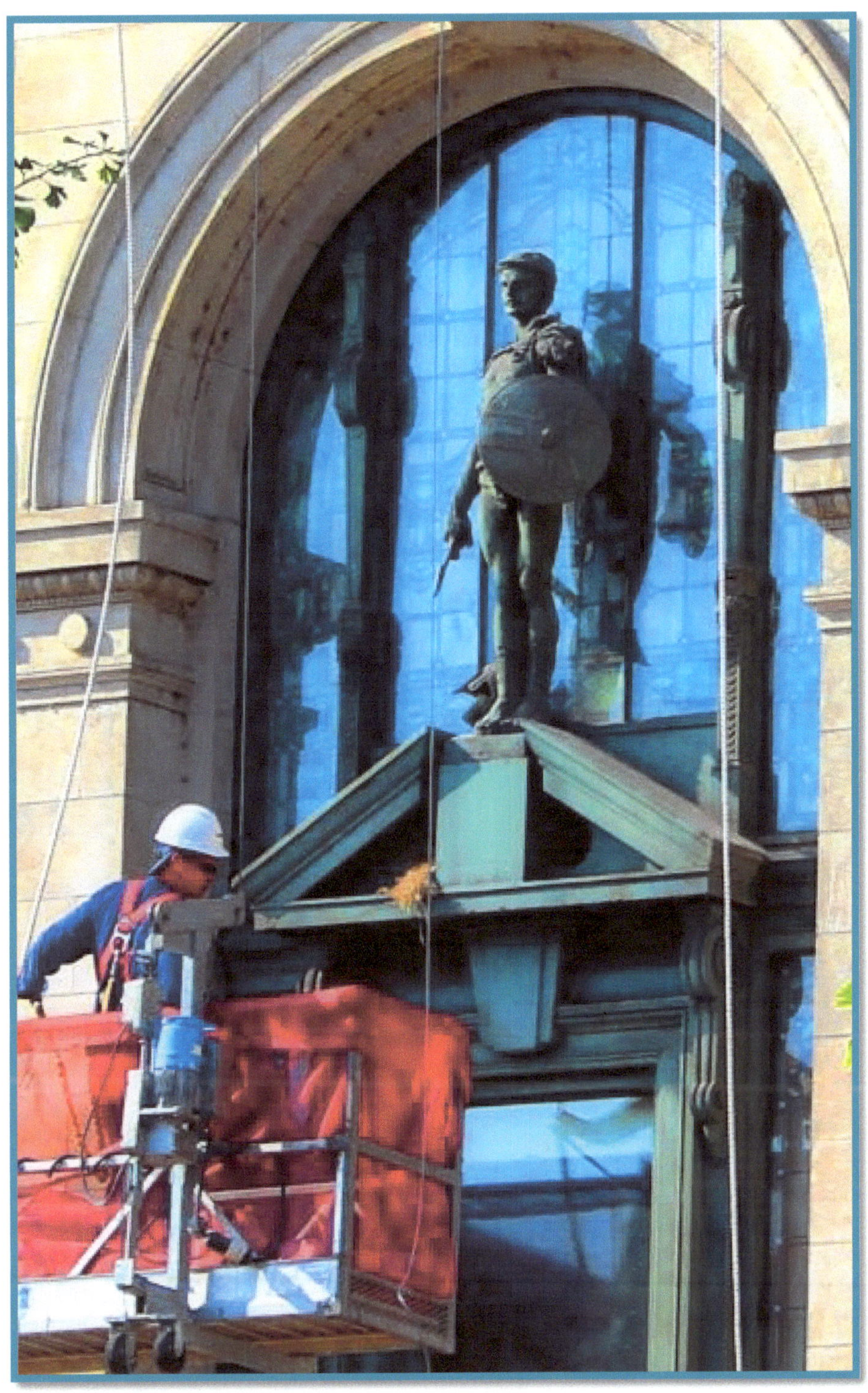

JACK was a swarthy, swaggering son-of-a-gun.
He worked thirty years on the railroad, ten hours a day, and his hands were tougher than sole leather.

Carl Sandburg,Chicago Poems

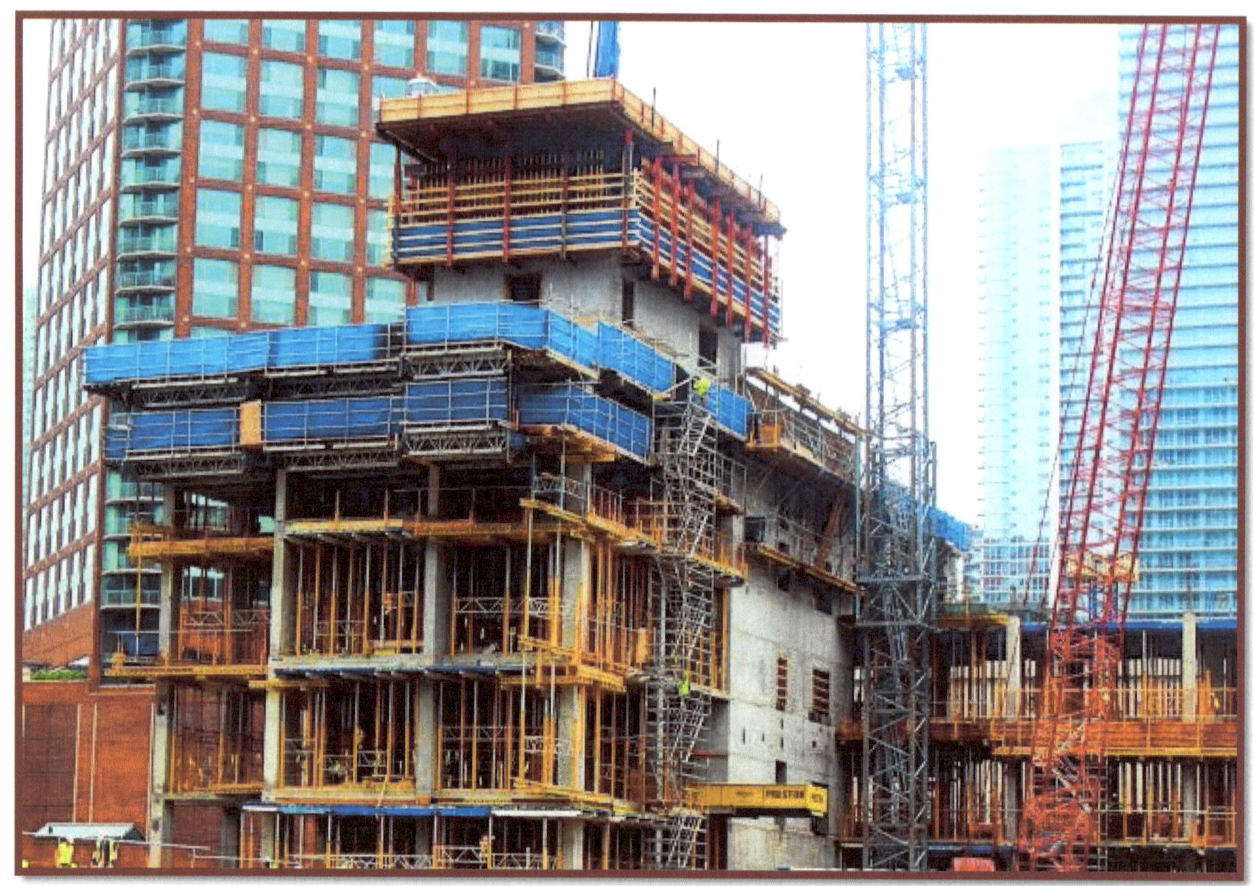

"The American city should be a collection of communities where every member has a right to belong. It should be a place where every man feels safe on his streets and in the house of his friends. It should be a place where each individual's dignity and self-respect is strengthened by the respect and affection of his neighbors. It should be a place where each of us can find the satisfaction and warmth which comes from being a member of the community of man. This is what man sought at the dawn of civilization. It is what we seek today". **President Lyndon B. Johnson, speech to Congress, Mar. 2, 1965**

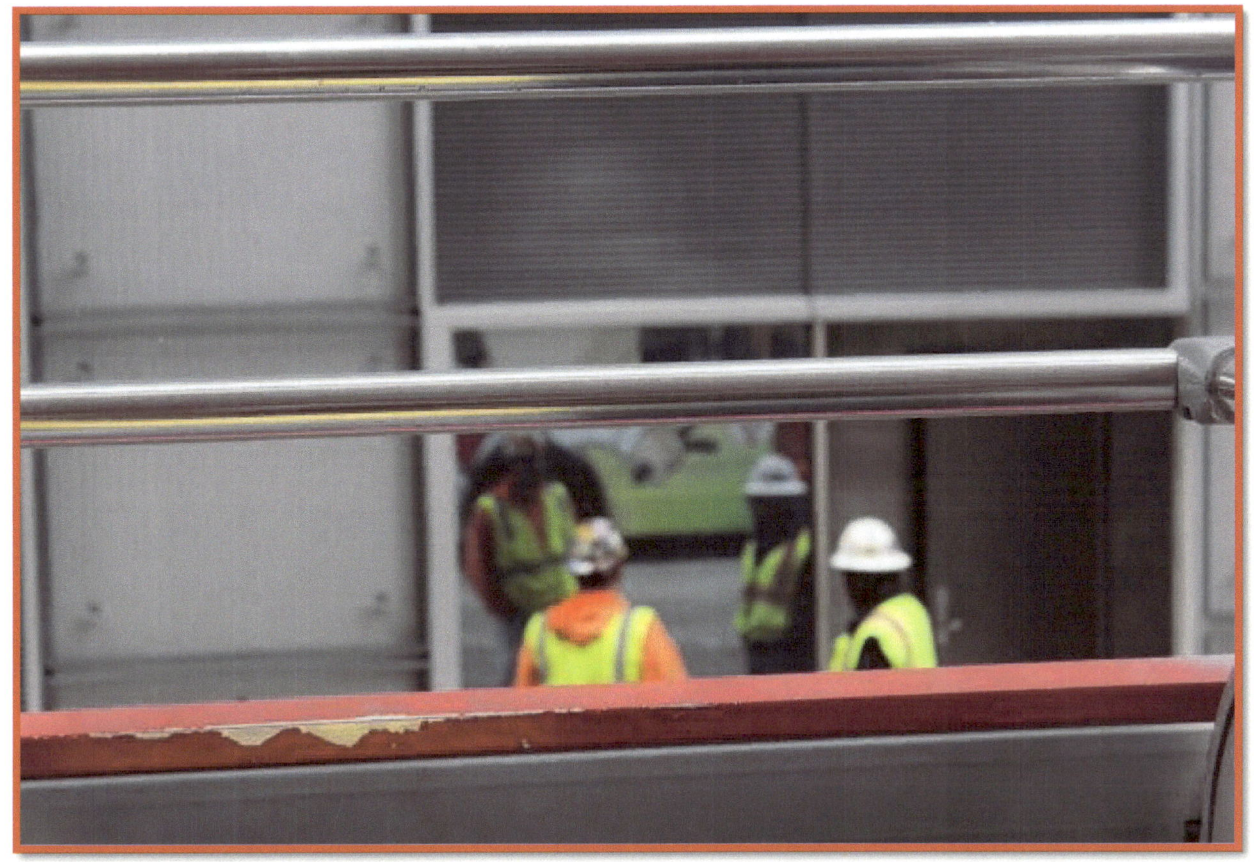

“I come from a pretty working-class neighborhood in Chicago. Hard work was just expected of you. It wasn't some noble thing you did; it was a prerequisite. It's what a man did. You get up, you put on your boots, and you work hard.” **John C. Reilly**

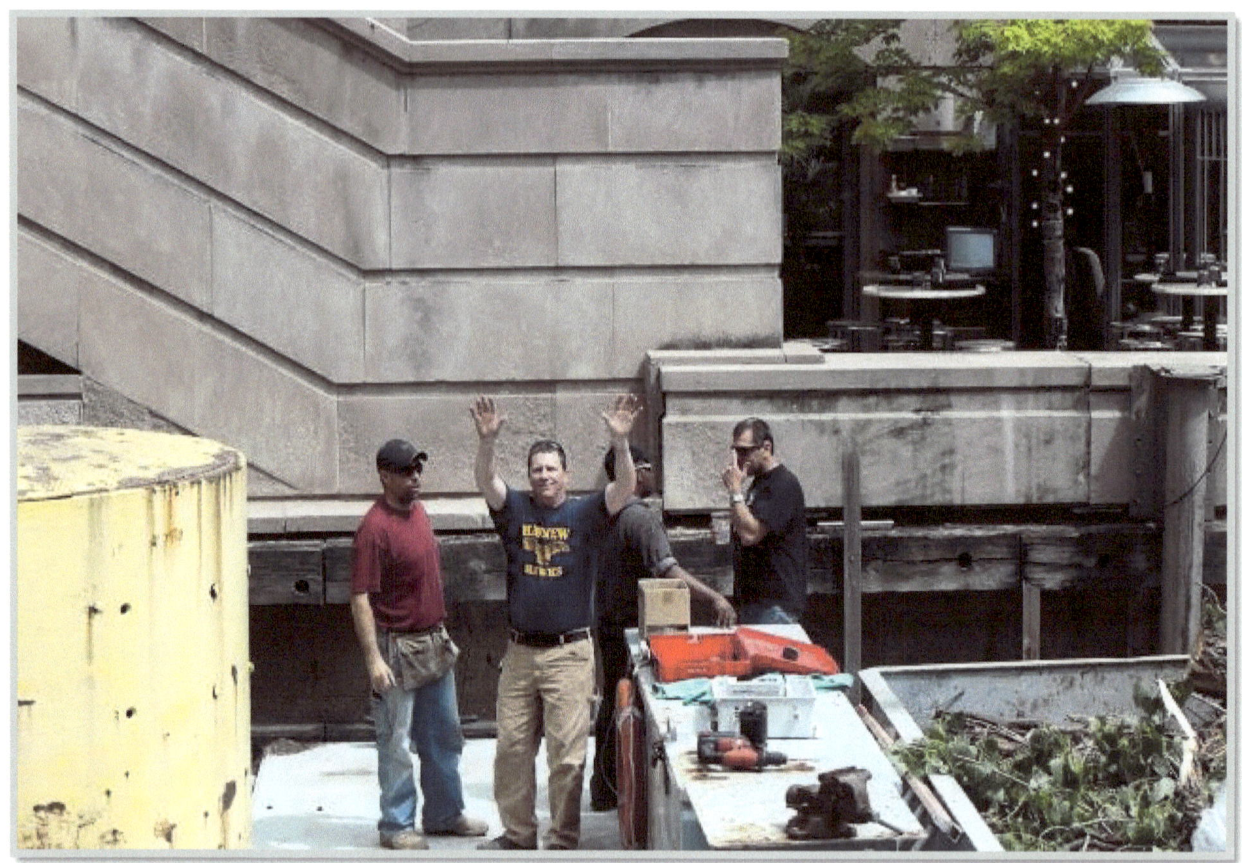

Well, that's what I heard. Cool people don't live there (in New York) anymore, They all live here. In Chicago." **Joe Meno, Office Girl**

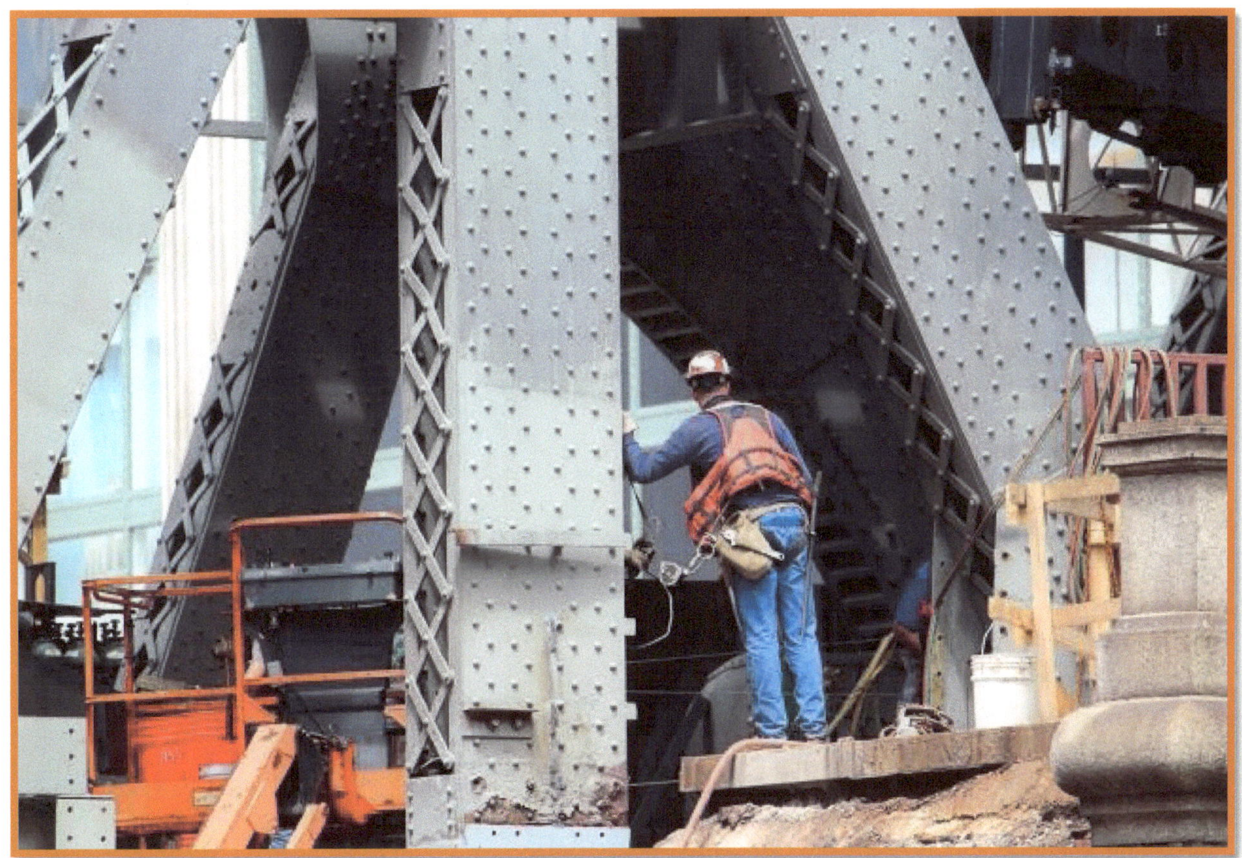

Men who sunk the pilings and mixed the mortar are laid in graves where the wind whistles a wild song without words.
And so are men who strung the wires and fixed the pipes and tubes and those who saw it rise floor by floor.
Souls of them all are here, even the hod carrier begging at back doors hundreds of miles away and the bricklayer who went to state's prison for shooting another man while drunk.

Carl Sandburg Chicago

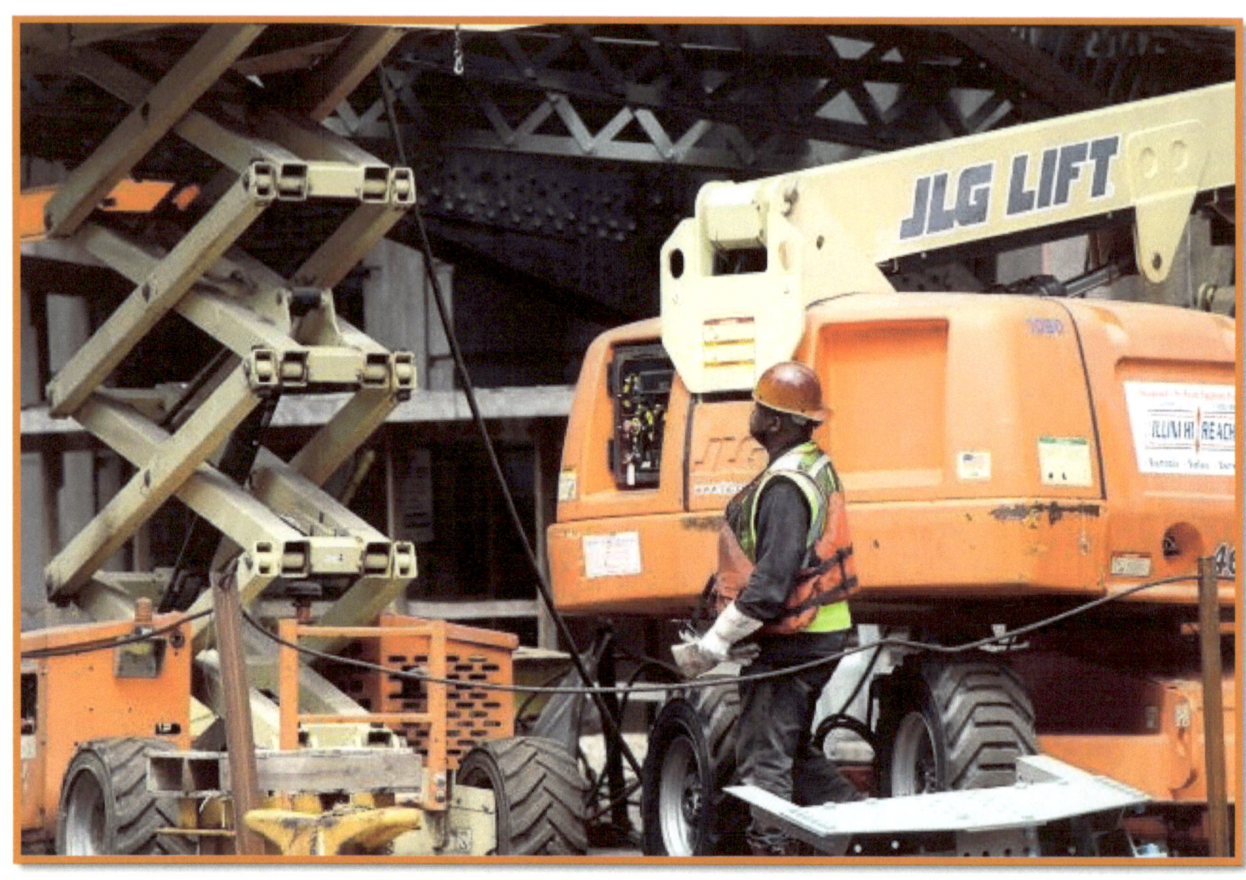

Stormy, husky, brawling,
City of big shoulders."
Carl Sandburg, "Chicago,"

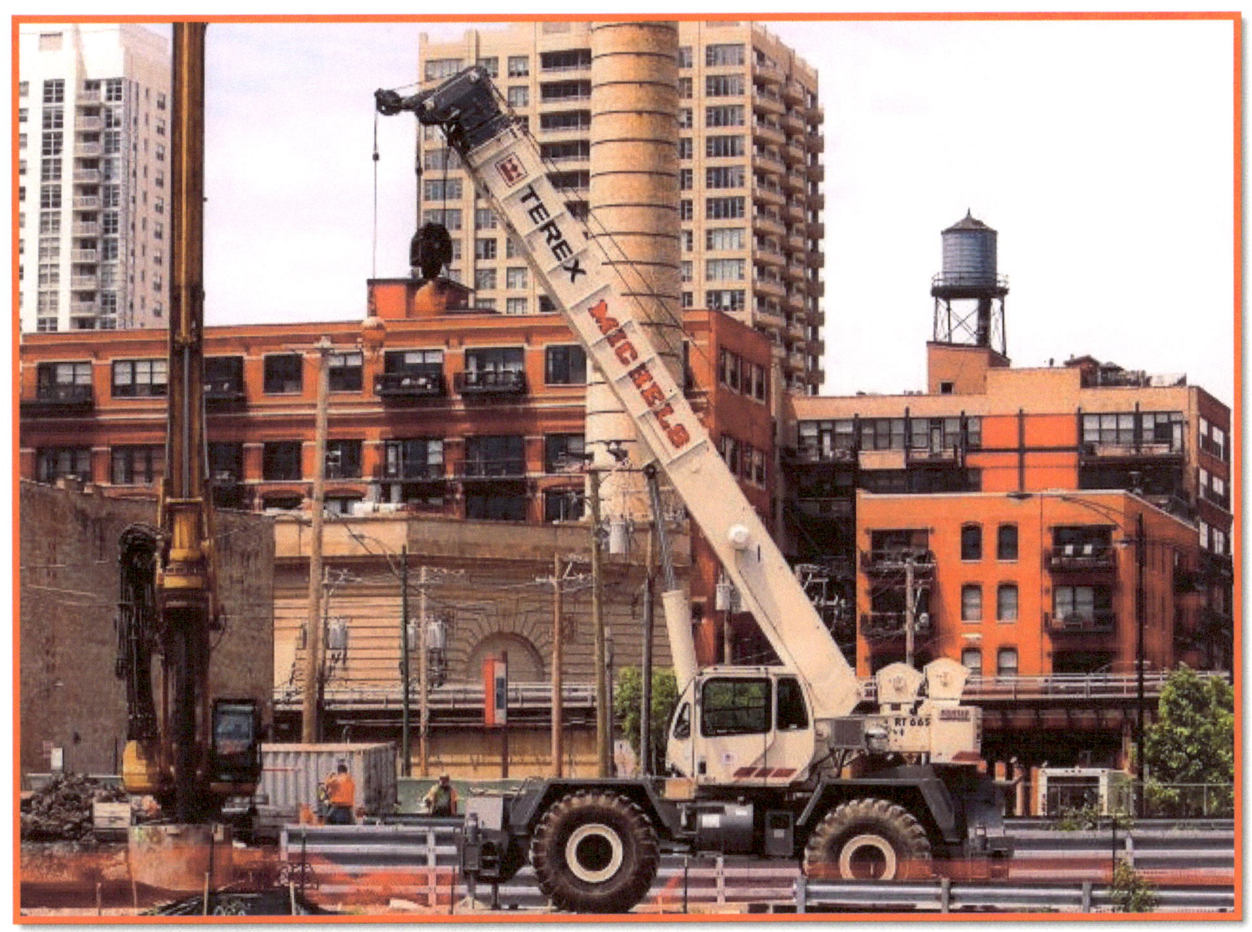

"Work is about a search for daily meaning as well as daily bread, for recognition as well as cash, for astonishment rather than torpor; in short, for a sort of life rather than a Monday through Friday sort of dying."
Studs Terkel

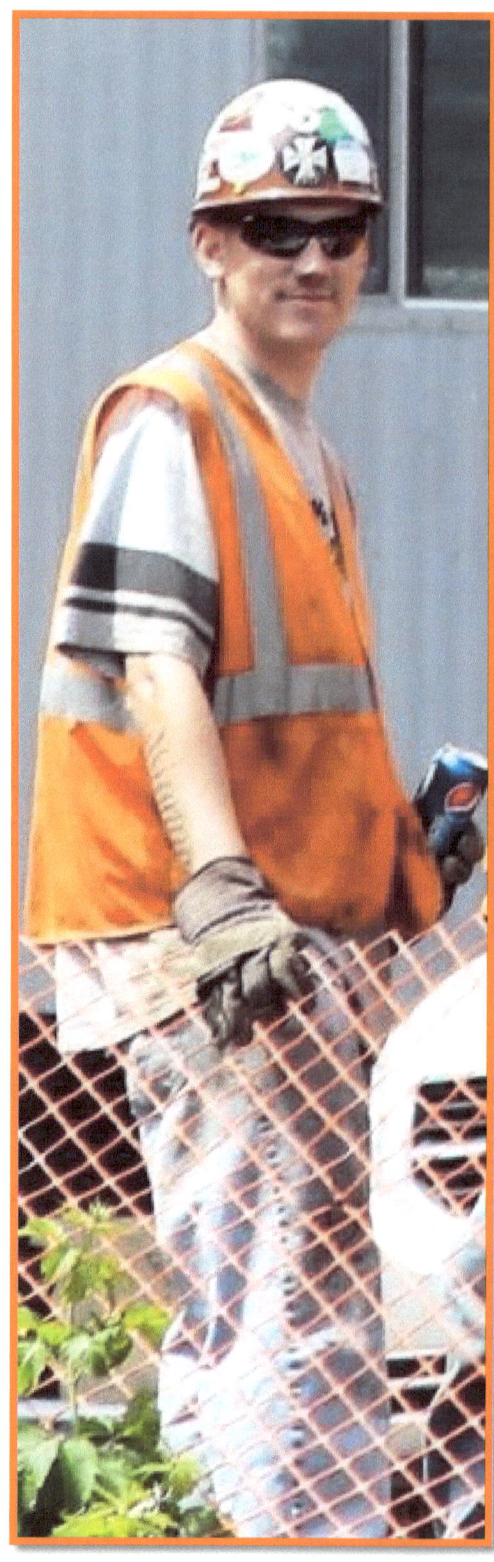

"Chicago will give you a chance. The sporting spirit is the spirit of Chicago." **Lincoln Steffens**

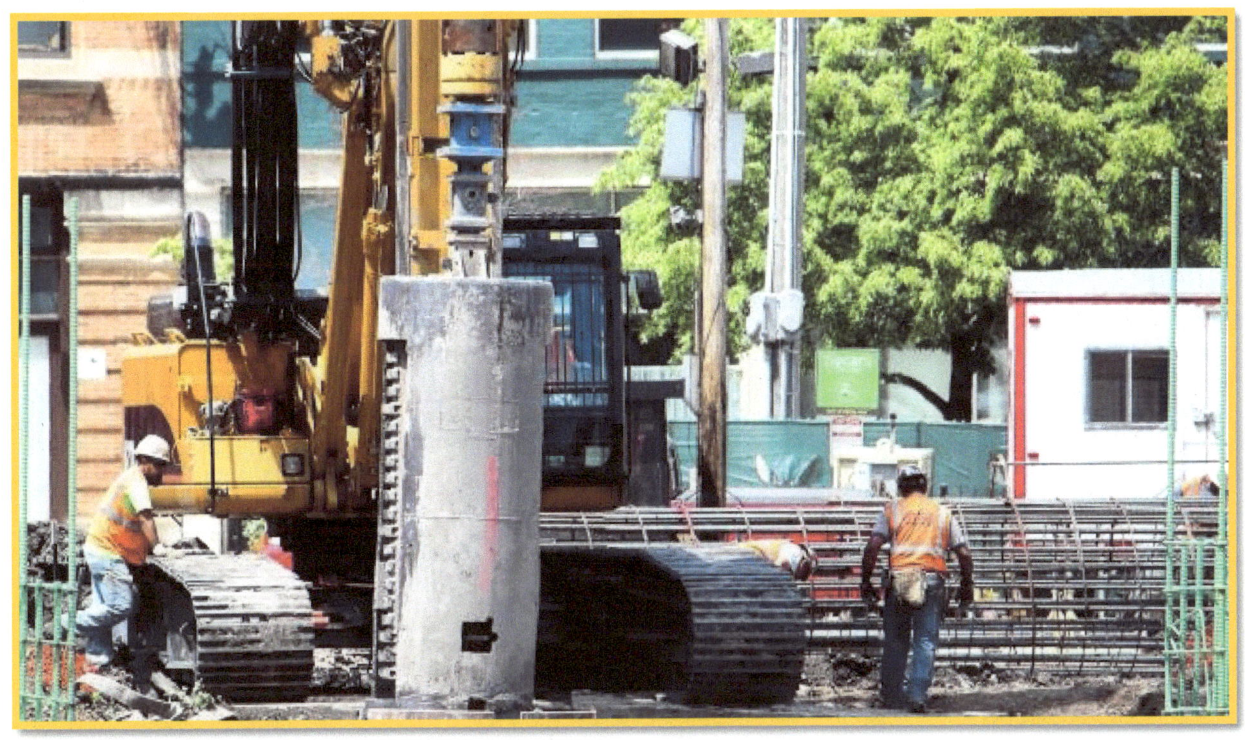

"I am stone and steel of your sleeping numbers;
I remember all you forget.
I will die as many times
as you make me over again."
— Carl Sandburg, *Selected Poems*

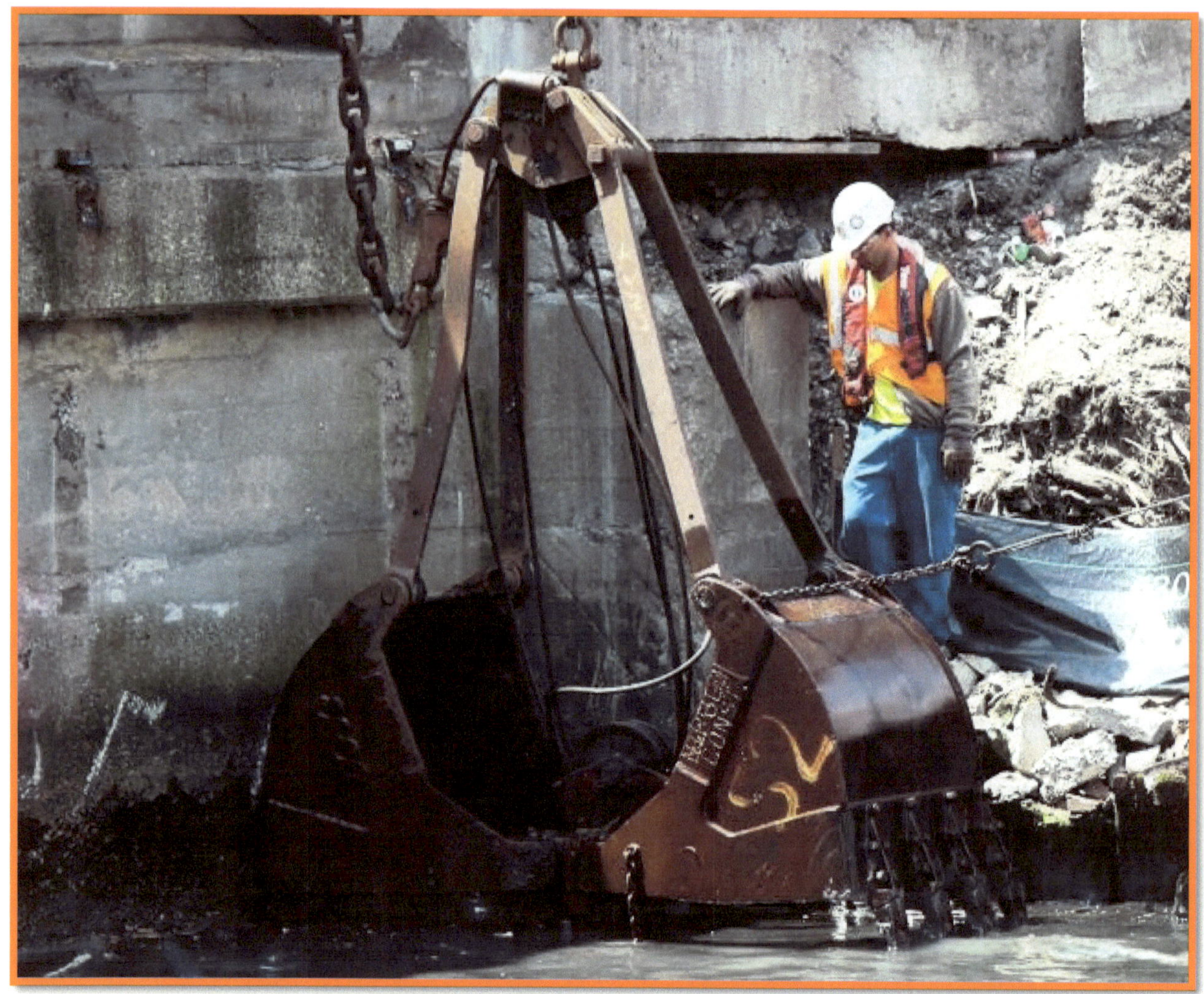

“Chicago happened slowly, like a migraine. First they were driving through countryside, then, imperceptibly, the occasional town became a low suburban sprawl, and the sprawl became the city.” — **Neil Gaiman, *American Gods***

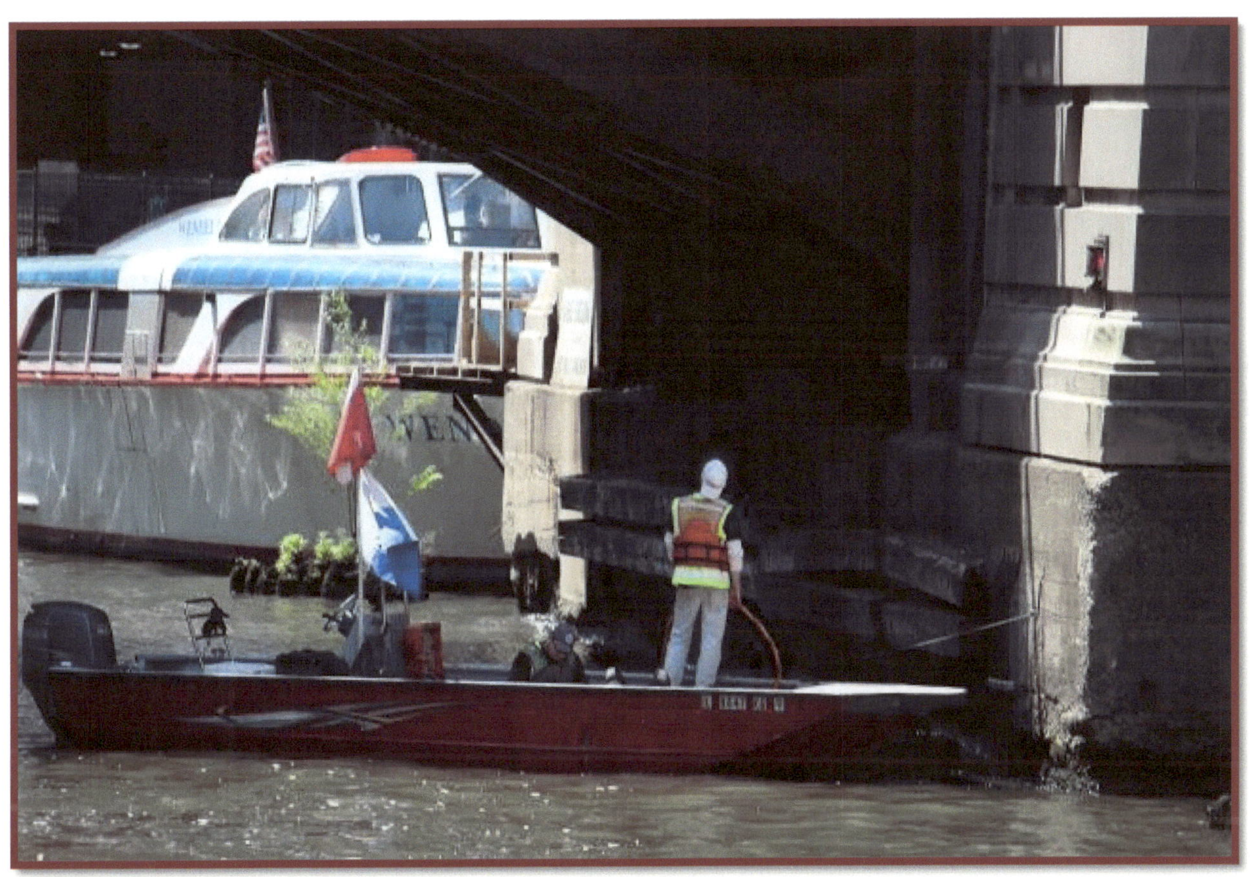

"I'm impressed with the people from Chicago. Hollywood is hype. New York is talk. Chicago is work." **Michael Douglas**

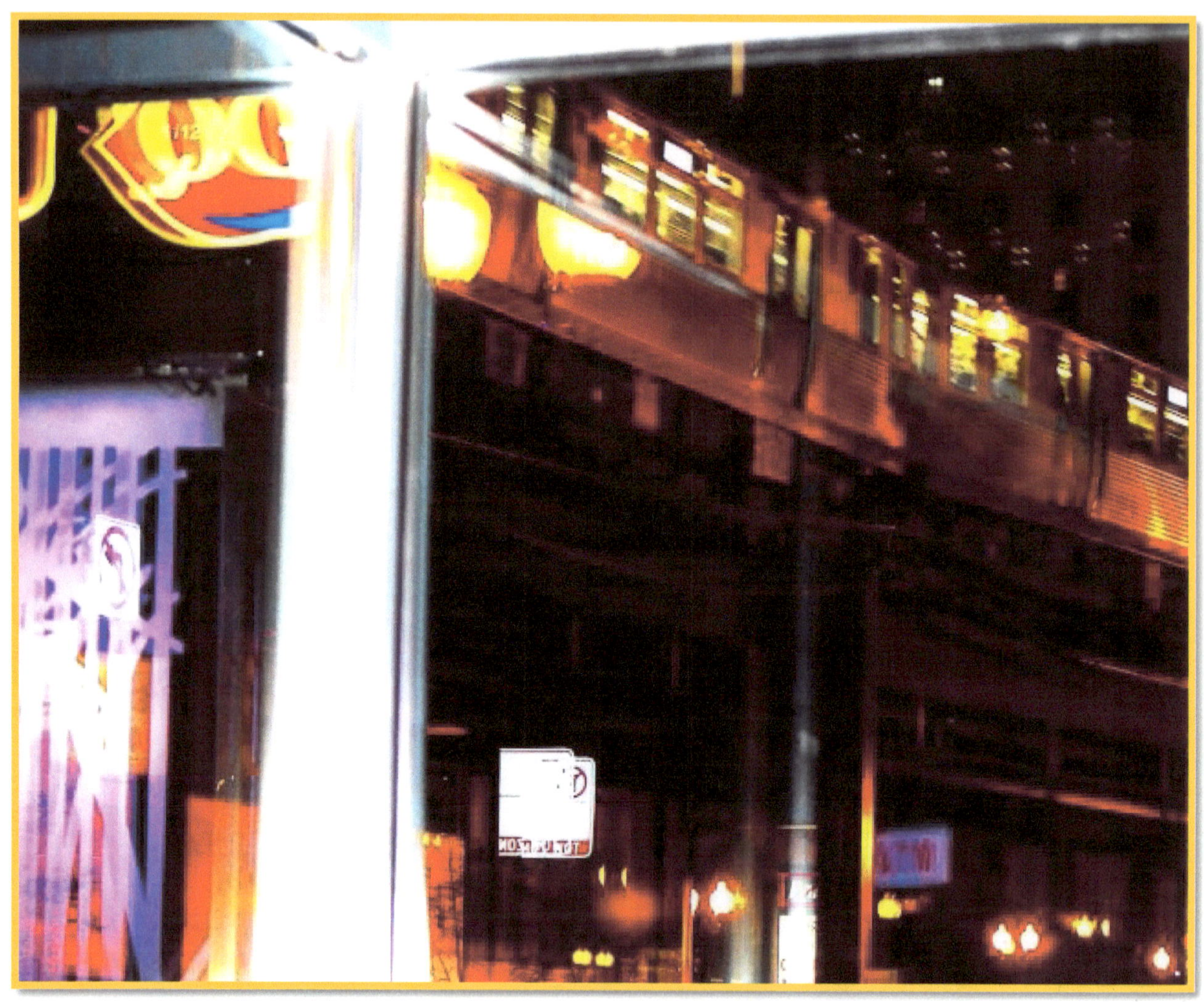

“The great trains howling from track to track all night. The taut and telegraphic murmur of ten thousand city wires, drawn most cruelly against a city sky. The rush of city waters, beneath the city streets. The passionate passing of the night's last El.” — **Nelson Algren, *Never Come Morning***

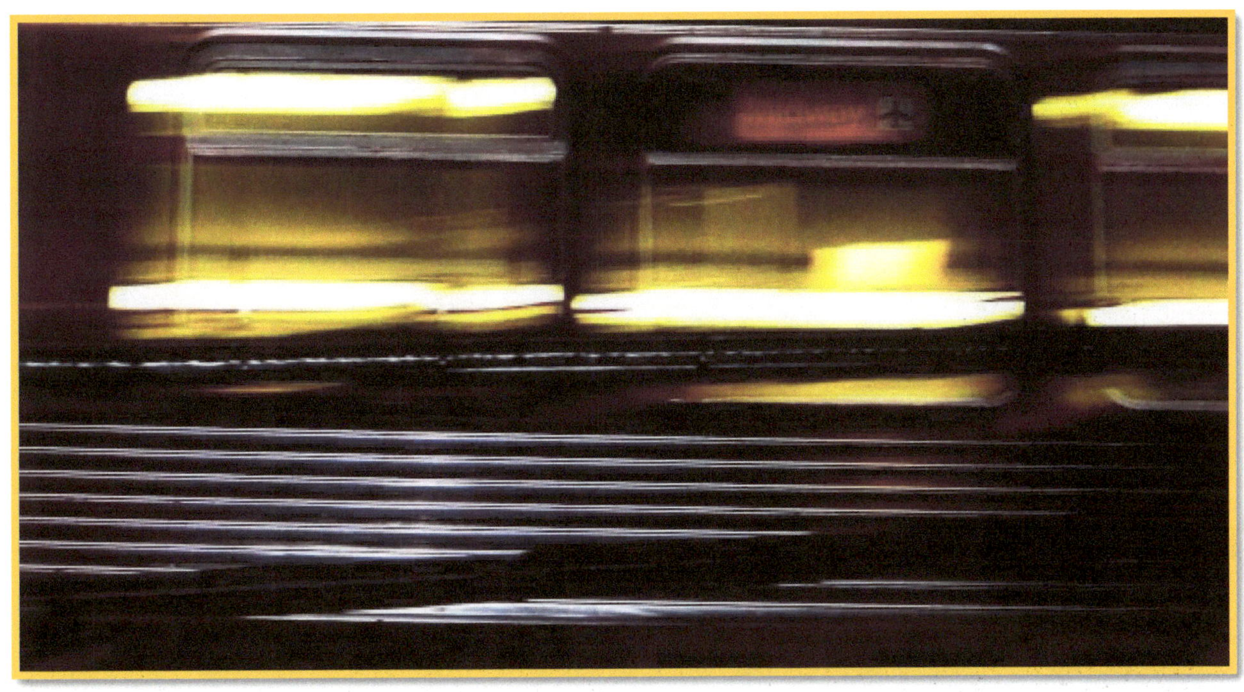

I like the roar of cities. In the mart,
Where busy toilers strive for place and gain,
I seem to read humanity's great heart,
And share its hopes, its pleasures, and its pain.
Ella Wheelr Wilcox "The City"

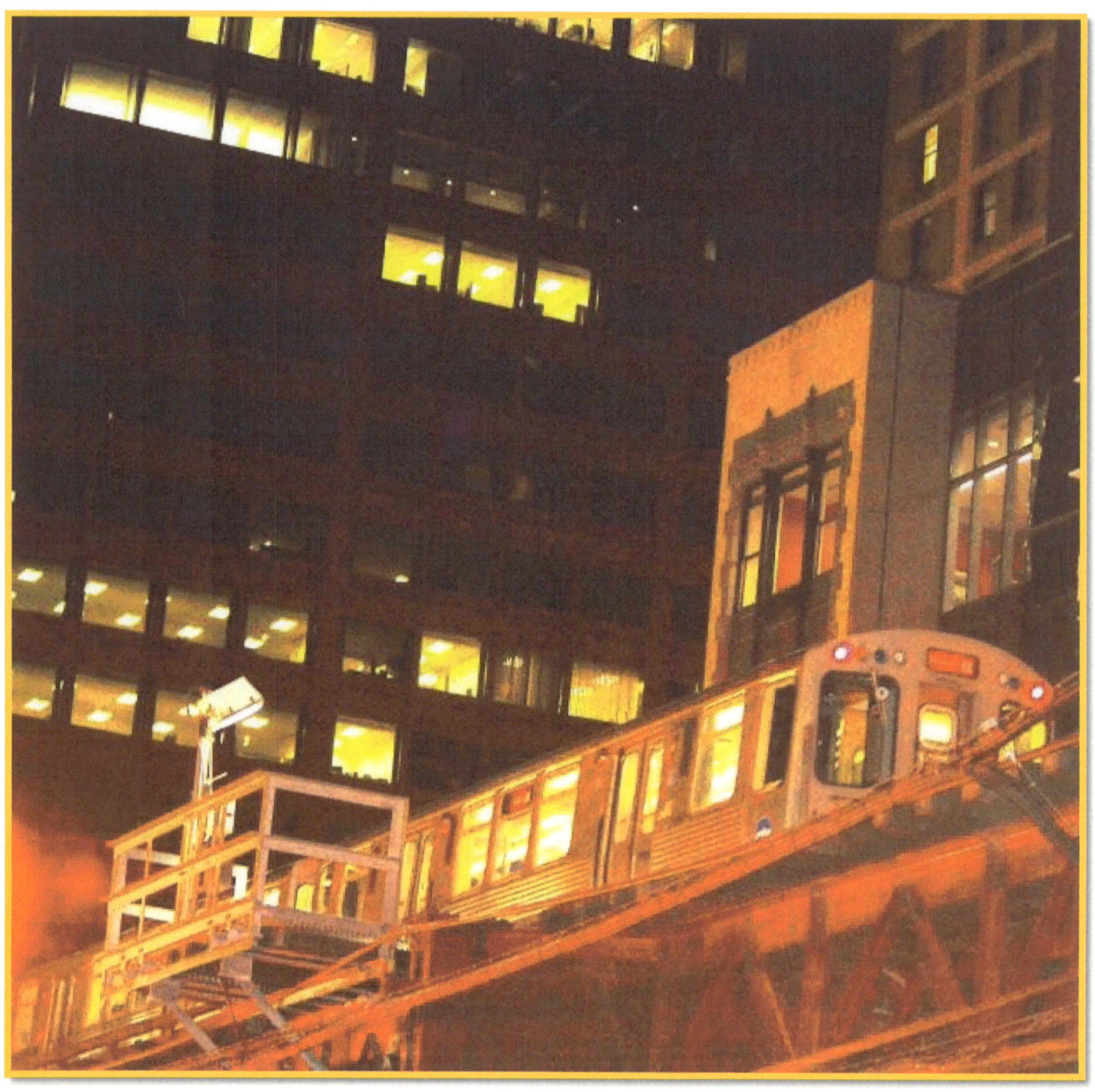

“They can print statistics and count the populations in hundreds of thousands, but to each man a city consists of no more than a few streets, a few houses, a few people. Remove those few and a city exists no longer except as a pain in the memory, like a pain of an amputated leg no longer there.” **Graham Greene, Our Man in Havana.**

"You can't understand a city without using its public transportation system." **Erol Ozan**

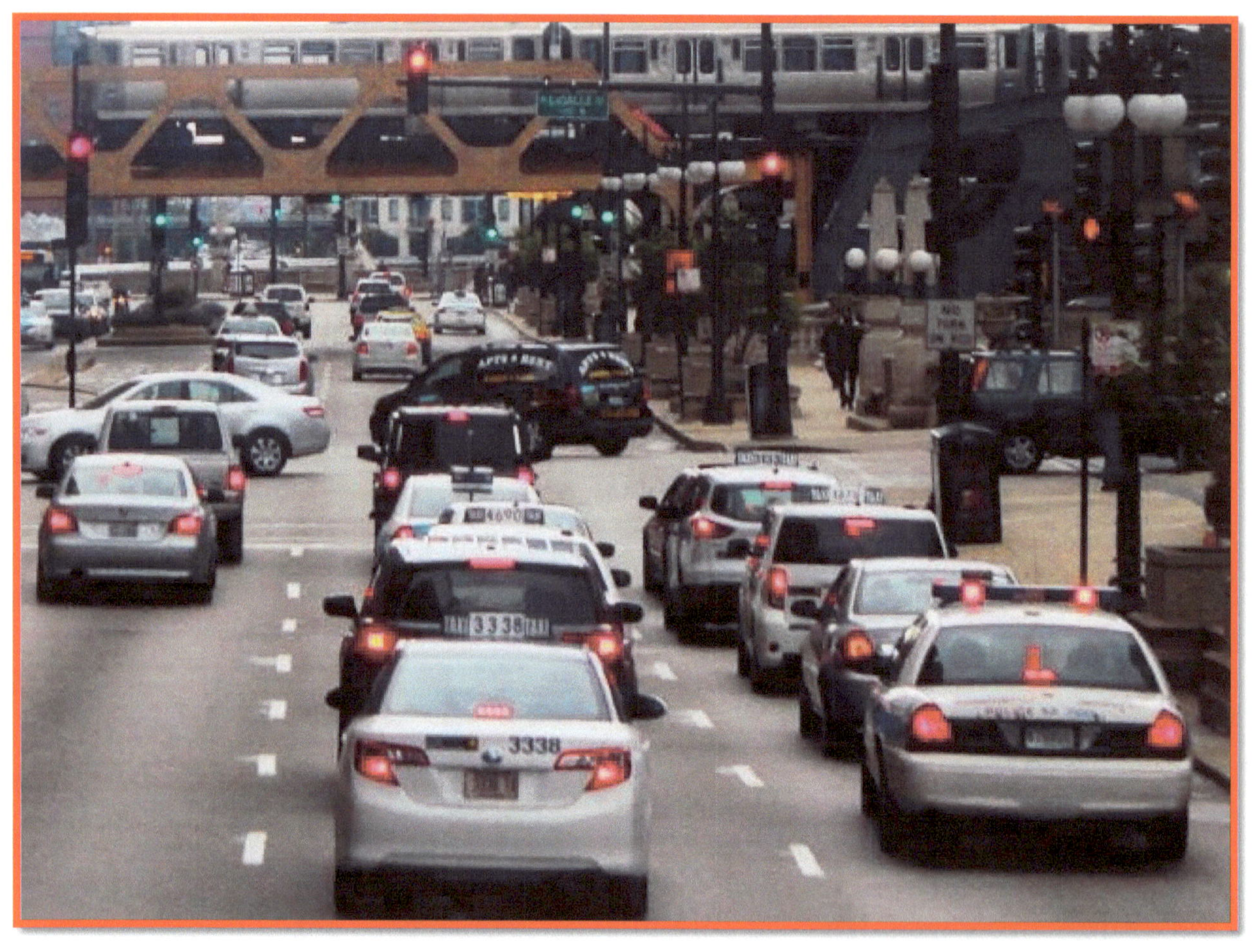

COME you, cartoonists,
Hang on a strap with me here
At seven o'clock in the morning
On a Halsted street car.
Halsted Street Car, Carl Sandburg Chicago Poems

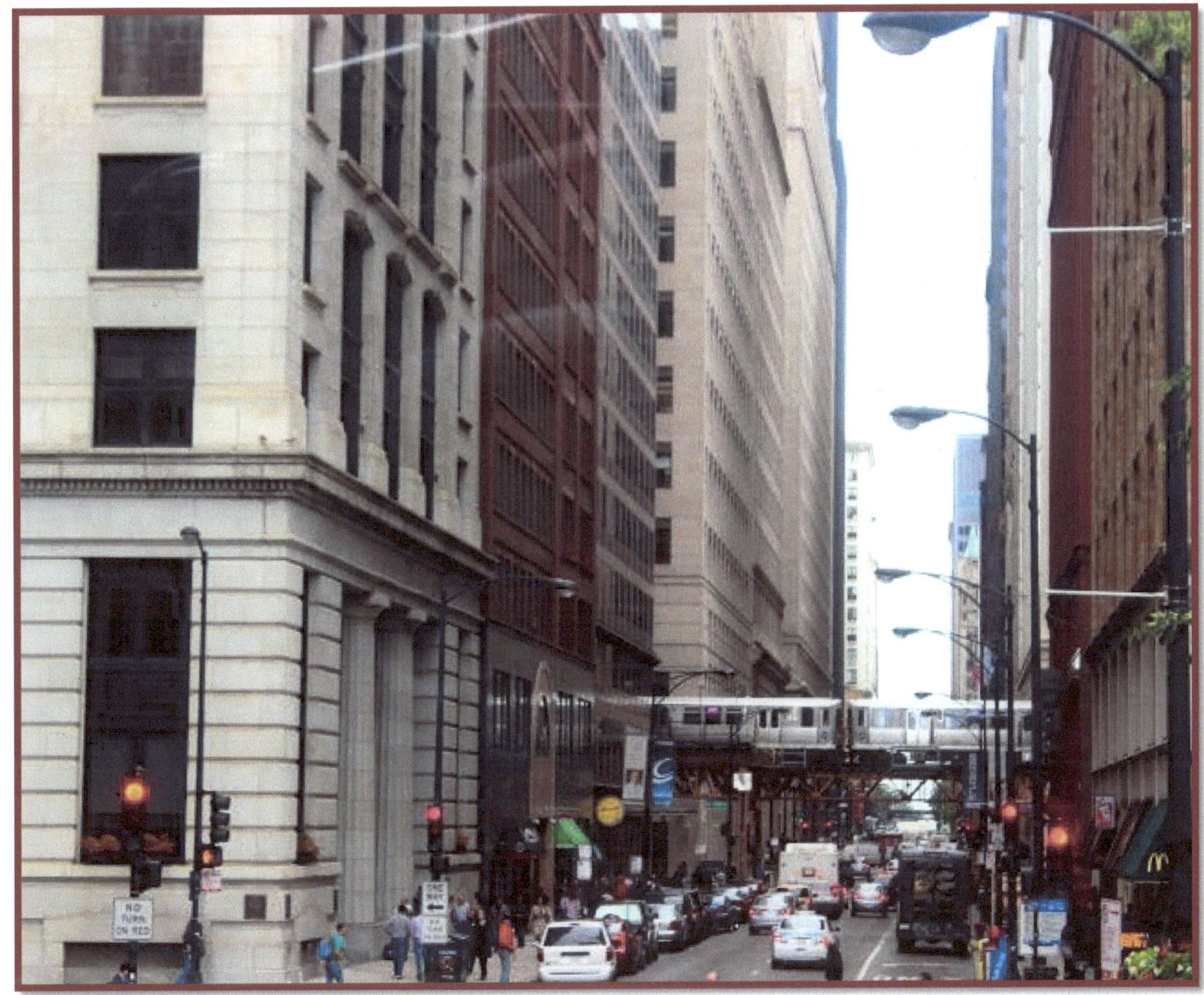

GOOD-BY now to the streets and the clash of wheels and locking hubs,
The sun coming on the brass buckles and harness knobs.
The muscles of the horses sliding under their heavy haunches,
Good-by now to the traffic policeman and his whistle,
The smash of the iron hoof on the stones,
All the crazy wonderful slamming roar of the street—
O God, there's noises I'm going to be hungry for.

Carl Sandburg, Chicago Poems.

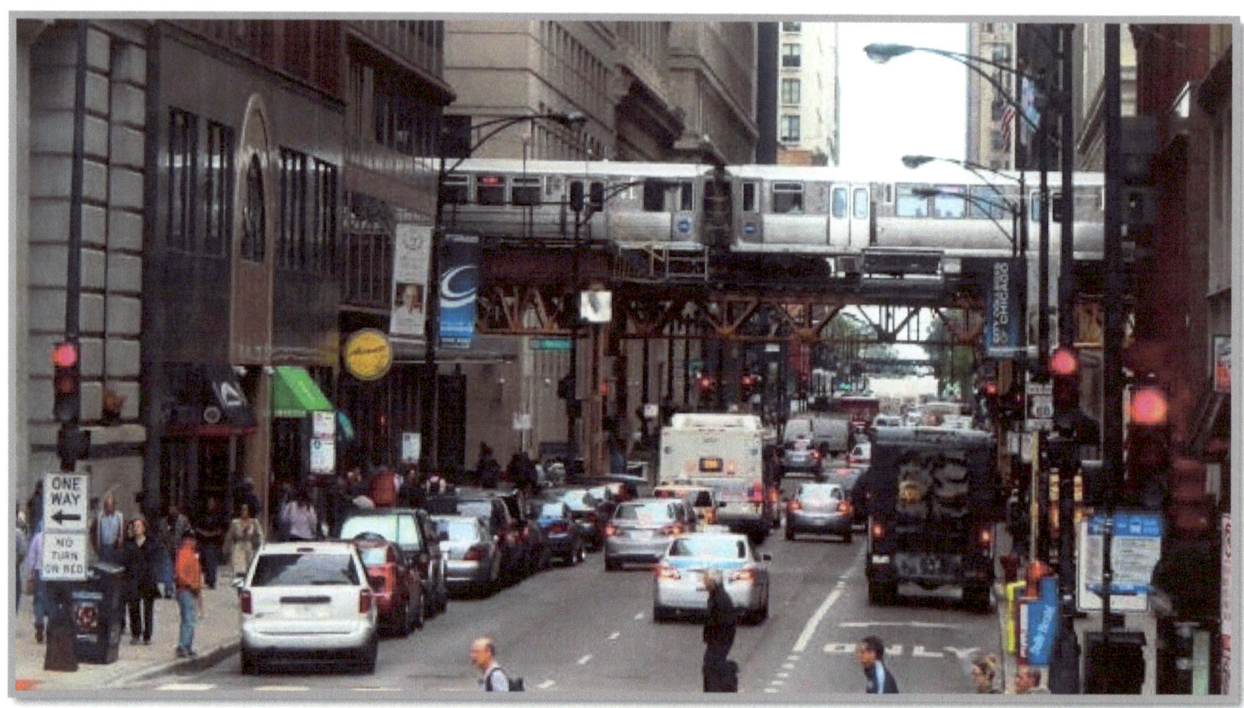

"He pulled her toward him and gathered her in his arms as his hand lovingly cradled the back of her neck. She stopped breathing as he leaned down—ohmigod, the Adonis was about to kiss her—and planted the softest, most sensual kiss on her lips. Time stood still on the busy Chicago street." - **Jennifer Lane, *With Good Behavior***

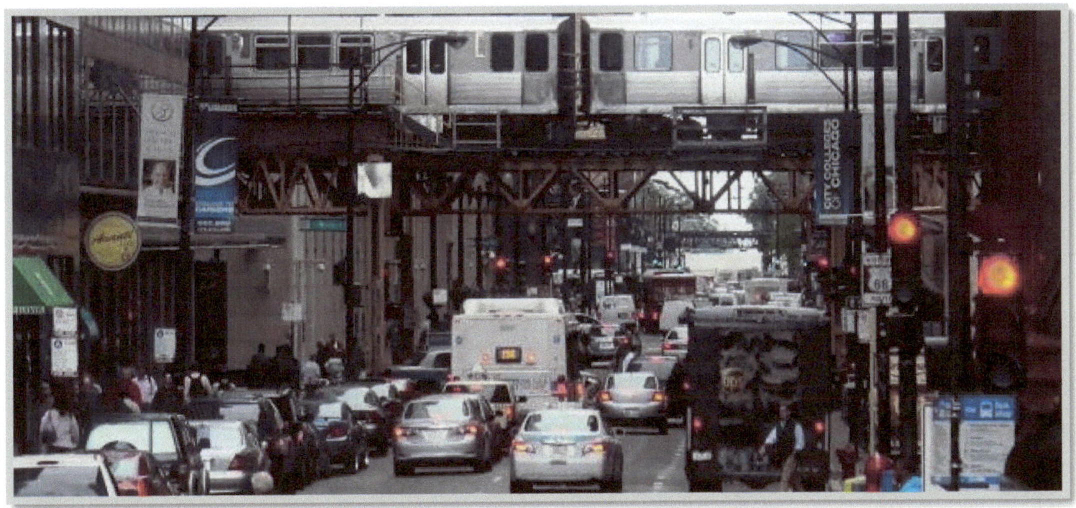

“The great trains howling from track to track all night. The taut and telegraphic murmur of ten thousand city wires, drawn most cruelly against a city sky. The rush of city waters, beneath the city streets. The passionate passing of the night's last El.” **Nelson Algren, Never Come Morning**

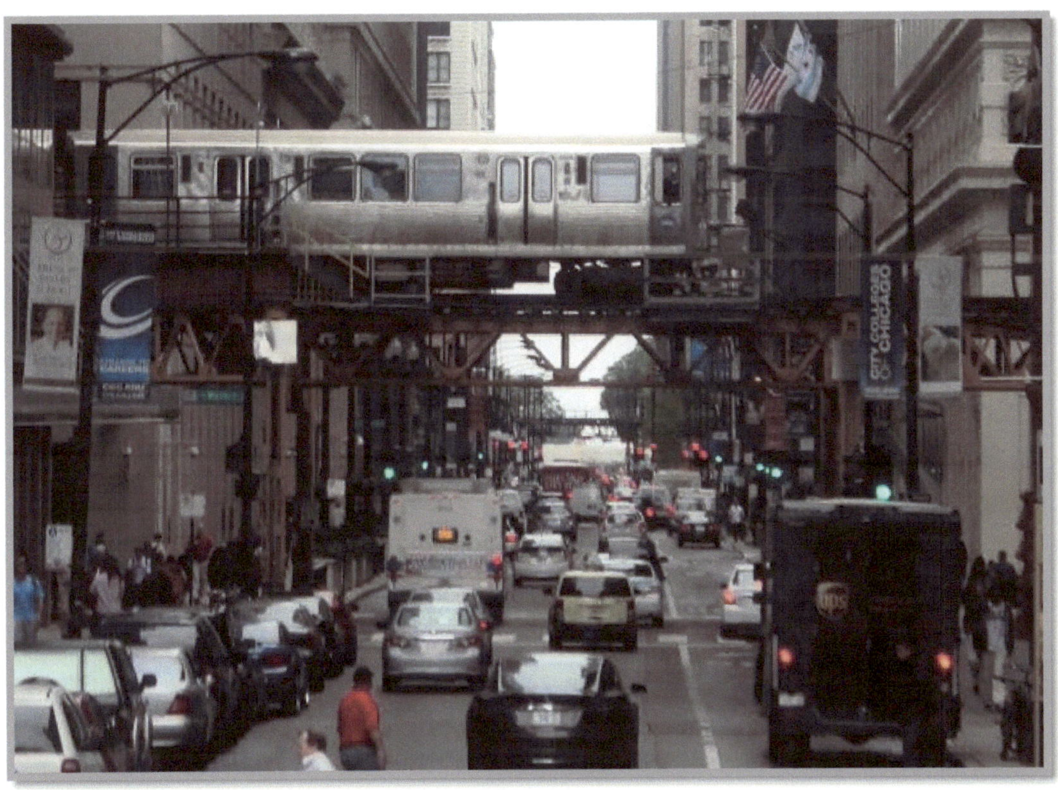

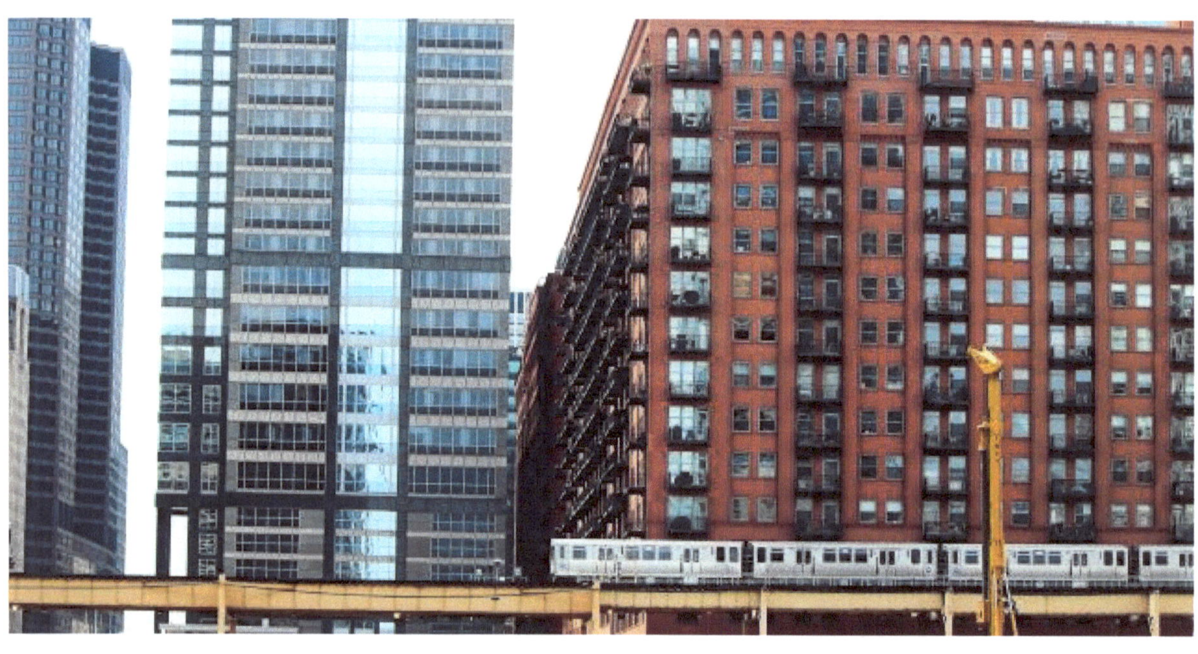

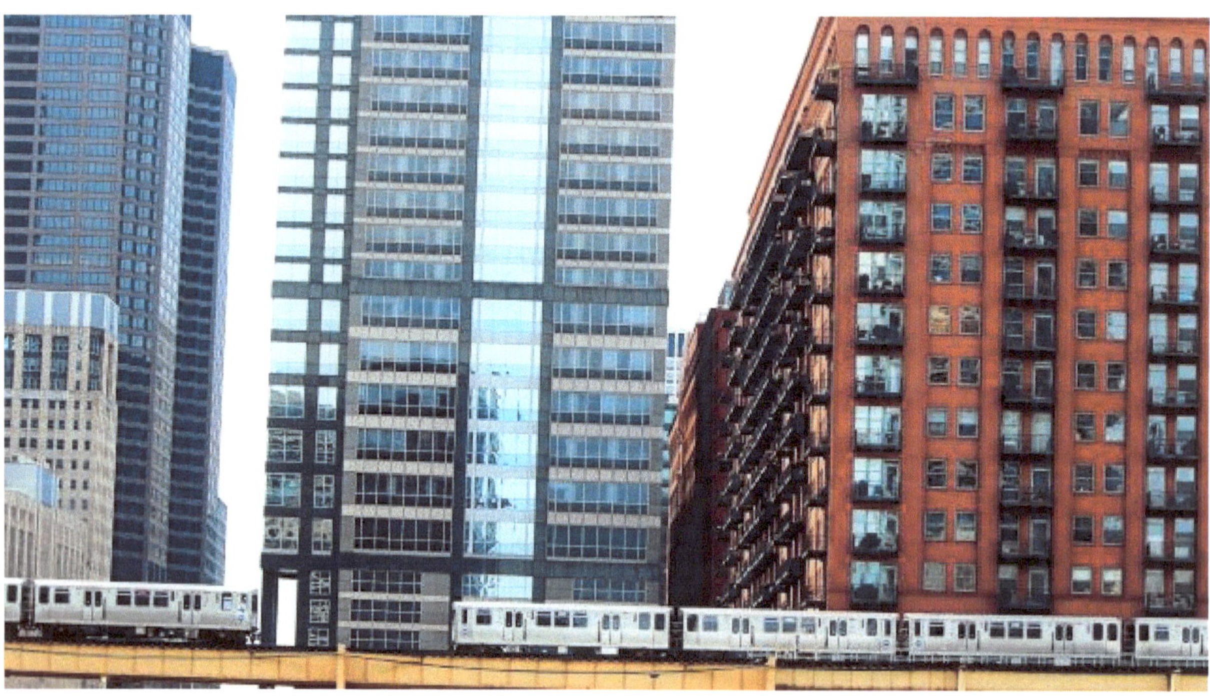

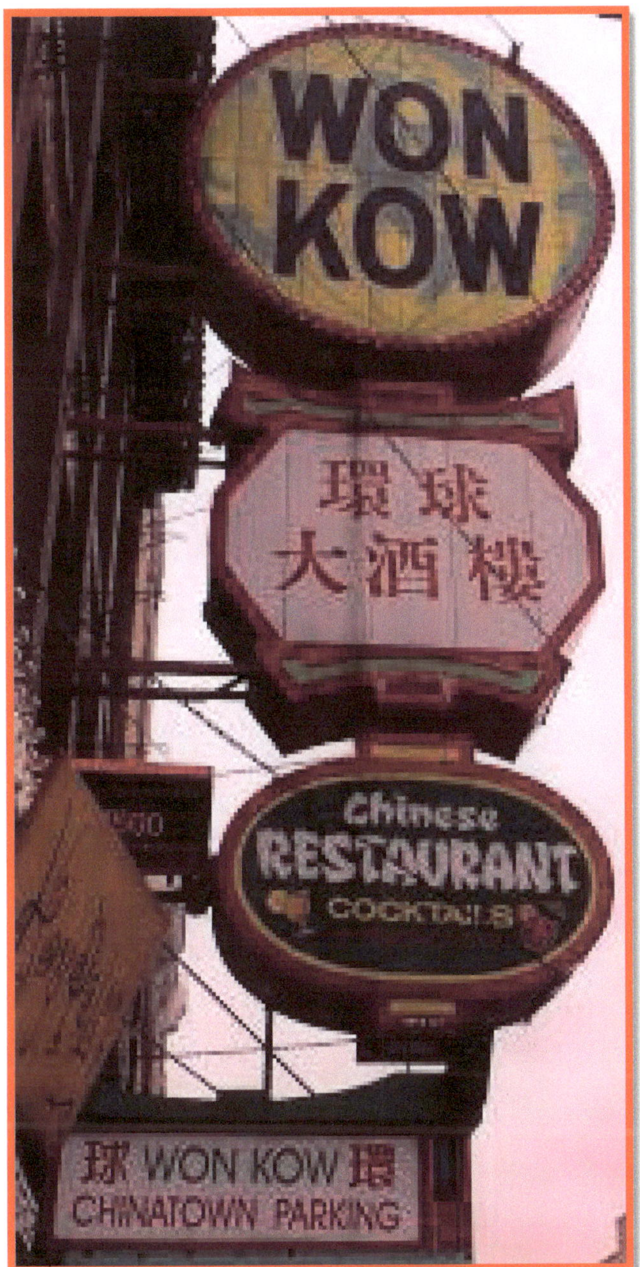

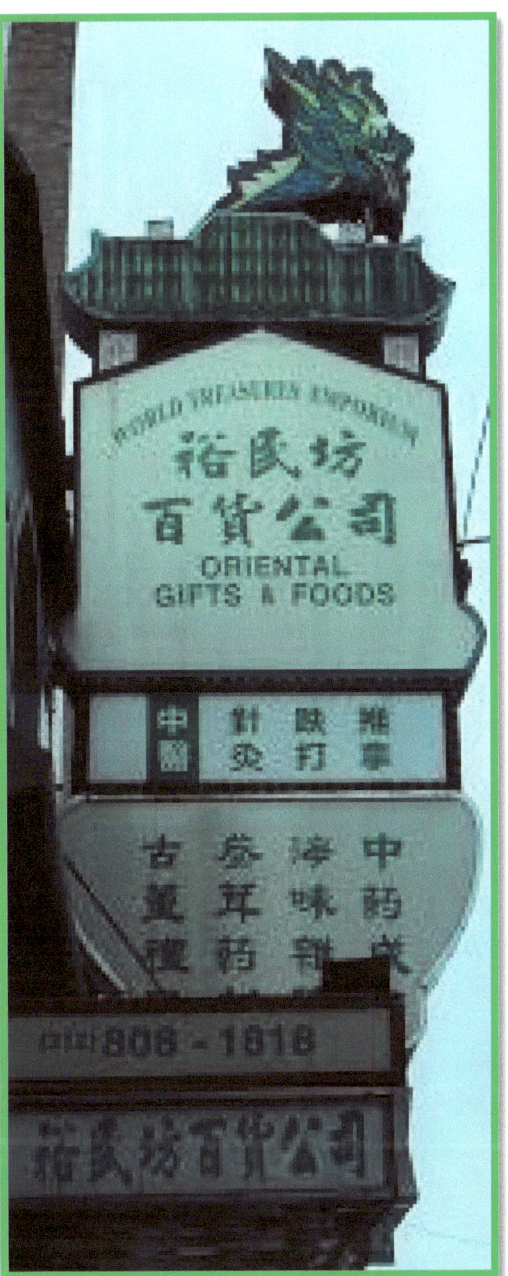

"Everyone is aware that tremendous numbers of people concentrate in city downtowns and that, if they did not, there would be no downtown to amount to anything--certainly not one with much downtown diversity."
Jane Jacobs, The Death and Life of Great American Cities

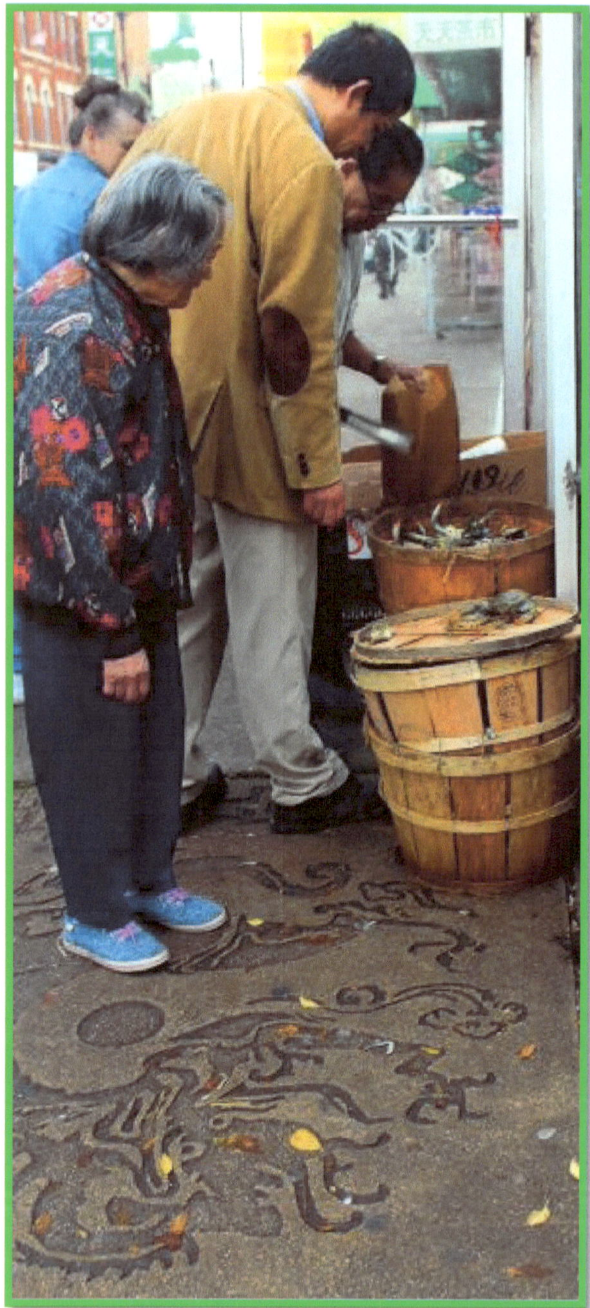

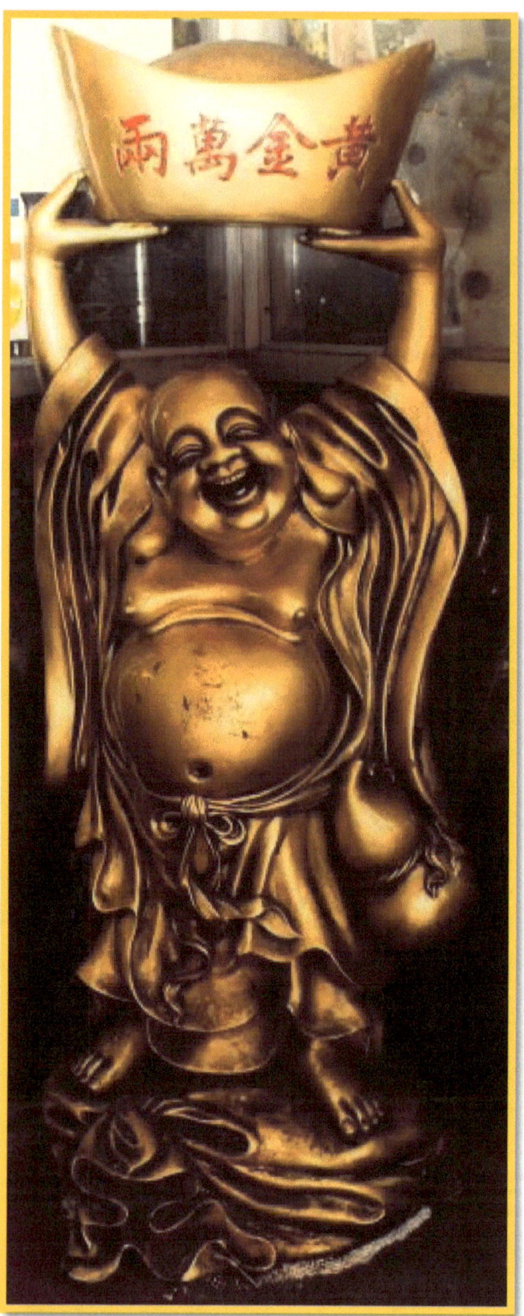

“When the Stranger says: "What is the meaning of this city? Do you huddle close together because you love each other?" What will you answer? "We all dwell together to make money from each other"? or "This is a community"? **T.S. Elliot, The Rock.**

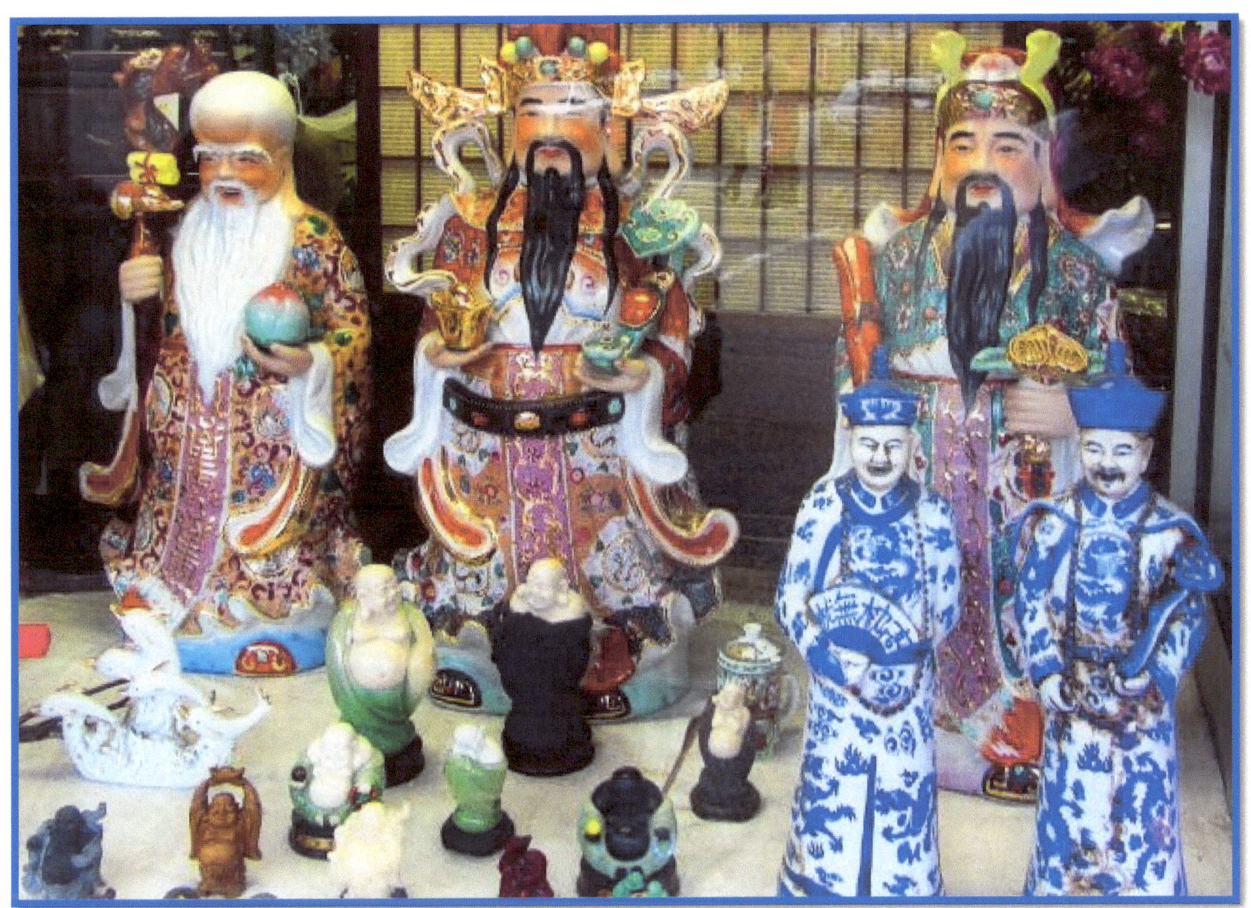

"A lot of real Chicago lives in the neighborhood taverns. It is the mixed German and Irish and Polish gift to the city, a bit of the old country grafted into a strong new plant in the new." **Bill Granger**

"I'd rather be a lamppost in Chicago than a millionaire in any other city." **William A. Hulbert**

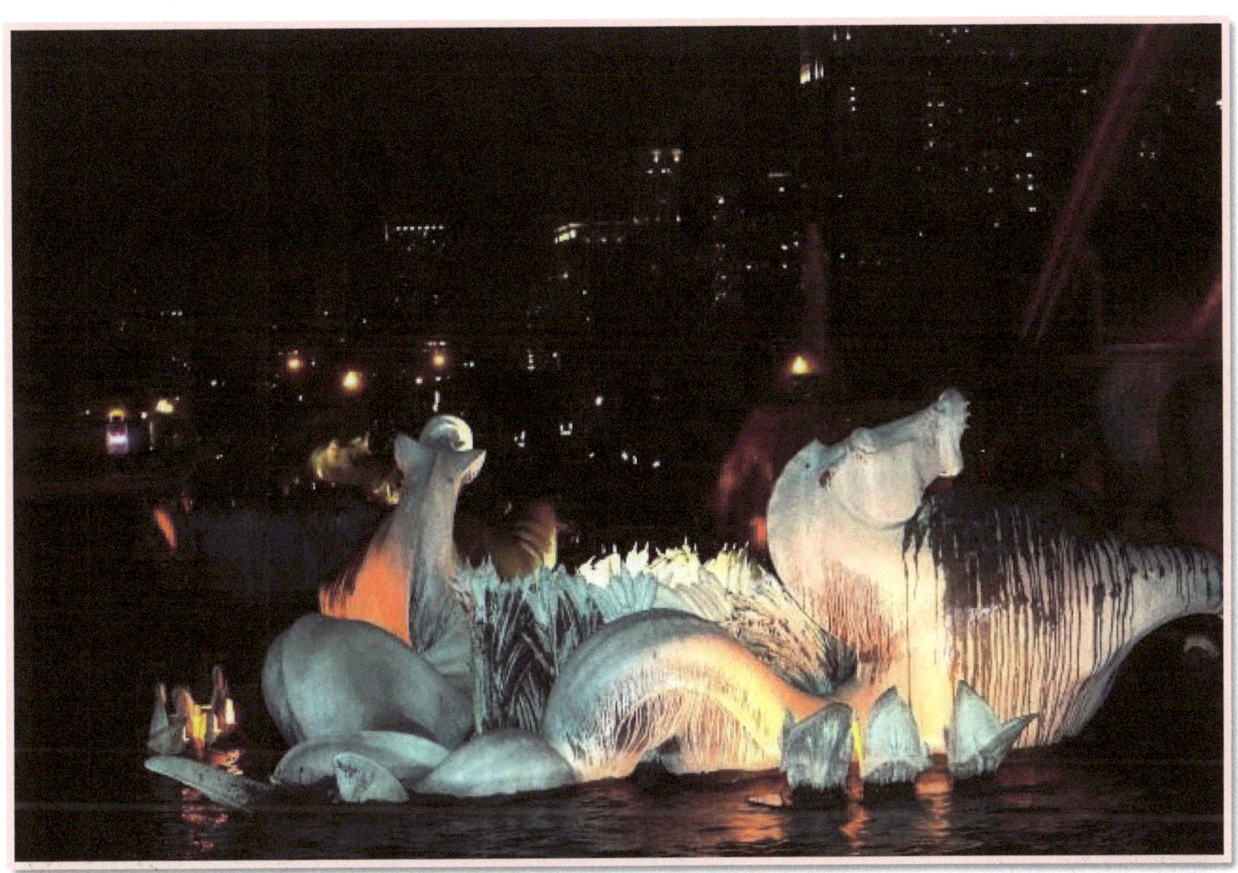

“Everything that's worth having goes to the city--the country takes what's left.” **Finley Peter Dunne**

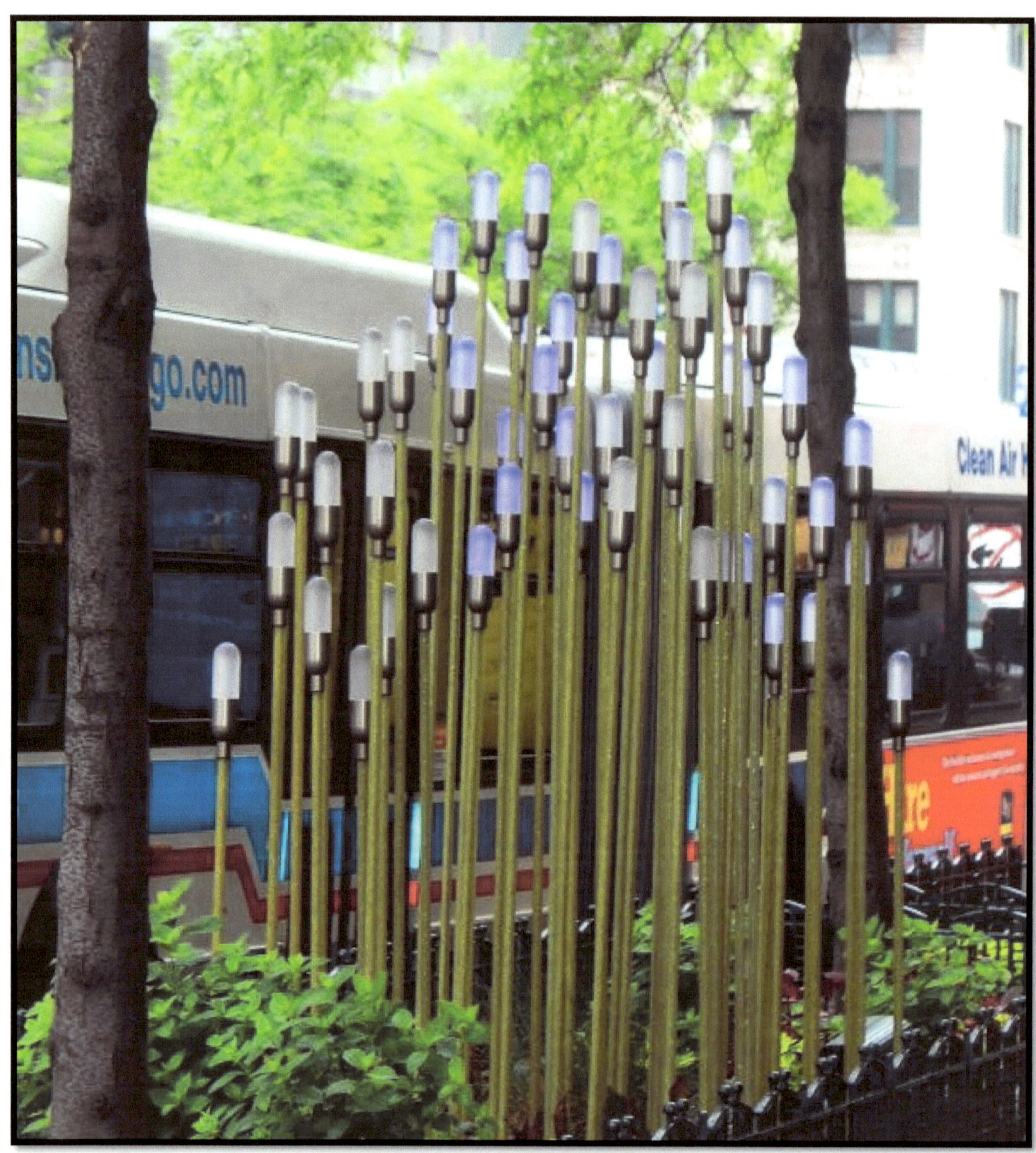

"A work of art which did not begin in emotion is not art." **Paul Cezanne**

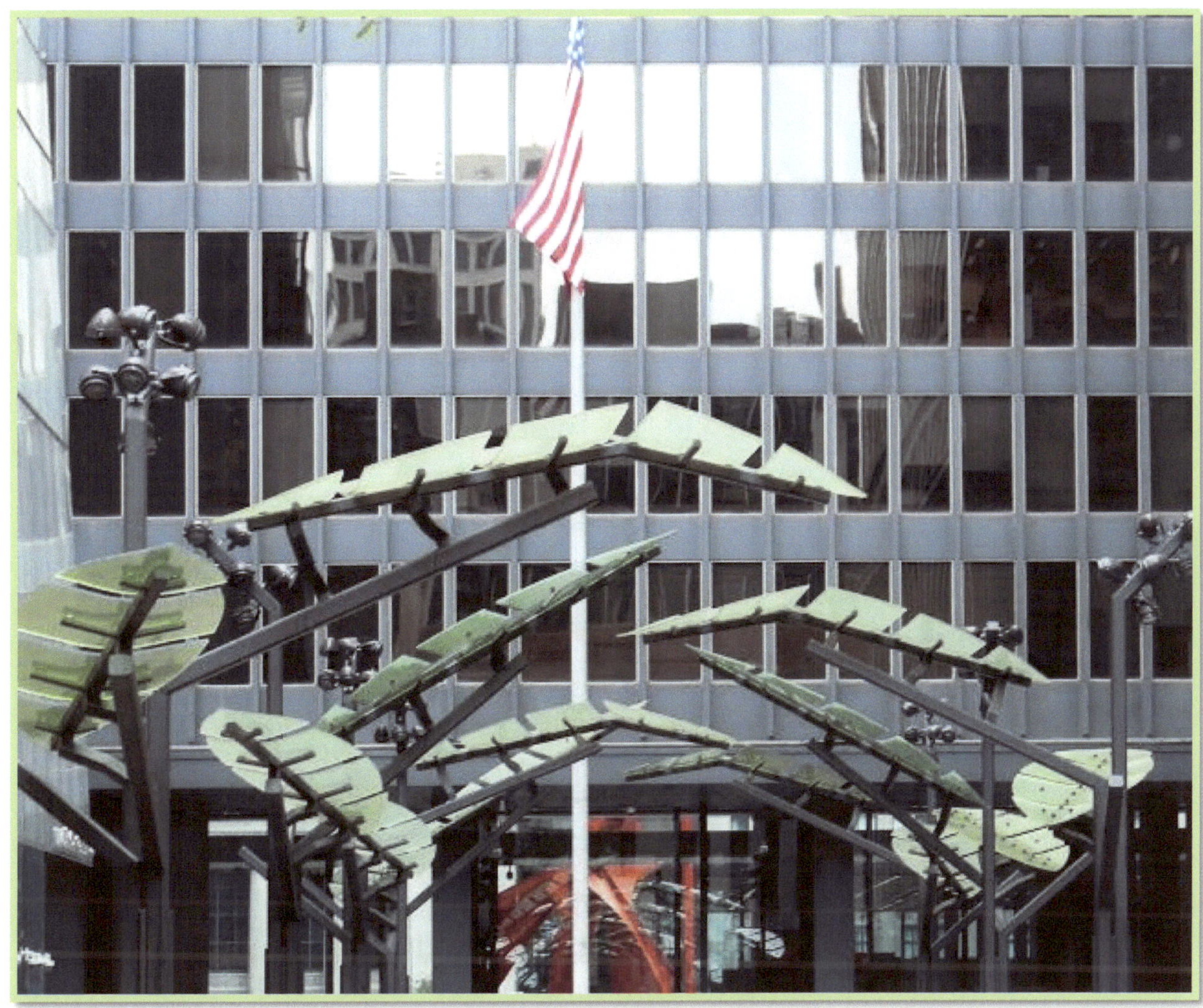

“Chicago does not go to the world, the world comes to Chicago! Who needs New York? Who has taller buildings than our tall buildings? Who's got a busier airport than our airport? You want Picasso? We got Picasso, big Picasso. Nobody can make heads or tails of it. It's a lion? No, a seahorse. Looks to me like a radiator with wings. Who gives a damn, people, a Picasso's a Picasso.” — **Peter Orner, *Love and Shame and Love***

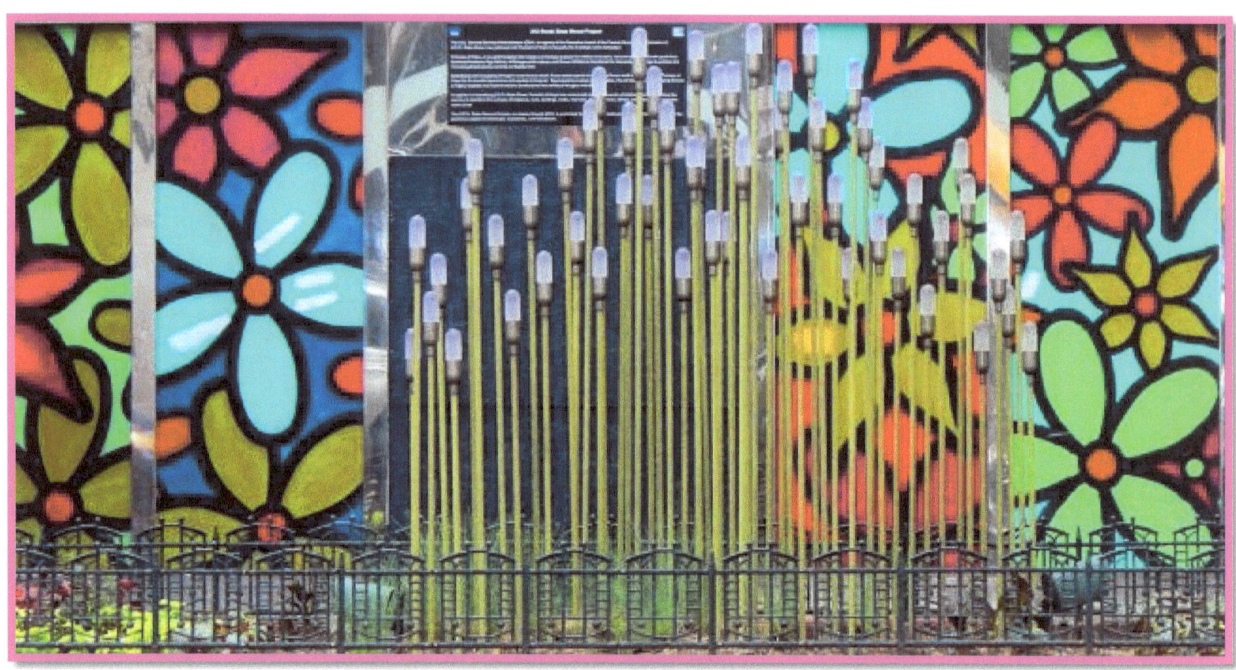

“Art works because it appeals to certain faculties of the mind. Music depends on details of the auditory system, painting and sculpture on the visual system. Poetry and literature depend on language.” **Steven Pinker**

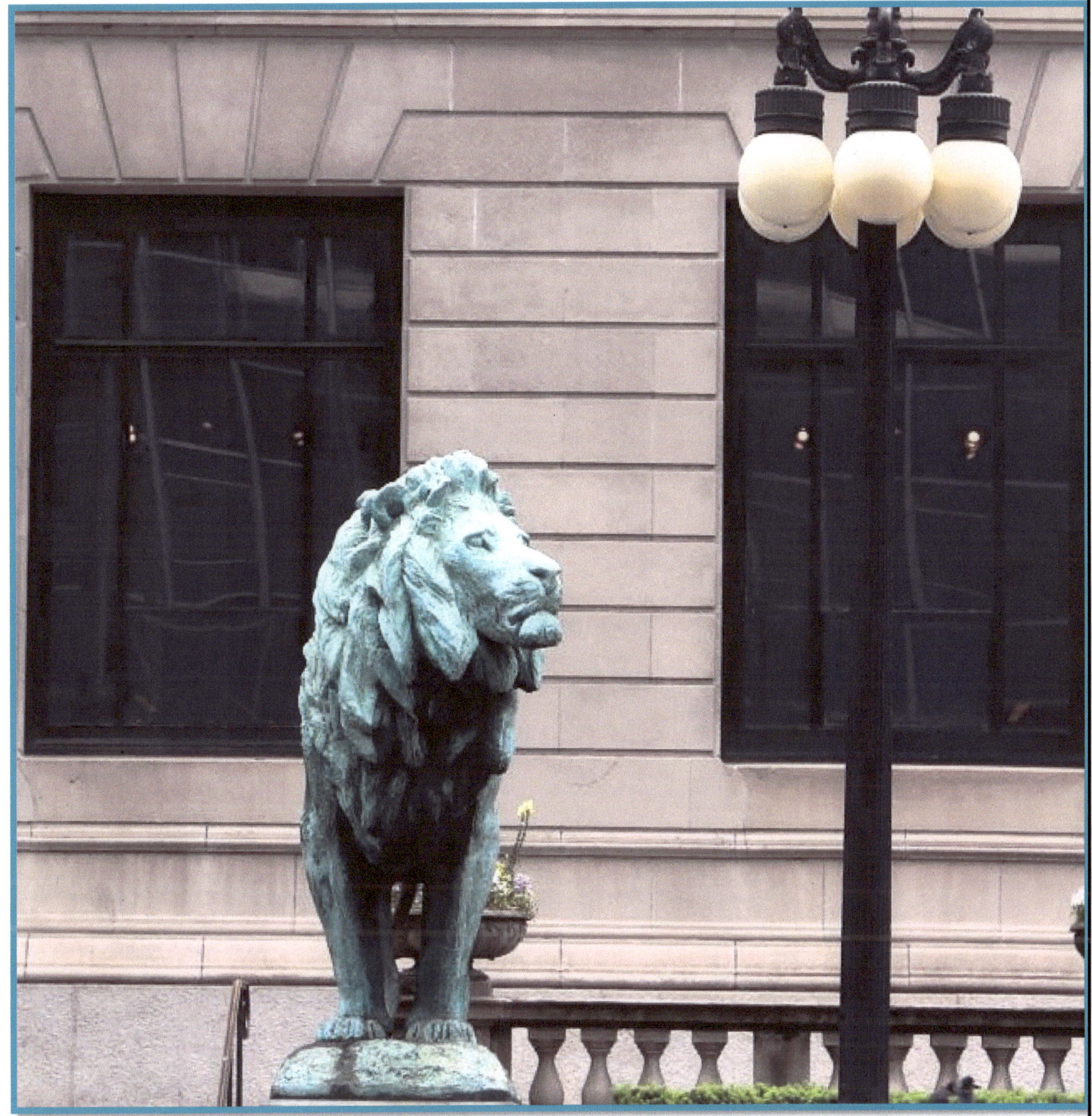

A city is a place where there is no need to wait for next week to get the answer to a question, to taste the food of any country, to find new voices to listen to and familiar ones to listen to again. **Margaret Mead**

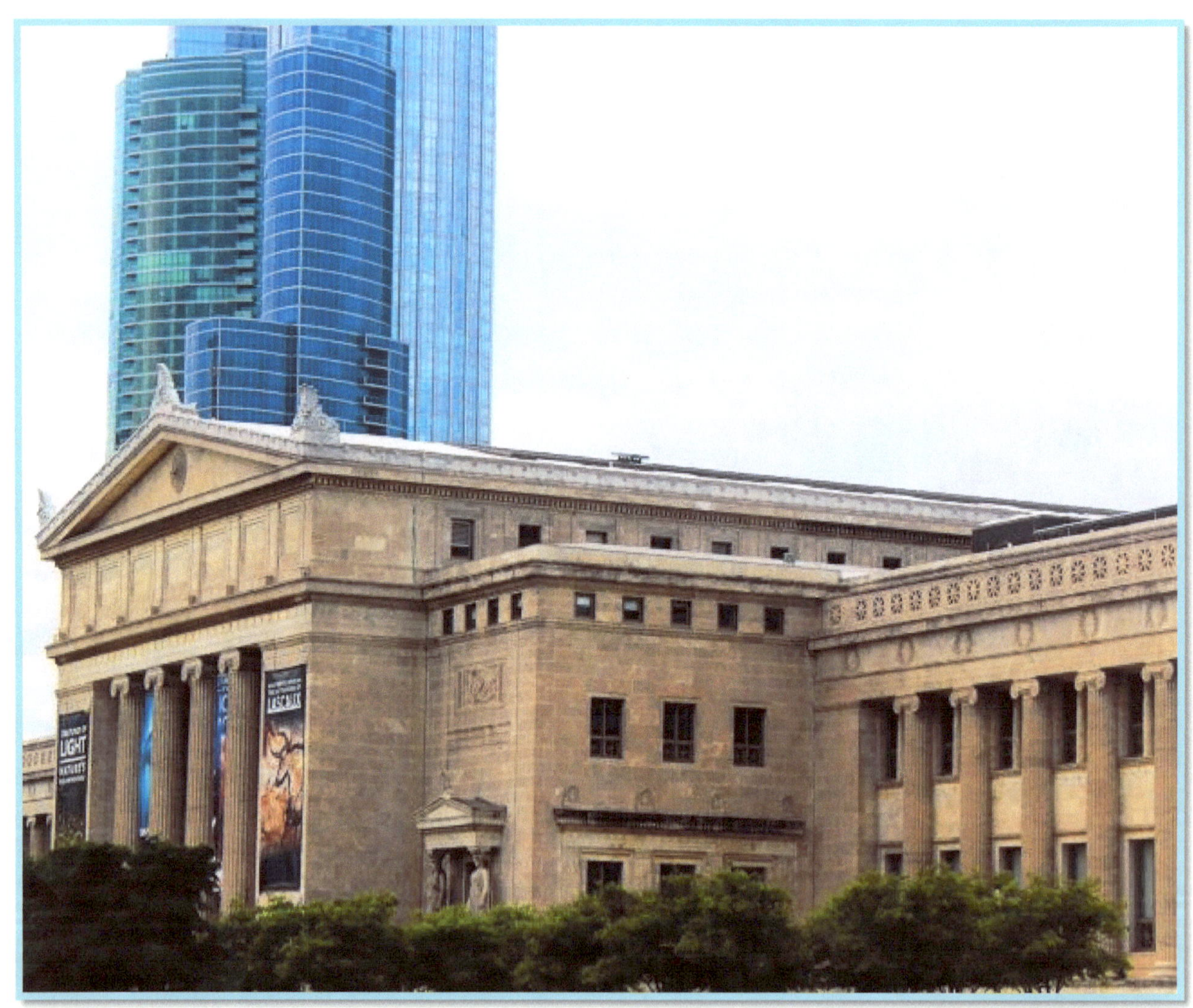

"Great buildings that move the spirit have always been rare. In every case they are unique, poetic, products of the heart." **Arthur Erickson**

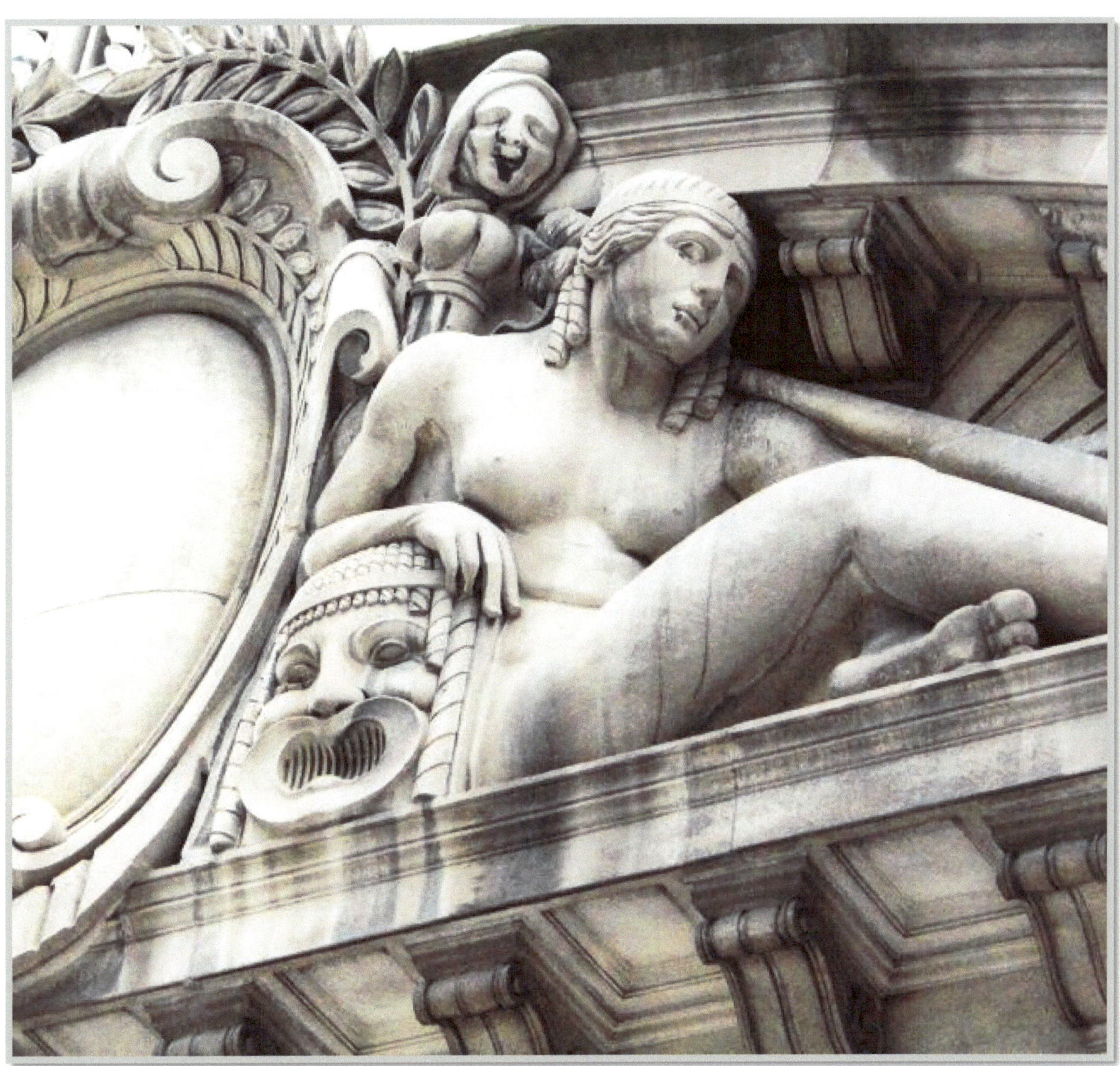

“The aim of art is to represent not the outward appearance of things, but their inward significance.” **Aristotle**

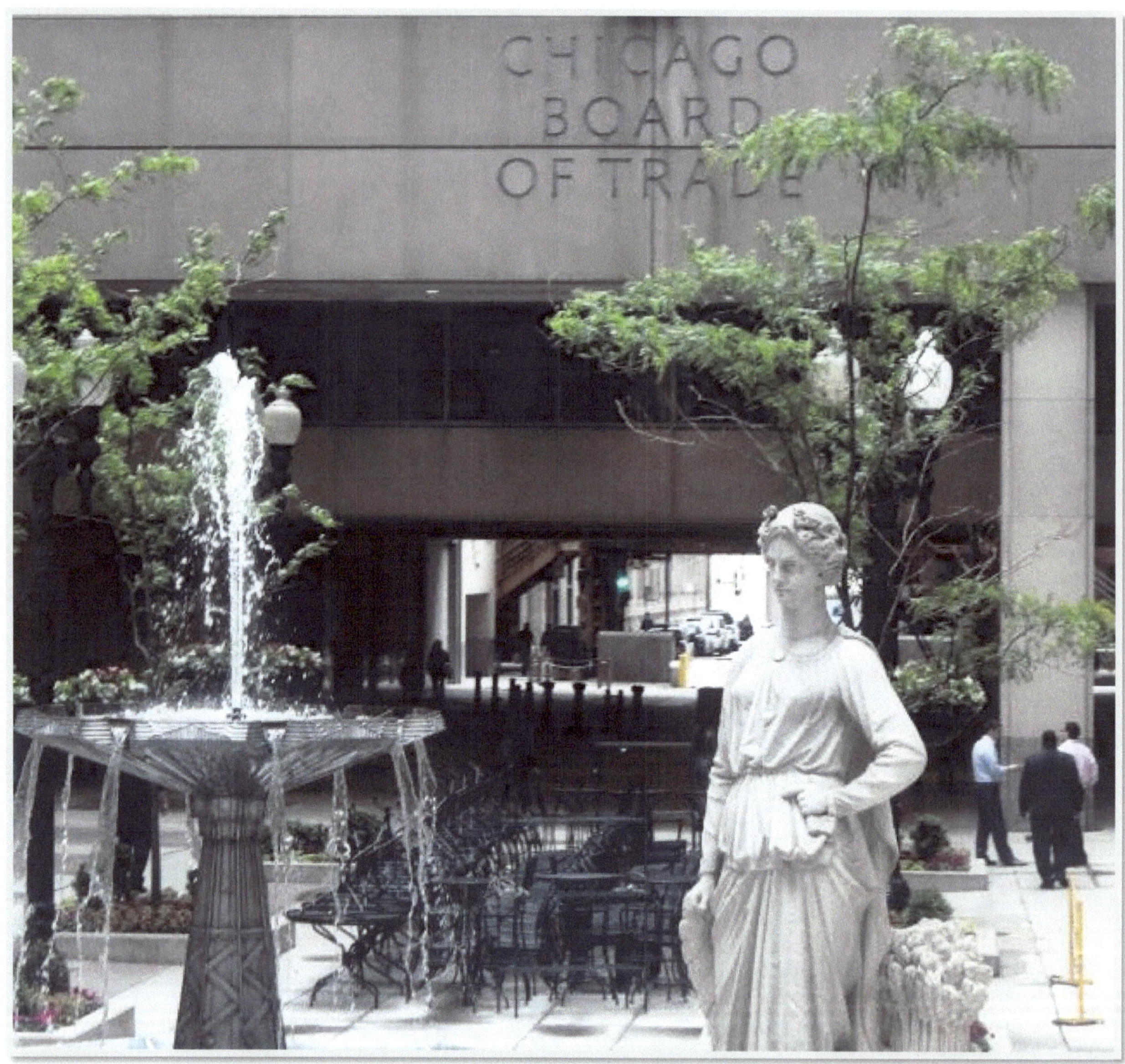

"How important are the visual arts in our society? I feel strongly that the visual arts are of vast and incalculable importance. Of course I could be prejudiced. I am a visual art." **Kermit the Frog**

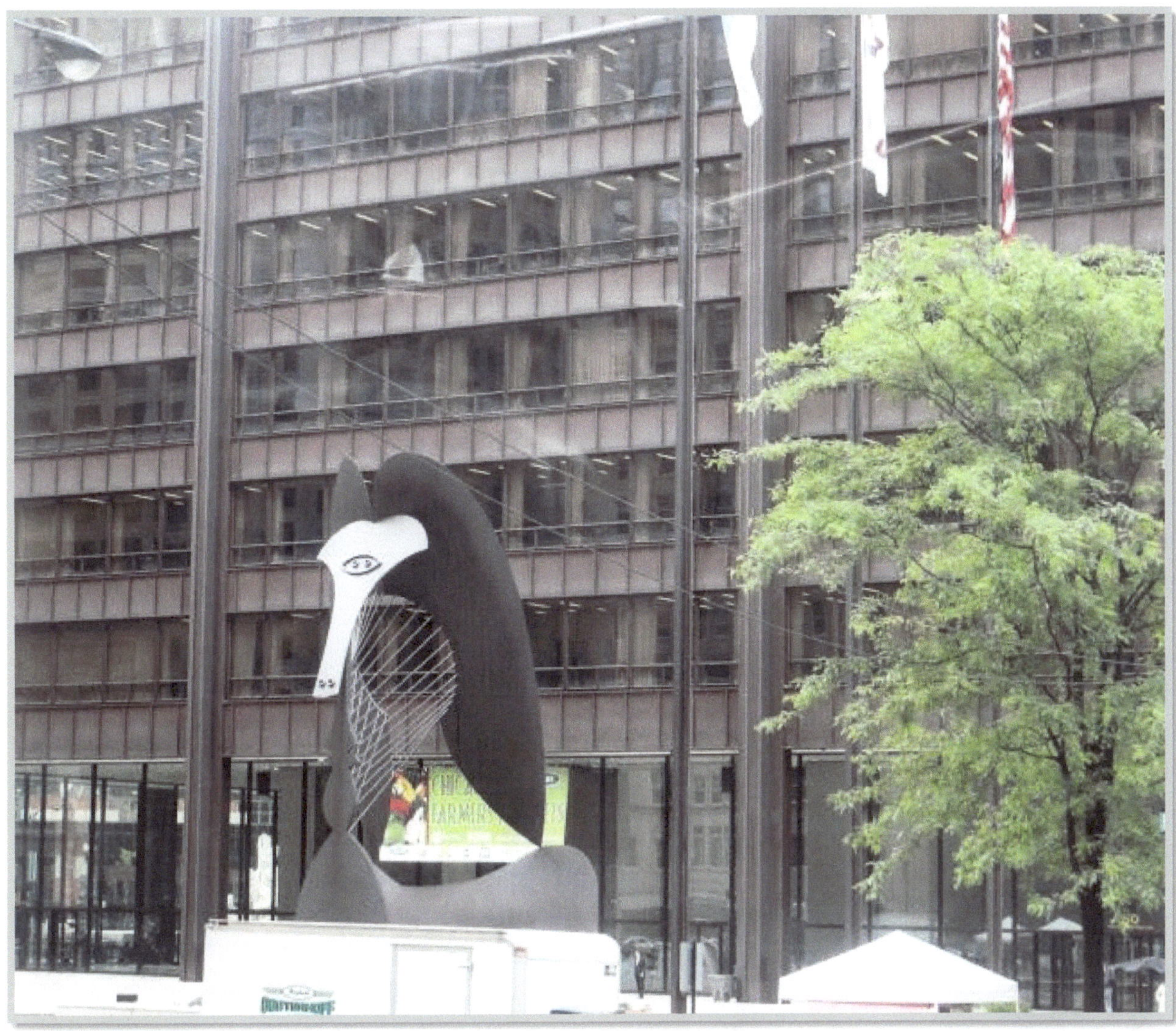

"In Chicago, we may not think the Picasso presiding over the Richard J. Daley Center plaza is art, but we know it's a big Picasso and it's the city's Picasso, and when the Cubs made the play-offs, the sculpture wore a baseball cap just like everything else." **Pat Colander**

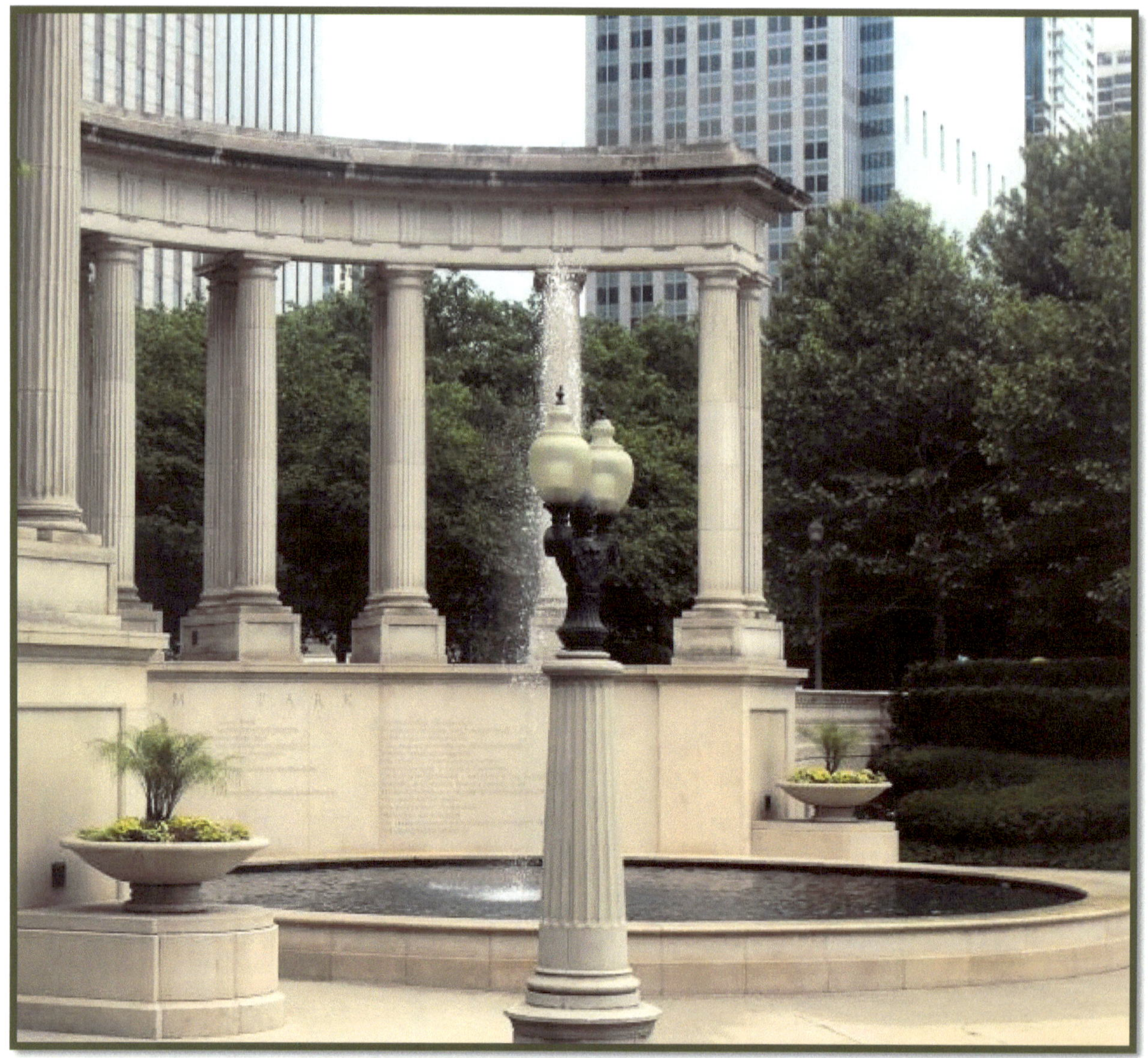

"There is one timeless way of building. It is a thousand years old, and the same today as it has ever been. The great traditional buildings of the past, the villages and tents and temples in which man feels at home, have always been made by people who were very close to the center of this way." **Christopher Alexander**

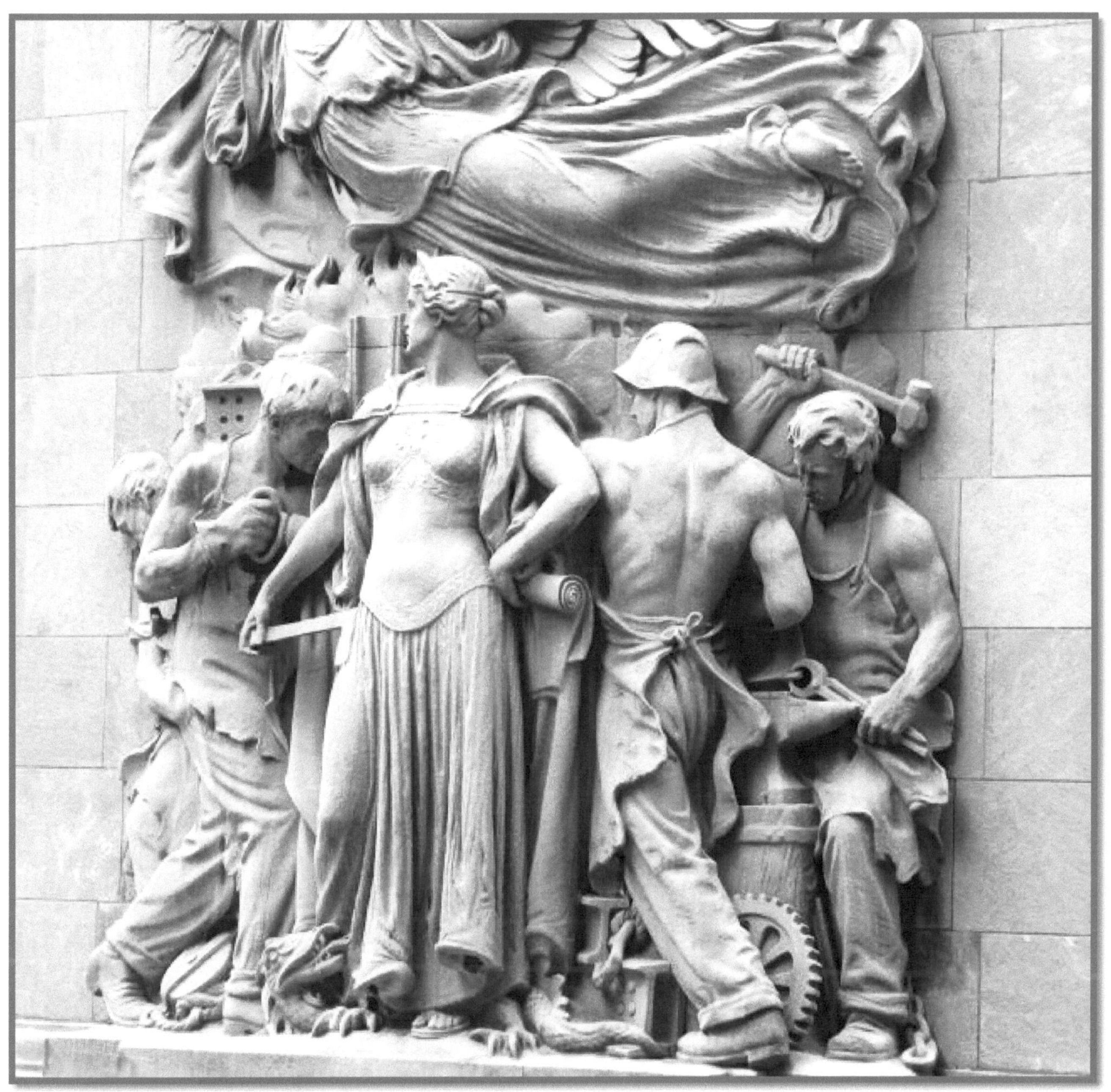

“Our architecture reflects truly as a mirror.” **Louis Henri Sullivan, Chicagoan by adoption.**

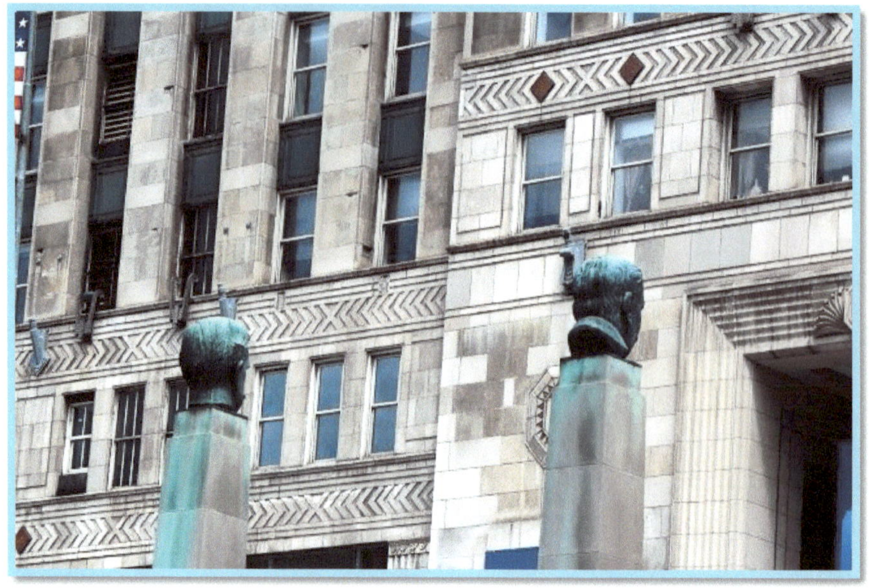

“Great minds are related to the brief span of time during which they live as great buildings are to a little square in which they stand: you cannot see them in all their magnitude because you are standing too close to them.” **Arthur Schopenhauer**

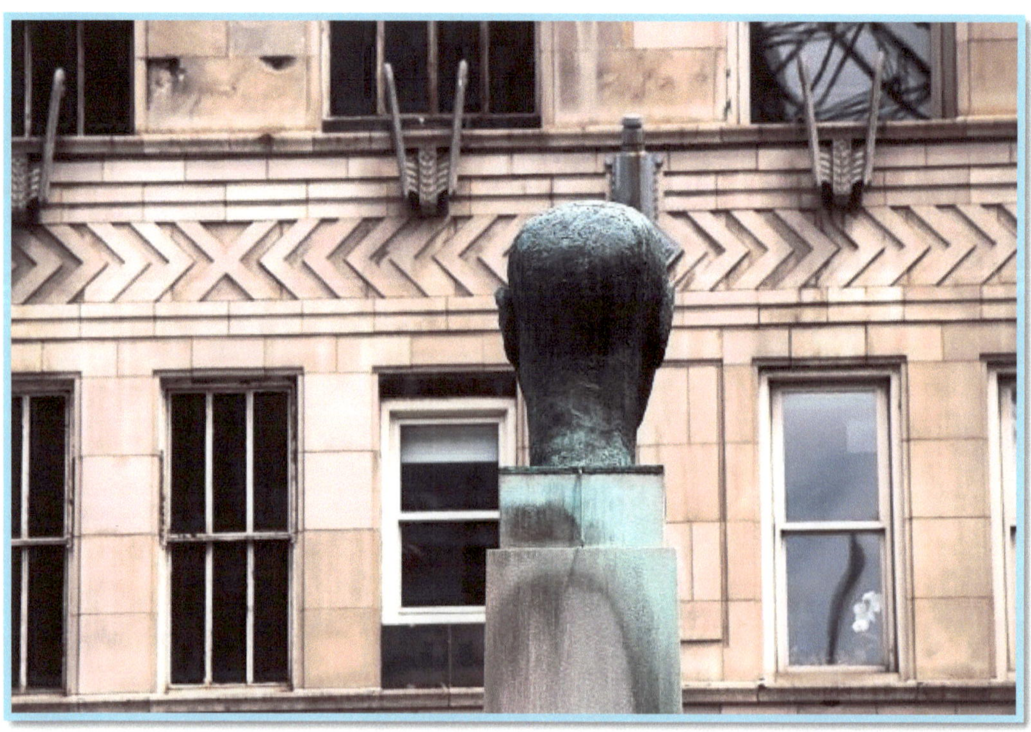

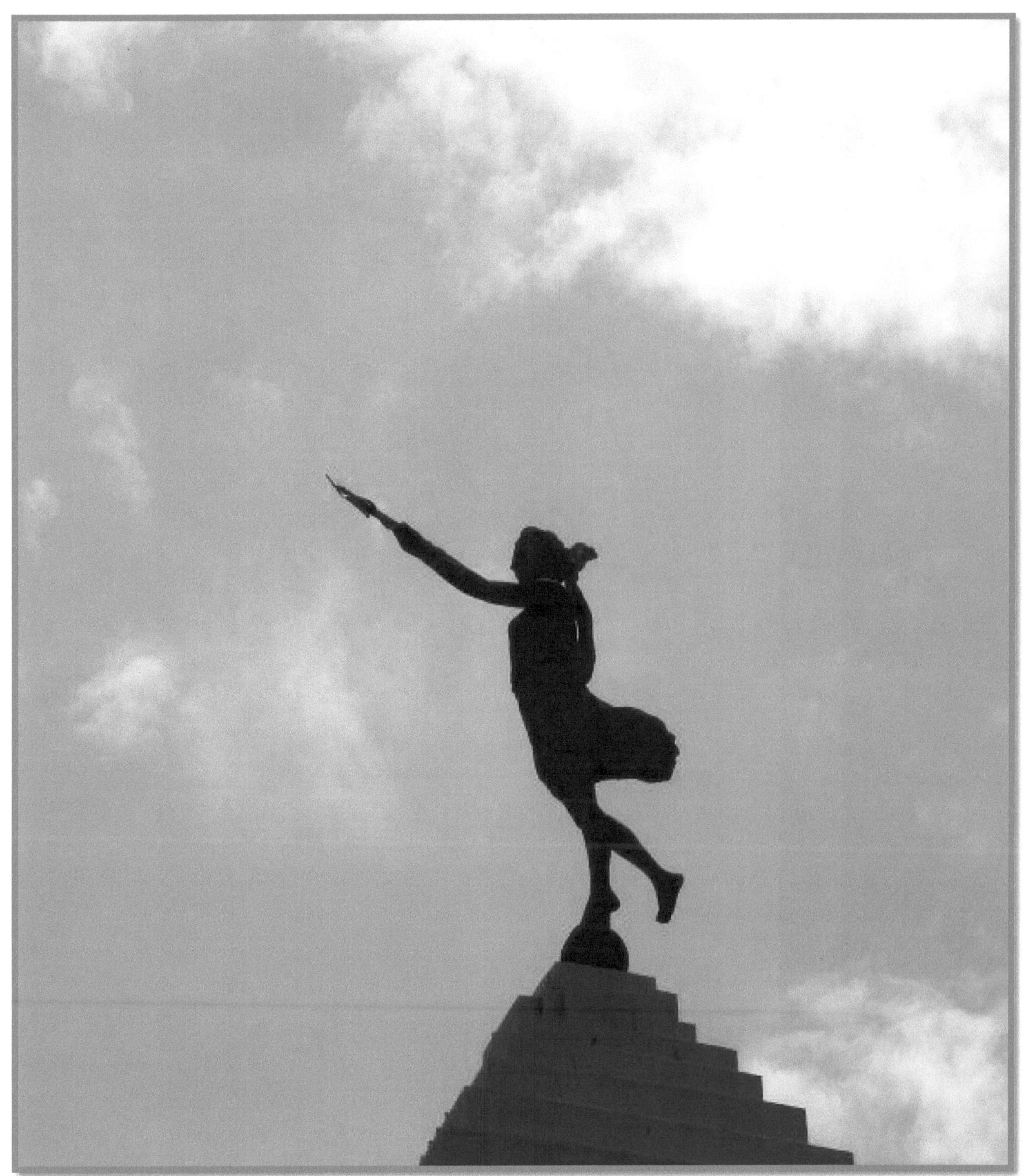

“The key to understanding any people is in its art: its writing, painting, sculpture.” **Louis L'Amour, Education of a Wandering Man**

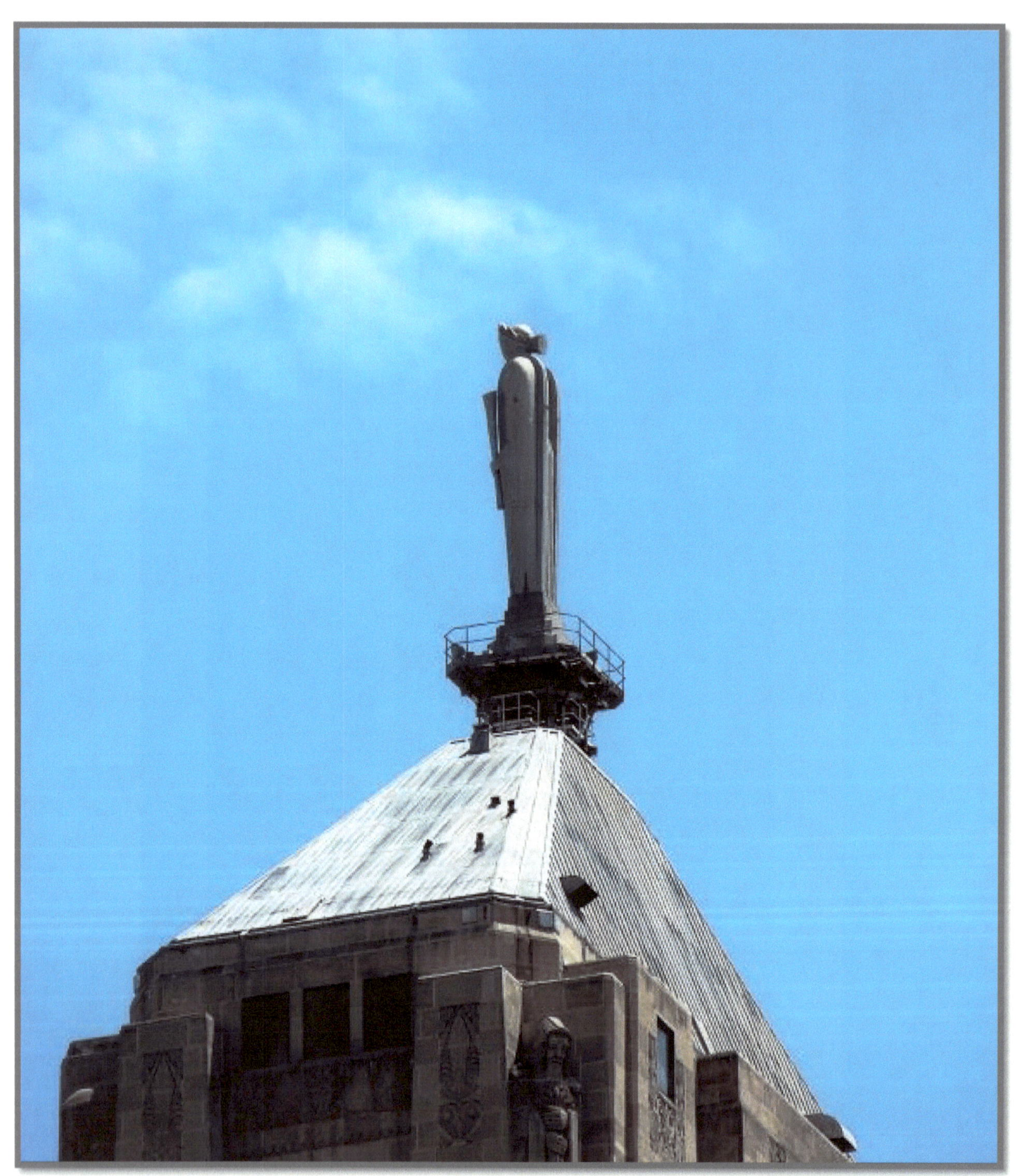

“Space is the breath of art.” **Frank Lloyd Wright**

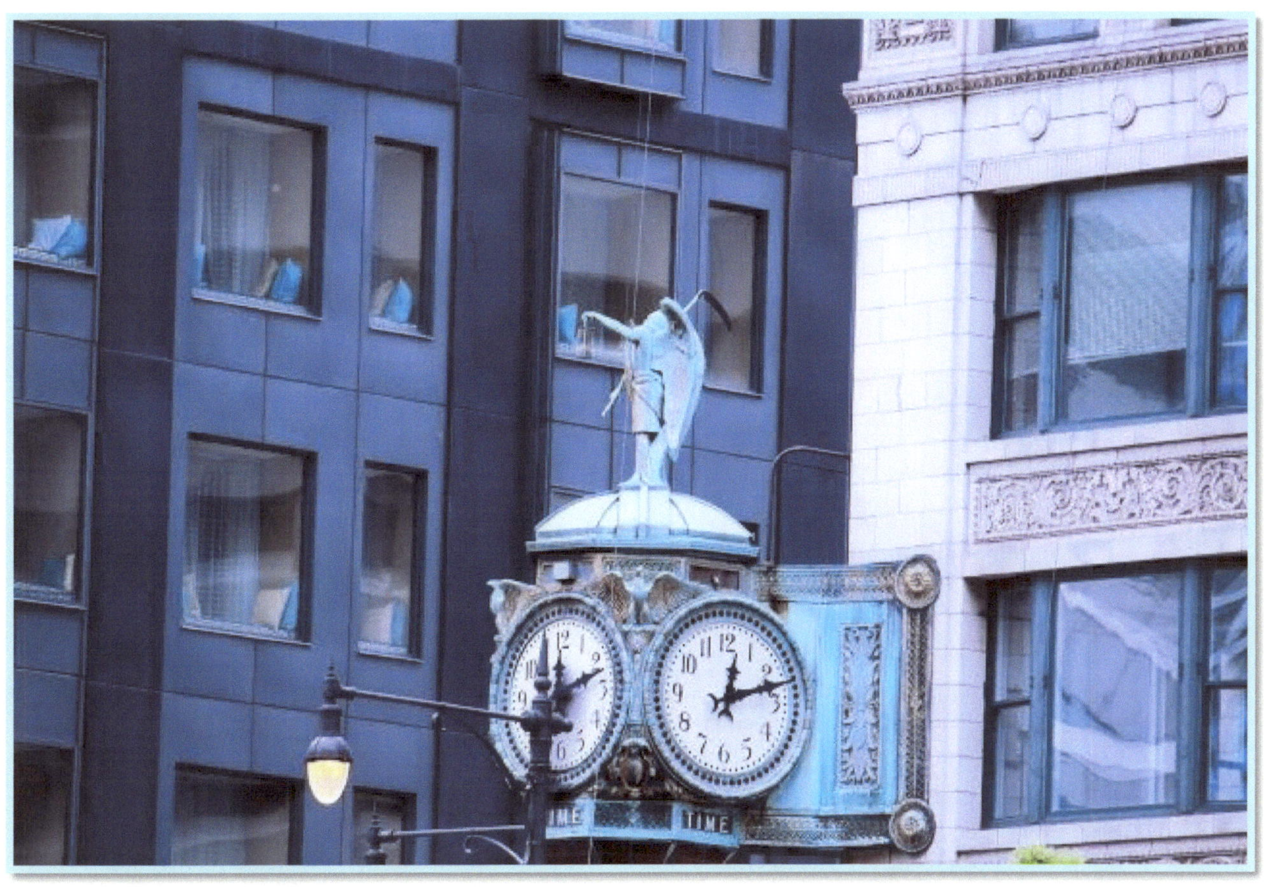

"In great cities, spaces as well as places are designed and built: walking, witnessing, being in public, are as much part of the design and purpose as is being inside to eat, sleep, make shoes or love or music. The word citizen has to do with cities, and the ideal city is organized around citizenship -- around participation in public life." **Rebecca Solnit, Wanderlust: A History of Walking**

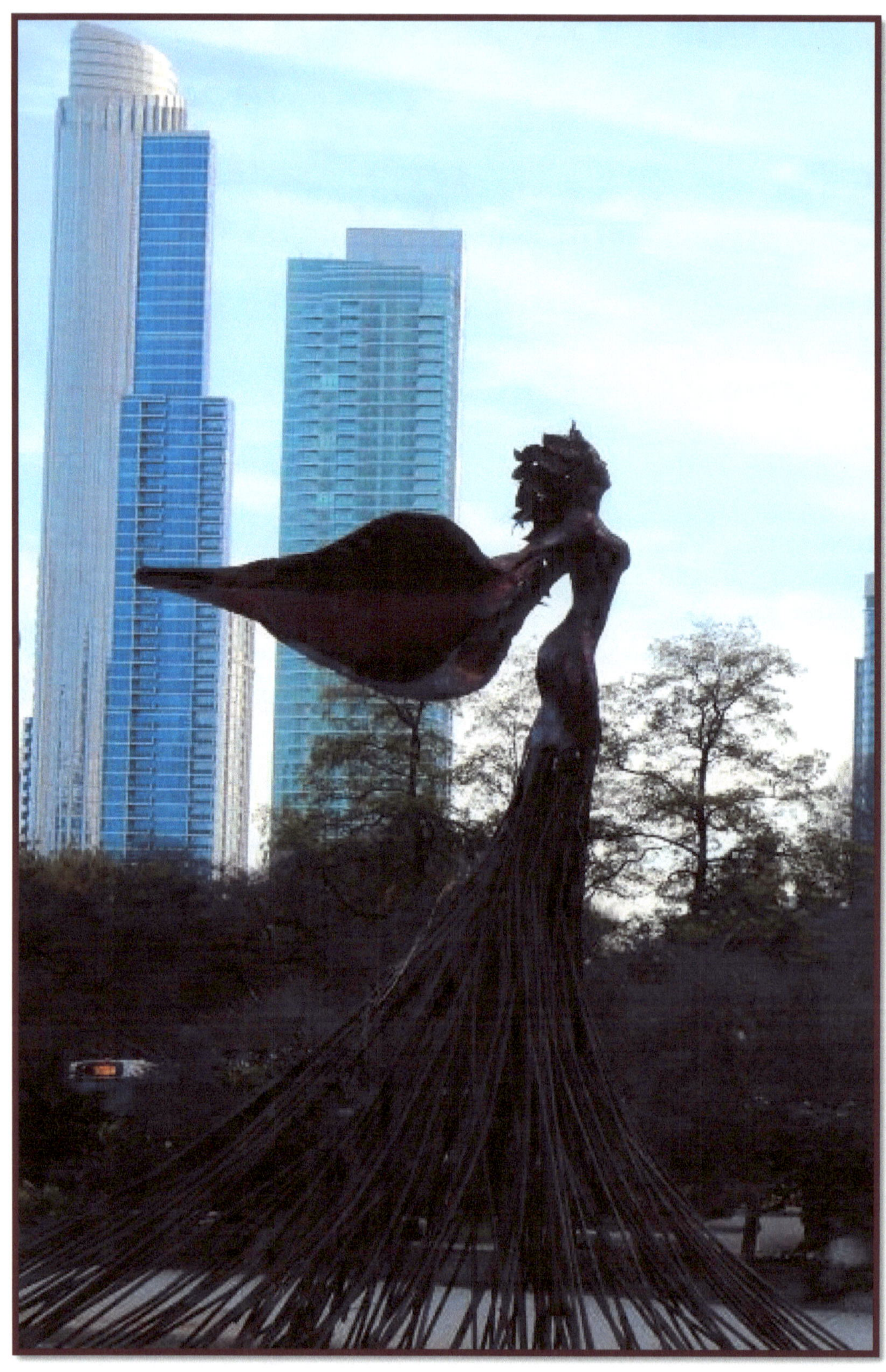

"I adore Chicago. It is the pulse of America." **Sarah Bernhardt**

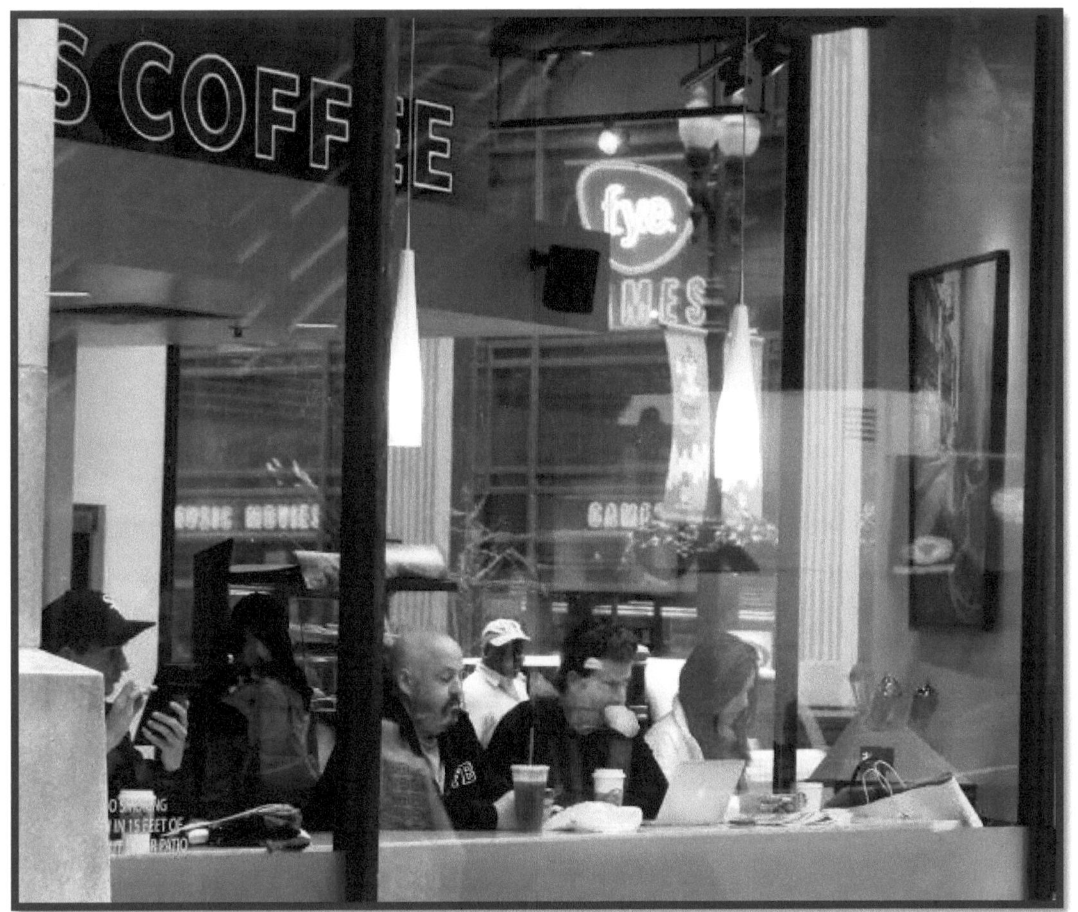

"Along the way I stopped into a coffee shop. All around me normal, everyday city types were going about their normal, everyday affairs. Lovers were whispering to each other, businessmen were poring over spread sheets, college kids were planning their next ski trip and discussing the new Police album. We could have been in any city in Japan. Transplant this coffee shop scene to Yokohama or Fukuoka and nothing would seem out of place. In spite of which -- or, rather, all the more because -- here I was, sitting in this coffee shop, drinking my coffee, feeling a desperate loneliness. I alone was the outsider. I had no place here. Of course, by the same token, I couldn't really say I belonged to Tokyo and its coffee shops. But I had never felt this loneliness there. I could drink my coffee, read my book, pass the time of day without any special thought, all because I was part of the regular scenery. Here I had no ties to anyone. Fact is, I'd come to reclaim myself." **Haruki Murakami, Dance Dance Dance**

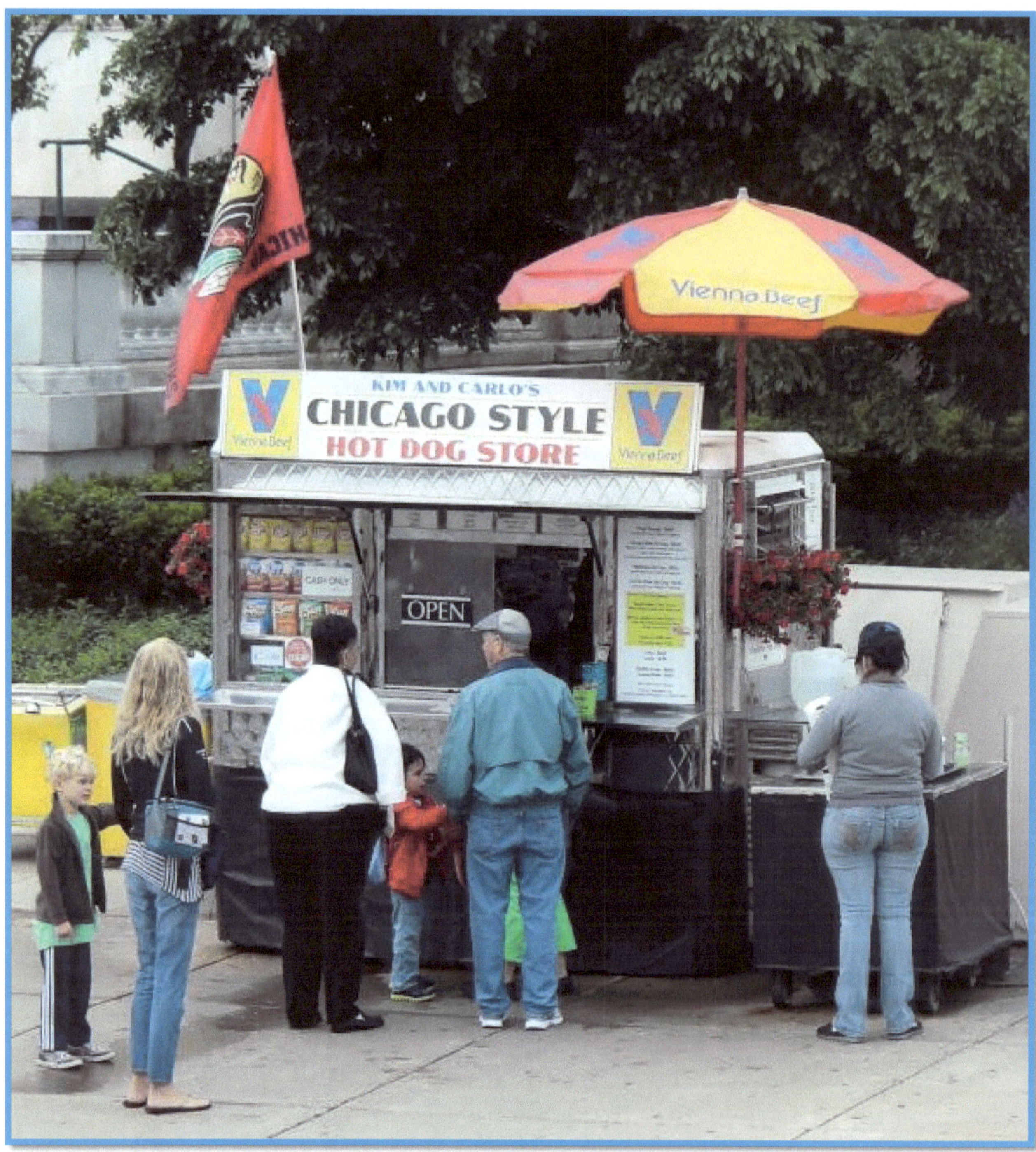

"Chicago is one city. We shall work as one people for our common good and our common goals." **Harold Washington**

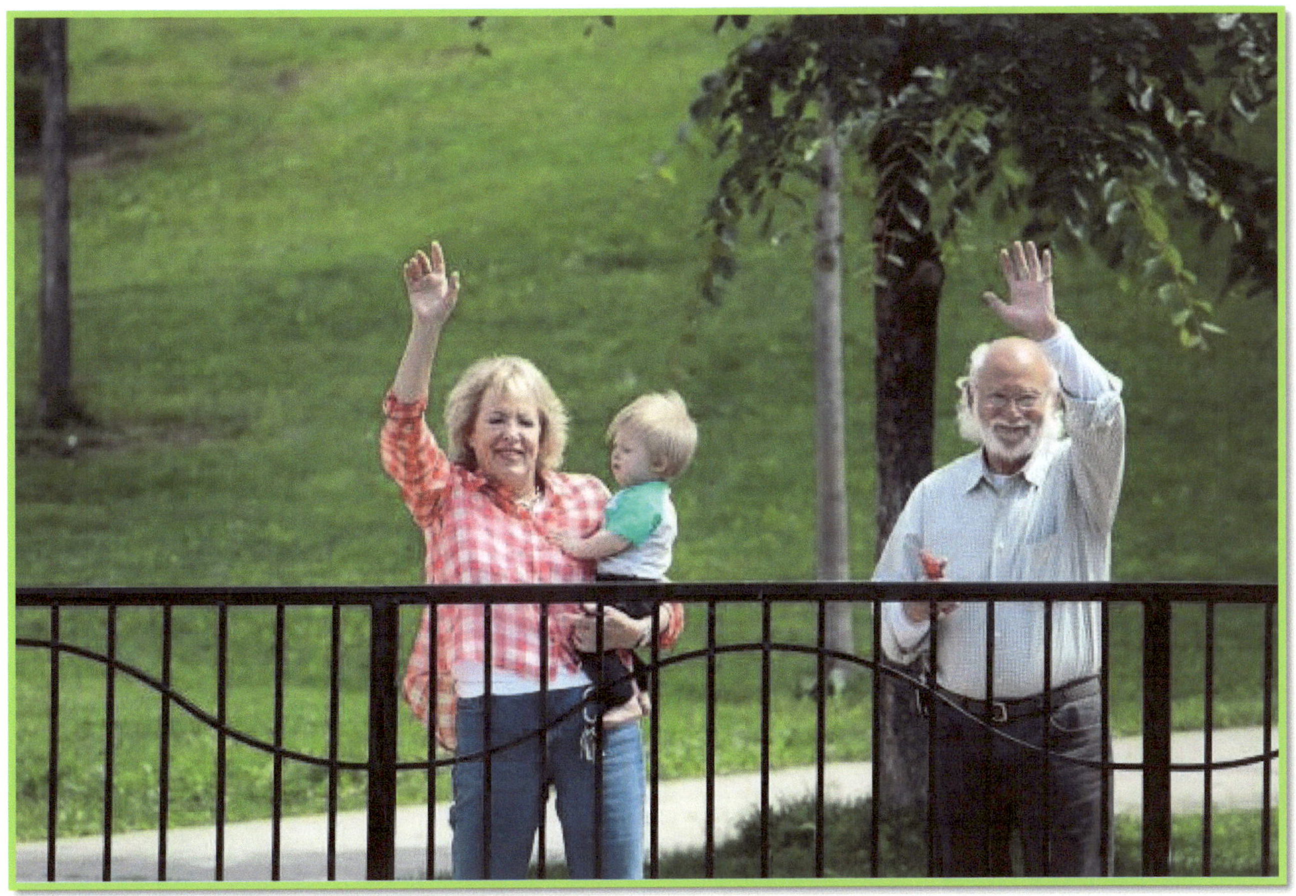

"I came to discover that Chicago is that most American of American cities, but one where citizens from more than 130 nations inhabit a rich tapestry of distinctive neighborhoods. Each one of those neighborhoods -- from Greektown to the Ukrainian Village; from Devon to Pilsen to Washington Park -- has its own unique character, its own unique history, its songs, its language. But each is also part of our city -- one city -- a city where I finally found a home." **Barack Obama**

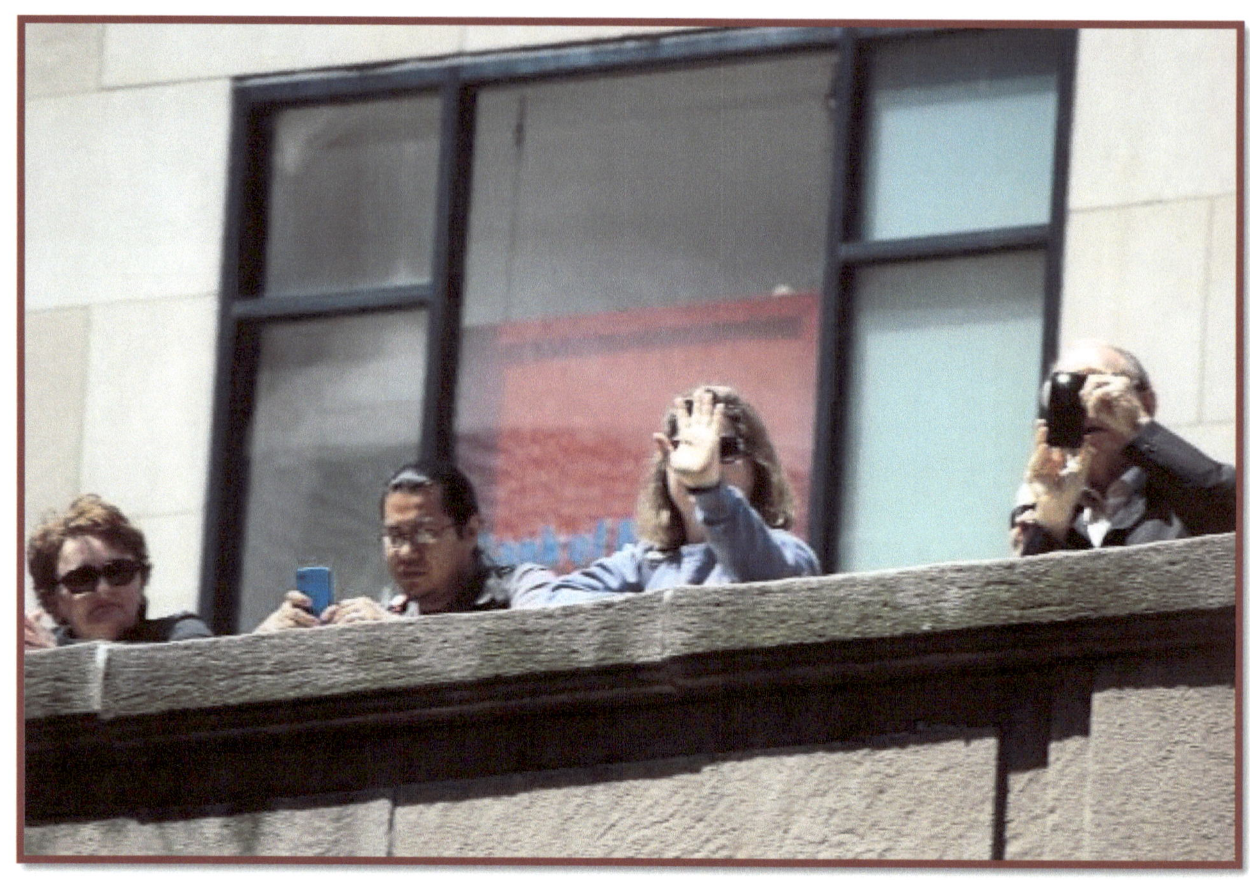

This is my kind of town, Chicago is
My kind of town, Chicago is
My kind of people too
People who, smile at you

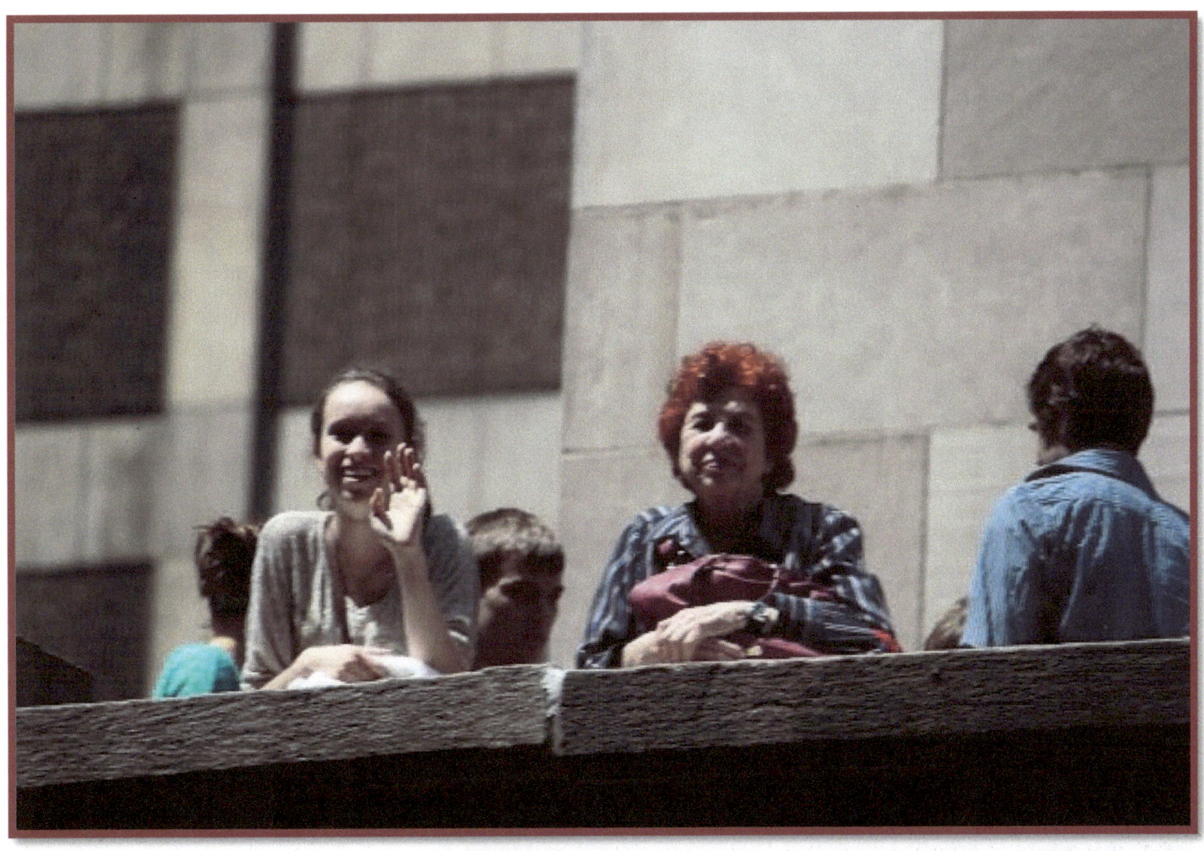

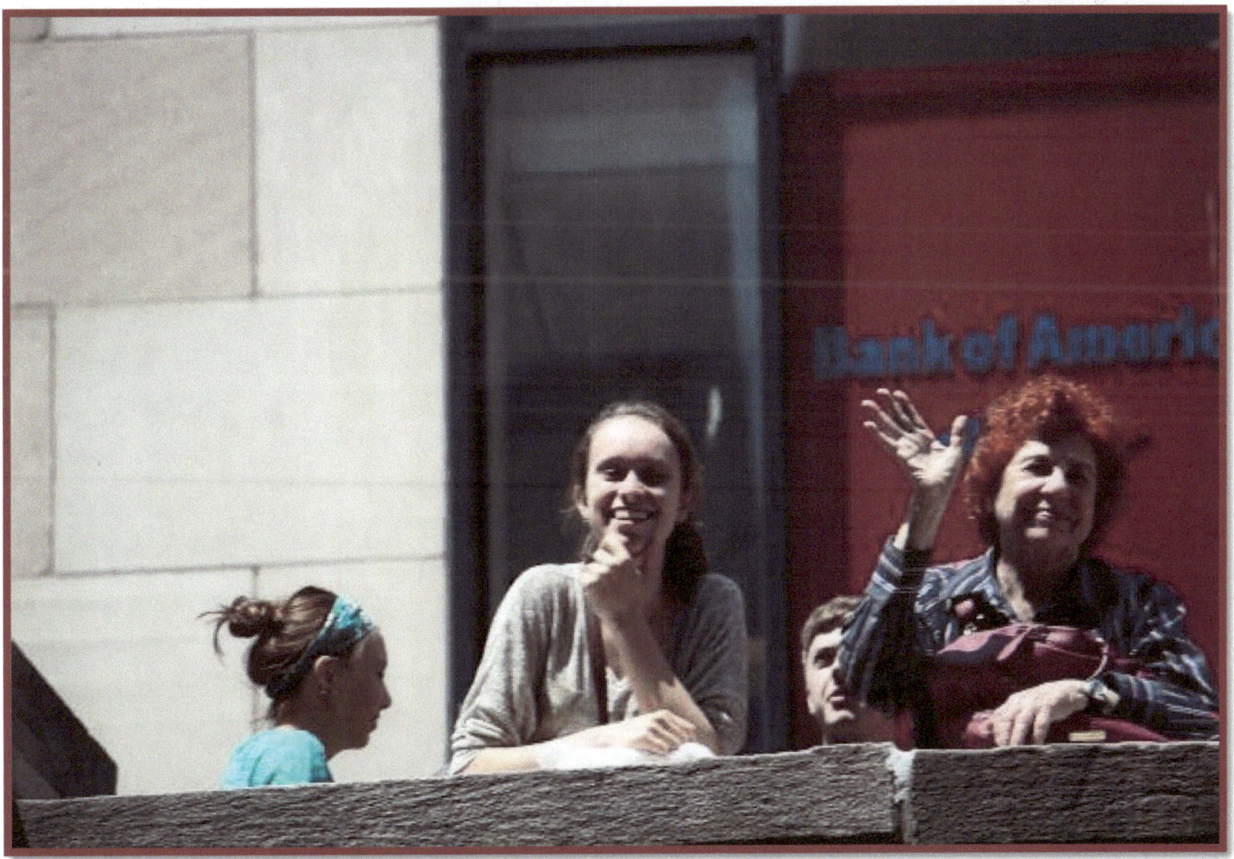

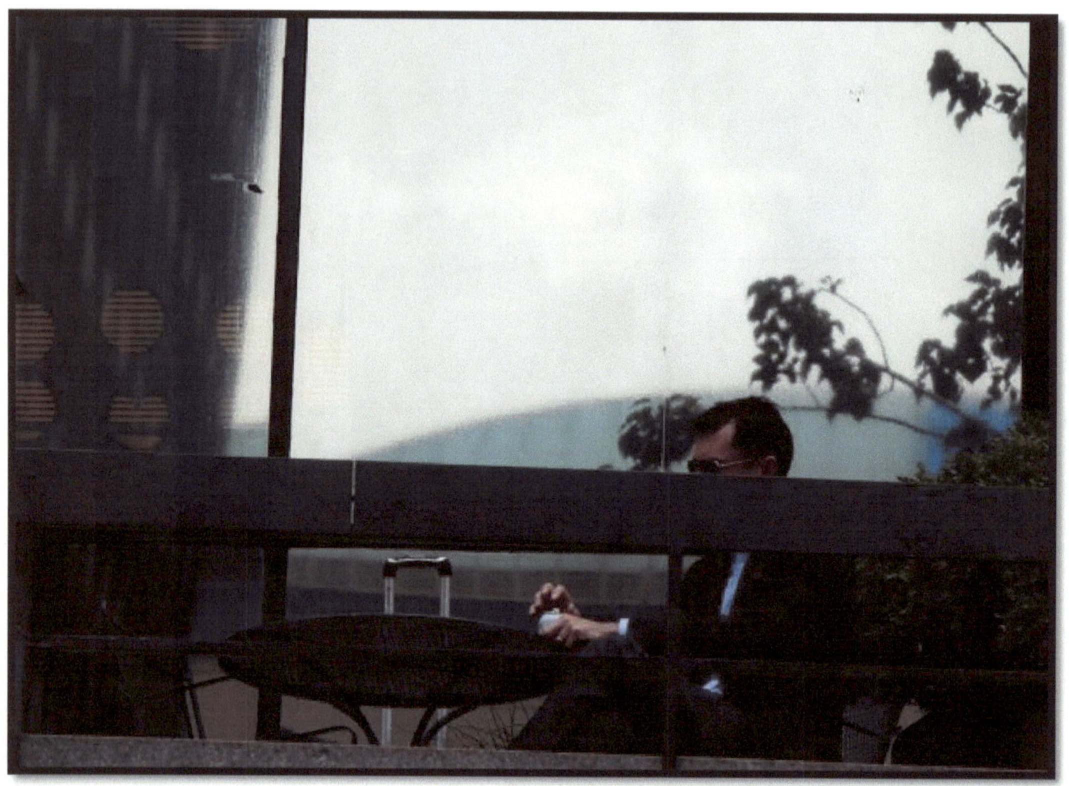

"I loved the city. We were anonymous, and even then I had the sense that cities were yielding; that they moved over and made room."
Sheridan Hay, The Secret of Lost Things

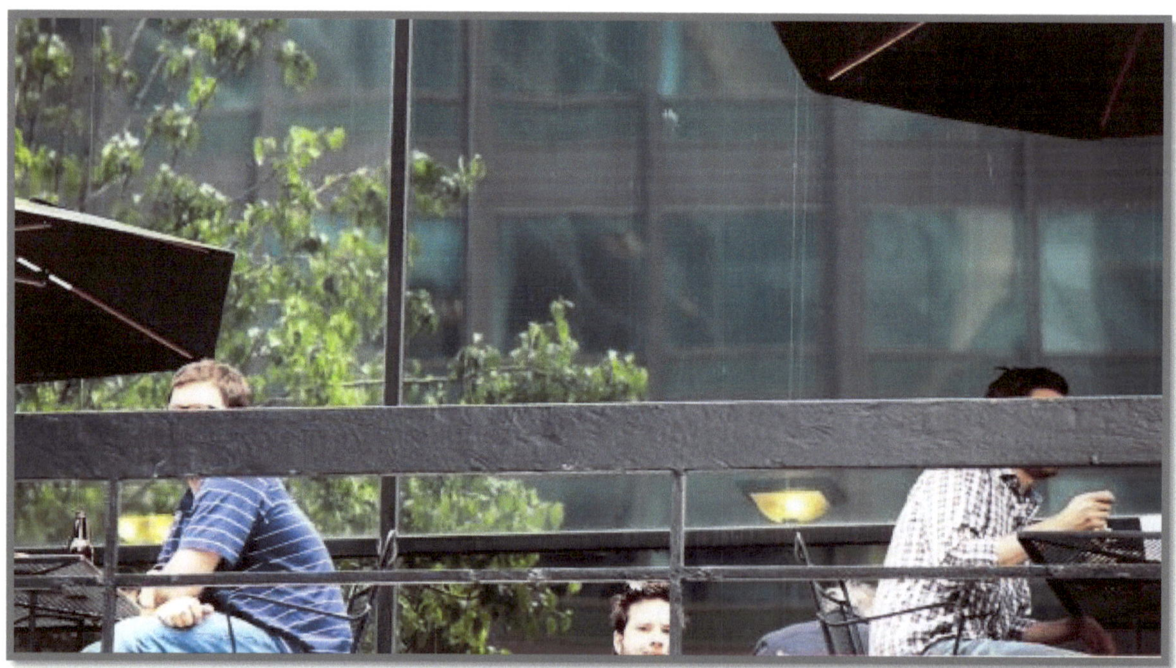

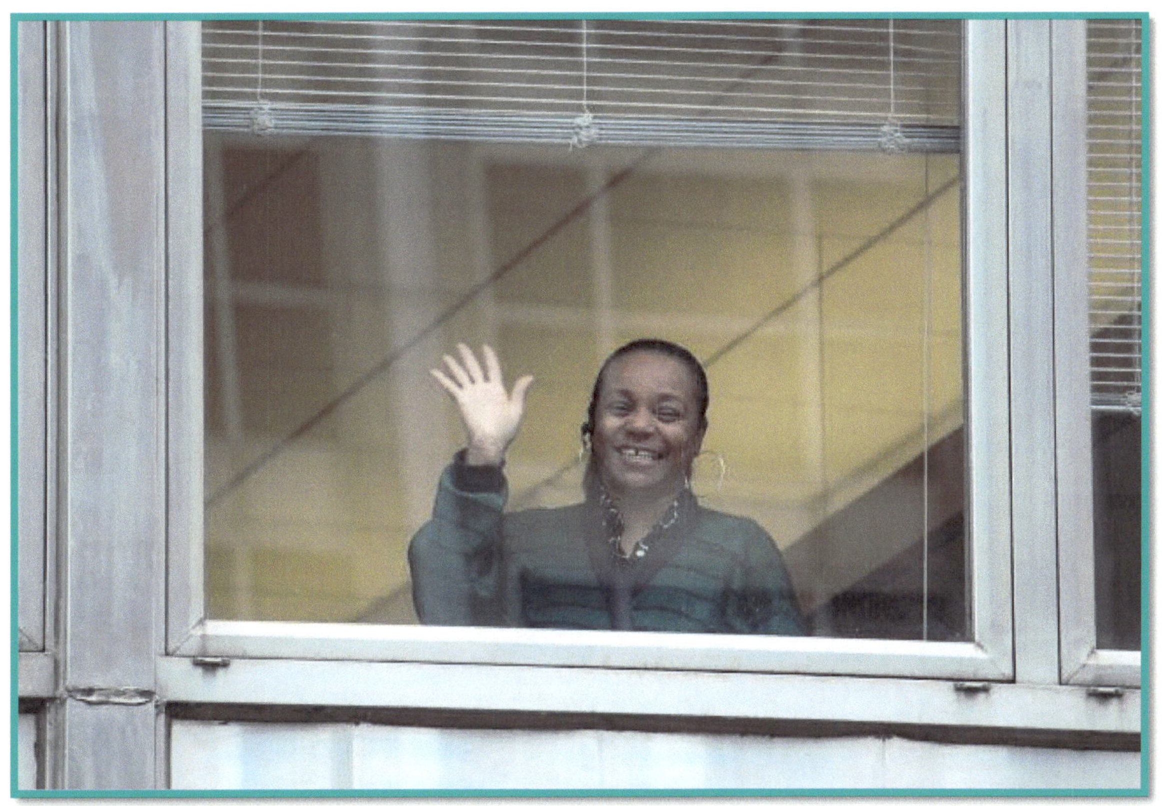

"This City is what it is because our citizens are what they are." **Plato**

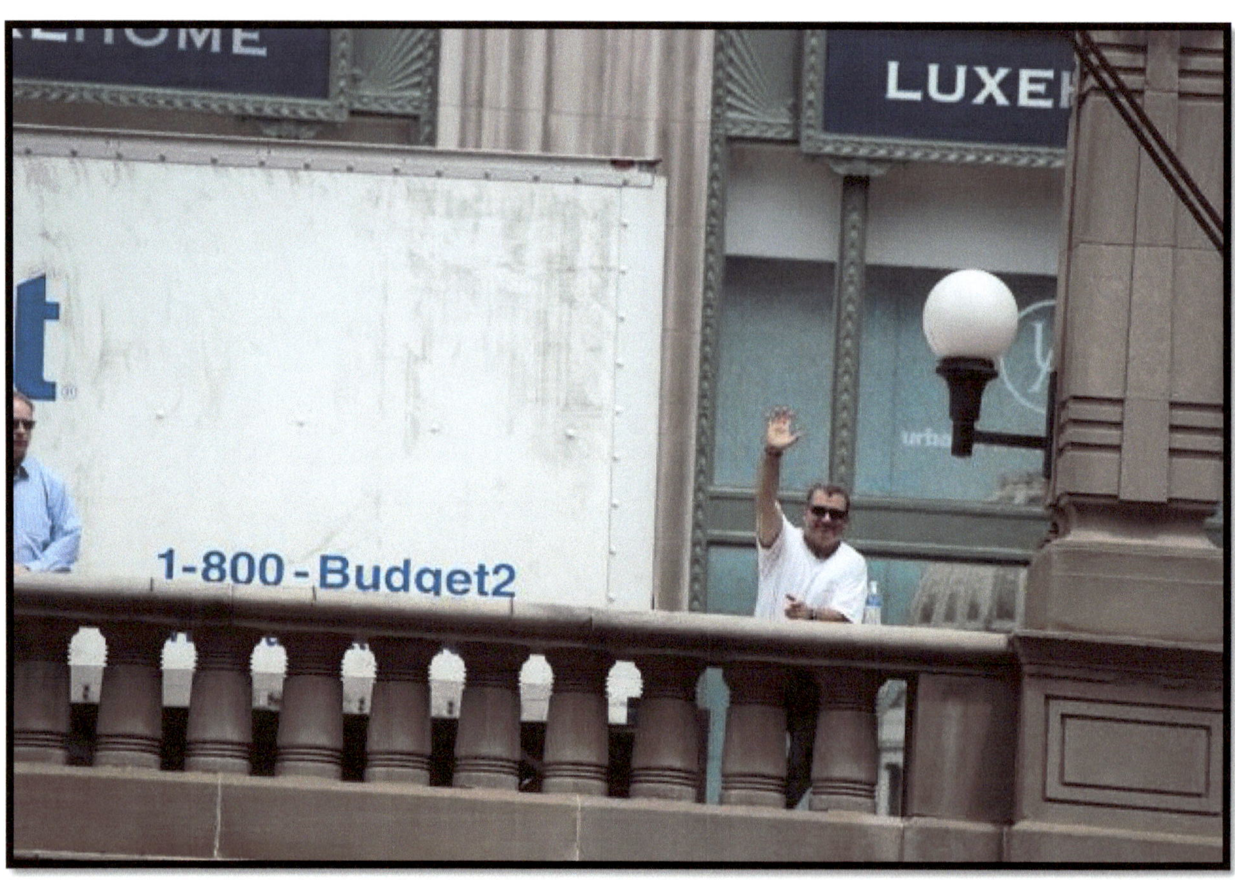

"It's a 106 miles to Chicago, we've got a full tank of gas, half a pack of cigarettes; it's dark and we're wearing sun glasses. Hit it!" ***The Blues Brothers***

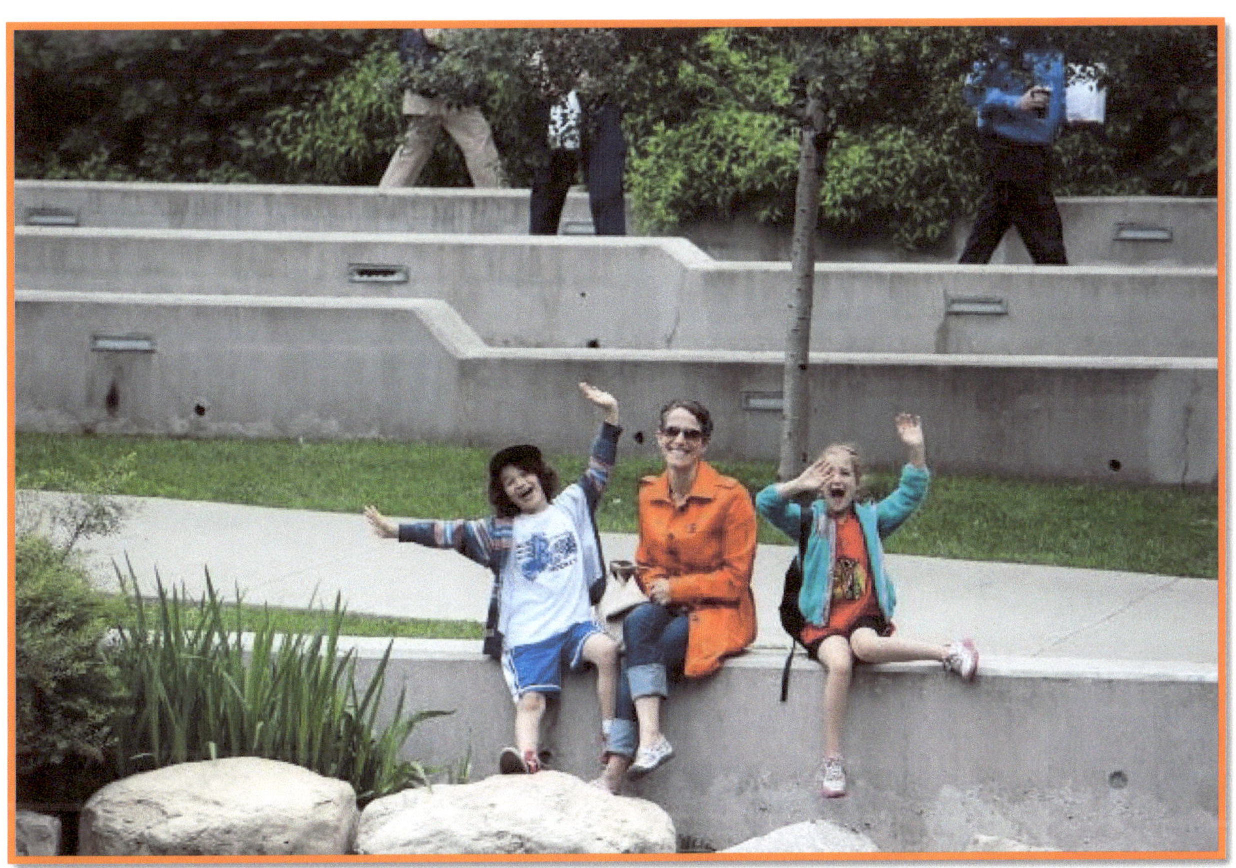

"Perhaps the most typically American place in America." **James Bryce, 1888**

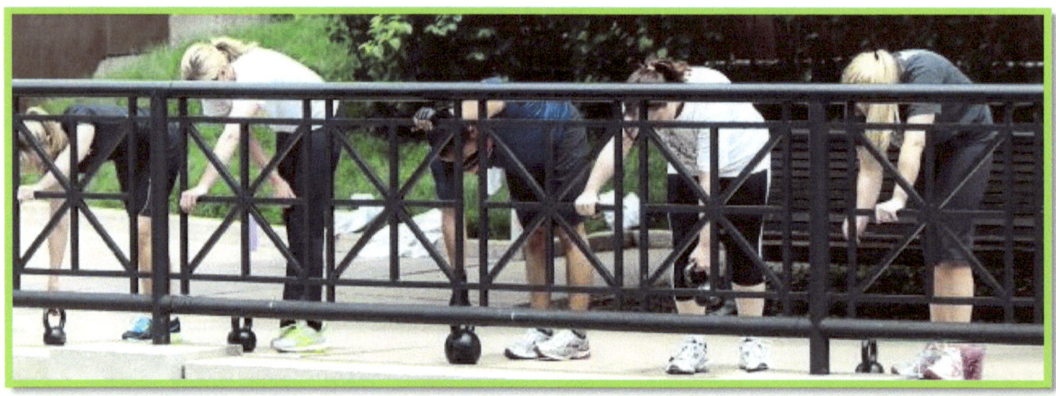

"Chicago, Chicago, that toddlin' town." **Fred Fisher "Chicago,"**

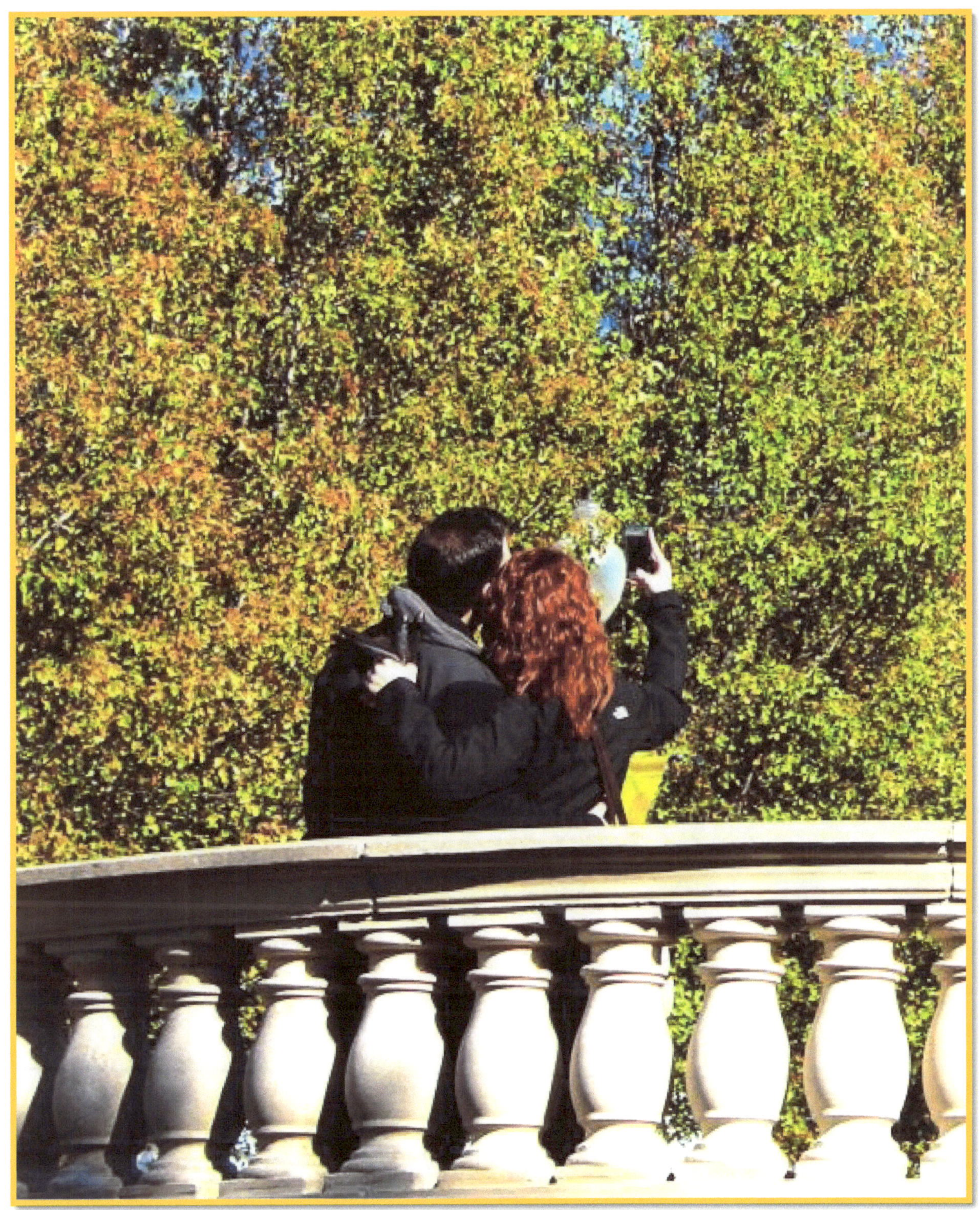

Think how different human societies would be if they were based on love rather than justice. But no such societies have ever existed on earth.
Mortimer Adler, Chicagoan

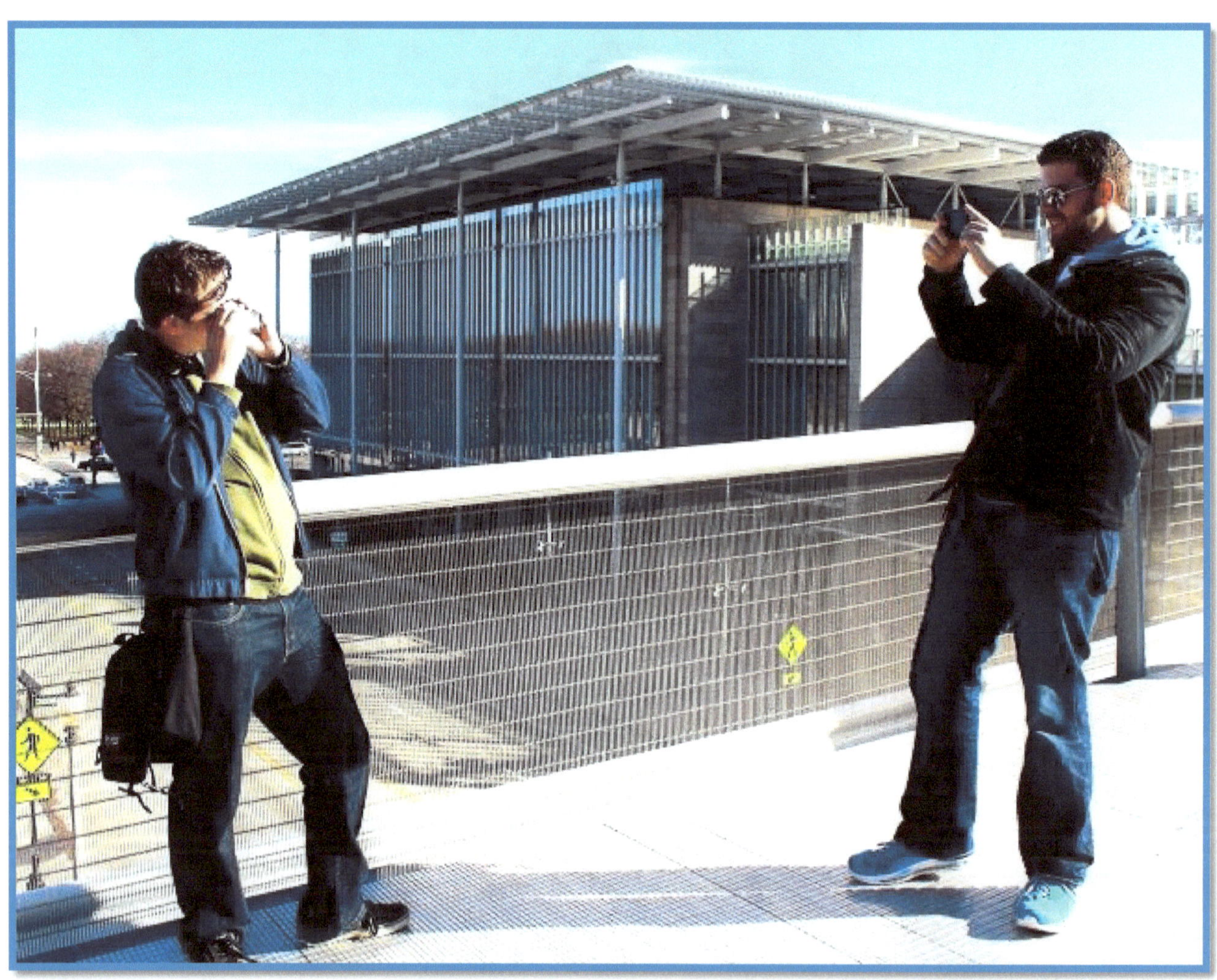

"It's one of the greatest cities on the planet. My heart beats differently when I'm in Chicago. It slows down and I feel more at ease." **Jeremy Piven**

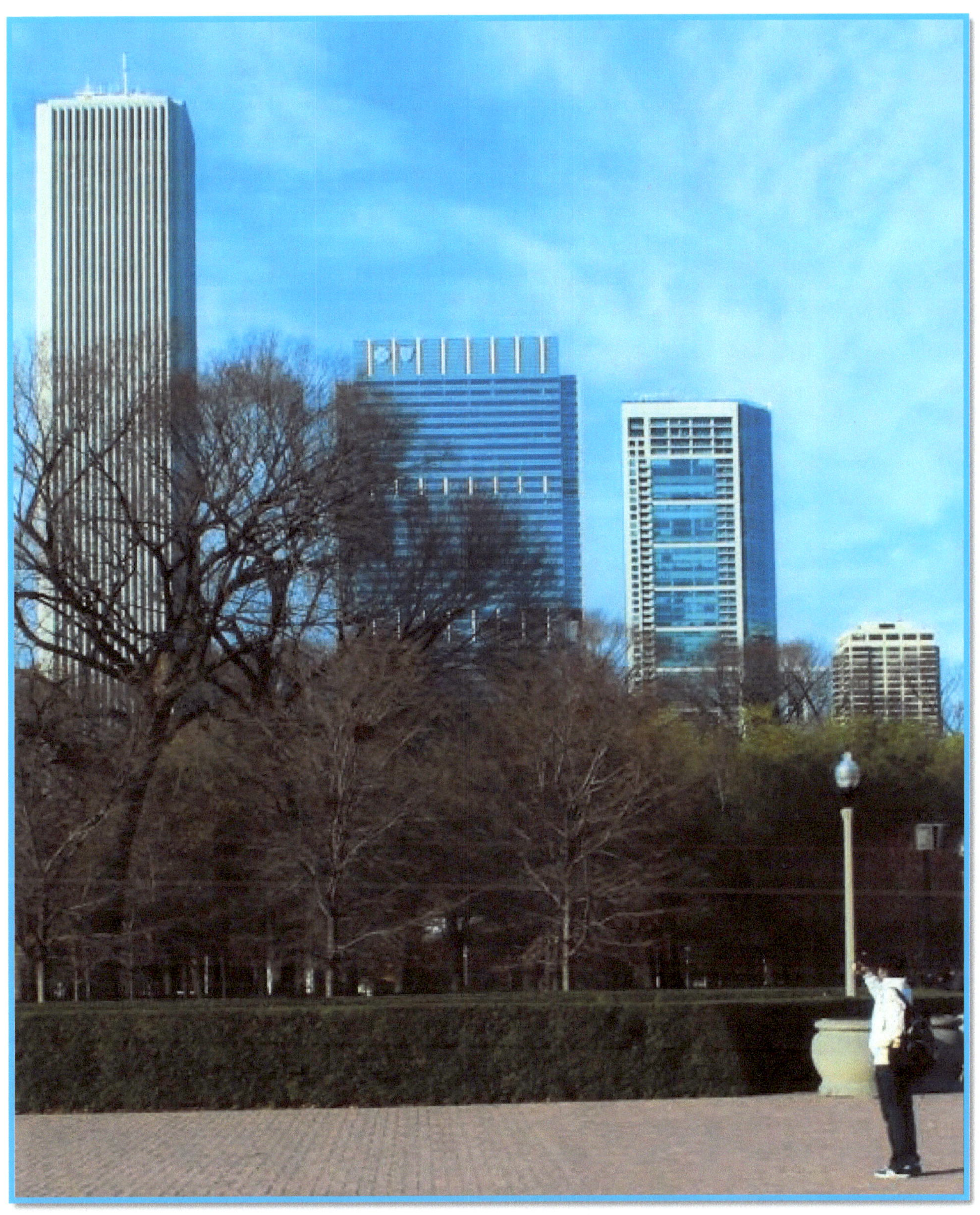

“Gigantic, willful, young, Chicago sitteth at the northwest gates."
William Vaughn Moody "An Ode in Time of Hesitation," 1901

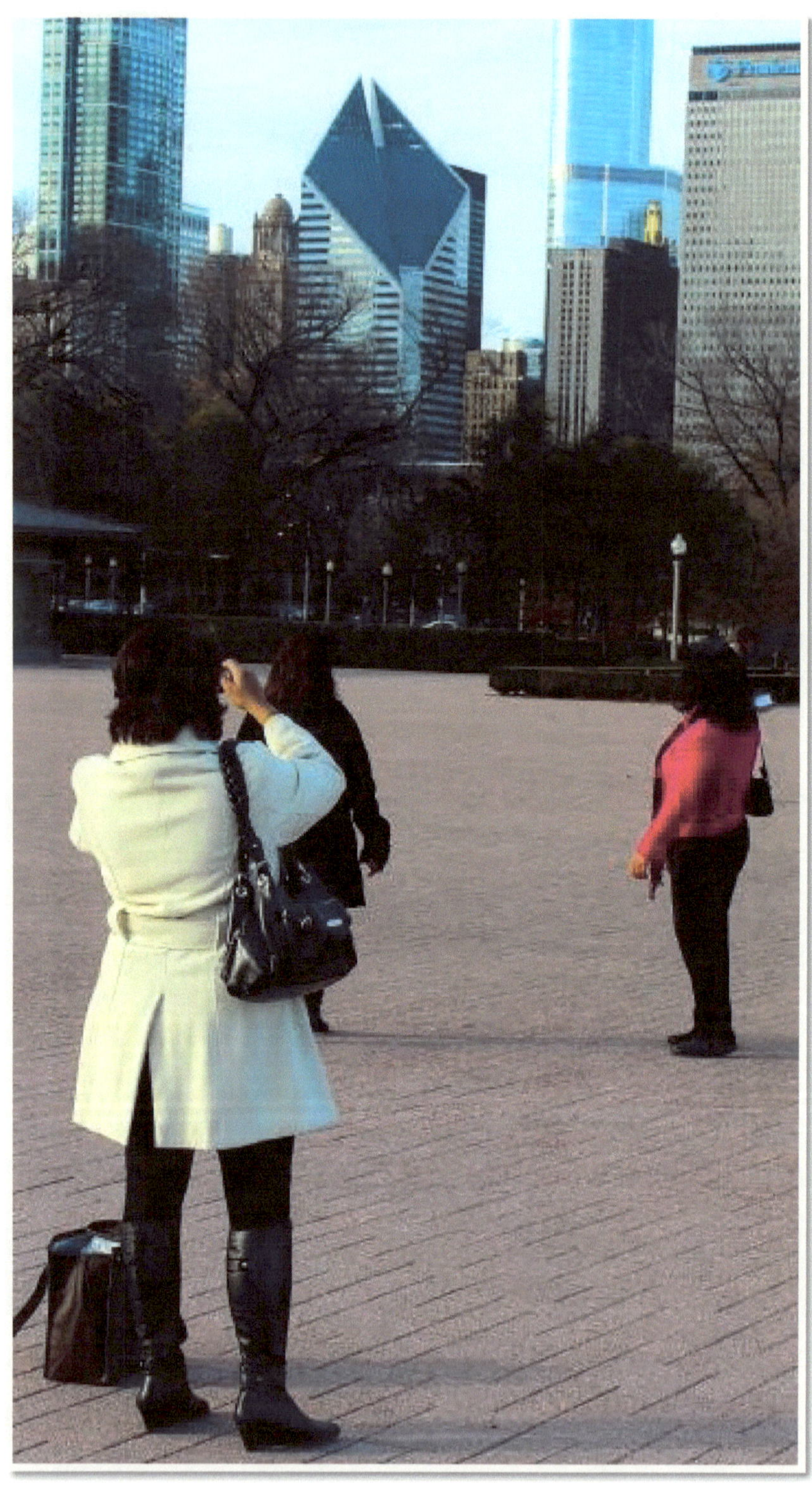

"You'd never think of taking a cab if you had to walk a mile down Chicago's Michigan Avenue." **Helmut Jahn**

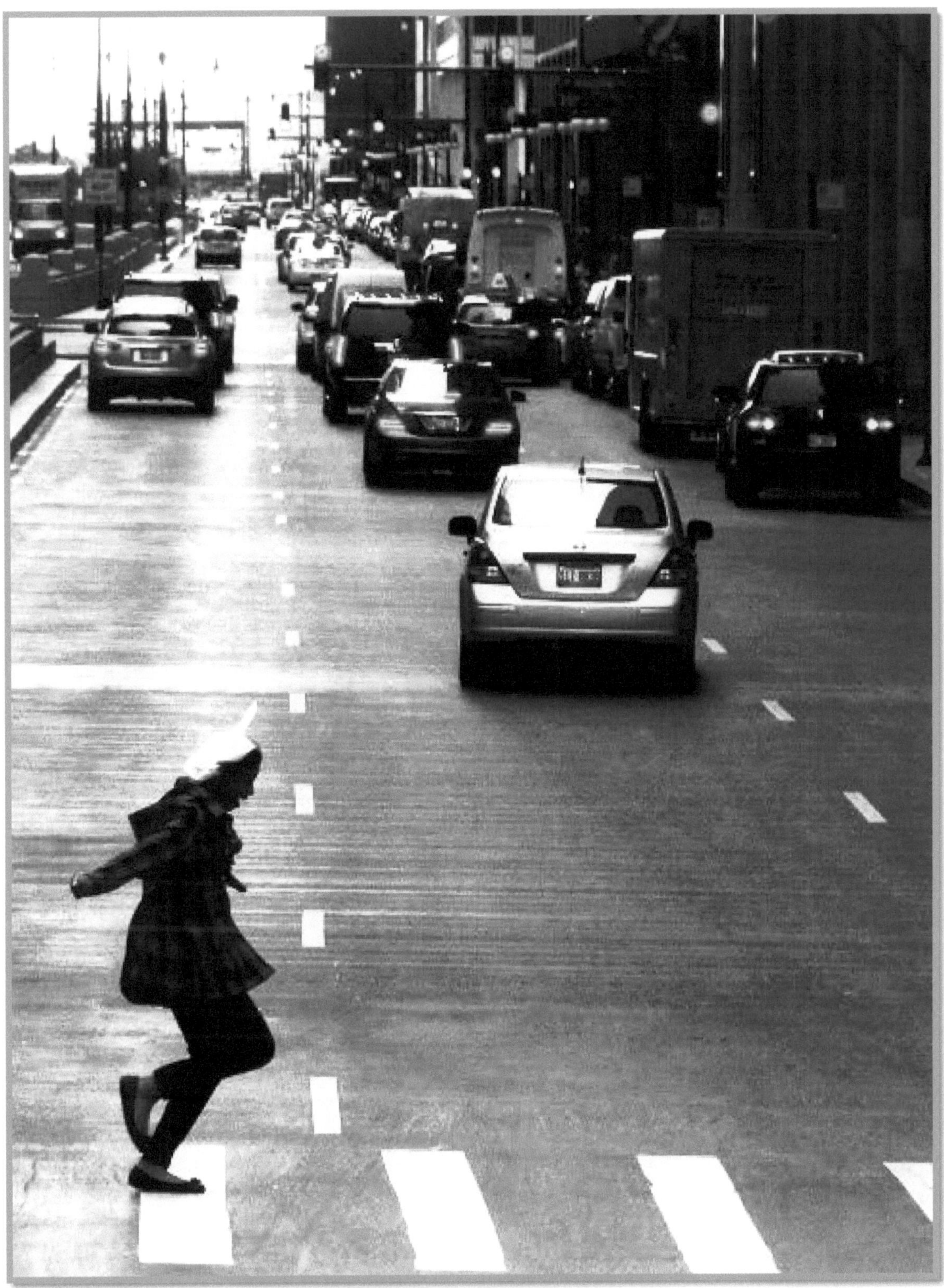

The search for human freedom can never be complete without freedom for women. **Betty Ford, Chicagoan**

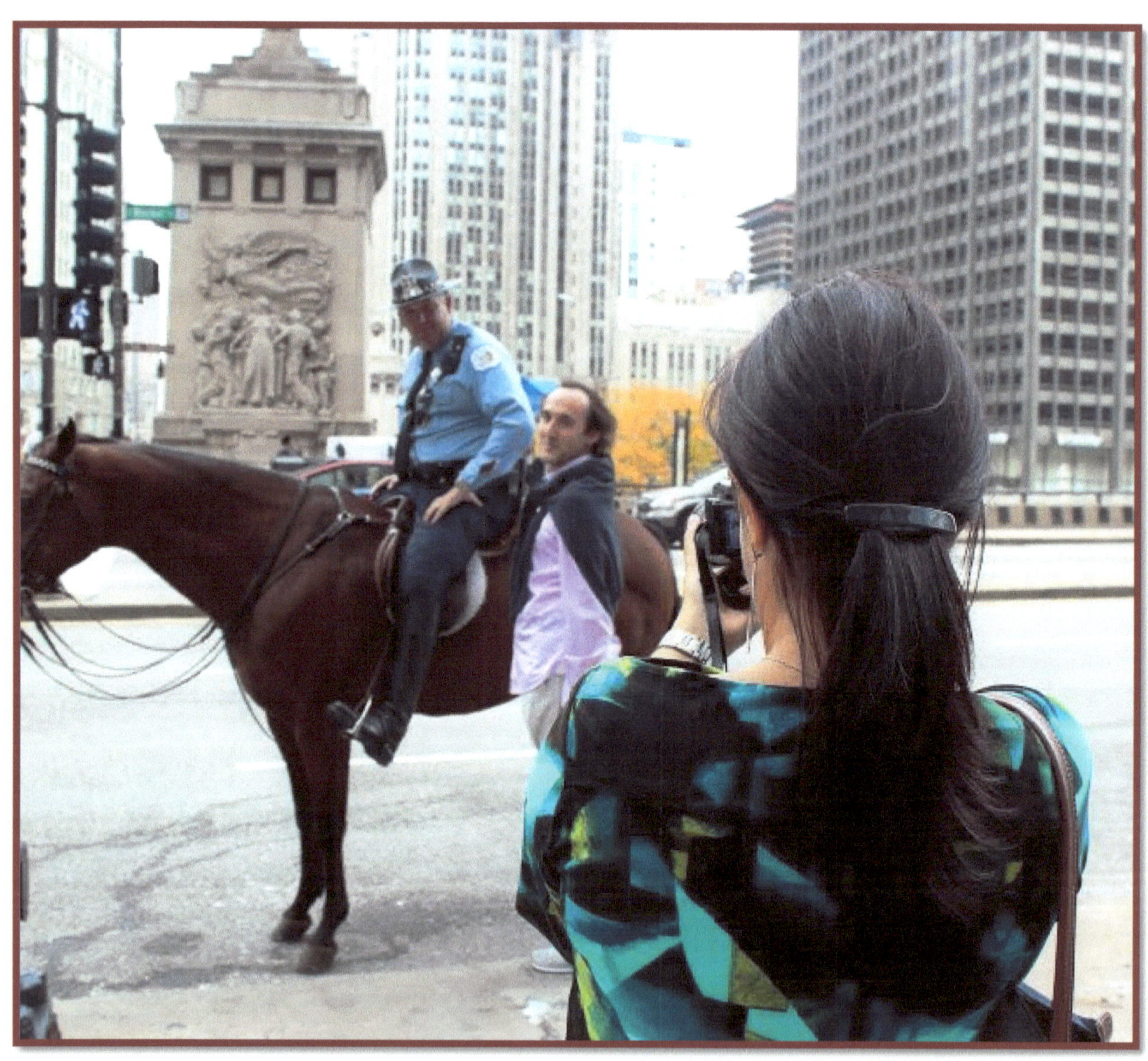

Dumped in the sea or fixed in a desert,
who would care for the building or speak its name
or ask a policeman the way to it?
Skyscraper*, Carl Sandburg, *Chicago Poems.

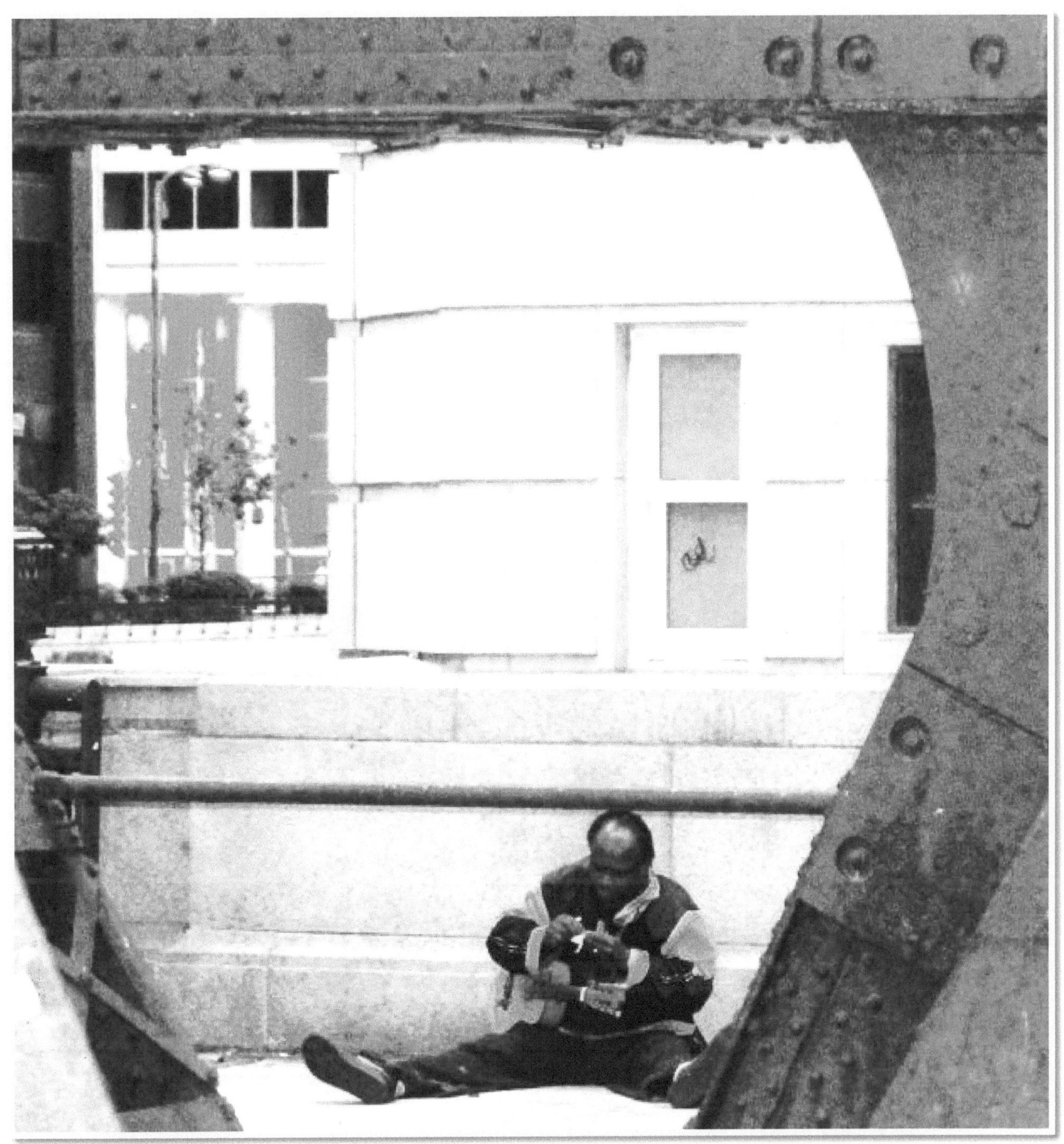

"As long as the world shall last there will be wrongs, and if no man objected and no man rebelled, those wrongs would last forever."
Clarence Darrow, Chicagoan

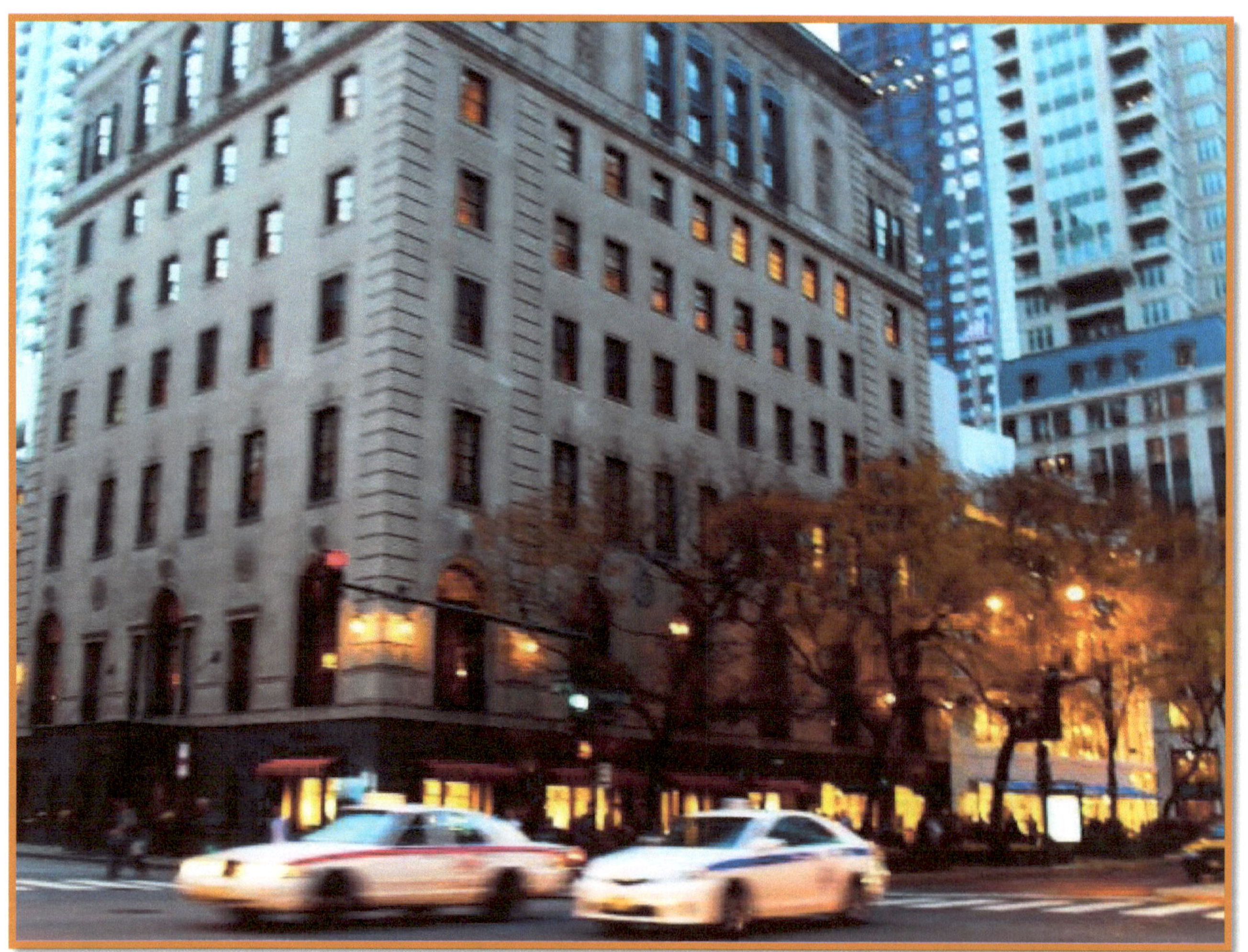

"After that, I started going downtown and doing a lot of theater shows in Chicago. When you go downtown there, it's like you're in New York, it's like going to Broadway" **Kel Mitchell**

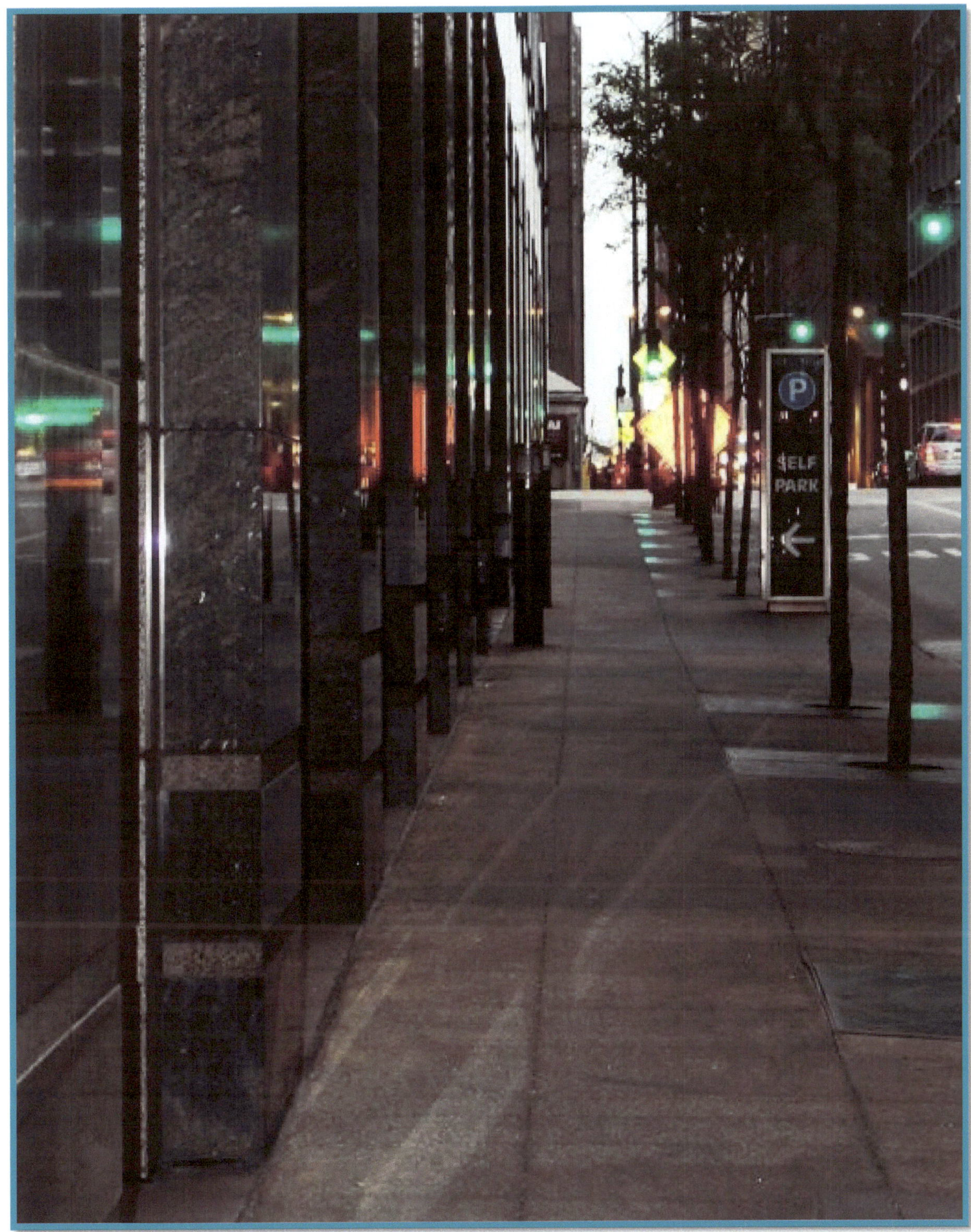
P
SELF
PARK

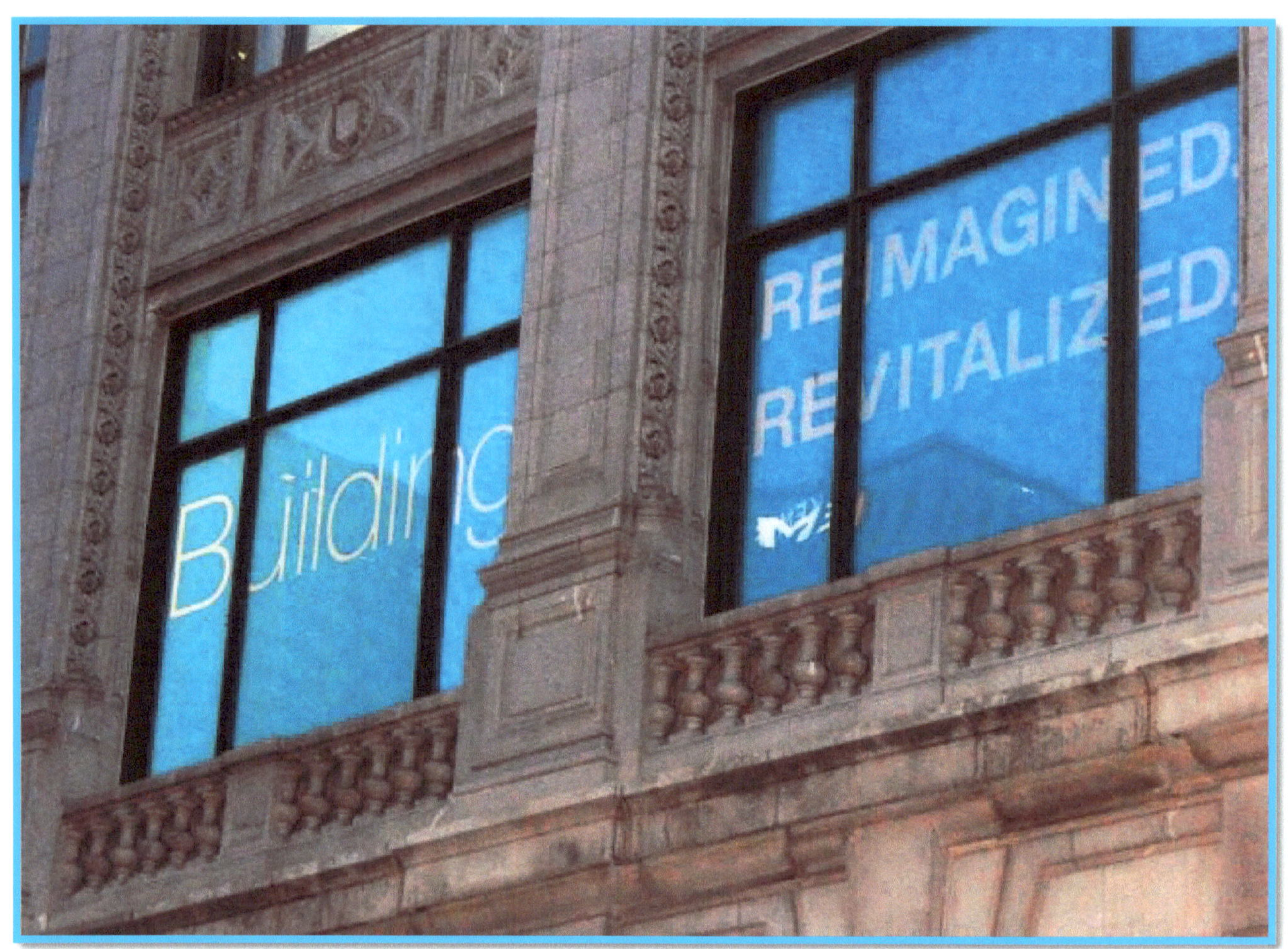

"... Chicago divided your heart. Leaving you loving the joint for keeps. Yet knowing it never can love you." — **Nelson Algren, Chicago: *City on the Make***

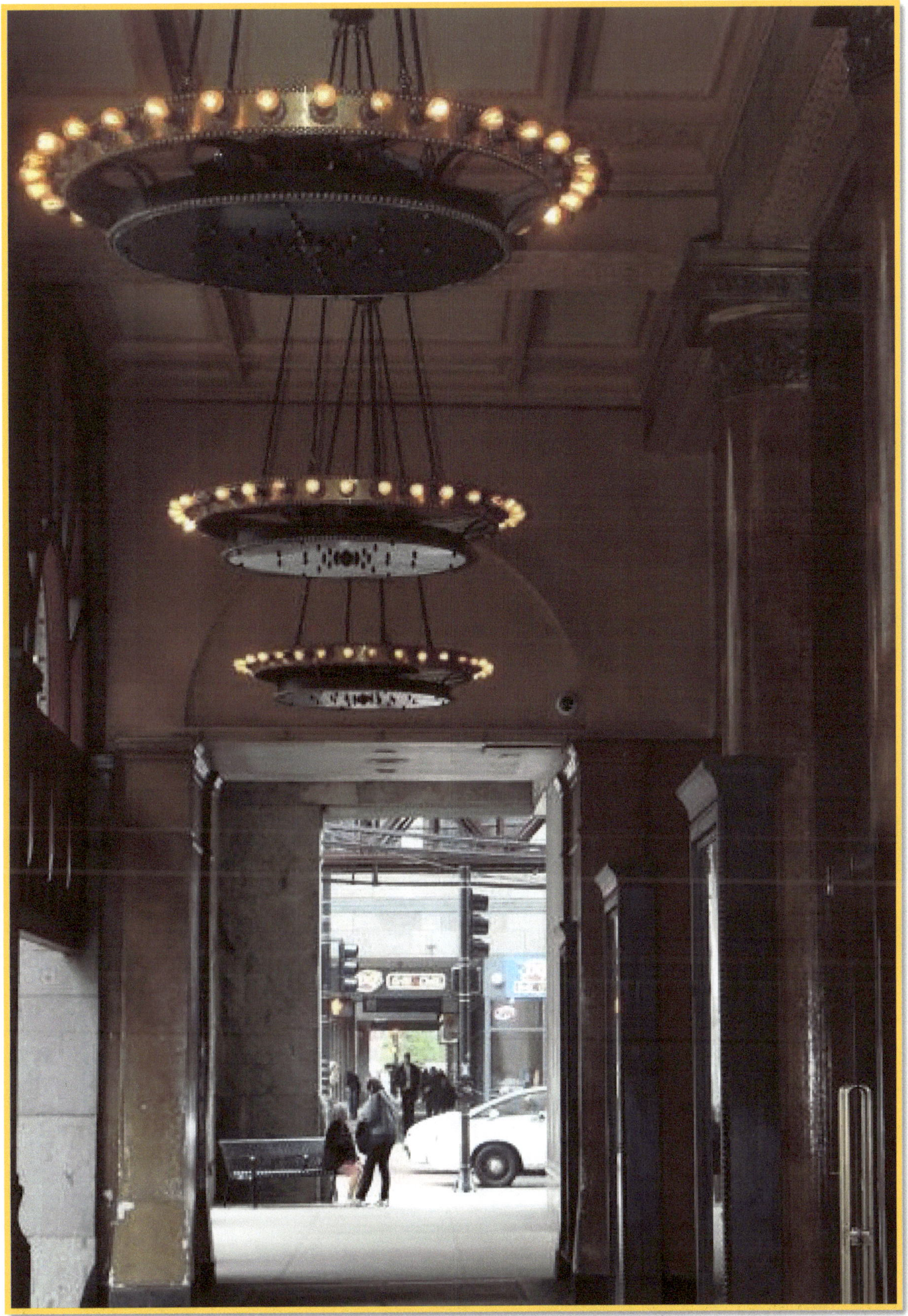

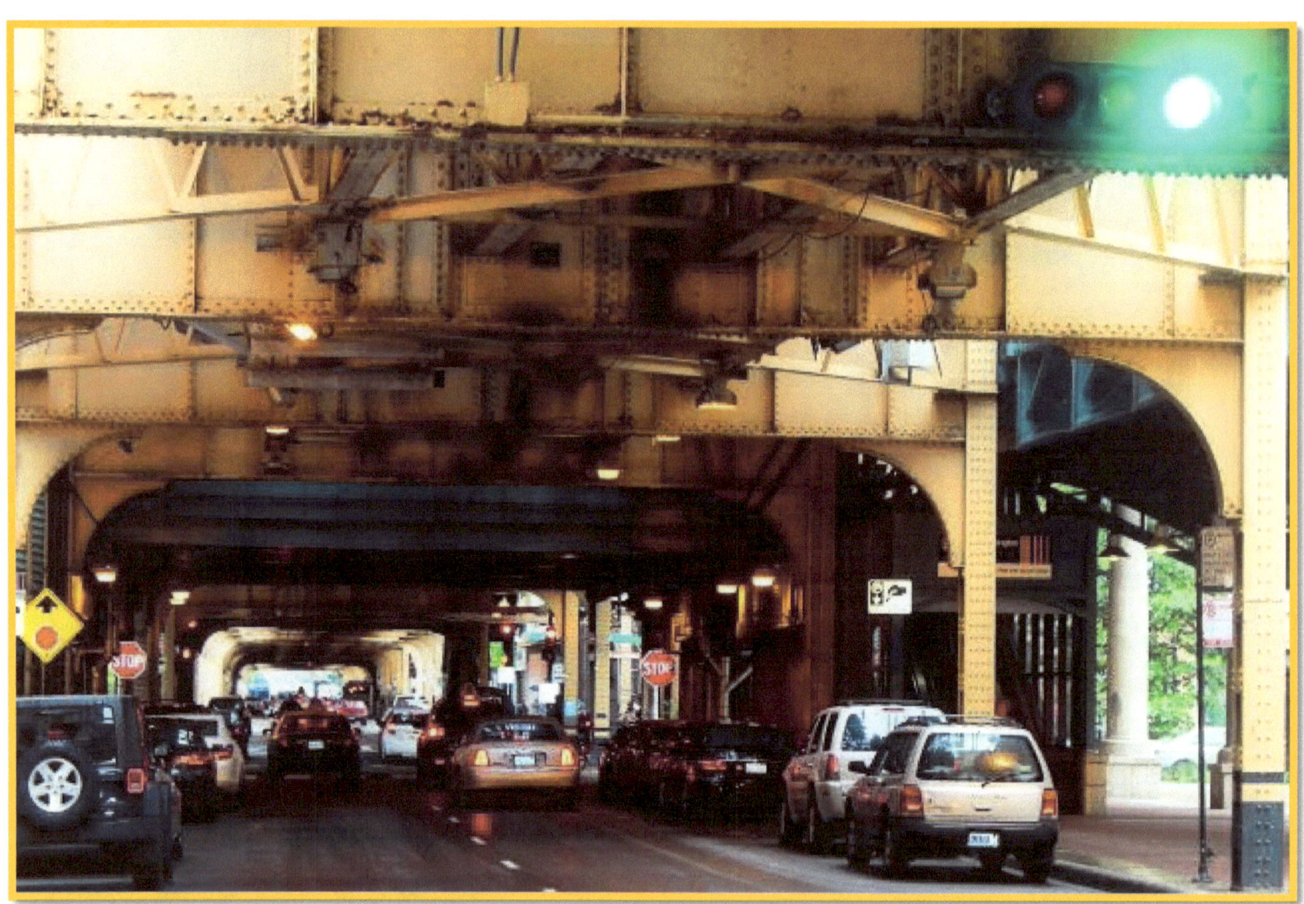

"I'm always going to get more of a charge playing Chicago than I will Duluth or some place like that. Just because of the history and the people there are way more knowledgeable than a lot of other cities. It's an amazing music scene with some great bands and great musicians." **Matt Cameron**

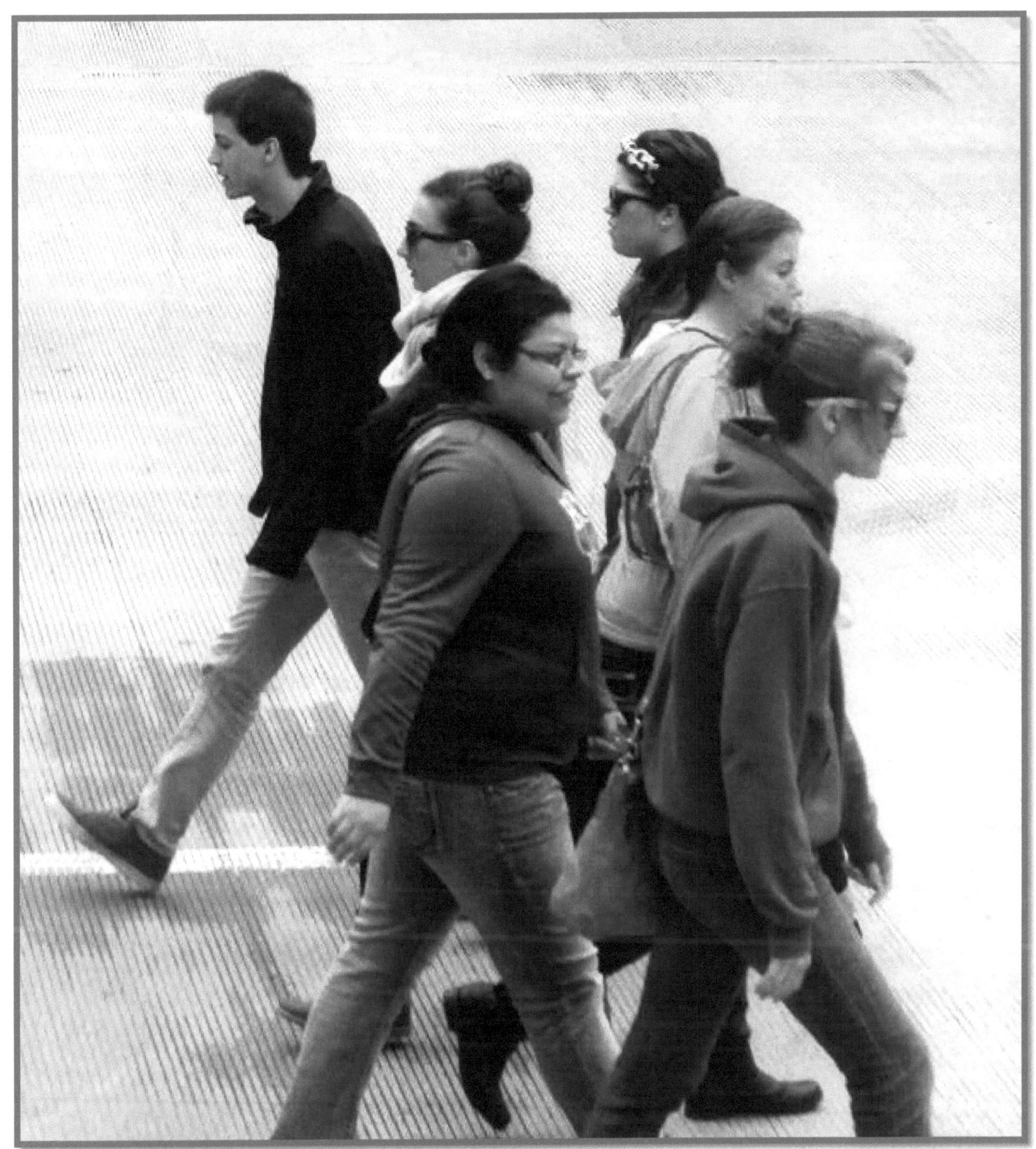

“Liberation was in the very scale of the city: a goldfish bowl one could never grow to fit.” **Sheridan Hay, The Secret of Lost Things**

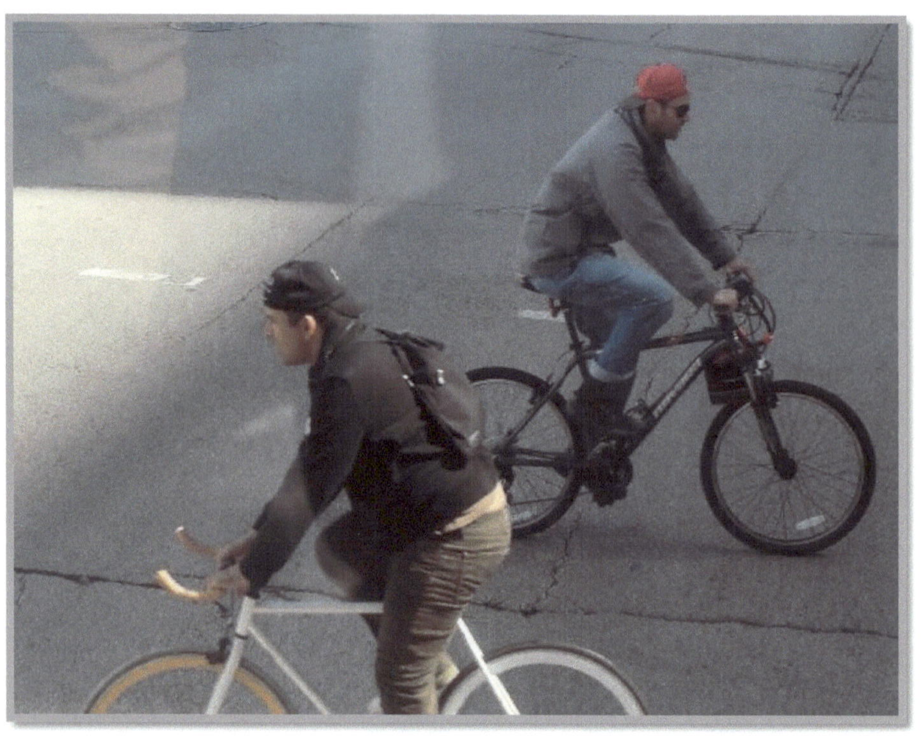

“Shortly before school started, I moved into a studio apartment on a quiet street near the bustle of the downtown in one of the most self-conscious bends of the world. The “Gold Coast” was a neighborhood that stretched five blocks along the lake in a sliver of land just south of Lincoln Park and north of River North. The streets were like fine necklaces and strung together were the brownstone houses and tall condominiums and tiny mansions like pearls, and when the day broke and the sun faded away, their lights burned like jewels shining gaudily in the night. The world’s most elegant bazaar, Michigan Avenue, jutted out from its eastern tip near The Drake Hotel and the timeless blue-green waters of Lake Michigan pressed its shores. The fractious make-up of the people that inhabited it, the flat squareness of its parks and the hint of the lake at the ends of its tree-lined streets squeezed together a domesticated cesspool of age and wealth and standing. It was a place one could readily dress up for an expensive dinner at one of the fashionable restaurants or have a drink miles high in the lounge of the looming John Hancock Building and five minutes later be out walking on the beach with pants cuffed and feet in the cool water at the lake’s edge.” — **Daniel Amory, *Minor Snobs***

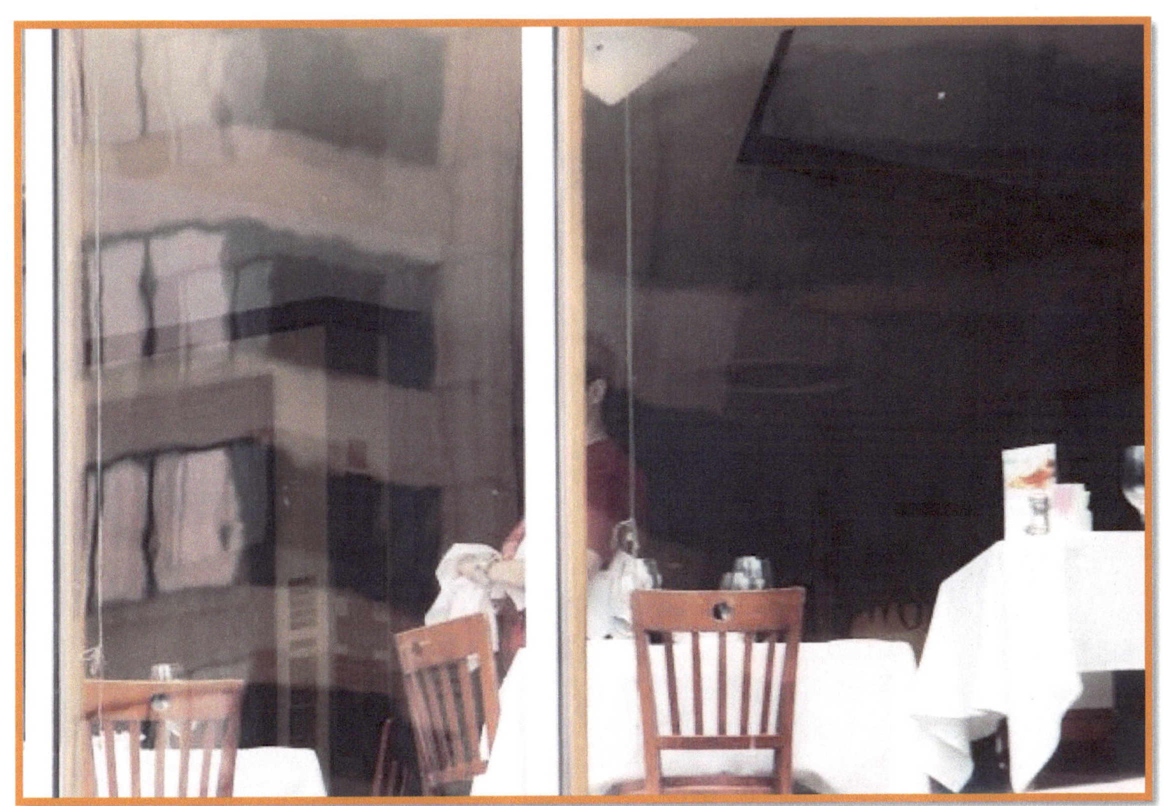

“Every day, my daddy told me the same thing. 'Once a task is just begun, never leave it till it's done. Be the labor great or small, do it well or not at all.'” **Quincy Jones, Chicagoan**

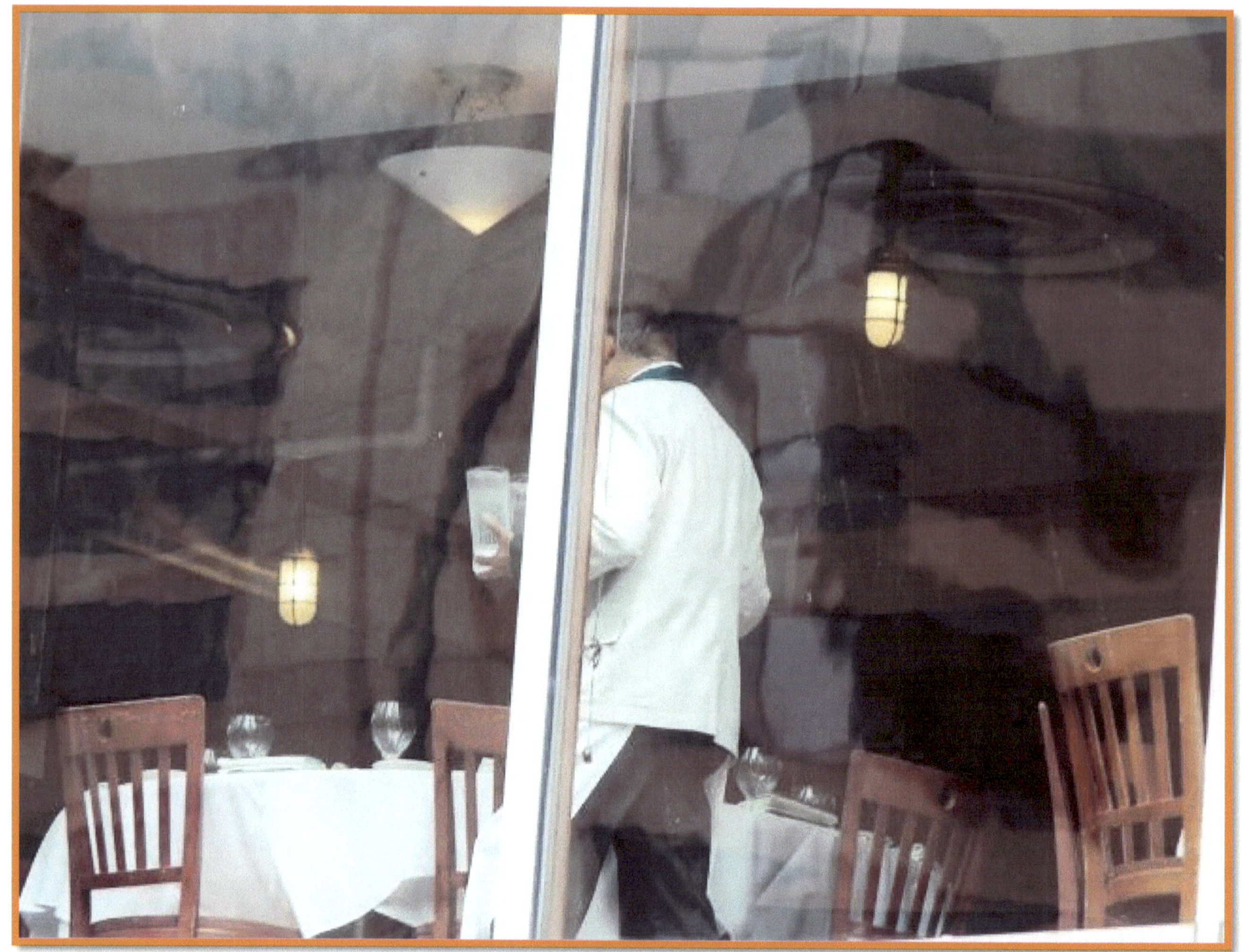

"Big-shot town, small-shot town, jet-propelled old-fashioned town, by old-world hands with new-world tools built into a place whose heartbeat carries farther than its shout, whose whispering in the night sounds less hollow than its roistering noontime laugh: they have builded a heavy-shouldered laughter here who went to work too young."
— **Nelson Algren, *Chicago: City on the Make***

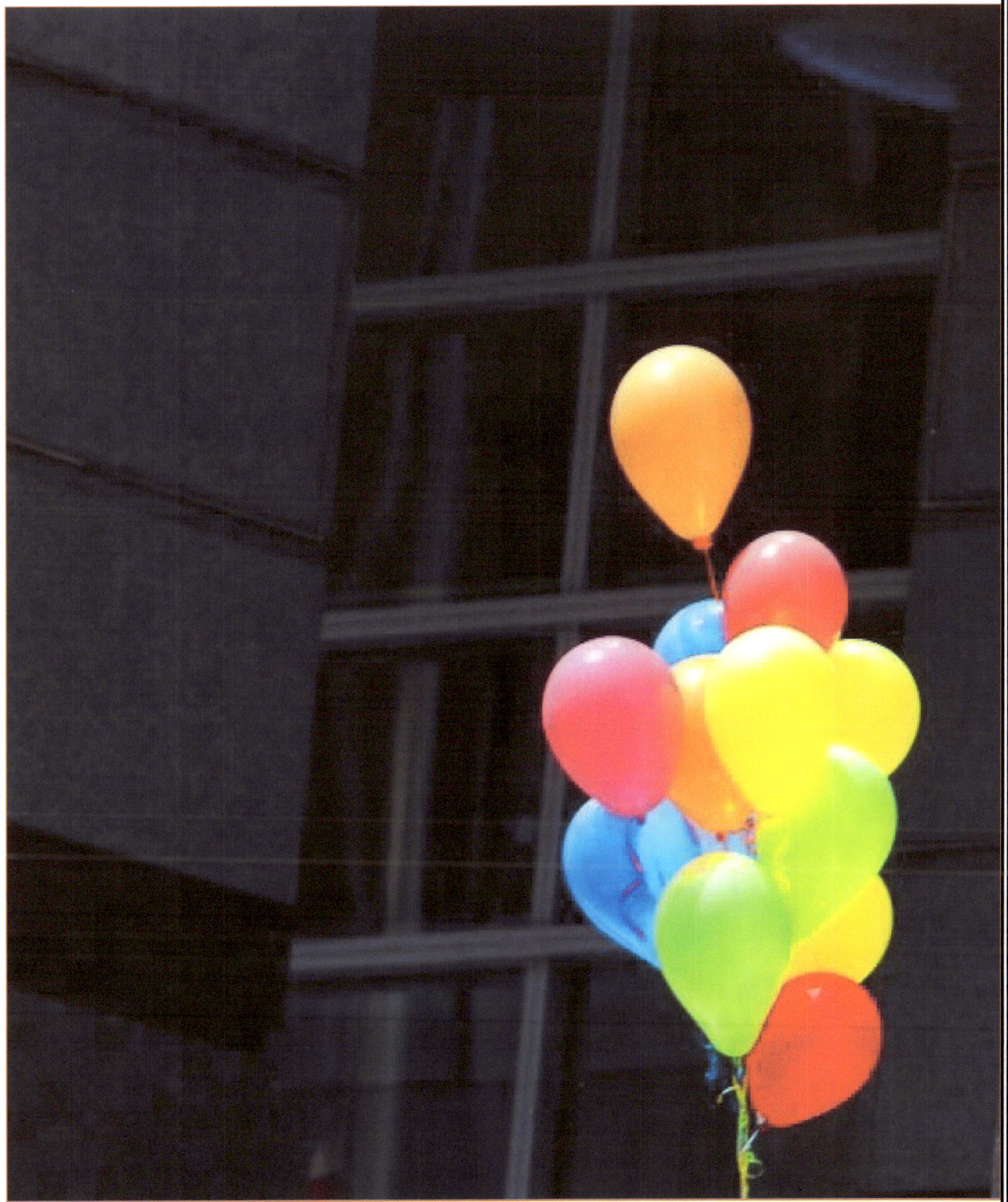

Creativity has more to do with the elimination of the inessential than with inventing something new. **Helmut Jahn, Chicagoan**

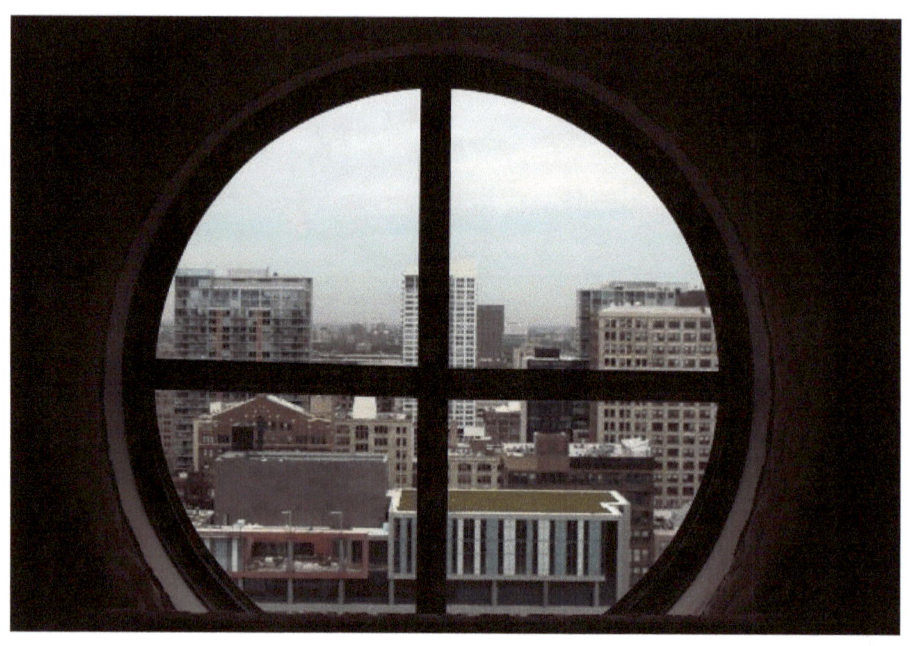

"When I burn please bury me deep
Somewhere on West Division Street
Put a bottle beneat' my head
'n a bottle beneat' my feet"
— Nelson Algren, *Never Come Morning*

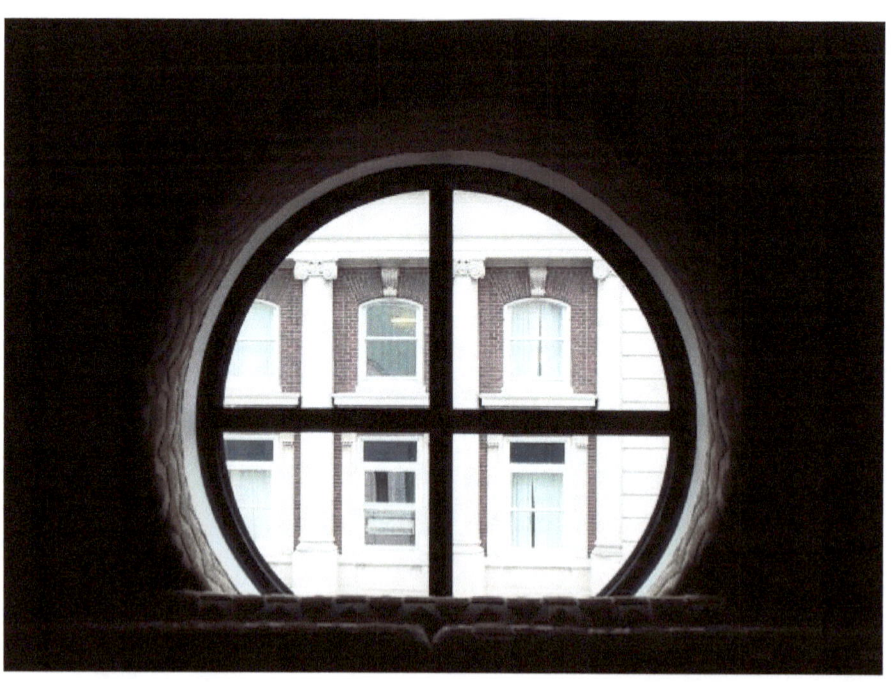

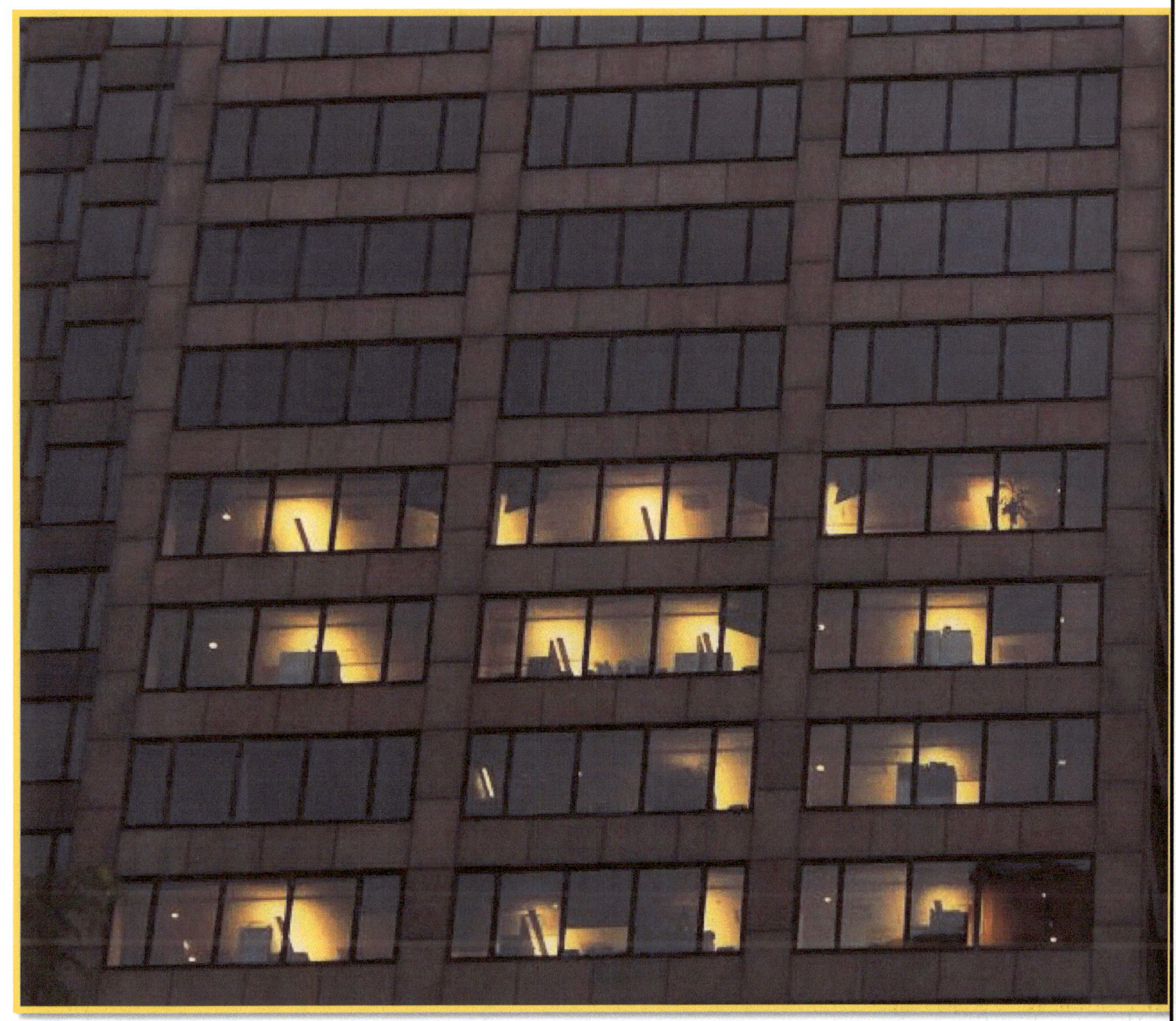

“It's the place built out of Man's ceaseless failure to overcome himself. Out of Man's endless war against himself we build our successes as well as our failures. Making it the city of all cities most like Man himself—loneliest creation of all this very old poor earth.” — **Nelson Algren, Chicago*: City on the Make***

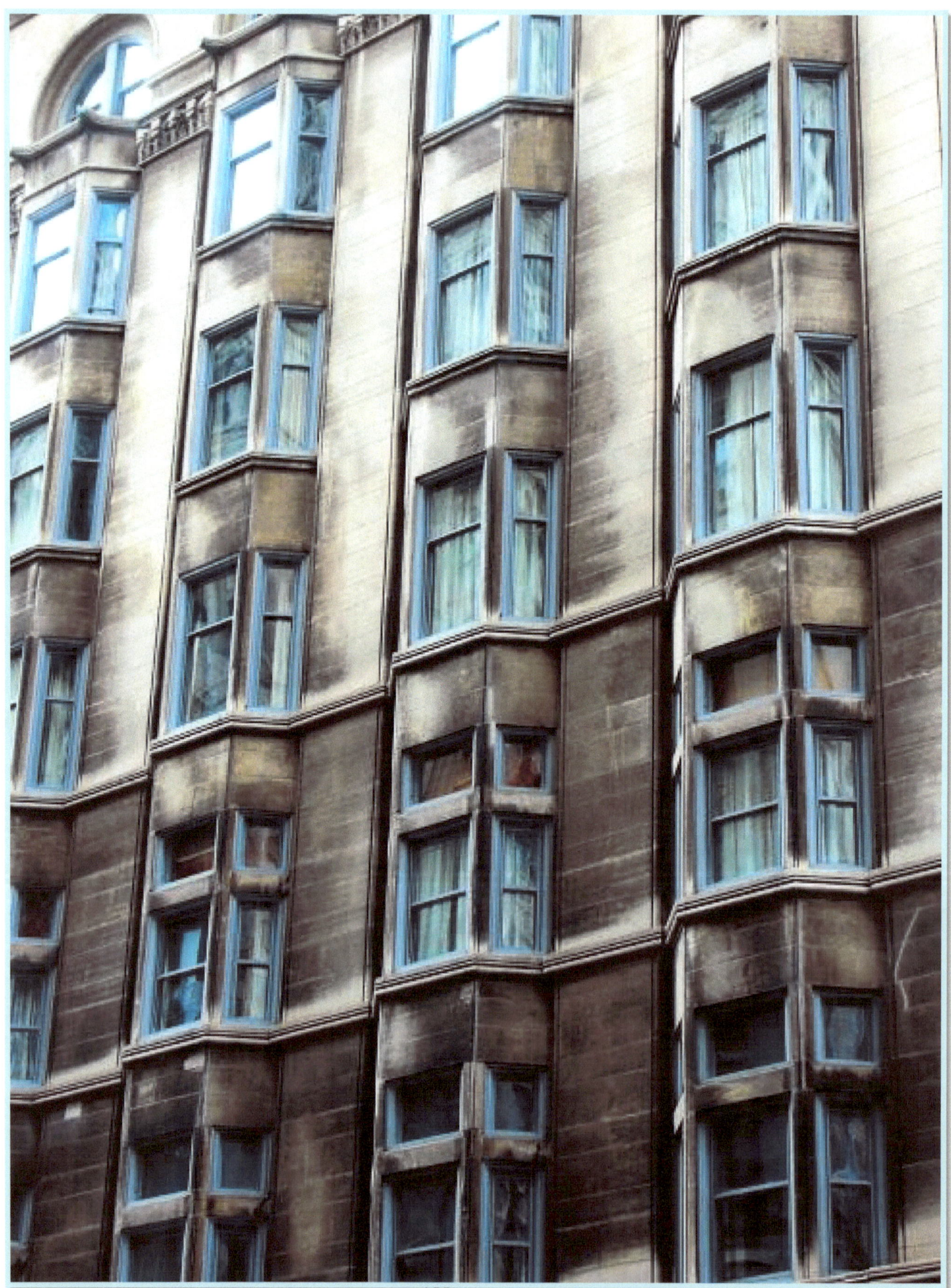

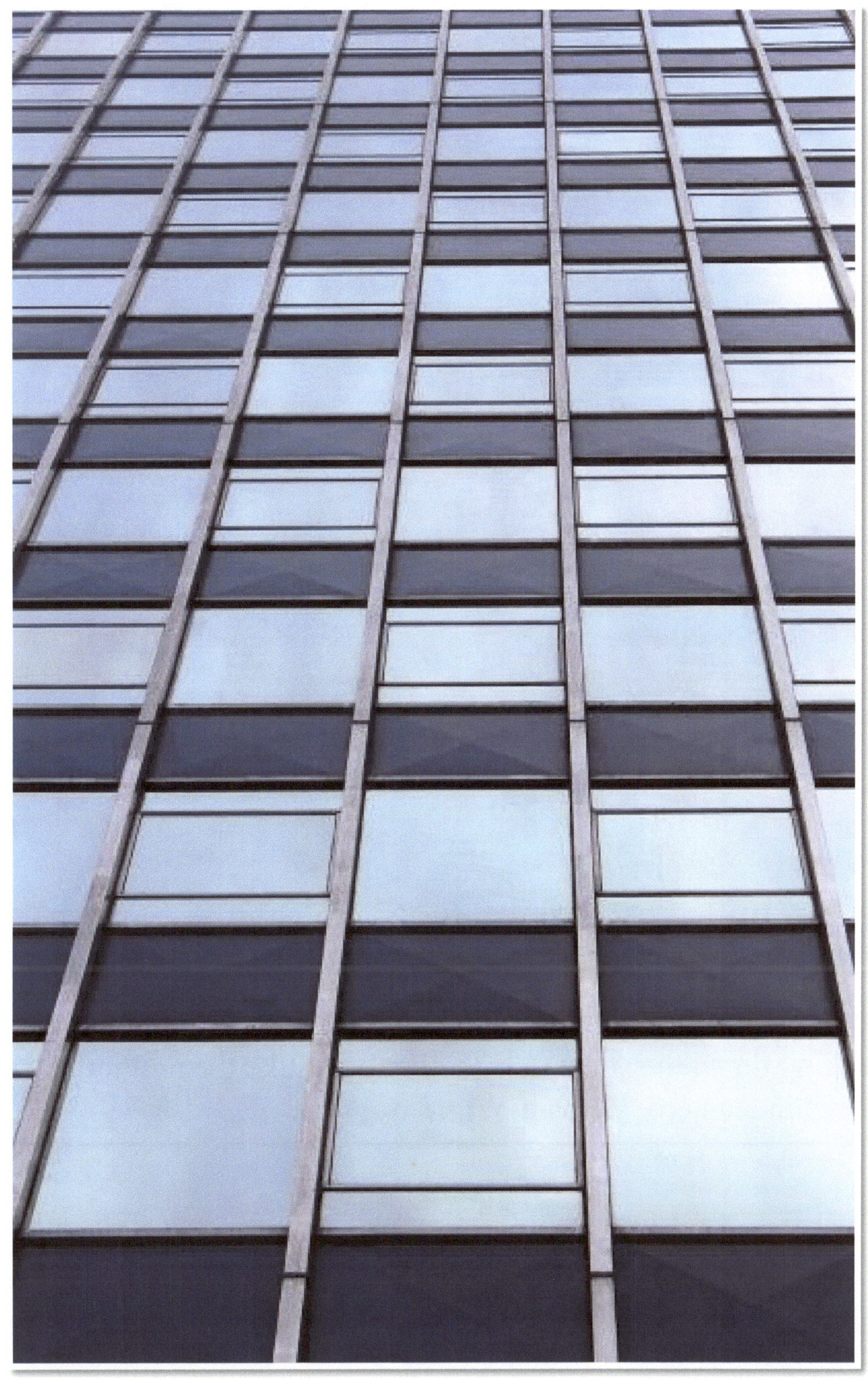

"Less is more." **Ludwig Mies van der Rohe**

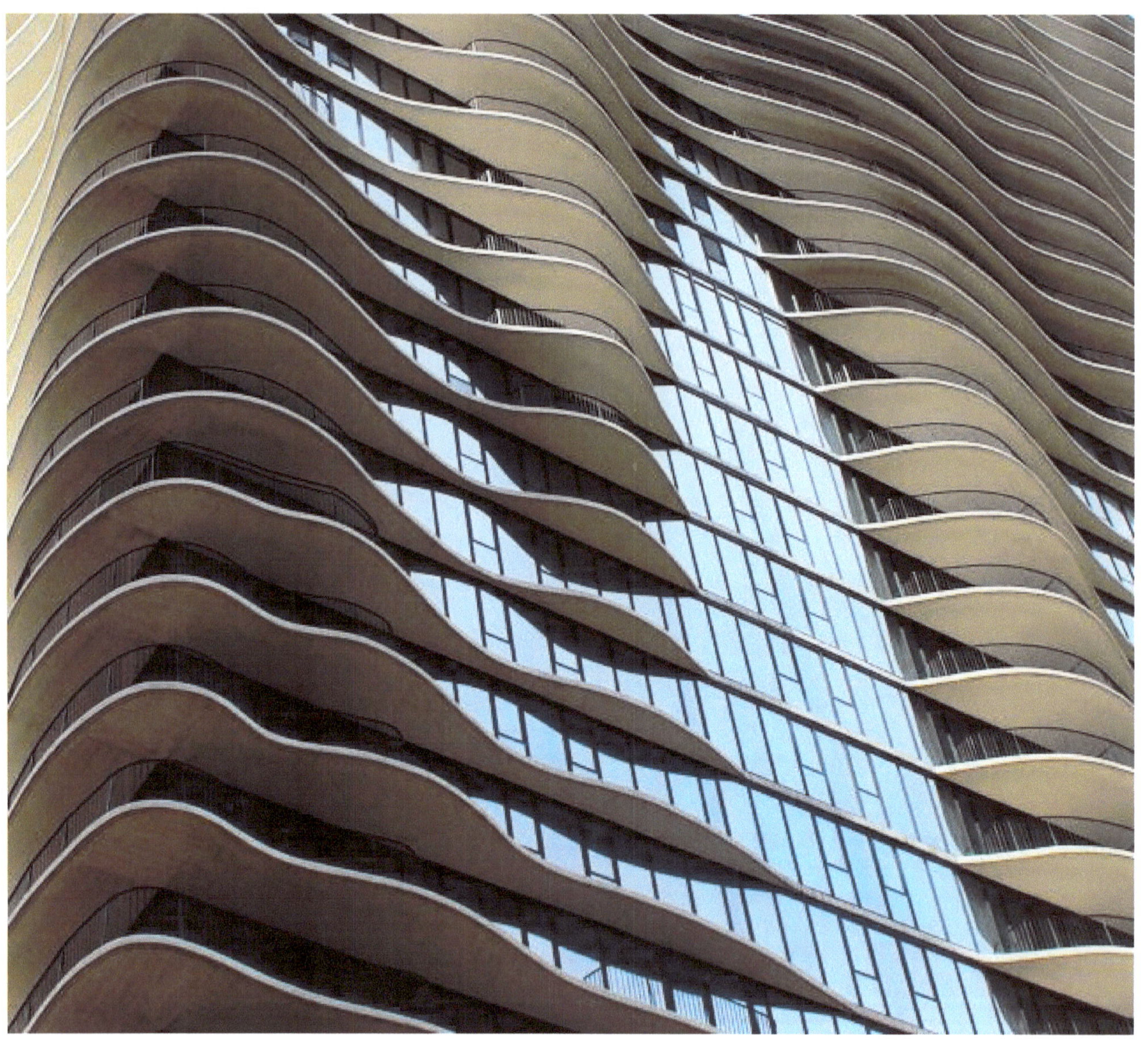

"My first day in Chicago, September 4, 1983. I set foot in this city, and just walking down the street, it was like roots, like the motherland. I knew I belonged here." **Oprah Winfrey**

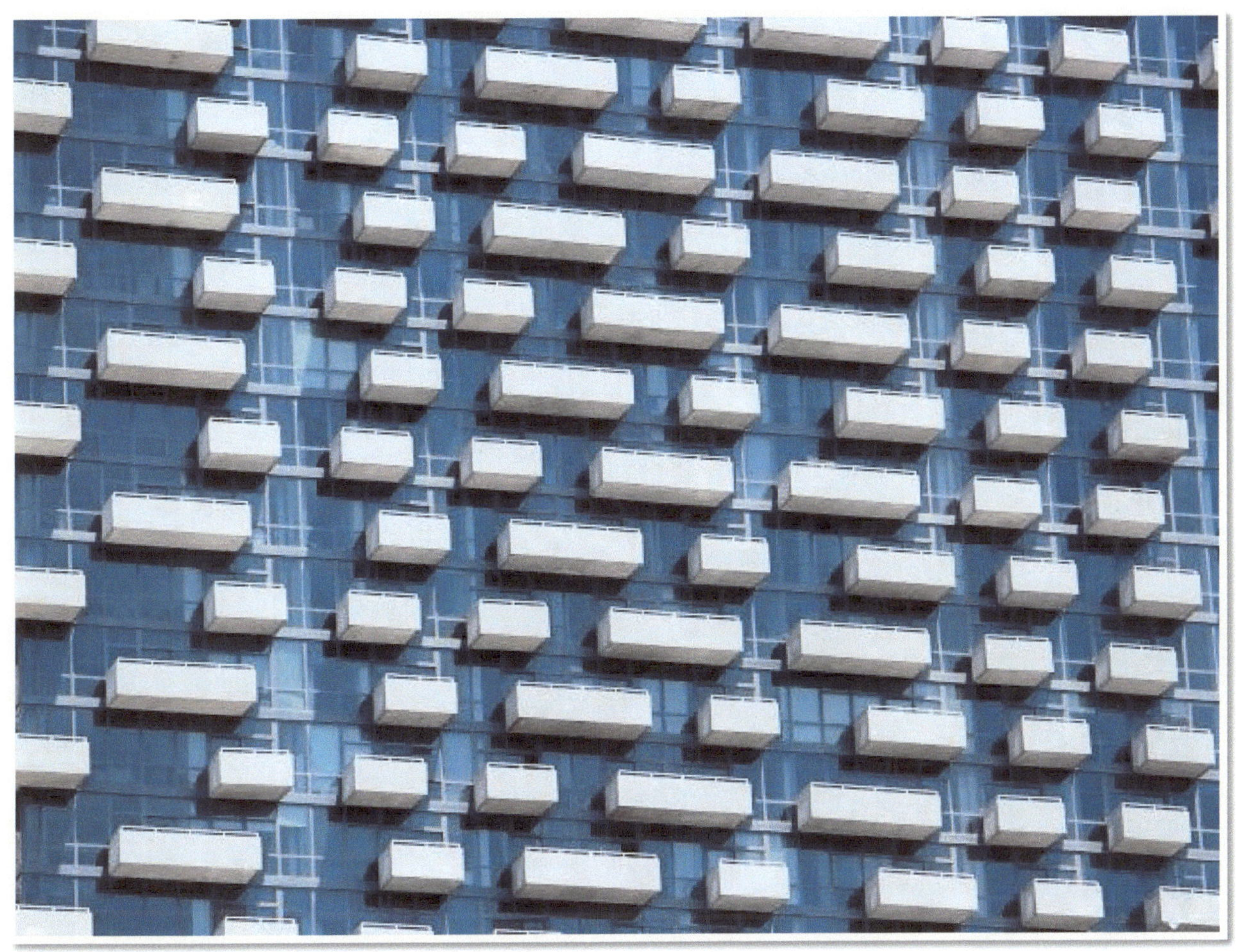

"With cities, it is as with dreams: everything imaginable can be dreamed, but even the most unexpected dream is a rebus that conceals a desire or, its reverse, a fear. Cities, like dreams, are made of desires and fears, even if the thread of their discourse is secret, their rules are absurd, their perspectives deceitful, and everything conceals something else." **Italo Calvino, Invisible Cities**

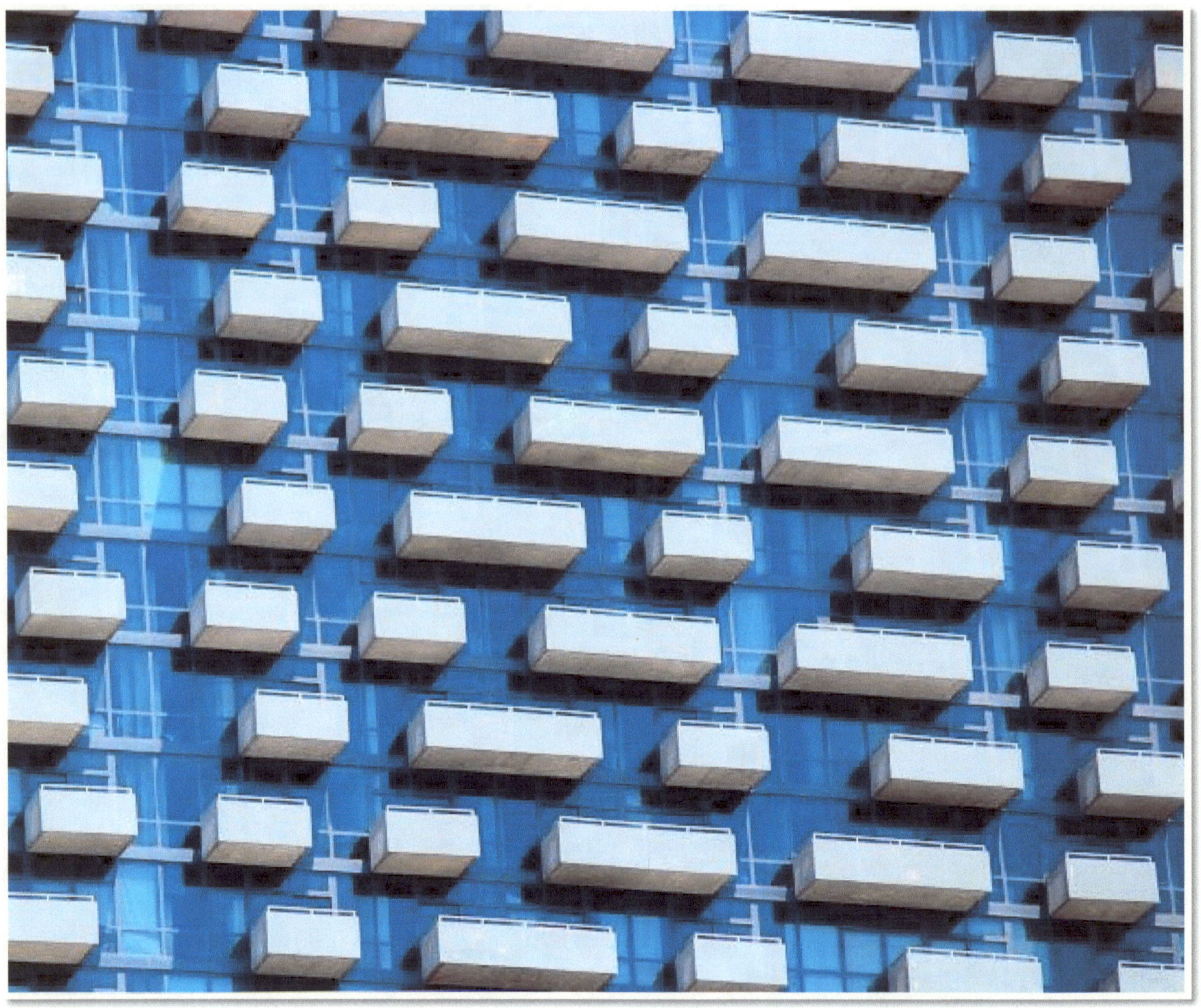

A city building, you experience when you walk; a suburban building, you experience when you drive. **Helmut Jahn, Chicagoan**

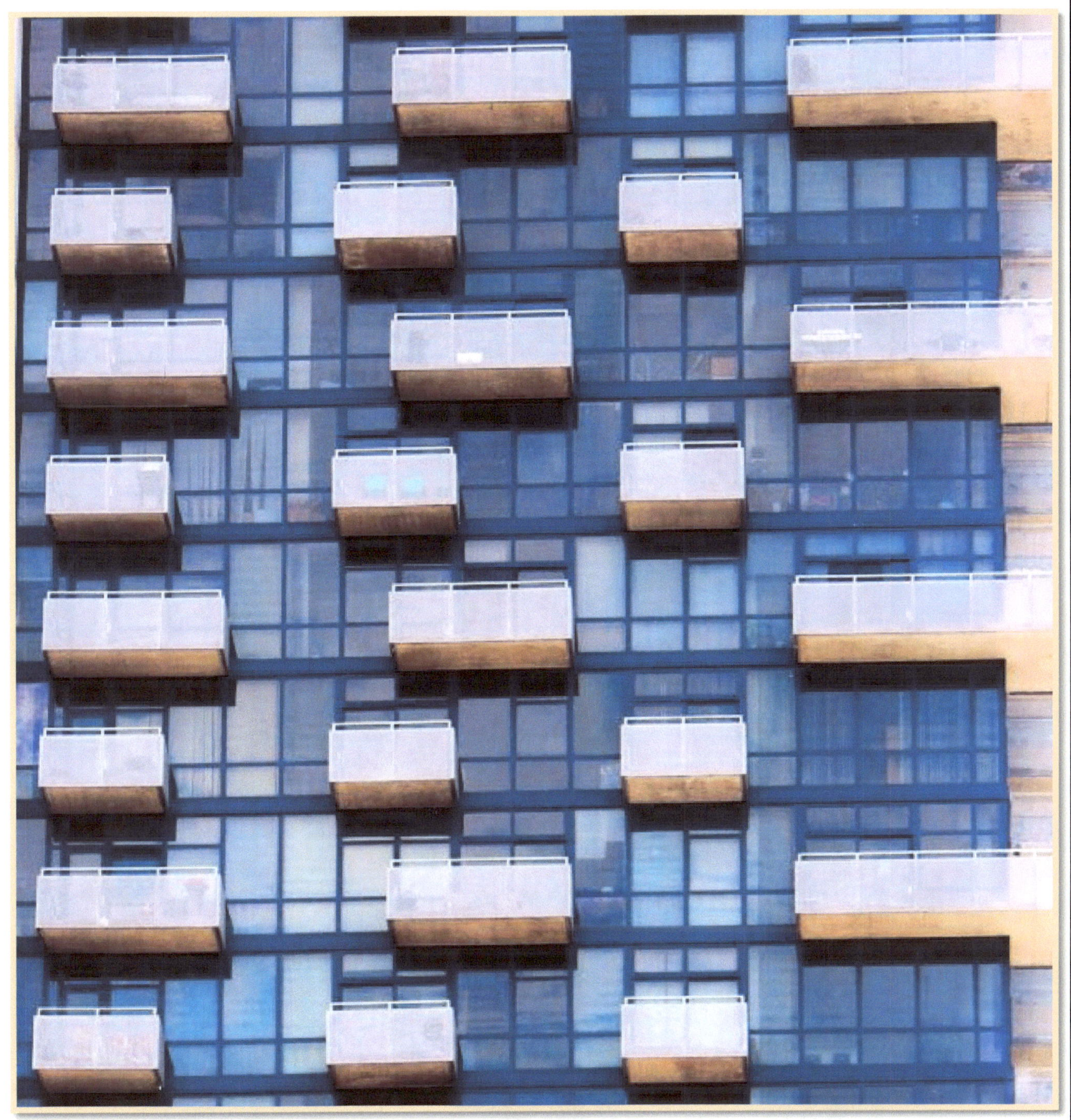

"There are almost no beautiful cities in America, though there are many beautiful parts of cities, and some sections that are glorious without being beautiful, like downtown Chicago." **Noel Perrin, Third Person Rural, 1983**

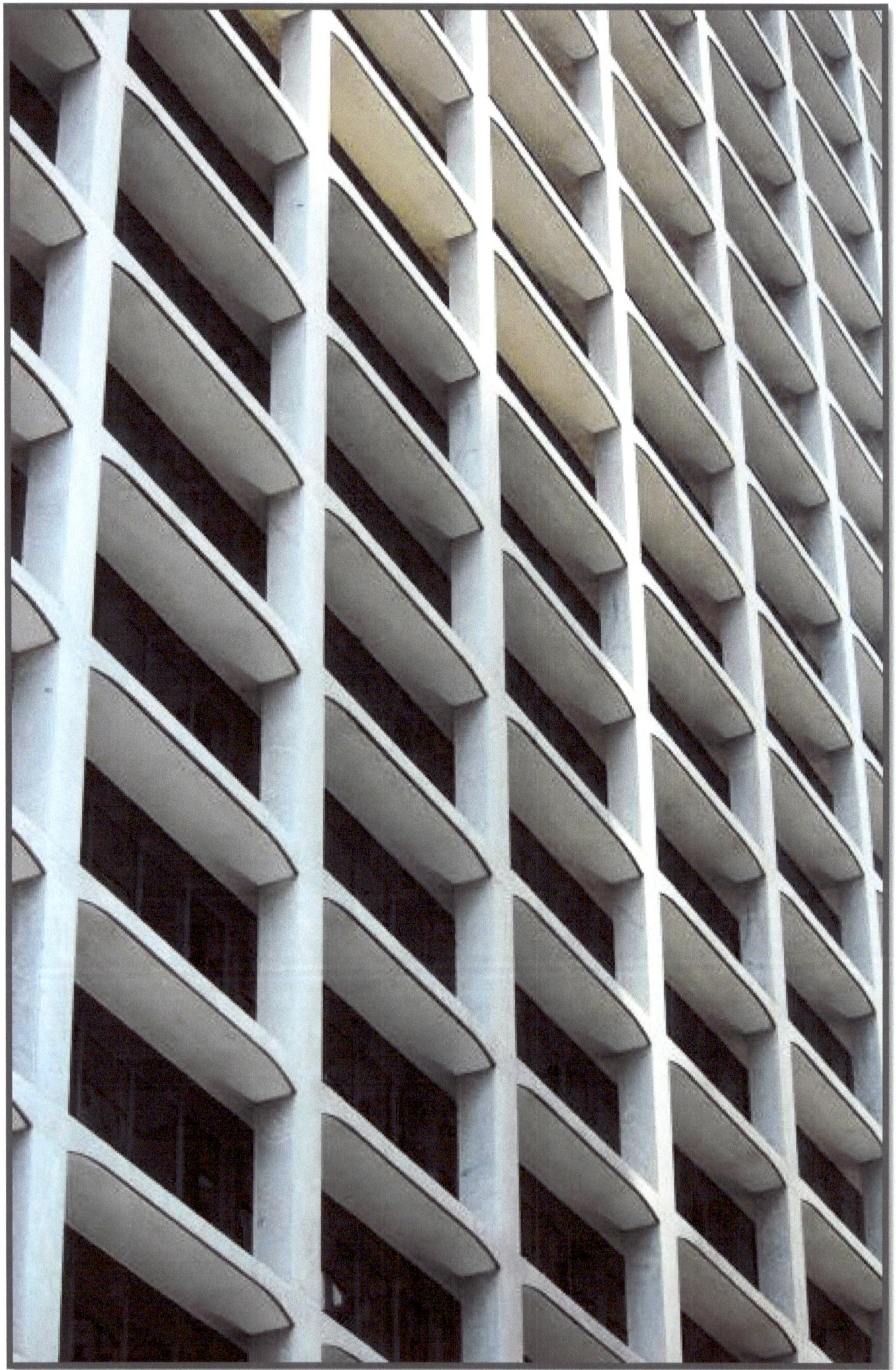

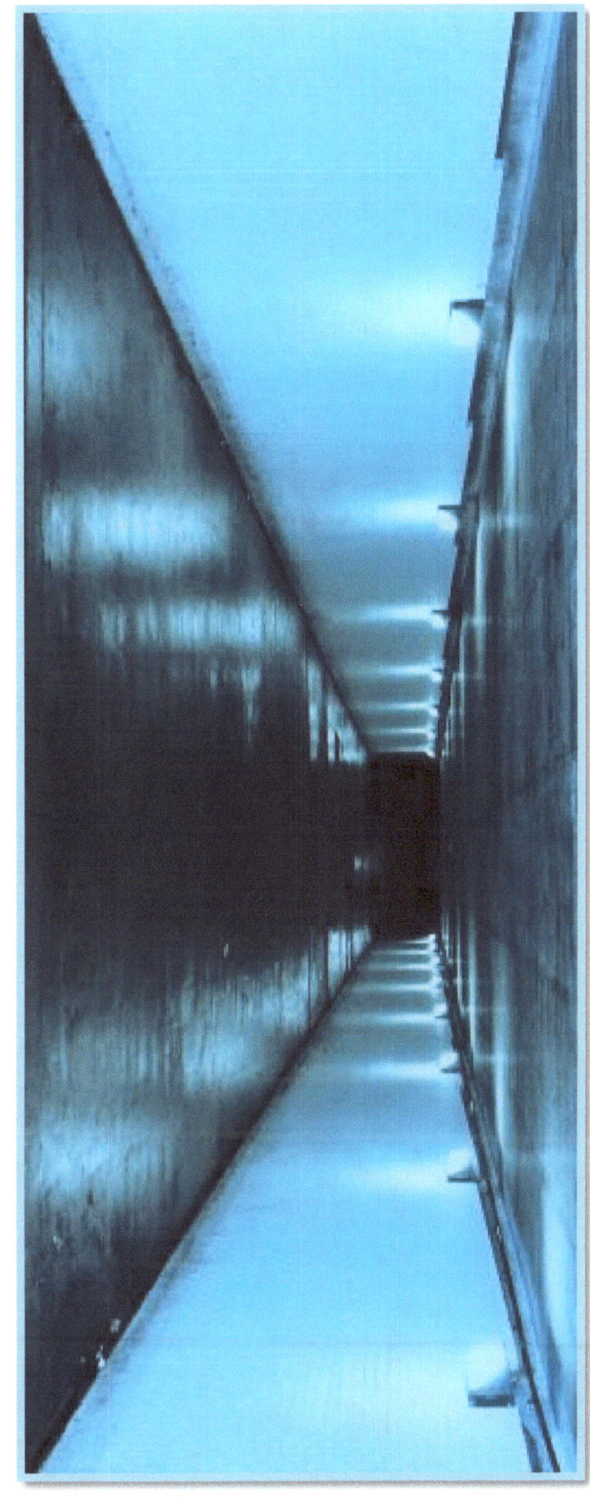

"Loving Chicago is like loving a woman with a broken nose." —**Nelson Algren**

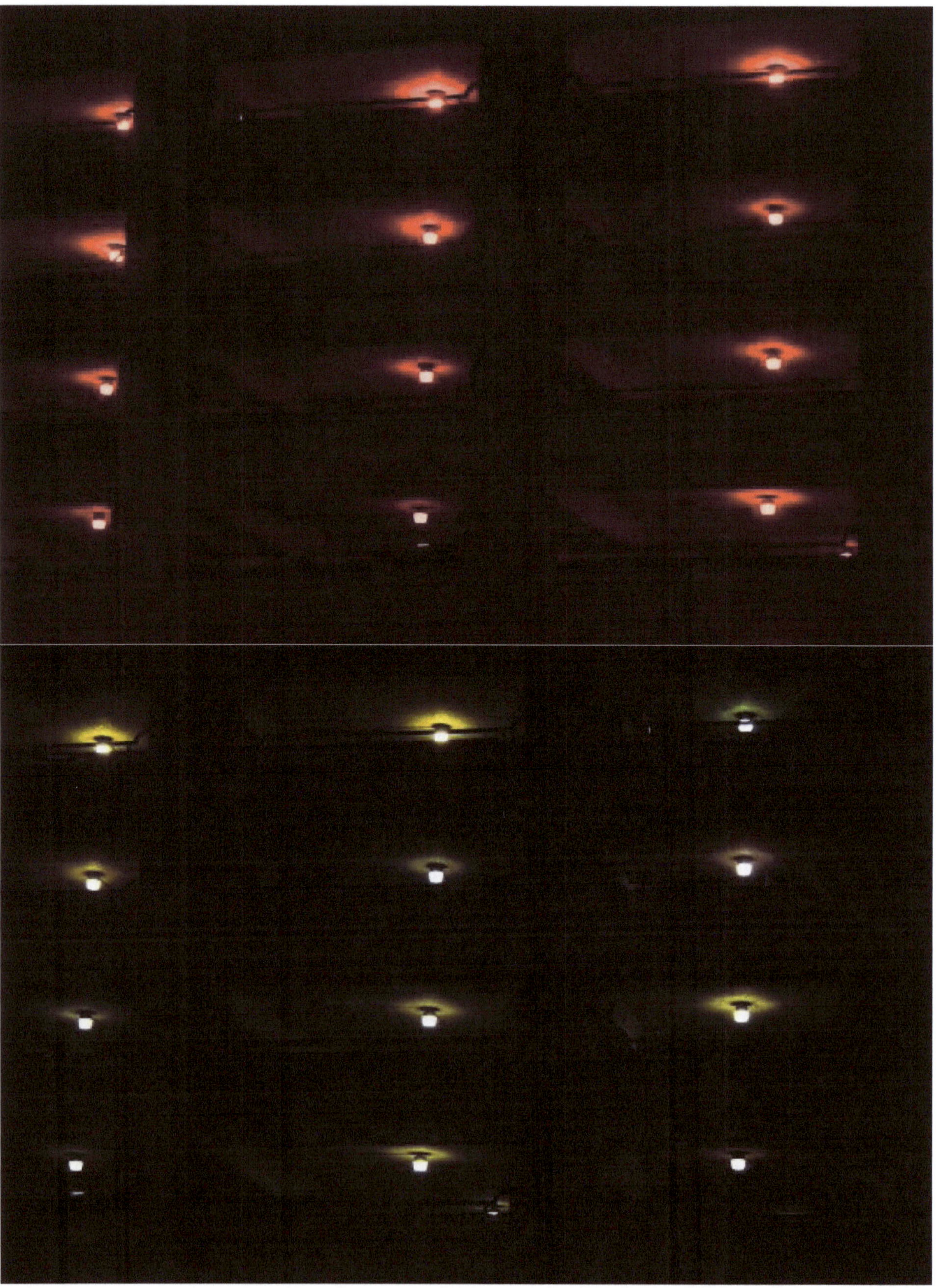

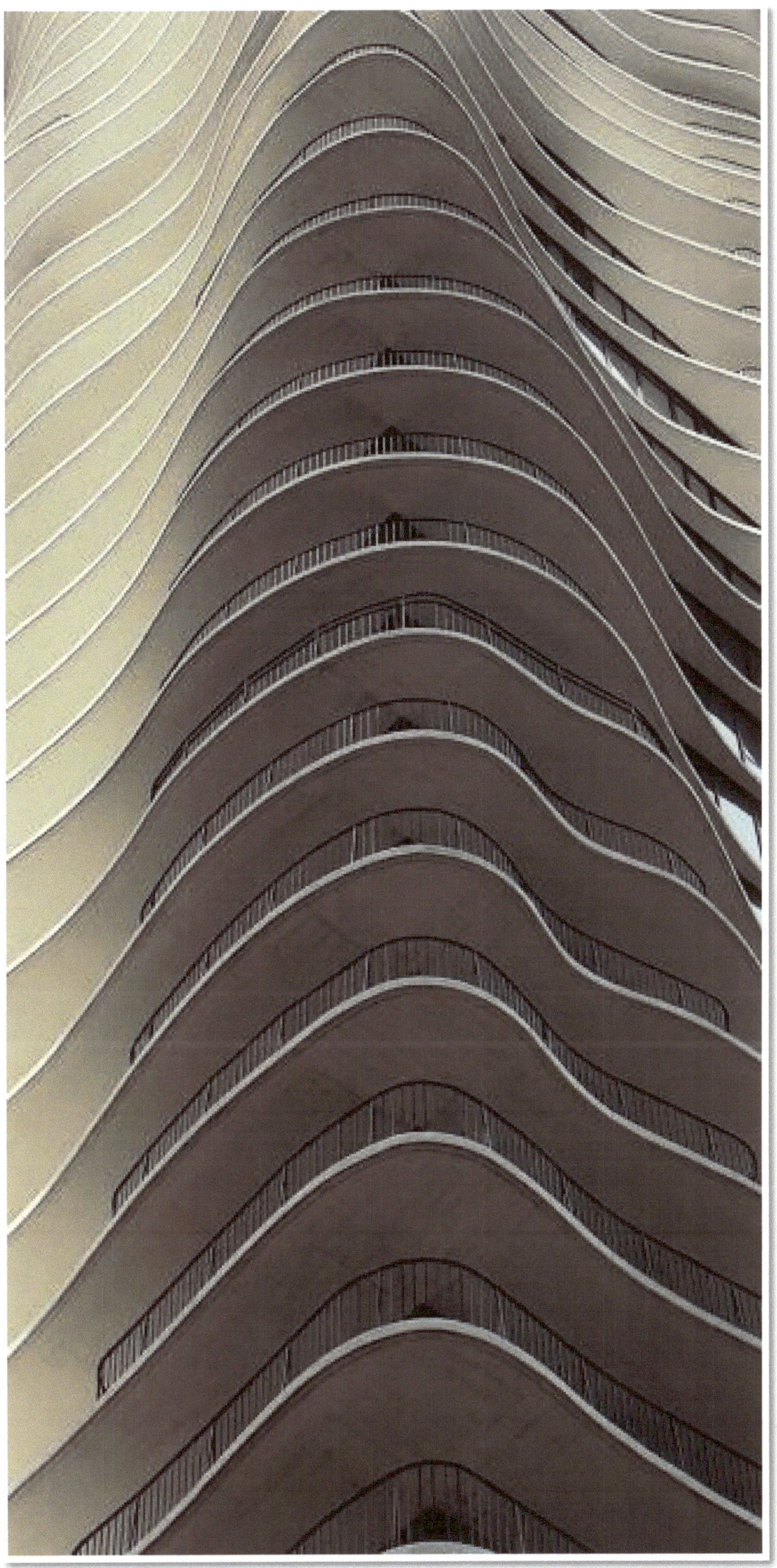

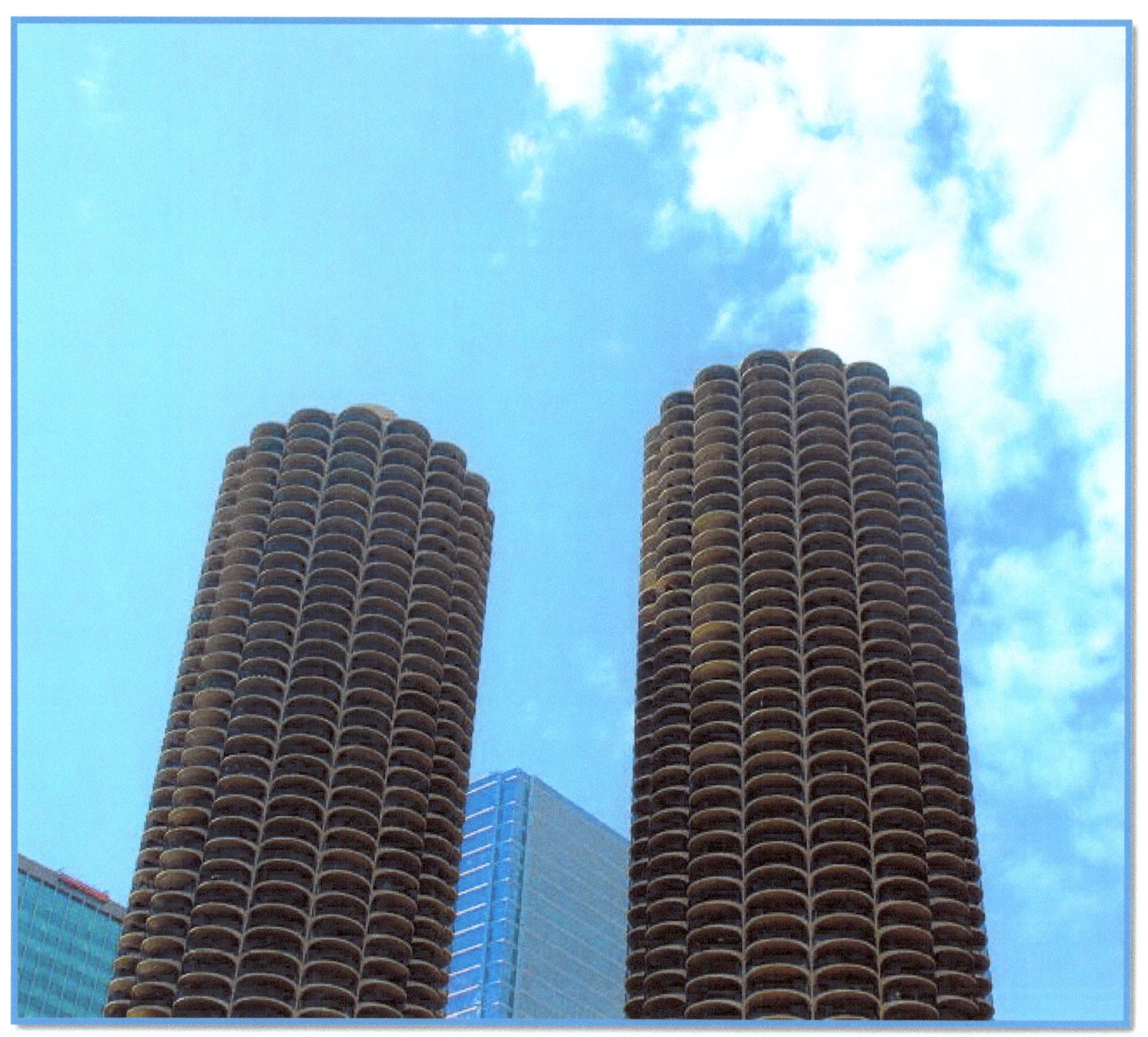

“Yet once you've come to be part of this particular patch, you'll never love another. Like loving a woman with a broken nose, you may well find lovelier lovelies. But never a lovely so real.” — **Nelson Algren, Chicago: *City on the Make***

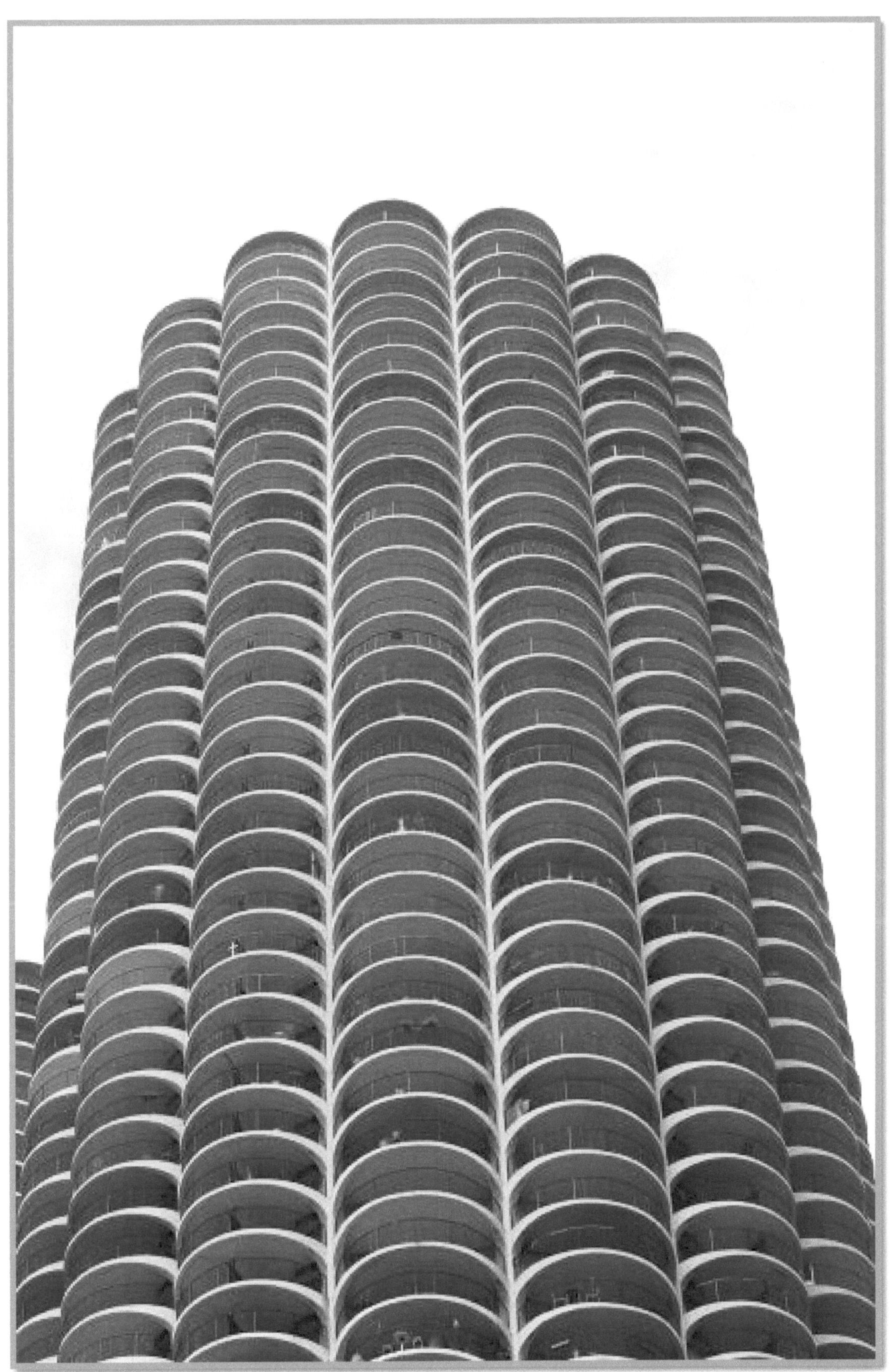

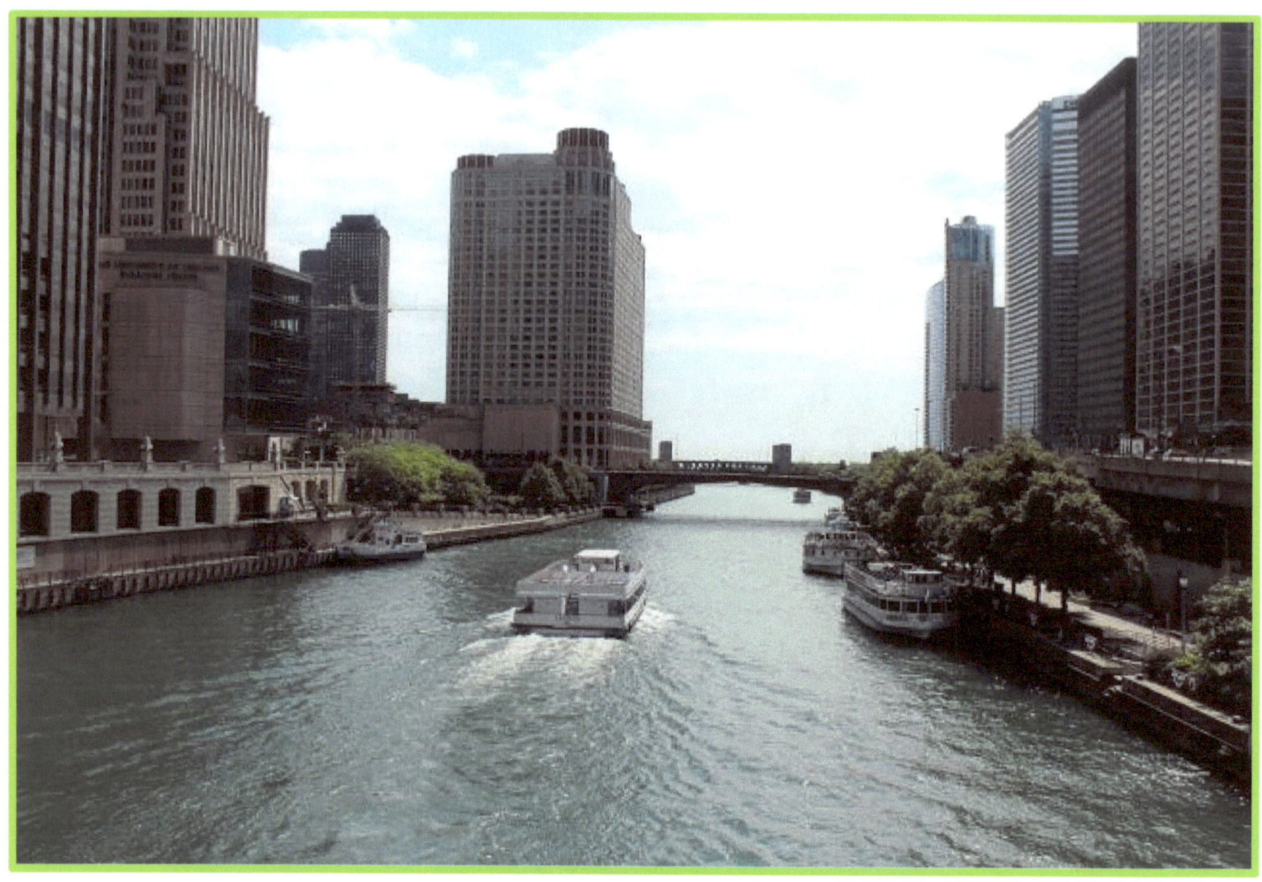

"I love Chicago. Chicago is my home." **Jonathan Toews**

www.ingramcontent.com/pod-product-compliance
Lightning Source LLC
LaVergne TN
LVHW070119110826
845147LV00002B/153

* 9 7 8 0 6 9 2 5 2 3 8 1 0 *